New Age in Norway

New Age in Norway

Edited by

Ingvild Sælid Gilhus, Siv Ellen Kraft and James R. Lewis

SHEFFIELD UK   BRISTOL CT

Published by Equinox Publishing Ltd.

UK: Office 415, The Workstation, 15 Paternoster Row, Sheffield S1 2BX
USA: ISD, 70 Enterprise Drive, Bristol, CT 06010
www.equinoxpub.com

First published 2017

ISBN–13: 978 1 78179 416 6 (hardback)
ISBN–13: 978 1 78179 417 3 (paperback)

British Library Cataloguing-in-Publication Data

A catalogue record for this book is available from the British Library.

Library of Congress Cataloging-in-Publication Data

Gilhus, Ingvild Sælid, editor.
New Age in Norway / edited by Ingvild Sælid Gilhus, Siv Ellen Kraft and James R. Lewis.
Includes bibliographical references and index.
LCCN 2015040158| ISBN 9781781794166 (hb) | ISBN 9781781794173 (pb)
1. LCSH: New Age movement—Norway. | Norway—Religion.
BP605.N48 N445 2016
DDC 299/.9309481—dc23

LC record available at http://lccn.loc.gov/2015040158

Edited and Typeset by Queenston Publishing, Hamilton, Ontario, Canada

Printed by Lightning Source Inc. (La Vergne, TN), and
Lightning Source UK Ltd. (Milton Keynes).

CONTENTS

List of Figures

List of Tables

CONTRIBUTORS

Bengt-Ove Andreassen is Associate Professor in the Study of Religion at the Department of Education, UiT—The Arctic university of Norway. Andreassen's doctoral thesis was an analysis of textbooks on religion used in teacher education. He has written a number of articles and books about RE, and especially addressed the lack of literature on conflict and violence in RE. He was also co-editor (with James R. Lewis) of *Textbook Gods* (Equinox Publishing 2014). Additionally, he has written several articles in various journals about the Study of Religions based Religion Education.

Asbjørn Dyrendal is Professor in History of Religion at the Norwegian University of Science and Technology, Trondheim, Norway. His research interests revolve around contemporary religion in society, particularly Satanism, popular occulture and conspiracy culture. He is also editor of the Norwegian sceptic's journal, *Skepsis*. And currently co-editor of *International Journal for the Study of New Religions*.

Trude Fonneland is currently professor in the Department of Culture studies at Tromsø Museum, UiT—The Arctic University of Norway. Her research interests revolve around contemporary religion in society, particularly Sami shamanism, tourism, and popular culture. She is the author of several scholarly articles on the subject. Recent publications include *Nordic Neoshamanisms* (2015) (co-edited with Siv Ellen Kraft and James Lewis), "Approval of the Shamanistic Association: A Local Norwegian Construct with Trans-Local Dynamics" (In *Nordic New* Religions), "Spiritual Entrepreneurship in the High North: The Case of Polmakmoen Guesthouse and the Pilgrimage 'the Seven Coffee Stops'"(*International Journal for the Study of New Religions* 2014) and "Spiritual Entrepreneurship: Tourism, Spirituality and Politics" (*Temenos* 2012).

Liselotte Frisk has been Professor of Religious Studies at Högskolan Dalarna since 2006. She has written several books about new religious movements and new age, and conducted several research projects in the same area of study. She is currently researching children in minority religions. Frisk is also chairperson of Finyar (the Nordic network for research on new religiosity) and is the co-editor of Aura (*The Nordic journal for the study of new religiosity*). She was the chairperson of ISSNR (International society for the study of new religions) between 2010 and 2013, and was the co-editor of IJSNR (*International journal for the study of new religions* between 2010 and 2013.

Ingvild Sælid Gilhus is Professor of History of Religions at the University of Bergen, Norway. Gilhus works in the areas of religion in late antiquity and new religious movements. Her publications include *Laughing Gods, Weeping Virgins: laughter in the history of religions* (1997), *Animals, Gods and Humans: changing attitudes to animals in Greek, Roman and early Christian ideas* (2006) and *New Age Spirituality: Rethinking Religion* (edited with Steven Sutcliffe 2013). She is book review editor of *Numen* and is an editorial board member of *Temenos*.

Anne Kalvig is Associate Professor of Religious Studies, Department of Cultural Studies and Languages, University of Stavanger, Norway. Her main research interests are new religious movements, alternative spirituality, popular culture, alternative and folk medicine, death, and gender studies. She has contributed to several international anthologies, edited two books and published the monographs Åndeleg *helse: Livssyn og menneskesyn hos alternative terapeutar* (2013), on views of life among alternative therapists, and *Spiritisme: Samtaler mellom levende og døde* (2016), on spiritualism in Norway.

Siv Ellen Kraft is professor of the History of Religions, UiT—The Arctic University of Norway. Kraft has written extensively on Theosophy, New Age spiritualities and religious revival among the Sami, including a number of articles, four edited books and four monographs. Recent books include *Nordic Neoshamanisms* (with Trude Fonneland and James R Lewis, Palgrave 2015), *Religion i pressen* (with Cora Alexa Døving, Universitetsforlaget 2013) and *Hva er nyreligiøsitet* (Universitetsforlaget 2011).

James R. Lewis is a highly published scholar in the field of New Religious Movements and Professor of Religious Studies at the UiT—The Arctic University of Norway. He currently edits or co-edits four academic book series, and is the general editor for two academic journals. Recent publications include (with Siv Ellen Kraft and Trude Fonneland), *Nordic Neoshamanisms*, (with Inga Tøllefsen) the *Oxford Handbook of New*

Religious Movements (2nd ed.), (co-edited Kjersti Hellesøy) the *Brill Handbook of Scientology*, and the *Cambridge Companion on Religion and Terrorism.*

Margrethe Løøv is a Ph.D. fellow at the Department of Archaeology, History, Cultural Studies and Religion at the University of Bergen. She holds a MA in Religious Studies from the University of Oslo and has previously studied in Hyderabad, Heidelberg and Montpellier. She has also been involved in a book project on the preface to the mission among the Sami people in Norway. Her research interests include the New Age movement and NRMs in general, quantitative approaches in the study of religion, the history of missions and the adaptation of Hindu/Buddhist meditation in the West.

Lisbeth Mikaelsson is professor emerita of Religion at the University of Bergen, Norway. Her research has focused on Christianity and NRM, and she has published numerous works about Norwegian mission literature, women and mission, religion and locality, pilgrimage, Theosophy, and New Age. Among her publications are *Kallets ekko. Studier i misjon og selvbiografi* (2003), and co-edited with Ingvild Sælid Gilhus, *Religion i skrift. Mellom mystikk og materialitet* (2013).

Mikael Rothstein. Ph.D., is Associate Professor of the History of Religions, University of Copenhagen, Denmark. He is also tenured Visiting Professor at the Vytautas Magnus University, Lithuania. He is author and editor of several volumes on new religions and comparative religion in general. Among his English language publications are *Belief Transformations* (1996), *Secular Theories in the Study of Religion* (edited with Tim Jensen, 2000), *New Age and Globalization* (edited volume, 2001), The Cambridge Companion to New Religious Movements (co-ed. with Olav Hammer, 2012), and *Handbook of the Theosophical Current* (also co-ed. with Olav Hammer, 2012).

Torunn Selberg, folklorist, is professor in Cultural Studies, department of Archaeology, History, Cultural Studies and Religion, University of Bergen. Her research interests revolve around folk religion, magic, ritualization, tourism, and cultural landscapes. Selberg is a prominent scholar of new religions in contemporary society and has written numerous chronicles, articles and books focusing on contemporary religious phenomena, pilgrimage, festivals and place construction.

Inga Bårdsen Tøllefsen (M.A University of Tromsø 2012) is a PhD student at the UiT—The Arctic University of Norway. Her research interests are New Religious Movements (especially Indian-oriented movements), religion and gender, the New Age, and religion and nature. Recent publications include, "Transcendental Meditation, the Art of Living Foundation and Public Relations: From Psychedelic Romanticism to Science and Schism" in *Controversial New Religions* (2nd edition 2014).

Oscar-Torjus Utaaker is currently a graduate student in Religious Studies at UiT—The Arctic University of Norway.

— Introduction —

New Age in Norway

INGVILD SÆLID GILHUS AND SIV ELLEN KRAFT

Images of the Nordic countries as among the most secularized in the world echo notions of proper "religion" and of church attendance and faith in the Christian gospel as suitable and sufficient indicators of religiosity. The Nordic countries, including Norway, have until recently been dominated by rather homogenous populations, the overwhelming majority of which have been members of state churches.[1] Church attendance at regular sermons is low, while membership and support of the main rituals remain high; 75 percent of the population were members of the Church of Norway in January 2014 (www.kirken.no). Statistics from 2013 show that the church performed 92 percent of burials; 61 percent of babies born were baptized and 64 percent of youngsters that year went through confirmation.

New Age ideas and practices reached Norway in the 1960s, along with other countercultural currents. They have since taken root and spread, in mainstream as well as countercultural circles, but have in public discourse tended to be ignored or marginalized—to be overlooked as "religion" or framed as quasi, bad or vulgar. One example of such tendencies is the white paper *Det livssynsåpne samfunn* (NOU 2013, 1), concerning the development of a comprehensive politics of religious beliefs and views of life. Based on a traditional view of religion and traditional indicators of religiosity, this otherwise informed and interesting report ignores some of the fundamental changes that have taken place over the course of the last generation. Chief among these changes are the diffusion of New Age spirituality, the role of popular culture as a primary source of religion and the important function

---

1. The Norwegian State Church was formally replaced by a folk church in 2012.

1

media play in the dissemination of religious ideas.

An attempt to question and challenge images of "proper" religion and a thoroughly secularized society, this book covers "alternative" spiritualities that increasingly cater to the mainstream, that are "here," "there" and "anywhere," according to the spatial terminology of Jonathan Z. Smith—to be later developed in more detail—and that today constitute "normal religion."

Our definition of New Age is three-fold: New Age is

1. a global discourse, consisting of a broadly recognizable cluster of ideas and practices, including self-spirituality, holistic perspectives, self-authority, perennialism and an esoteric dimension.
2. organized in small groups, networks, specific events and on-line forums, and disseminated through old and new media.
3. a relational term, to some extent shaped by a particular national setting, including official notions of proper religion, folk religious traditions, boundaries between the religious and the secular, and hegemonic discourses about knowledge.

We will be dealing with New Age both in a restricted (*sensu stricto*) and a wide sense (*sensu lato*),[2] focusing mainly on the period from the mid-1990s and onwards, with particular emphasis on developments after the turn of the century. Principal tendencies and fields of manifestation will be discussed in relation to both global influences and local frames of reference. Few, if any, of the ideas and practices to be discussed in this book are uniquely Norwegian, but local soil and climate still matter, as habitats for particular movements and developments. Globalizing currents are here—as elsewhere in the world—shaped and molded by local religious history and contemporary religio-political systems, along with random incidences, such as the establishment of an angel-business by Norwegian Princess Märtha Louise. The position of Lutheran Protestantism as the "national religion" is, for instance, likely to impact on the development and perception of religious competitors. Christianity is still sovereign in its role as master of national ceremonies, as the "heritage" of Norwegians (according to the Constitution),[3] and probably as the Norwegian version of a prototype for religion—of what it is and should be.

---

2. The distinction between New Age in a restricted and a wide sense was introduced by Wouter Hanegraaff. For a further explanation of the terms, see page 8, this chapter.

3. The state-church reform in 2012 included a revision of the paragraph pertaining to the relationship between the church and state. The Constitution of Norway, from 1814, stated that "The Evangelical-Lutheran religion shall remain the official religion of the State. The inhabitants professing it are bound to bring up their children in the same" (§2; cf. E. Smith 2010). The new paragraph (from 2012) states that "Our values will remain our Christian and humanist heritage."

Ingvild Sælid Gilhus and Siv Ellen Kraft

New Age and New Age research in Norway:
First, second and third wave

Several new religious movements had representatives in Norway by the early 1970s, including movements of Asian provenance, the Sufi-inspired Eckankar, the Christian-inspired Children of God, and already well-established movements like The Theosophical Society and Anthroposophical Society, founded in Norway in 1893 and 1923 respectively. Together with the anti-war movement, hippie-culture and a growing ecological awareness, these movements contributed to an increase in the general awareness of especially Asian religions. There were several distribution centers for alternative and religious lifestyles at that time, and several new magazines and periodicals helped channel alternative ideas and practices (Ahlberg 1980). Two meditation organizations were particularly influential: Maharishi Mahesh Yogi's organization (MIKI) and the organization ACEM, initiated by Are Holen.

While the 1970s and 1980s were characterized by small, marginal groups, the 1990s saw a wider circulation of religious ideas, networking and new organizations, with New Age gradually established as a part of mainstream culture. The organization *Alternativt Nettverk* (Alternative Network, founded in 1992) has played an important part in these developments. As the first, and the still most comprehensive and well known New Age organization in Norway, Alternative Network has spread its visions through a magazine (originally called *Alternativt Nettverk*; since 2006 titled *Visjon* [*Vision*]),[4] through a web site with news on activities, as an active participant in public debates, and increasingly as spokespersons for New Age vis a vis the church. Last but not least, so-called alternative fairs (*Alternativmesser*), organized annually in several Norwegian towns and cities, have proven highly successful. The fairs, like the journal, constitute a combination of business and spirituality—arenas in which professional New Agers can offer their products and meet colleagues and customers. In addition, and unlike the journal, the fairs have documented mainstream appeal and media appeal. By 2014, approximately 50 alternative fairs were being organized annually across the country, and visitor numbers are impressive. The Oslo fair alone attracts some 9000 visitors, and is today the largest alternative fair in Scandinavia. Media interest in these happenings can be related partly to visitor numbers, partly—one may assume—to pragmatic concerns. The fairs are occasions for journalists to literally "have it all" in one location, easily available and readily mediated.

Perhaps the most important of later organizational innovations, and one that partly grew out of Alternative Network and shares its main visions, is *Holistisk Forbund* (The Holistic Federation of Norway), founded in 2002. The Holistic Federation offers a full set of life passage rituals, thus making New

---

4. The original name was *Nettverksnytt* (*News of the network*), then *Alternativt Nettverk* (*Alternative Network*) before it became *Visjon* (*Vision*).

3

Age into a more comprehensive way of life, as well as a well-defined alternative to Christianity.

Research on Norwegian New Age dates back to the seventies[5] and has since the mid-1990s been rather extensive, including academic books, articles, PhD-dissertations and several master theses.[6] Most of these studies are written in Norwegian, implying that their influence have been limited to the Scandinavian countries. They belong, with some notable exceptions, to what Steven Sutcliffe has called "second wave" studies of New Age (Sutcliffe 2003). The first wave comprised macro level analyses, focusing on the content and boundaries of what was going on during the 1980s and 1990s, and referred to as the New Age movement (Sutcliffe 2003; Sutcliffe and Gilhus, eds. 2013, 6). It was followed by contextualized case studies, increasingly from around the world, but based primarily in European and US localities, and with England, Holland and North America as international strongholds.

The research project "Myth, Magic and Miracle meet Modernity (MMMM)" (1994–1998) has been vital in the Norwegian context. MMMM was led by historians of religion Ingvild Sælid Gilhus and Lisbeth Mikaelsson, and folklorists Bente Alver and Torunn Selberg, and contributed—as an early, ambitious and wide-ranging study of New Age in Scandinavia—in important ways to opening up and charting the course for this field of study on Norwegian grounds. The project was critical to phenomenologically-based approaches to religion as necessarily bounded, deep, serious, and pure, in the sense of being uniquely regulated by "religious" sensitivities and motivations. New Age was approached as a fluid and dynamic field, comprised of loosely organized networks and centers, professional entrepreneurs of various sorts, the gradual establishment of a market, and in addition as thinly spread across popular- and mainstream culture. We are, to quote the title of one of the books published on this phenomenon, facing a "re-enchantment of culture" (kulturens refortrylling)—one in which boundaries between different religions, and between the religious and the secular, are increasingly challenged (Gilhus and Mikaelsson 1998). Multi-religious actors are typical of this setting (Gilhus and Mikaelsson 2000), and New Age—rather than being limited to a particular sector—is located "all over the place" (Gilhus 2013).

A different sort of approach to New Age has been conducted at KIFO (Foundation for Church Research) and the University of Agder. Here sociological

---

5. The theologian Arild Romarheim was a pioneer in the study of new religious movements (1977, 1988).

6. Gilhus and Mikaelsson have provided an overview of scholarly and student studies of New Age and new religious movements in Norway (Gilhus and Mikaelsson 2012). Many of the studies included are directly (and explicitly) inspired by what has been known as "the Bergen milieu," and many of them—including most of the contributors to this book—either started their studies in Bergen or have been taught by teachers with a background from the University of Bergen.

approaches and quantitative research have dominated,[7] with stress placed on questions about belief and especially on the relationship of New Age to the church, and less on cultural impulses and hermeneutics.[8]

One main goal of this book is to make Norwegian-based research available to international scholarship. A second goal is to further develop major contributions, and thereby address a third wave of New Age-studies, "one that takes seriously the theoretical potential of New Age for general studies of "religion" (Sutcliffe and Gilhus, eds. 2013, 7), as well as contributes to the theorizing of New Age studies. Our chapters will approach these tasks differently, in relation to their chosen topics and particular directions of interest. Among common threads are the relationships between local/national and global currents and currencies. Several local or regional studies of New Age appeared during the first decade of the 21st century (Heelas and Woodhead 2005; Aupers and Houtman 2005; Frisk and Åkerbäck 2013; cf. also Frisk 1998), but national or state boundaries and traditions have rarely been considered. A concern with multi-religious actors, and with religion "outside of the box" (a particular sector) constitute yet another thread; we are interested in the presence and impact of religion in anticipated as well as in more unexpected places and spaces, in the form of both deep and shallow versions. We define religion as a particular type of communication, regardless of the types of systemicity involved. Religion, according to this perspective, comprises "people's communication with and about superhuman beings" (Gilhus and Mikaelsson 2001, 29). It thus includes religious beliefs and practices, in the ordinary sense of these terms, as well as the broader circulation of religious ideas and images, for instance through films, commercials, well-being culture and news media debates.

Religion here, there, anywhere and everywhere

Among the recent suggestions for theoretical advances in the field of New Age-studies is a spatial approach, developed by Jonathan Z. Smith and further adapted by Ingvild Sælid Gilhus (Smith 2003; Gilhus 2013). Originally constructed for the study of religion in the late ancient world, Smith's model focuses on *where* in society religion is situated (*here, there* or *anywhere*) and *how* it is practiced (Smith 2003). Gilhus has added "religion everywhere" to this as a fourth location and field of practice (Gilhus 2013, 38–39).

We thus have, with examples drawn from contemporary Norwegian society: (1) *religion there* as civic national religion, closely connected to a monarchical institution, and largely based on Christian churches and cathedrals. Christianity is described in the Constitution as "our heritage," and is accord-

---

7. Pål Ketil Botvar has in books and several articles discussed New Age currents in Norway from a statistic and sociological perspective (cf. Botvar 1993, 2009).

8. The challenges to the Church have also been treated by the historian of ideas Per Magne Aadnanes (2008) and the theologian Arild Romarheim (1977, 1988).

ingly central to official definitions of Norwegian identity, expressed through the monarchy, national ceremonies, through the school system, and to some extent through politics, for instance through debates on immigration. 2) *Religion here* is domestic religion, located primarily in homes, and belonging to the family, to former generations and generations to come (cf. Smith 2003, 24–27), and connected to the "continuation of the family as a biological and social unity" (Gilhus 2013, 38). *Religion anywhere* (3) occupies an interstitial space between the other two loci. Smith describes magicians, astrologers and various associations as typical of this space (Smith 2003, 30–36). In late modern Norway, a more or less professional New Age market is the most obvious example, characterized—as with the magicians and astrologers of the late ancient world depicted by Smith—by combinations of elements from *here* and *there* (Gilhus 2013, 38). Finally, (4) *Religion everywhere* comprises communication *about* religion, a dimension that is public and to which everyone in principle is exposed and has access. In contemporary societies, however, this dimension is particularly strong, with "the mediatization of religion" as a general and pervasive cultural process, providing religion here, there and everywhere with a rich and ever-expanding resource of religious ideas, notions, symbols and practices (cf. Gilhus 2013, 39).

Stig Hjarvard defines the mediatization of society as "the process whereby society to an increasing degree is submitted to, or become dependent on, the media and their logic" (2008a, 113). Media, accordingly, are agents of religious change, and institutionalized religions are no longer the prime source of mediatization. Rather, religious issues "are produced and edited by the media and delivered through genres like news, documentaries, drama, comedy, entertainment and so on. Through these genres, the media provide a constant fare of religious representations that mixes institutionalized religion and other spiritual elements in new ways" (Hjarvard 2008b, 12).

Hjarvard has contributed in important ways to the theorizing of these fields, particularly in regard to institutionalized religions, but his theory of mediatization fails to take seriously New Age. One may—and we in this book do—suggest that New Age, more than "normal" institutionalized religions, are uniquely suited for late modern media-scapes, and thrives partly because of them.

Religion *there* is vulnerable to mediatized scandals, to media focus on internal conflicts, and to value conflicts with secular society. But a powerful institution like the Church of Norway can strategically meet and negotiate mediatized demands and images, in ways that are quite different from individual New Age entrepreneurs. An extensive media focus on gay marriage has, for instance, forced church leaders to deal with this issue, but has not—despite more or less univocal demands from the press—resulted in reforms.

Religion *here* is in principle controlled by private actors, who can draw on resources from everywhere and anywhere, as well as from institutionalized religions. Religion *everywhere* and *anywhere* are regulated by legal terms and conditions only, such as freedom of speech restrictions with respect to racism. Otherwise, these are the fields of free float, with religion produced through complex, but to some extent predictable, processes. Different media formats tend, for instance, to produce quite different images of the same phenomena. Ideas and practices that are ignored or scandalized in Norwegian news media, are, in popular cultural media formats, such as weekly magazines and prime-time television programs, taken more seriously and/or used as entertainment. The angel school co-founded and run by Princess Märtha Louise is one example of this tendency. Coverage of alternative medicine and spiritism are others.

The question of definition and demarcation

The issue of what it *is*, has haunted New Age-studies from the start. The increasing preference for alternative self-designations among "New Agers" has further complicated things, along with the spread of New Age geographically, and in the direction of mainstream culture. In Norway, the preferred insider-terms are *spirituell* and *åndelig*, which function as synonyms and can both be translated "spiritual" (cf. Løøv and Melvær 2014).

One may, as do Steven Sutcliffe and Ingvild Gilhus, argue that the field of New Age studies has "not yet produced a clearly defined and cumulative set of research questions," and that "the most common question remains the basic problem of demarcating 'new age' phenomena within wider cultural formations" (2013, 6).

Dramatically different evaluations of impact, significance and extent are one consequence of this situation. Evaluations range from references to a revolution (Heelas and Woodhead 2005) and a re-enchantment of mainstream culture (Gilhus and Mikaelsson 1998, Aupers and Houtman, eds 2010; Partridge 2004, 2005) to the more or less non-existent remains of a dying movement (Bruce 2002). Scholars supportive of the latter find no common ground between the ideas and practices categorized as New Age, and consider New Age as not only eclectic in the extreme, but as trivial, superficial and socially insignificant—and accordingly as unlikely to survive over time. Linda Woodhead has claimed of Steve Bruce, and other representatives of this position, that their knowledge of New Age tends to be limited and to lack foundation in empirical research, and that they, in addition, tend to be shaped by an "inadequacy approach" (Woodhead 2010; see also Kraft 2014). New Age is judged (and found wanting) in relation to an implicit, Christian-based norm for "real" religion: it does not look like the religions known to us from Western church history, and is accordingly not a proper religion.

Woodhead prefers "spiritualities" for New Age, as do several other scholars in these fields. However, a shift in terminologies would not seem to solve definitional problems, and in addition introduces some new ones (see Gilhus 2013). Our decision to keep the category New Age is based on the need for an etic term, and New Age is still—recent competitors notwithstanding—the most established one. Most important, however, is the presence of a loose and varied but nevertheless recognizable, New Age discourse. In the words of Olav Hammer, "diverse components of a popular religious milieu that can be traced back to the spiritual ferment of the 1970s remain highly visible in the contemporary cultural landscape" (Hammer 2013, 239). Similarly, Stef Aupers and Dick Houtman have argued that "New Age spirituality is remarkably less eclectic and incoherent than typically assumed" (Aupers and Houtman 2013, 175). The diversity of the spiritual milieu, they claim, "results from rather than contradicts the existence of [...] coherent doctrine[s]" (Aupers and Houtman 2013, 179). In brief: "If it is believed that the sacred resides in the deeper layers of the self, after all, what else can be expected than people following their own personal paths, experimenting freely with a range of traditions in a highly heterogeneous spiritual milieu?" (Aupers and Houtman 2013, 179). Scholars should, at the same time, distinguish between emic rhetoric and etic realities, between the ideology of "truth as a pathless land" (to use then Theosophist Jiddu Krishnamurti's famous expression), and practices on the ground. The latter tend to cluster along shared paths, in line with a varied, but hardly boundless repertoire of New Age ideas and symbols. Modes of organization, socialization and distribution, similarly, are new and unfamiliar, but neither non-existent nor lacking in systematic forms (Taves and Kinsella 2013). New Age lacks church-like institutions, but is organized through networks, through markets and through new and old media (Hammer 2013, 224). Its boundaries are no doubt fuzzy and fluid, but not necessarily more so than other fields of "lived religion"—of religion as actually practiced by people, rather than imagined and systematized by their theological elites (see McGuire 2008). We must, as Jonathan Smith has taught us, live with the fact that map is not territory (Smith 1978), but the alternative—with religion, as with culture more generally—is rarely complete chaos, lacking anything resembling directives and guidelines. Some of the New Age directives and guidelines have had a global reach; available literally anywhere and everywhere (cf. Rothstein, ed. 2001). Others are local variations on global tendencies, including a seemingly endless and ever-changing variety of courses, workshops, books, and specialized methods, all of it fertilized by the increasing professionalization of the New Age market (Redden 2005).

Wouter Hanegraaff's highly influential distinction between New Age in a limited (*sensu stricto*) and a wide sense (*sensu lato*) is helpful in regard to the history of New Age as well as to current conditions (Hanegraaff 1996).[9] By New Age *sensu stricto*, he means a millenarian movement that emerged in England during the late 1960s, and for which the imminent coming of a New Age (the Age of Aquarius) was a central focus. By New Age *sensu lato* he refers to a broader current, one in which this earlier and more narrow movement

---

9. The distinction between a restricted and a broader version has also been adopted outside of New Age circles, with for instance Satanism defined in a *sensu stricto* and a *sensu lato sense*. See for instance Faxneld 2014.

merged with a broader mixture of American New Thought, metaphysical movements and counter cultural currents, that became visible in California during the 1970s (1996, 47). Towards the end of the 1970s, what had started out as a loose cultic milieu became "conscious of itself." Spiritual seekers from around the world came to acknowledge and recognize connections between these highly variegated currents, practices and ideas (Hanegraaff 1996, 522), and was accordingly able to relate to a sense of "we-ness" and commonality.

New Age disappeared as a self-designation during the 1980s, more or less simultaneously with the appearance of "spirituality," and due partly to the downplaying of millenarianism and the derogatory connotations it had over time acquired (Sutcliffe and Gilhus 2013, 4). This, then, is the situation: "New Age" is no longer an emic term of self-designation; the sense of "we-ness" among countercultural milieus has been replaced by a bewildering variety of networks, centers, festivals and businesses, catering to a broad variety of interests and motivations, and connected to mainstream as well as counter-cultural positions, and admixtures of the two.

What, then, are the core New Age practices and ideas? Self-spirituality remains strong, whether in the form of explicit references to inner gods, or vaguer notions of personal shortcomings, and connected to highly diverse directions of development, such as health, work, personal relationships and spiritual conditions (Heelas 1996; Gilhus and Mikaelsson 1998; Hammer 2013).

References to holistic perspectives are more or less mandatory, along with notions of the underlying "stuff" of the universe as comprised of energy and consciousness. Human beings are connected to this stuff, and are commonly granted the power of tapping into or manipulating it (Hammer 2013). Self-authority—*trust your personal experiences and intuitions only*—belongs to the level of dogma. Finally, esotericism seems to be widespread. Esotericism has in recent scholarship been defined both in terms of a focus on secrecy and concealment (Stuckrad 2005) and in the form of "rejected knowledge" (Hanegraaff 2012). Per Faxneld in a study of satanic feminism combines these two versions, defining esotericism as designating "a set of discourses that share a strong rhetorical focus on secrecy and concealment in relation to a supposed higher knowledge (in Stuckrad's sense), and which represent a form of rejected knowledge at odds with hegemonic discourses (in Hane-graaff's sense)" (Faxneld 2014; see also Asprem and Dyrendal 2015). Actual secrecy is not a requirement, according to this definition. Rather, stress is placed on rhetoric and emic conceptions. As for New Age discourse, a dis-trust in authorities has clearly outlived the earlier counterculture, whether in the form of medical institutions and knowledge, science in general or the doctrines and dogmas of established religions. The idea, for instance, that the medical establishment is either ignorant of, or gains from hiding, truths regarding sickness and health, appears to be common among distributors and practitioners of alternative medicine.

Stef Aupers and Dick Houtman have called attention to a lack of scholarly interest in the social construction of New Age spiritualities. New Age, they argue, should, like other religions, be approached and explored with respect to how it "is socially constructed, transmitted and reinforced" (Aupers and Houtman 2013, 195). Ann Taves and Michael Kinsella, similarly, have stressed the importance of assessing formative processes and the organizational forms of the apparently "unorganized" New Age (Taves and Kinsella 2013). Alternative Network has in the Norwegian context been vital, obviously in organizational terms. The flora of alternative centers, shops and individual entrepreneurs constitute other examples, along with the constant formation of small groups—some of them short-lived, others more permanent, and, in recent years, even fully established religions, some of which continue to participate in the New Age (economic) market, and continue to spill over into New Age spirituality more generally. Sami neo-shamanism, Maharishi Mahesh Yoga and Art of Living are examples of such tendencies.

New Age in Norway—unique traits and standardized imports

New Age is a global or globalizing religion, which is at the same time shaped by local/national landscapes—of the *there,* as well as the *anywhere* and *everywhere.*

On the one hand, and as nicely put by Mikael Rothstein, "basic tenets of New Age are quite intelligible even if concepts of modernity and postmodernity are disregarded" (Rothstein 2013, 129). Religious imagination is universal and New Age comparable to other types of religion (Rothstein 2013, 129–130). Core New Age ideas and practices, moreover, have during the last decades moved freely across cultures and national boundaries. On the other hand, and in line with basic tenets of theories of globalization, places still matter, along with culturally and socially specific frames of reference. Globalizing New Age discourses will to some extent be shaped by local and national conditions and expressed through local and nationally specific languages and vocabularies. Its impact on the *here* and *there* can similarly be expected to vary according to different local/national landscapes and trajectories.

What, then, are the typical and homegrown traits of Norwegian New Age? Our chapters will add flesh and color to this issue; for a brief and overarching introduction, the following characteristics can be noted.

First, the presence of one highly dominant religious institution is likely to shape the development of other religions, including New Age spiritualities. In the Norwegian context, The Church of Norway and Christianity in the form of Lutheran Protestantism has for centuries more or less monopolized the religious market, as well as been the favored religion of the state. Public discourses on religion and religious education in schools, similarly, have until recent decades been based primarily on Christian premises. What Norwegians have learnt about religion (their own and others) have thus been shaped by Christian views of what religion is and should be; of what constitutes proper, authentic and fake religiosity; and of where the distinction between the secular and the religious ought be placed.

New Age can be expected to thrive on a certain degree of tension with hegemonic formations and normative models of "authentic religion." The issue of where to draw the boundaries between one and the other has, at the same time, since the 1990s been hotly debated, inside and outside of the church, due partly—one may assume—to the fact that they are increasingly ignored and transgressed. In a piece published in 2000, Ingvild Gilhus and Lisbeth Mikaelsson apply the term "multi-religious actors" to individuals who belong to, or participate in, both Christian and New Age milieus and activities. Thirteen years later, Ketil Botvar and Ann Kristin Gresaker refer to an increasing number of "switchers" (pendlere)—individuals who move between Christian and New Age-milieus (Botwar and Gresaker 2013, see also Kraft 2015). Many of our chapters deal with border issues along these lines, and with the negotiations currently taking place regarding the dwellings and crossings (Tweed 2008) of people, symbols and rituals.

Folk religious traditions constitute another likely source of New Age-diversity. In the Norwegian context, New Age has to some extent merged with folk religious traditions, some of which have for centuries lingered on the margins of the Church. In contrast to these older traditions, however, opposition from the church may, in the case of New Age, have supported identity formation and a sense of collectivity. New Agers, due to their lack of submissiveness vis-a-vis religious authorities, feel free to take what they wish from the Christian traditions that Norwegians—regardless of their faith or lack thereof—are familiar with, and revise these as they see fit. The use of Christian folk religious traditions, or other Christian symbols and figures that belong to the margins of Church theology, constitute particularly rich resources. The use of angels is an obvious example; channeling from Maria Magdalene a more unusual, but equally interesting one. Pilgrimages constitute a third.

Second, the presence of New Age celebrities distinguishes the Norwegian field from its Nordic neighbors, and perhaps from other national contexts more generally. Princess Märtha Louise and Elisabeth Nordeng have, since the founding of their Angel school, belonged to a select group of persons with a more or less emblematic function in relation to New Age. The retired bell-ringer, Joralf Gjerstad (Snåsamannen), similarly, has won national fame as a warm hands (healing hands) healer. Gjerstad professes Christianity and his activity has in the main been accepted by the Church, as belonging to a Christian tradition of healing miracles, justified in the gospels. The emblematic position of single persons is not, moreover, a recent phenomena. The theologian and vicar Helge Hognestad became a household name during the 1970s in the wake of his support of New Age perspectives and attempts to combine these with Lutheran Christianity. The bestselling historical fantasy and pulp fiction author Margit Sandemo held a similar position during the

1980s and 1990s. The author of 172 novels, many of them wildly popular, Sandemo based her literary production on a combination of Norwegian folk beliefs and New Age ideas, and has for this been accused by theologians of playing with the dark forces and promoting an occult worldview (Penny 1997; cf. Gilhus 2012). Norway's relatively small population may to some extent explain this tradition of national New Age celebrities. Ideals of uniformity in a relatively homogenous culture constitute another possible source of explanation.

Third, the importance placed on nature and ecological thinking—of green style New Age—has been pronounced in the Norwegian setting. The founding leaders of *Alternativt Network*, Øyvind and Eirik Solum, have helped shape this development. *Alternativt Network* has from the very beginning highlighted ecological awareness and downplayed, for instance, the "prosperity consciousness" of New Age gurus like Depak Chopra. Additionally, established traditions of nature as essential to Norwegian culture and identity may have contributed to the importance of nature, the natural and ecology in New Age circles. Nature is commonly described as integral to Norwegianness (Gullestad 1990; Witoszek 1998), typically in relation to farming, leisure and expeditions, and increasingly in relation to the wilderness. The Norwegian philosopher Arne Næss (1912–2009) combined interests in outdoor life and environmentalism (Næss 1974). An important inspirational figure within the environmental movement of the late twentieth century, Næss coined the term "deep ecology" and helped add a spiritual basis to environmentalism as it developed on Norwegian grounds. Næss was himself inspired by the Neo-Hinduism of Mahatma Gandhi, and is an example of what Tarjei Rønnow has described as the increasingly important notion of nature as in itself a sacred cosmos (Rønnow 2007).

Fourth and finally, at least one new movement can be defined as homegrown. Shamanism comes in various versions in contemporary Norwegian society, most of them imported and having blurred boundaries with the New Age arena. Sami neo-Shamanism, although similarly shaped by global currents, is oriented towards the pre-Christian traditions of Sami religion. Sami neo-shamanism can be connected to New Age and Michael Harner-style shamanism, but draws upon and articulates resources from the ancient pre-Christian Sami religion, and combines these with ethno-political agendas and recent discourses in what one might term indigenous spirituality (Fonneland and Kraft 2013). Organizational innovation in these fields speak, moreover, explicitly to Norwegian politics of religion. The so-called Shamanistic Association, a group that has from the start been dominated by Sami shamanism, was in March 2012, after a first round of applications in which they failed to meet all the criteria demanded, granted status as an official religious community. They can thus offer rites of passage, like weddings, baptism and burials, and are entitled to government funding relative to the size of their membership.

Outline of the book

The book consists of 12 chapters, all of which are based on Norwegian material.[10] Chapter One (Mikaelsson) deals with the relationship between Christianity and New Age. It begins with a brief history of Christian-New Age relations on Norwegian grounds, and covers recent conditions, including official policies towards New Age on the part of the church on the one hand, and activities on the ground, on the other. "Lived religion" Christian style appears to be increasingly influenced by New Age-religion; boundaries are continuously discussed and negotiated, and border-zone groups and individuals continue to test and question their legitimacy.

Chapter Two (Løøv) covers "*Alternative Network/VisionWorks,*" the most influential of formal New Age-networks to emerge on Norwegian grounds, and in the international context exceptionally successful. In the words of the author, "no other countries have fostered a similarly broad and national network for alternative thought and practice." Founded in 1992, *Alternativt Nettverk* (later *VisionWorks*) has offered common platforms and agendas, including the magazine *Visjon*, annual alternative fairs, lectures and a website with news on various relevant activities. It has probably been vital to a sense of common identity among (at least parts of) the alternative milieu, and to the perception of "it" as a fluid, but nevertheless recognizable field. The influence of a few, talented persons, moreover, is striking, in comparison with Nordic countries more generally.

Chapters Three to Five deal with media, mediatization and texts, through a focus on New Age in news media and popular media (Kraft), spiritual tourism (Selberg), and educational politics over school curriculums (Andreassen). Chapter Three provides an overview of tendencies concerning coverage of New Age in news media and popular culture respectively, arguing that these differ considerably. Contrasting sparse treatment and a predominantly "bad religion" discourse in the news media, New Age constitutes a dominant religion in popular media, and one that is presented in positive ways. Kraft in the second part of her chapter uses this overview to critically discuss the mediatization of religion thesis developed by Stig Hjarvard, focusing in particular on his concept of banal religion and lack of focus on what Kraft describes as the New Age logic of popular media.

Chapter Four deals with the relationship between New Age and tourism, drawing upon local (Norwegian) examples, and discussed in the context

10. The ideas and chapters of this book were the theme of conferences at Solstrand Fjordhotel outside Bergen in 2013 and 2014. We wish to thank Liselotte Frisk, Knut Melvær, Liv Ingeborg Lied and Mikael Rothstein, who contributed very much to the book with their helpful comments. We extend our thanks to the Department of Archaeology, History, Cultural Studies and Religion, University of Bergen and the Department of History and Religious Studies, UiT—the Arctic University of Norway for financial support to the two conferences.

of globalizing trends. Torunn Selberg has chosen three examples through which to discuss these in more detail: the Norwegian enterprise Gaia Travel (earlier Totalhelse), and two package tours—one of which is based on the best-selling alternative (light) novel and movie *Eat. Pray. Love*, the other a pilgrimage along the Camino de Santiago.

Religion as a school subject has, during the last several decades, been a hotspot of Norwegian educational politics. Bengt Ove Andreassen, in Chapter Five, discusses the relative lack of attention granted to New Age and new religions, based on a study of national curricula and textbooks for Religious Education (RE) in primary, secondary and upper-secondary school in Norway in the period from 1996 to 2008. He is concerned, moreover, with representations of New Age within the world religion paradigm that has framed, and to a large extent still frames, religious education in the Norwegian school system.

Chapters Six to Nine discusses a select number of important New Age topics, starting with alternative medicine (Kalvig), and including chapters on the (Norwegian style) angel craze (Gilhus), conspirituality (Dyrendal) and spiritism (Kalvig). Alternative medicine is by far the most popular of New Age products in the Norwegian setting, as probably in Europe and the US more generally. Chapter Six, by Anne Kalvig, provides an overview of the field, including the increasing extent and importance of the alternative medical market, and important government actors. Moving on to a more specific, but highly popular phenomenon, Ingvild Sælid Gilhus discusses the Norwegian version of what for the American setting has been termed "the angel craze." Angels "travel light," Gilhus claims in her chapter, and have proven adaptable to highly different cultural and social circumstances. An introductory historical review adds flesh to some of their historical transformations and functions, as well as context to their contemporary texture. Moving on, Gilhus discusses the "spaces for angels," based on Jonathan Smith's spatial model, along with some of their main functions in contemporary Norway, as companions and therapists, messengers and guardians. Finally, contested issues are covered, including that between New Age and Lutheran protestant angel discourses, and the ways they have been played out in the Norwegian context.

Asbjørn Dyrendal (Chapter Eight) discusses conspirituality in the Norwegian New Age context. Originally coined by Charlotte Ward and David Voas (2011) "conspirituality" refers to a fairly recent development, based on the fusion of New Age spirituality and conspiracy culture. The specific scene selected for investigation is the Norwegian group blog *Nyhetsspeilet*, as the most important Norwegian example of international conspirituality, and, for a time, "the hub where Norwegian conspiracy culture met 'New Age' concerns." Dyrendal discusses issues concerning its rise and later developments, focusing particularly on the role of "epistemic authority" in regard to the construction of enemies, and—towards the end—the "apocalyptic wave" of its rise and fall.

Anne Kalvig (Chapter Nine) covers spiritualism in contemporary Norway, a major trend that so far has received little scholarly attention. She begins with an overview of organizations and more loosely organized market-oriented actors and practices, and moves on to a focus on "lived spiritualism." In the final section, she explores spiritualism in Norway through the model of religion here, there, anywhere and everywhere.

The three last chapters (10–12) discuss groups and milieus that are positioned ambiguously with regard to boundaries between New Age and new religious movements. Trude Fonneland (Chapter Ten) explores the Norwegian shamanic arena, with a particular focus on Sami neo-shamanism. Although today a "religion" in the formal or legal sense of the term, Sami neo-shamanism remains closely connected to basic New Age ideas and practices, and many of the shamans involved still offer their services on the New Age marketplace. In addition to qualifying for status as a homegrown New Age religion, Sami neo-shamanism also exemplifies the importance of national frameworks and regulations with respect to religious development, in this case in the sense of legal definitions of what constitutes a religion.

The Art of Living (AoL), discussed in Inga Bårdsen Tøllefsen's chapter, is another example of ambiguity concerning boundaries between New Age and—in this case—an Indian-oriented new religious movement, as well as the national framing that typically follows immigrant religions. Contrasting the stricter boundaries of AoL in India and the greater importance placed on gurus among Indian devotees, Norwegian AoL members have a somewhat different relationship with the organization, and seem to be less interested in gurus. AoL-Norway, in effect, has more blurred boundaries with the New Age market, in contrast to fellow members in India.

The last chapter is written by James Lewis and Oscar Torjus and provides a discussion of key sociological concepts in the study of New Age and new religious movements, in relation to statistical material concerning New Age and new religious movements.

Finally, Mikael Rothstein and Liselotte Frisk have contributed a comparative view from Denmark and Sweden respectively, focusing on the ways in which this situation in these countries differs and coincides with New Age in Norway.

References

Aadnanes, Per Magne. 2008. *Gud for kvarmann. Kyrkja og den nye religiøsiteten.* Oslo: University Publishing House.

Ahlberg, Nora. 1980. "Religiøs motkultur i Norge, 1967–1978." Unpublished PhD thesis, History of Religions, University of Oslo.

Asprem, Egil and Asbjørn Dyrendal. 2015. "Conspirituality reconsidered: How surprising and how new is the confluence of spirituality and conspiracy theory?" *Journal of Contemporary Religion* 30: 367–382.

Aupers, Stef and Dick Houtman, eds. 2010. *Religions of Modernity: Relocating the Sacred to the Self and the Digital.* Leiden: Brill.

Aupers, Stef and Dick Houtman. 2013. "Beyond the spiritual supermarket: The social and public significance of New Age spirituality." In *New Age Spirituality: Rethinking Religion,* edited by Steven Sutcliffe and Ingvild Sælid Gilhus, 174–196. Sheffield: Equinox.

Botvar, Pål Ketil. 1993. *Religion uten kirke: ikke-institusjonell religiøsitet i Norge, Storbritannia og Tyskland.* Diaforsk rapport nr. 10. Oslo: Diakonhjemmets høgskolesenter.

———. 2009. *Skjebnetro, selvutvikling og samfunnsengasjement: Den politiske betydningen av ulike former for religiøsitet blant norske velgere.* Ph.D dissertation. University of Oslo.

Botvar, Pål Ketil and Ann Kristin Gresaker. 2013. *Når troen tar nye veier. En studie av pendling mellom kristne og nyåndelige miljøer.* KIFO rapport 2013: 1.

Bruce, Steve. 2002. *God is Dead: Seculariation in the West.* Oxford: Blackwell.

Faxneld, Per. 2014. *Satanic Feminism. Lucifer as the Liberator of Woman in Nineteenth-Century Culture.* Stockholm: Molin & Sorgenfrei.

Fonneland, Trude and Siv Ellen Kraft. 2013. "New Age, Sami Shamanism and indigenous spirituality." In *New Age Spiritualities. Rethinking Religion,* edited by Ingvild Sælid Gilhus and Steven Sutcliffe, 132–145. Durham: Acumen.

Frisk, Liselotte. 1998. *Nyreligiöstitet i Sverige: ett religionsvetenskapeligt perspektiv.* Nora: Nya Doxa.

Frisk, Liselotte and Peter Åkerbäck. 2013. *Den mediterande Dalahästen.* Stockholm: Dialogos Förlag.

Gilhus, Ingvild Sælid. 2012. "Post-secular religion and the therapeutic turn: Three Norwegian examples." In *Post-Secular Religious Practices,* edited by Tore Ahlbäck, 62–75. Scripta Instituti Donneriani Aboensis 24. Åbo, Finland: Donner Institute for Research in Religious and Cultural History.

———. 2013. "All over the place": The contribution of New Age to a spatial model of religion." In *New Age Spirituality: Rethinking Religion,* edited by Steven Sutcliffe and Ingvild Sælid Gilhus, 35–49. Sheffield: Equinox.

Gilhus, Ingvild Sælid and Lisbeth Mikaelsson. 1998. *Kulturens refortrylling. Nyreligiøsitet i moderne samfunn.* Oslo: University Publishing House.

———. 2000. "Multireligiøse aktører og kulturens refortrylling. *Sosiologi i dag* 30(2): 5–22.

———. 2001. *Nytt blikk på religion.* Oslo: Pax forlag.

———. 2012. "Bibliografisk oversikt over nyreligiøsitetsforskningen i Norge." *Aura* 4(2012): 21–45.

Gullestad, Marianne. 1990. "Naturen i norsk kultur. Foreløpige refleksjoner." In *Kulturanalyse,* edited by Trine Deichmann-Sørensen and Ivar Frønes, 8–96. Oslo: Gyldendal.

Hammer, Olav. 2013. "Cognitively optimal religiosity. New Age as a case study." In *New Age Spirituality: Rethinking Religion,* edited by Steven Sutcliffe and Ingvild Sælid Gilhus, 212–226. Equinox.

Hanegraaff, Wouter J. 1996. *New Age Religion and Western Culture: Esotericism in the Mirror of Secular Thought.* Leiden: Brill.

———. 2012. *Esotericism and the Academy: Rejected Knowledge in Western Culture.* Cambridge: Cambridge University Press.

Heelas, Paul and Linda Woodhead. 2005. *The Spiritual Revolution: Why Religion is Giving Way to Spirituality.* Oxford: Blackwell.

Hjarvard, Stig. 2008a. "The Mediatization of Society: A Theory of the Media as Agents of Social and Cultural Change." *Nordicom Review* 29 (2): 105–134.

———. 2008b. "The mediatization of society: A theory of the media as agents of religious change." *Northern Lights* 6: 9–26.

Kraft, Siv Ellen. 2014. "New Age Spiritualities." In *Controversial New Religions,* edited by James Lewis, 302–314. Oxford: Oxford University Press.

———. 2015. "Royal angels in the News. The case of Märtha Louise, Astarte Education and the Norwegian News Press." In *Nordic New Religions,* edited by James Lewis and Inga Bårdsen Tøllefsen, 190–202. Brill Handbooks on Contemporary Religion 11. Leiden: Brill.

Løøv, Margrethe and Knut Melvær. 2014. "Spirituell, religiøs eller åndelig? Om selvbetegnelser i det norske alternativmiljøet." *Tidsskrift for religion og kultur* 1(2014): 113–133.

McGuire, Meredith B. 2008. *Lived Religion: Faith and Practice in Everyday Life.* Oxford: Oxford University Press.

Næss, Arne. 1974. *Økologi, samfunn og livsstil, utkast til en økosofi.* Oslo: Universitets-forlaget.

NOU 2013: 1 *Det livssynsåpne samfunn.* Oslo: Kulturdepartementet.

Partridge, Christopher. 2004. *The Re-Enchantment of the West, Volume 1: Alternative Spiritualities, Sacralization, Popular Culture and Occulture.* London: Clark International.

———. 2005. *The Re-Enchantment of the West, Volume 2: Alternative Spiritualities, Sacralization, Popular Culture and Occulture.* London: Clark International.

Penny, Bridget. 1997. *Margit Sandemo. Forfatter og religiøs inspirator i et moderne samfunn.* Hovedoppgave i religionsvitenskap. Bergen: Universitetet i Bergen.

Redden, Guy. 2005. "The New Age: Towards a market model." *Journal of Contemporary Religion* 20(2): 231–246.

Romarheim, Arild. 1977. *Moderne religiøsitet, en oversikt over ca. 30 nyere bevegelser og retninger som arbeider aktivt i Skandinavia.* Oslo: Aschehoug.

———. 1988. *Kristus i Vannmannens tegn. Nyreligiøse oppfatninger av Jesus Kristus.* Oslo: Credo forlag.

Rønnow, Tarjei. 2007. *Saving Nature: Religion as Environmentalism. Environmentalism as Religion.* Berlin: Lit Verlag.

Rothstein, Mikael, ed. 2001. *New Age Religion and Globalization.* Aarhus: Aarhus University Press.

Rothstein, Mikael. 2013. "Dolphins and other humans: New Age identities in comparative perspective." In *New Age Spirituality: Rethinking Religion*, edited by Steven J. Sutcliffe and Ingvild S. Gilhus, 117–131. Durham: Acumen.

Smith, E. 2010. "And they lived happily together? On the relationship between confessionalism, establishment and secularism under the constitution of Norway." In *Law and Religion in the 21st Century—Nordic Perspectives*, edited by L. Christoffersen, L. Å. Modèer and S. Andersen, 123–143. Copenhagen: Djøf Publishing.

Smith, Jonathan Z. 1978. *Map is not Territory: Studies in the History of Religions*. Chigaco, IL: University of Chicago Press.

———. 2003. "Here, there, and anywere." In *Prayer, Magic, and the Stars in the Ancient and Late Antique World*, edited by S. Noegel, J. Walker and B. Wheeler, 21–36. University Park: Pensylvania State University Press.

Stuckrad, Kocku von. 2005. *Western Esotericism: A Brief History of Secret Knowledge*. London: Equinox.

Sutcliffe, Steven. 2003. "Category formation and the History of 'New Age.'" *Culture and Religion: An Interdisciplinary Journal* 4(1): 5–29.

———. 2013. "New Age, world religions and elementary forms." In *New Age Spirituality: Rethinking Religion*, edited by Steven J. Sutcliffe and Ingvild S. Gilhus, 17–34. Durham: Acumen.

Sutcliffe, Steven J. and Ingvild Sælid Gilhus, eds. 2013. *New Age Spirituality: Rethinking Religion*. Durham: Acumen.

Taves, Ann and Michael Kinsella. 2013. "Hiding in plain sight: The organizational forms of "unorganized religion." In *New Age Spirituality: Rethinking Religion*, edited by Steven J. Sutcliffe and Ingvild S. Gilhus, 84–98. Durham: Acumen.

Tweed, Thomas A. 2008. *Crossing and Dwelling: A Theory of Religion*. Cambridge, MA: Harvard University Press.

Witoszek, Nina. 1998. *Norske naturmytologier fra Edda til økofilosofi*. Oslo: Pax Forlag.

Woodhead, Linda. 2010. "Real Religion and Fuzzy Spirituality? Taking sides in the Sociology of Religion." In *Religions of Modernity: Relocating the Sacred to the Self and the Digital*, edited by Stef Aupers and Dick Houtman, 31–48. Leiden: Brill.

— 1 —

Church Religion and New Age:
An Encounter between Rivals?

LISBETH MIKAELSSON

Church religion in this chapter refers to the Church of Norway, the main religious institution in the country, belonging to the family of Lutheran churches. Until 2012, it was a state church according to the Norwegian constitution. Its new position means that constitutionally the church will continue to occupy a privileged religious role in society as *folkekirke*.[1] Today its membership comprises about 75 percent of the total population of five million people.[2] In addition various Protestant denominations, Catholic and Orthodox churches are represented here, as are Islam, Hinduism, Buddhism, Sikhism and a number of other religions.

Scholars and officials attached to the Church of Norway have discussed the spiritual current we are calling New Age[3] in this book for decades,[4]

---

1. The literal translation would be "folk church."

2. www.kirken.no.

3. Confer the discussion of the New Age concept in the introductory chapter of the book. Other terms covering more or less the same bouquet of phenomena used by Scandinavian scholars are "popular religion" (*populærreligion*) (Frisk 2013), "new religiosity" (*nyreligiøsitet*) (Kraft 2011), and "new spirituality" (*nyåndelighet*) (Botvar and Gresaker 2013). A term frequently used by both insiders and outsiders in Norway has been "the alternative movement" (*alternativbevegelsen*).

4. Central publications are Arild Romarheim, *Kristus i vannmannens tegn* (1988), Helge Hognestad, *Morgendemring. En ny spiritualitet?* (1989) and *Den indre kilde. Vår tids religiøsitet i lys av historien* (1994), Leif Gunnar Engedal and Arne Tord Sveinall (eds.), *Troen er løs. Bidrag til belysning av forholdet mellom folkereligiøsitet, nyreligiøsitet og kristen tro* (2000), Per M. Aadnanes, *Gud for kvarmann. Kyrkja og den nye religiøsiteten* (2008), Notto R. Thelle, *Prinsessens engler: Invitasjon til en samtale om alternativ spirit-*

a proof that New Age spirituality has been taken seriously as a religious challenge. The lack of distinct religious borders concerning teachings, leadership, organization, followers and practice in the New Age complicates how it should be assessed for scholars, and the same is true for church representatives. Is it a passing fad or a religious renewal that may benefit the church, or maybe a rival on a par with other religions, only more demanding because it does not sail under the usual kind of religious flag? A diffuse competitor may be more difficult to handle than a clear-cut one, and, as Jonathan Smith has argued, the closest and most similar religious "others" are the most interesting ones in theological thinking (Smith 2004, 27). The allegation that New Age is indeed a rival religion has been a significant part of the international evangelical/fundamentalist attack on the movement. Inspired by demonic forces, it may infiltrate Christian groups and infect Christian beliefs without the danger being realized because of its dispersed appearance. This polemic is also found in Norway, and books by some of the primary exponents of "devilish conspiracy"-accusers such as Constance Cumbey (1984) and Carol Matrisciana (1988) have been translated into Norwegian (cf. Mikaelsson 2008a; Saliba 1999). Yet, demonization of New Age spirituality is not generally representative of the attitude of members of the Church of Norway.

Since its publication in 2005, Paul Heelas and Linda Woodhead's book, *The Spiritual Revolution*, with its assertation that subjective spirituality is superseding established, traditional Christianity, has frequently been taken as a point of departure when discussing the relationship between church religion and New Age. Undeniably, New Age spirituality has changed the Norwegian religious scene; however, prophesising its religious usurpation seems rather presumptuous at this point. A more reasonable conjecture is that the Church of Norway will continue to influence religious life in the future due to its integration into Norwegian culture. As Pål Ketil Botvar and Jan-Olav Henriksen have argued, a real spiritual revolution would imply that fundamental patterns in Norwegian society rooted in church religion would change, which is not a very likely scenario at this point (Botvar and Henriksen 2010, 80). Yet, many church members today behave like "multi-religious actors," combining church religion and New Age elements at will. Such individualist pluralism may become even more common in the future (Gilhus and Mikaelsson 2000). Another line of development would be to accommodate such spirituality into the church itself, which is already taking place to a considerable extent.

A central item in Heelas and Woodhead's analysis is a distinction betweeen two different religious modes having key values declared to be incompatible. One is characterized by conformity with external authority called "life-as" religion that is said to be typical of established church religion. The

---

ualitet (2010), Tormod Engelsviken, Rolv Olsen and Notto R. Thelle (eds.), *Nye guder for hvermann? Femti år med alternativ spiritualitet* (2011), Jan-Olav Henriksen and Kathrin Pabst (2013), *Uventet og ubedt. Paranormale erfaringer i møte med tradisjonell tro.*

other mode, called "subjective-life" spirituality, is described as "authentic connection with the inner depths of one's unique life-in-relation" (Heelas and Woodhead 2005, 4). Personal experience and states of consciousness, feelings, memories, thoughts, dreams and inner conscience become subjective sources of meaning and authority instead of established traditions (2005, 3–4). Such a distinction throws light on many sides of the encounter between church religion and New Age spirituality, i. e. characters and conflicts, strategic approaches, religious commuting, and changes in church religion that can be attributed to the impact of the new spirituality—all matters that will be accounted for in this chapter. By way of introduction the character of the Church of Norway as an inclusive *folkekirke* will be discussed. For generations the church has been able to harbour factions and keep the loyalty of secularized members. Its ability to house disagreements and tolerate the passivity of its members is relevant for the framing and development of New Age in Norwegian society. On the other side there are influential strata in the church, not least the Christian newspapers and magazines, displaying critical, if not hostile, positions towards non-Christian religion. Thus church religion does not speak with one voice. None the less, the dominant role of the institution is an important structural aspect affecting New Age spirituality and other parts of contemporary religious pluralism.

The Church of Norway

The Norwegian monarchy adopted Christianity approximately one thousand years ago. Church religion was subsequently established by law as a religious monopoly in the country. First in the shape of Catholicism, and then, following the Protestant reformation in 1537, membership in the Lutheran-Evangelical state church was obligatory for all citizens until 1845. Since the nineteenth century, religious pluralism has been on the rise. In the wake of pietist revivals, several lay organizations for inner and foreign mission were established from the middle of the ninteteenth century onwards. The lay organizations gave new social strata power in religious matters, and fostered elites whose influence and authority became comparable to that of the clergy. Having different theological profiles, the organizations were not homogenous in all respects, and some of the most energetic bridge-builders between the church and the New Age have a background in foreign missions. Yet, the most conservative lay segment, tending towards biblicism, has been very critical of aspects of modern developments, resulting in a series of long-lasting struggles in the twentieth century on the topics of liberal theology, female clergy, abortion and homosexuality; the last two are issues still on the agenda. Thus a significant tension in church religion exists between conservative theologians and ditto lay believers on the one hand, and advocates of the church as an inclusive, national institution on the other. The tension has been a marked trait for almost two centuries. Assisted by the Labour Party when in power, liberal troops won important victories in the period after World War II. Women priests and bishops are, for instance, now widely accepted. There is good reason to expect that the distance to new religious movements is most pronounced in the conservative group.

A third segment in the church is the large group of passive members who seldom or never participate in church activities.[5] How to make the church more attractive to this group, whether in style or message, has been on the agenda for a long time. Secularization has been a standard explanation of the situation, but why people maintain their membership is a more puzzling issue. A common ecclestical supposition has been the "master of ceremony" thesis; i.e. that people still need the church to solemnize important life transitions. This is a likely interpretation as far as it goes, but the spiritual upsurge has indicated that people's passivitiy is not that easily explained.

One factor to keep in mind, regarding both the position of the church and the lack of participation, is cultural identity. To be Christian in the sense of belonging to the Church of Norway has been part of national identity for centuries and has provided the institution with an incomparable national status as "folk" church, the church of the Norwegian people.[6] In the modern era, this has had the curious effect that many people have regarded themselves as Christian but not religious, to repeat my mother's self-definition. The adjective "religious" has correspondingly been reserved for active lay people and free church members (cf. Hegstad 1996, 27–28). For passive Christians, church membership has not necessitated piety, belief in God and Christian dogmas, or regular church attendance. The rites of passage, however, have been respected; the reason for this loyalty is likely to be more complex than the "master of ceremonies" thesis. Rather, it can be assumed that a changeable blend of family and local traditions, national identity, aesthetic and religious motives is at work. Harald Hegstad, who has made a thorough study of the division between *"folkekirke"* and *"trosfellesskap"*[7] groupings in three local congregations, warns against simplifying or degrading the religious and cultural values of the *folkekirke* segment (Hegstad 1996, 411).

The concept of popular religion represents another gateway to the beliefs and practices of common members. According to Torunn Selberg, popular religion (*folkelig religiøsitet*) comprises religious forms primarily existing in everday life that "can be personal, creative and related to experience rather than dogmas and institutions" (Selberg 2011, 10). Referring to statistical surveys in the 1980s, Arild Romarheim argues that popular religion in Norway

---

5. Grace Davie's concept of "vicarious religion" is relevant here. Vicarious religion characterizes churches in which a religious minority is active, so to speak, on behalf of the passive majority (cf. Davie 2007).

6. The sociological concept of "civil religion" is relevant to understand the national role of the church, cf. for instance Margit Warburg *et al.*, *Civilreligion i Danmark* (2013).

7. The word means "community of believers."

is becoming progressively more influenced by ideas derived from New Age spirituality. In his book *Kristus i Vannmannens tegn* (1988), he draws a scenario of common people sceptical of the church, but positive towards Christianity (1988, 134). His investigations of popular religious elements in weekly magazines published from the 1960s until the present show a marked increase of subject matter involving occultism, astrology, divination, healing and magic, while during the last decade an increased belief in spirits is observable (Romarheim 1988, 135–136; 2011, 55). Taking into account the enormous popularity of weekly magazines in the Norwegian population—almost 100 million magazines are printed every year and on average each one is read by 4–5 persons—their influence on ordinary people's religious orientation appears to be significant (Romarheim 2011, 52).

The concept of *folkekirke* gained a new status in 2012 when the Constitution was changed. "The Evangelical-Lutheran Religion" is no longer the "official religion" of the Norwegian state; it has been replaced with The Church of Norway defined as *"Norges Folkekirke."*[8] The church is still constitutionally declared to continue as "Evangelical–Lutheran" and be supported by the state, and a number of special relations between the church organization and the state are not yet dissolved. A mixture of ecclesiastical and political motives is encapsulated in *folkekirke* terminology. The result is a phrasing that specifies the church as an inclusive religious community, yet retaining its old confessional identity.

The constitutional solution represents a halfway position between a state church and a free church, and entails that the religio-cultural functions of the church in Norwegian society should be carried on. Esteem of social cohesion and cultural heritage are included in the *folkekirke* concept, a way of thinking that allows members to identify themselves as *kulturkristen* ("cultural Christian"), a designation sometimes heard nowadays. More consciousness about the ties linking a large majority of Norwegians to the church and consideration for their spiritual needs and preferences can be registered in various church-related contexts, for instance in the research institution KIFO,[9] which regularly publishes statistics, reports and books about church life and the religious situation in Norway.[10]

The ties between church and common people incarnated in the local sanctuary is a significant aspect of the *folkekirke* function. Affection for the local

---

8. Cf. §§ 2 and 16 in the Constitution.

9. Its official name is KIFO, *Institutt for kirke-, religions- og livssynsforskning*. It is primarily funded by the state.

10. Much public discussion within and outside the church has accompanied its formal secession from the state. In 2013 a committee appointed by state authorities led by theologian Sturla Stålsett published its report *Det livssynsåpne samfunn*. The report called for a new state politics based on more regard for the existent pluralism and less privileging of the Church of Norway. A remarkable omission in the report is any mention of New Age spirituality.

church building, especially if it is old and beautiful, became visible in the 1990s during a period of church burnings. Inspired by Satanism, local black metal musicians in 1992 set fire to a medieval stave church in the city of Bergen.[11] This shock was followed by a series of church burnings elsewhere; within five years, about thirty churches had been set on fire, half of which were demolished (Aadnanes 2008, 235). The sorrowful reactions in local communities and the zeal evinced in having the churches rebuilt indicate the strong symbolic function of the local sanctuares for many people. Somewhat surprisingly, the sense of loss went far beyond regular church-goers (Aadnanes 2008, 243; Aagedal 2003). The comforting role the church has taken in moments of local and national disasters is another *folkekirke* function, reaching beyond the phalanx of believers. This was most convincingly demonstrated after the 22 July 2011 terrorist incident, when 77 people, most of them youngsters, were killed and government buildings demolished. Great numbers of people afterwards sought the local churches and used them as common arenas for expressing their grief (cf. Aagedal *et al.* 2013).

The rites of passage offered by the church still have considerable support as the figures reveal: According to statistics from 2013, 62 percent of the babies born in Norway were baptized, about 63 percent of all youngsters went through the rite of confirmation, and 90 percent of all burials were performed by the church (Holberg and Brottveit 2014, 13–14, 17, 20). Yet there is no way of denying the fact that church religion, including the lay organizations, has suffered decline. In ten years, membership in the church has gone down about ten percent, a decline mostly explained by immigration. But withdrawals and a decrease in baptisms are also part of the picture (Holberg and Brottveit 2014, 43). The marked decline in baptism has become a matter of ecclesiastical concern. Even babies born to church members are no longer regularly baptized. Figures are uncertain, but about 80 percent of the babies in this category are stipulated to have undergone the rite (Holberg and Brottveit 2014, 14). How to attract and activate the estranged segment is thus a strategic as well as missional challenge for the church. The decline in baptisms has, for instance, prompted a minister to suggest a new rite combining blessing and intercessory prayer for babies whose parents desist from baptism due to the religious promises involved (Skaar 2015). A local church in Trondheim has initiated a simplified drop-in baptism, following a model practised in the Church of Sweden for the purpose of inducing more parents to choose baptism (Friestad 2015).

The upsurge of New Age spirituality kindled an unexpected hope that secularization is not an inevitable process after all. Awareness that this spirituality, and now also spiritualism, attract thousands of people have prompted

---

11. The Norwegian version of black metal has fans in all parts of the world. The new stave church, carefully built in the old manner and raised in the same place, has become a well-known pilgrimage site for Satanists and black metal fans. Bergen is reckoned as "the capital" of black metal in Europe (Aasen 2015).

strategic reflections and measures in church contexts. Besides, many common members have by word and deed demonstrated their appreciation of the "spiritual supermarket" and the possibilty of religious commuting.

Grassroot combination of Church Religion and New Age Spirituality

Commitment to New Age ideas has produced one national "life stance" organization in Norway with a clear New Age profile; i. e. *Holistisk Forbund* (Holistic Society), founded in 2001 as a replica of the successful *Human-etisk Forbund* (The Humanistic Association).[12] Both organizations offer rites of passage corresponding to those of the church, thus being alternative and competing options. In Norway, it is forbidden by law to be a member of more than one religious or life stance community due to the economic support provided by public authorities to these organizations; the size of the sum is calculated on the basis of membership. The membership of *Holistisk Forbund* is remarkably small; registered members number about 1000 people.[13] Considering the country's lively New Age scene, the number is puzzling. For instance, about 100 000 people annually visit the large alternative fairs being held annually in a number of Norwegian cities (Mikaelsson 2011, 80). The well-known hostility against organized religion in New Age circles is a possible factor, but it can hardly be a complete explanation of the modest membership. The idea that people are allowed to function as multi-religious actors probably provids a significant clue (Gilhus and Mikaelsson 2000). Persons outside the reach of both formal and informal control mechanisms are free to combine church membership and New Age affinities more or less as they like. Ordinary members may thus enjoy both the benefits of solemn rituals of passage in the church and the benefits of spiritual experimentation provided by the New Age market.

A recent investigation of religious commuting between Christian and New Age milieus (Botvar and Gresaker 2013) substantiates the assumption that a number of people behave like multi-religious actors in the above-mentioned sense. Conclusions were based on questionnaires from about 500 people affiliated with the organization *Alternativt Nettverk*,[14] and in-depth interviews with seven informants selected from the questionnaire respondents (2013, 9). The concept "religious commuting" is roughly defined as "in many cases a gradual transition from one world of conceptions to another, without necessarily changing one's formal connection to a religious or life stance community" (2013, 13, my translation). Most relevant for the line of reasoning being pursued here is that commuting may mean regular travel between

---

12. The organization was founded in 1956 and its members counted 84300 1 January 2014. www.ssb.no/kultur–og–fritid/statistikker/trosamf/aar/2014-11-18

13. www.trooglivssyn.no/?id=135240

14. *Alternativt Nettverk* was founded in 1992 as a network organization for practitioners of New Age spirituality and alternative therapies.

two different places. Thus the word can function as a metaphor for alternation between church religion and New Age milieus.

Analysis of the questionnaires indicated that one fifth of respondents had been in touch with a Christian group for a shorter or longer period. Another group, about ten per cent, had switched between the two milieus several times. The minority with such contacts are characterized as commuters. Most of these had retained their membership in the Church of Norway, but were not active in Christian contexts (2013, 49). A significant difference between the commuters and the rest was more involvement in Christian milieus during adolescence. This is said to have made them more positive toward church religion (2013, 25). All seven informants were church members when young, four were members at the time of the interviews, and the group as a whole had moved in and out of the church more than people in general. They can be characterized as definitely being more seekers than shoppers, being reflective about religious matters and engaged in various spiritual activities. All the church members emphasized that the church is a natural part of Norwegian culture, and therefore important to preserve as a source of identity. Four had used church rites to mark significant occasions in life (2013, 40–41, 50). One of the three who had resigned nevertheless describes her positive reaction when present at a baptism in the family:

> [...] The building, the beauty, the music, the rituals, it was something there that was so beautiful, and really gave me something on the inside.
>
> (Johanne, Botvar and Gresaker 2013, 40, my translation)

Yet, comments about boring services and outsider sentiments also express an ambivalence to church religion among the members. For those whose attitude is so positive that they might become active in a Christian group, it is decisive that the church is inclusive as regards the ideas and experiences common in New Age circles. Interestingly, informants seem satisfied with a loose connection to spiritual milieus as well; the data indicate that reading religious literature is more important than participating in alternative religious communities (2013, 50–51).

The most famous commuter in Norway is the royal princess Märtha Louise. Probably no single person has done more to awaken public interest in the new spirituality (cf. Gilhus 2012; Kraft 2008). As a royal, Märtha Louise is hardly a grassroot representative, but theologically she is, being educated as a physiotherapist and in later years attaining remarkable success as a spiritual entrepreneur and expert on relations with angels. The controversial princess has renounced her royal apanage, but neither her title nor church membership. Her marriage was celebrated with much pomp and circumstance in the grand cathedral Nidarosdomen, and her three children have been baptized. The princess can be seen as a personal model of the union between the old church and New Age spirituality. Her father the king, until 2012 formal head of the church and professedly identifying with it, has desisted from publicly criticizing his daughter's activities. What his silence implies is not evident, but it might be taken as royal support of a church that is generous enough to include people like his daughter.

Neither Märtha Louise nor the commuters in the above-mentioned project are "spiritual shoppers." To draw a strong dividing line between (serious) seekers and (superficial) shoppers is not adviseable, given the spectrum of attitudes, possibly turbid as well as changeable. Yet, the present capitalist market of New Age does allow individuals a consumer role that disregards their motives and use of products (Mikaelsson 2011 and 2013; Redden 2005). People may, for instance, visit alternative fairs for fun, curiosity, stimulation, health problems and social reasons. On the individual level, the alternation between church religion and New Age need not be a serious affair. Also, as mentioned, even religiously minded people are not keen to find a social anchorage in the holistic milieu. The individual combination of church affiliation and spiritual attractions may thus take different forms. Arguably a primary point is that commuting contributes to upholding both the church and the New Age market. Secondly, commuters aid the inclusive *folkekirke* position of the church, while it can be surmised that the growth of *Holistisk Forbund* is hampered.

Helge Hognestad: Priest and New Age advocate

In spite of all the sensational press reports about the princess, the person causing most commotion for his New Age ideas has been Helge Hognestad (1940–). His public revolt against the traditional bearing of the church, played out in academic and ecclesiastical arenas, has no parallels in the history of church religion and New Age in Norway. Having a doctor's degree in theology and years of experience as chaplain and vicar, Hognestad has been an elite opponent to central Christian doctrines, voicing his views in a number of articles in the press and in the volumes *En kirke for folket* (1982), *Morgendemring. En ny spiritualitet* (1989), *Den indre kilde. Vår tids religiøsitet i lys av historien* (1994). His religious journey is sketched in his autobiography *Fra alter til våpenhus. På leting etter Gud bak dogmer og bastante meninger* (2000). Essentially, the text is an apology defending the author's wish to return to ministry, allegedly with a deeper spiritual understanding of Christ, the church and himself.

In the period between the late 1960s and the mid-1980s, Hognestad became the country's principal critic of ecclesiastical rituals and preaching. Instead of lamenting secularization, he attacked the church itself for causing people's estrangement. A summit was reached in 1978 when Hognestad obtained a doctorate for a sociologically-oriented study of preaching.[15] His contention

---

15. Helge Hognestad, *Forkynnelse som legitimering. Eksegetisk-homiletiske studier til Matteus-evangeliet.* Vol. 1 *Forkynnelse til oppbrudd. Studier i Matteus-evangeliet og kirkens bruk av det.* Vol 2. *Forkynnelsen—kirkens forsvar? Studier i Matteus-evangeliet og kirkens bruk av det.*

in this period was that ecclesiastical discourse, based on formulations origi-
nating in the primitive church and the Protestant reformation, constructs a
version of reality, a "church-created reality." This construct legitimates the
existent church institution and its power, but does not meet people's needs
in today's world. He claims that the church pushes its own church-created
reality on people in an authoritarian way without heeding their experiences
and life situations. Moreover, the church overlooks the ethical challenges of
poverty and suppression in our time by pointing to the individual's broken
relationship to God as the source of all human problems, while the solace
preached is the restoration of this relationship as conveyed by the church.
As a controversial chaplain in Høvik near Oslo, Hognestad instead practised
"theology from below." This was meant to be an open and unfinished theology, created in cooperation with the congregation (Hognestad 2000, 28).
A popularized version of his radical thinking in this period was imparted in
En kirke for folket (1982). It concludes with the following declaration:

> Our task is to see how God operates and creates today. We shall identify
> God in our everyday life, in our psychic and social reality. Reap experi-
> ences of God. And pass it on to others. In our own words.
>
> (Hognestad 1982, 140, my translation)

It all became too much for the bishop of Oslo, Andreas Aarflot, who pressed
Hognestad to go on study leave in 1984. In 1989 Hognestad asked to be untied
from his ordination promise after having reoriented himself in the alternative spiritual milieu. The search for spiritual enlightenment had brought
Hognestad into contact with the well-known spritual teacher Jes Bertelsen
in Denmark. Bertelsen's idea of the "Christ process," described in his book
Kristusprocessen (1989), influenced Hognestad's reflections.

Hognestad's book Morgendemring (1989) appears as a piece of standard New
Age conceptions about the self, human consciousness and cosmic energies
contextualizing his interpretation of Jesus: Jesus did not make atonement
for human sin. What he had attained was a realization of his higher, spiritual
self. Thus he could function, not as a saviour, but as a model and guide for
humans in their own spiritual development. In Den indre kilde (1994), Hognestad delineates a historical evolution linking religion, culture and gender. The first phase is said to have been dominated by a collective feminine
consciousness expressed through goddess worship and a unity-with-nature
mentality. The second phase revolutionized human life when a male ego-
consciousness marked by rationality and exploitation of nature developed.
As time went by, religion became dominated by patriarchal structures and
cults of male gods. The third phase means that the opposition between the
feminine and the masculine will gradually be replaced by a holistic gender
synthesis and development of the Self. This phase started with Jesus and
his teachings of a kingdom of God within, but the insight of Jesus has been
repressed by the power-seeking church through the centuries. Now, how-

ever, the time is ripe for the "Christ process" in the human psyche.

Hognestad's views obviously conflicts with Lutheran teachings, yet in 1996 he contacted bishop Aarflot in order to have his rights as priest restored. He was met with no sympathy by the bishop, but the bishop of Hamar, Rosemarie Køhn, the first woman bishop in Norway, allowed Hognestad to take a deputyship in her diocese. After a process involving bishops as well as government politicians, Hognestad's rights were restored in 2000 (2000, 104–105). His account to Den norske kirkes lærenemd[16] dated 16 April, 2000,[17] is formulated in a way that does not collide with church tenets concerning God, Christ, salvation, and the Bible (2000, 106–108). Eventually it appeared that his views were not materially changed, and in 2010 Hognestad had to resign from his ecclesiastical office owing to divergent views on central Christian teachings (Jordheim 2010).

His autobiographical narrative focuses on the author's psychic-spiritual development. Attention is directed away from church and society to the inner journey, from institutional critique to criticism of self. The narrator's self is sketched in a way congruent with the New Age self-development paradigm. The resultant self-theology is inspired by Jes Bertelsen's idea of "the Christ process" as an evolutionary stage when the individual shall learn his way to his own higher Christ self and become transformed by its energies of love (Hognestad 2000, 84). This idea is a point of departure for Hognestad's vision of a church that is open for seekers, guides them and offers them a silent room in their development process (2000, 85–86). The new understanding of his own priestly calling agrees with the vision: "To be priest, and that means to explore the spiritual part of reality and give others room to do the same; give support to the best in man" (2000, 91, my translation).

Hognestad is a seismograph for contemporary religious tendencies. His life history sums up frustration over a church felt to be irrelevant, a seeker's experimentations, and reconciliation with the church on individualist, spiritual terms. This particular blend, magnified in the life of a self-conscious priest with a prophetic disposition, may in fact be a model of many people's religious commuting in our time. The spiritual platform established for church religion by Hognestad is thus partly grounded in theology and theory, and partly in his own illustrative life story.

An indefinite number of common church members have welcomed his views with interest and sympathy, yet Hognestad's priestly career has clearly demonstrated existing limits to the public teachings of a minister in the church. In contrast to Jes Bertelsen, Hognestad is not a spiritual entrepreneur;[18] he did not create a spiritual centre, and he has no publicly

---

16. A church committe evaluating dogmatic issues.

17. The text is included in the autobiography, pp. 106–108.

18. Jes Bertelsen founded the "spiritual growth" centre *Vækstsenteret* i Nørre Snede in 1982.

well-known disciples; the lasting effect of his work is therefore difficult to estimate. In later years his revolutionary voice has no longer been heard as before, but Hognestad's books still have readers. Among the influential authors mentioned by informants in Botvar and Gresaker's project were both princess Märtha Louise and Helge Hognestad (Botvar and Gresaker 2013, 30).

An unsuccessful border crossing

Apart from Helge Hognestad's literary testimony, his role in the history of church religion and New Age is mainly about the challenge his teachings have represented for clerical and theological elites. The manifestation of the New Age movement described in the following also challenged church religion, but in this case the affected parties represented a Lutheran lay organization, circles within the church influenced by the charismatic movement, a Pentecostal congregation, and two independent charismatic congregations. The short history of the movement is interwoven with its representation in the media. The leading Christian daily Vårt Land had an active role in the course of events, displaying its habitual apologetic and warning position when treating new religious movements (cf. Aadnanes 2008, 38).

The Lightbearers (Lysbærerne) is the name of this awakening. It originated in the city of Trondheim's New Age milieu during the autumn of 1997. Its history illustrates how religious borders may be challenged, redrawn, and consolidated. For the participants in this history, the vital question concerned whether New Age activities could be accepted and possibly integrated into established Christian communities.

The awakening centred around Svein Erik Hellstrøm, who was proclaimed by a medium to be permeated by cleansing light (gjennomstrålende lys) at a seance in the home of an alternative therapist. Hellstrøm explained it as the light of Jesus Christ that dwelled in himself.[19] This event sparkled the awakening, with Hellstrøm in the role of prophet. A growing number of seekers and converts testified to have experienced the loving presence of Jesus (Jørgensen 1997). Propehetic messages were accompanied by references to biblical texts, thus belief in the Bible as revelation was gaining ground. Stories of remarkable signs and propehecies made the awakening sensational, and hopes were nourished that this particular milieu would be used by God to instigate a new revival. Thus the Lightbearers were invited to give witness accounts in established Christian communities. An evangelist in the lay organization Inner Mission (Indremisjonen) in Trondheim[20] was permitted by

---

19. Eikeland and Morken in Vårt Land, 13 March 1999, p. 16, and an anonymous interview with Inger Handberg in Santalen, no. 8, 21 August 1998.

20. A local association belonging to the nation-wide organization Det norske lutherske Indremisjonsselskap. This organization has played a significant role in the lay movement related to the Church of Norway since the nineteenth century.

the organization's board to be engaged in the awakening. The Lightbearers themselves wished to have such contacts and be guided in their process towards a Christian conviction (cf. Handberg 1998). The evangelist knew Olav Garcia de Presno, a well-known minister in the Storsalen Inner Mission congregation in Oslo, who was enthusiastic about the tidings from Trondheim. [21] As subsequent events demonstrated, the contact with Oslo determined the further course of the movement.

Olav Garcia de Presno belonged to an influential group of 15 ministers and pastors led by Kjell Aasmundrud, founder and pastor of the charismatic Oslo Vineyard congregation. For more than three years, these men had been praying for revival, inspired by prophecies of a grand revival in Norway by the English charismatic leader Mark Stibbe and American prophets Paul Cain and David Saunders from Kansas City.[22] Thus in 1997, this group, or at least some of them, were quite ready to welcome the news of an awakening to Jesus in New Age circles.[23]

Kjell Aasmundrud whole-heartedly joined the revival after having been told by Hellstrøm of a vision appointing him, together with Garcia de Presno and the prominent Pentecostal Pastor Egil Svartdahl, as Hellstrøm's guides and pastoral leaders of the awakening.[24] Another well-known pastor, Jan-Aage Torp of the charismatic *Seierskirken*, later became a fourth member of the core group. Thus a rather unique relationship between the New Age milieu and leading personalities of charismatic, Pentecostal and Lutheran circles was established. For a short time optimism was high. During the winter and spring of 1998, Lightbearers travelled widely with their message, to Sweden, Denmark, India and Kansas City in USA. Eschatological expectations seemed to be confirmed by signs, prophecies and the mission fervour mushroomed.[25]

Yet the momentous conversions did not manifest, and in Oslo Vineyard Aasmundrud's preaching created misgivings.[26] Moreover, rumours that he, a married man with five children, had entered into an allegedly "spiritual" relationship with a Lightbearer woman circulated. Aasmundrud was then

---

21. Eikeland and Morken in *Vårt Land*, 13. March 1999, p. 17.

22. Saunders had visited Norway in 1997 and met parliament member Kjell Magne Bondevik, chairman of the Kristelig Folkeparti, who was told by the American that he would become prime mininster after the election; a prophecy fulfilled in September the same year. Eikeland and Morken in *Vårt Land*, 15 March, 1999, p. 9. Another harbinger of the forthcoming grand revival was the woman Esther Teo, who came to Norway all the way from Singapore in 1997 to impart the message.

23. Eikeland and Morken in *Vårt Land*, 15 March, 1999, p. 10–11.

24. Eikeland and Morken in *Vårt Land*, 16 March, 1999, p. 7.

25. Rasmussen 1998; Eikeland and Morken in *Vårt Land*, 18 March 1999, p. 10.

26. He was said to have mentioned prophecies calling Jesus created, accepting belief in reincarnation and common law marriage, and launching grandiose ideas about the importance of the Lightbearers. Eikeland and Morken in *Vårt Land*, 18 March 1999, p. 12.

pressed by Scandinavian Vineyard leaders; i.e. the Swedish pastors Hans Sundberg and Torbjörn Freij, to give up his position as pastor of Oslo Vineyard in August 1998.[27]

The conflict in Oslo Vineyard grew into a public scandal. Accusations of lies, contacts with occult forces, high-strung prophecies, and unbiblical conceptions were listed against the Lightbearers. Besides, suspicions of improper relationships between men and women were dramatized by rumours of a prophecy allowing leaders in the awakening to have "spiritual wives" in addition to their married partners (cf. Aure 1998; Gudvangen 1999a, 1999b; Sandsmark 1999a, 1999b). In their public account, Sundberg and Freij emphasized the idea of "spiritual wives," drawing a parallel to practices in the Children of God movement.[28] The reference to the Children of God sect was no accident; many people probably remembered the strong accusations against this movement in Norwegian media during the 1970s. Even the bishops at the time joined in the warnings against its autoritarian leadership and sexual practices (Aadnanes 2008, 42). According to a Vineyard member, contact with the Lightbearer movement had been designed by "our greatest enemy" to destroy the congregation (Gudvangen 1999a). Incidentally, pastor Torbjörn Frej, a disciple of Constance Cumbey (Frej 1986, 5), had formerly warned against the wily New Age infiltration by Lucifer in his book New Age—de nygamle løgnene fra Eden (1986).

Undoubtedly the awakening's relations with influential Christian leaders explains the press coverage of the Lightbearers. Initially it was met with surprise and enthusiasm in Christian media (cf. Haavet 1998). Religion scholar Arild Romarheim, whose apologetic stance in favour of Christianity was well-known, publicly supported the awakening, testifying that the main ideas were sound (Romarheim 1998). A positive editiorial in Vårt Land January 1998 approvingly cited bishop Finn Wagle in Trondheim, who recommended that alternative communities in the church could supplement regular services,[29] a liberal embrace by a man in this position. Yet gradually the coverage became more critical and negative. Referring to the happenings in Oslo Vineyard, the chief editor later the same year concluded that the awakening was no more than reinspikka svermeri, i.e. pure religious delusion (Lund 1998). The newspaper's Lightbearer series of seven rather detailed articles published in March 1999, written by journalists Jan Eikeland and Johannes Morken, paint a picture of megalomaniacal revival expectations in the group of pastors that prevented a timely crititique of the extravagant prophecies coming from Hellstrøm and others. The articles represented a decisive blow against the movement and created a heated debate, including criticism of the newspaper's role (cf. Garcia de Presno 1999; Karlsen 1999;

---

27. Eikeland and Morken in Vårt Land, 18 March 1999, p. 15.

28. The Children of God was known for its method of "flirty fishing."

29. "Alternativ," Vårt Land, 5 January 1998.

Olsen 1999; Romarheim 1999). Egil Svartdahl questioned *Vårt Land*'s objectivity on the basis that one of its editors belonged to the leadership in Oslo Vineyard and was personally affected by the Aasmundrud case, (Svartdahl 1999). Romarheim turned in the series to *Pressens faglige utvalg* (PFU), a committee assessing whether press material breaks the norms and standards of the press. His critique was not recognized by the PFU as weighty enough, however (Omdahl *et al.* 1999).

Vårt Land played such a role in the course of events that it is justifiable to call it a key agent. What the Lightbearer awakening would have come to without the intervention of the press is, however, pure speculation. Its following was uncertain; core members were said to be dozens, while hundreds were affected. The harsh confrontation with the Christian media probably eliminated the possibility of its growing into a New Age Jesus movement. After 1999, it disappeared from the national newspapers. Eventually it lost a powerful ally in 2000 when the central leadership of Inner Mission ceased its engagement with the movement (Bjartvik 2000). The Lightbearers are still registered on the internet in 2015, but no activities are indicated.

Hostile prejudices on two sides were thus strenghtened by the Lighbearer incident: new agers were confirmed in the belief that dialogue with established Christian communities is impossible, and dualistic charismatics and like-minded lay people might see the workings of evil forces in Oslo Vineyard as they had earlier operated in the Children of God sect, and, indeed, in every manifestation of modern "occultism." Yet, the Lightbearer affair also documented optimistic expectations in Christian circles of the New Age as a spiritual renewal that might benefit church religion and Christian congregations.

Seekers, goals, and borders

Besides beliefs in signs and prophecies, the Lightbearers and the established Christians shared a common understanding that many people are spiritual seekers. The seeker has become a key identity notion. According to Steven Sutcliffe, the typical actor in the New Age milieu is a person on a spiritual quest, who subjectively adopts and mixes the cultural resources at hand (Sucliffe 2003, 200). It is quite likely, however, that the Lightbearers and the Christians in contact with them had different ideas about seekership. Comments from the Christian side seem to imply hopes that the Lightbearers would eventually accept central Christian teachings and find their place in some existing Christian community. This is in accordance with a time-honoured Christian model as exemplified by the apostle Paul and the church father Augustin: both had a religious breakthrough caused by supernatural intervention that was followed by belief in the divine truth of the gospel and the holiness of the church. Similarly, the Christian idea of a pilgrim is a seeker on his way to a specific goal. The Lightbearers, however, did not seem willing to be guided into ending their "occult" practices. They also stuck by their religious phrasing, finding it the most adequate for expressing their own experiences.

The crux of the matter is that many seekers are not looking for a final answer to their "spiritual longing" or whatever it is that motivates their search. Some versions of seekership may rather be seen as rooted in a deep-seated, individualist mentality corresponding with the enormous choice of spiritual offers in today's religious market. The fascinating cornucopia at hand may dispose people to prefer a continuous multi-religious actor role. Nowadays the attractiveness of a traditional Christian home-coming may be seriously affected by its imagined costs: restricted openness, avoidance of engaging activities, and the individual's religious path fixed and explained by Christian dogma. Märtha Louise demonstrates a resistance against the traditional model in her book *Fra hjerte til hjerte* (2002), where the princess exclaims that she will always be a pilgrim, on an everlasting journey for her inner church, her high altar (2002, 14). Hellstrøm's motives for seeking guidance from the core group of well-known pastors are not evident from the source material used here, but other requests for guidance among the Lighbearers express a desire for being accepted as alternative seekers with a Jesus devotion they wished to ponder with experienced Christians (cf. Handberg 1998). Yet, it is an open question whether the Lightbearers really wanted to settle into a Christian "home," contrary to the expectation voiced on the Christian side.

This case illustrates that a major challenge for the church today is to communicate with individuals insisting on a continuous spiritual quest outside the borders raised by traditional Christendom. One such border is implied in the goal of turning persons into "normal" Christians.

Operating dialogue: Areopagos

One mission organization in Norway has a long experience with this kind of challenge; i.e. the Areopagos Foundation. This organization plays a significant role in the current religious scene, partly due to its dialogue approach, partly to its economic muscles and networking capacities. Areopagos is a Danish-Norwegian mission organization dating back to 1925–1926 when the Norwegian China missionary Karl Ludvig Reichelt (1877–1952) left the Norwegian Missionary Society (NMS: *Det Norske Misjonsselskap*) and founded *Den Kristne Buddhistmisjonen*. Reichelt serves as a model in Areopagos missionary thinking. Cherishing a profound respect for Buddhism, his unusual missionary method was to practice friendship and dialogue with Buddhist monks. So controversial were his views and activities that he withdrew from NMS on the basis of accusations of syncretism. Particularly controversial was his wish to include extracts from *Tripitaka*, the Buddhist canon, in rituals and education in the Chinese church organization he founded (Sharpe 1984, 61). In 1929, Reichelt and his collaborator Notto Normann Thelle settled in Hongkong and built the centre Tao Fong Shan in Chinese architectural style.[30]

---

30. Its meaning is "the mountain from where the Christ wind blows."

Sale of land in Hongkong in 1994 made the organization one of the most prosperous mission agencies in the world.[31] In the period 1986–2000, the name of the organization was *Den Nordiske Kristne Buddhistmisjon* (the Nordic Christian Buddhist Mission); thereafter, the name has been Areopagos.

Its activities are dispersed across several countries, with centres in Scandinavia and Hongkong and the main office in Oslo. Rooted in the Lutheran tradition, the organization's approach is ecumenical and gives priority to religion studies, interreligious dialogue and spirituality. It provides arenas for seminars and retreats, and support various kinds of projects and agencies. For instance it was Aropagos grants that financed the project by Pål Ketil Botvar and Ann Kristin Gresaker referred to above, and the publication of *Uventet og ubedt* by Jan-Olav Henriksen and Kathrin Pabst to be mentioned later.

Partners include *I Mesterens Lys*,[32] a Danish fellowship geared to be a bridge between the Danish state church and New Age spirituality, and the Norwegian Egede Instituttet, an institution supporting academic studies on missions and new religious movements. Influential persons in the Areopagos network are the theologians Tore Laugerud and Notto R. Thelle, both public spokesmen for dialogue and spiritual renewal in the church. Thelle, son of Notto Normann Thelle, is the author of a number of popular books in the Christian spirituality genre (cf. Thelle 1991 and 1993).

Alternative fairs are conspicuous local events where many kinds of spiritual entrepreneurs and trades present their offers for the common public. They are places to recruit clients and initiate discussions. Areopagos is annually present at about ten such fairs, viewing them as significant arenas for church personnel to gain knowledge of New Age spiritulity.[33] The Areopagos-financed dialogue centre Emmaus, first established in Oslo in 1990 and closed down in 2009, also had stands at alternative fairs.[34] Emmaus' strategy was anchored in the belief that God exists in every human being and that knowledge of God can be reached in meditation and contemplation. These notions were the basis for recognizing the religious experiences of people of other faiths in a dialogue whose purpose was to bring everyone closer to God (Nybråten 2000, 17). Courses in so-called Christian deep meditation, retreats, dialogue meetings, and services were arranged by the centres. Emmaus was replaced by *Kirkelig dialogsenter* in Oslo in 2010, a joint agency by the diocese and Areopagos. Parallel centres have been established in Bergen and Stavan-

---

31. Areopagos is not as affluent as before, after having handed over Tao Fong Chan and part of the revenue fund to a Chinese Christian organization in Hong Kong.

32. "In the light of the master."

33. Such attendance started in 2003. Personal communication by Tore Laugerud, 6 June, 2015.

34. Emmaus centres were also founded in five more cities: Bergen, Fredrikstad, Sarpsborg, Stavanger, Tromsø.

ger. They are meant to be competence and resource agencies that create networks and initiate activities promoting spirituality, professional cooperation, and dialogue between people of diverse religions and world views in cooperation with local congregations.[35]

A recurrent concept in the Areopagos milieu is "spiritual longing."[36] This was launched as a key conception at the Council of the Church of Norway in 1999 where the assembly discussed how the church should relate to "the new turn to the spiritual"; i.e. "spiritual" in a broad sense, specified as philosophcal questions, feelings, values, the mystical and the religious (Laugerud 1999, 8). Spiritual longing is described as the longing for the presence of God, the longing for human community and unity, and the longing for the wholeness of creation; an array of different phenomena is therefore collocated in the concept. A report had been prepared for the delegates, Kirken i møte med den åndelige lengsel i vår tid (1999), written by Tore Laugerud, director of Egede Instituttet in cooperation with a consulting group consisting of representatives from various Christian research institutions as well as Emmaus and Buddhistmisjonen. Thus the foremost institutions affiliated with the church were involved in the preparation of the subject matter, which was treated at the highest organizational level within the church.

The report is an important strategy document, and a testimony of how central persons in the church are still thinking about its role vis-a-vis New Age spirituality. A missionary intent is in evidence; moreover, the report calls for a spiritual renewal in the church itself. The summary concludes that neither lay piety in the traditional sense, the activism of social-ethics, nor charismatic expressions give adequate responses to present-day questions about human identity. Additionally, scholarly theology is viewed as meeting challenges of authenticity and relevance (1999, 53). The call to the church is sketched in the following way:

> In this situation we are called to seek beyond the polarized church reality for a more holistic spirituality; a spirituality in which bible reading and prayer, mission and evangelism, ritual services and the display of charismatic gifts go hand in hand with engagement for justice, human rights, and protection of creation. [...] Further we are called to rebuild the connection between the dogmatic structure of the church as it is imparted by scholarly theology and personal piety.
>
> [...] Perhaps the most important question for our church at the threshold of a new millennium is this: What do we have to relinquish, what do we have to renounce in order to enable the creation of a church that lives near, and of, the source?
>
> (Laugerud 1999, 53, my translation)

---

35. Cf. kirkeligdialogsenter.no

36. Cf. *Areopagos. Strategidokument 2002-2004*. Vedtaget af Areopagos repræsentantskab den 5. april 2002.

The debate revealed that it was not that simple to attain common agreement about an ecclesiastical strategy under the heading of spiritual longing (Aadnanes 2008, 316). In his book *Gud for kvarmann. Kyrkja og den nye religiøsiteten* (2008), so far the most comprehensive study of the encounter between church religion and New Age spirituality, theologian Per M. Aadnanes gives a pointed summary of the positions and arguments, including a theological essay pointing out the hinderances that, from a Lutheran perspective, complicate the spiritual longing approach delineated in Laugerud's report (2008, 324–326).[37]

The report suggests a number of enterprises and changes that, it is conjectured, will improve the church as a relevant spiritual agency; i.e. meditation, pilgrimages, dialogues, and spiritual councelling; suggestions to a varying extent, being implemented centrally and locally. Since the 1990s, the church has had an active role in a pilgrimage renaissance whose primary focus is the cathedral in Trondheim. For the ecclesiastical authorities involved, a major issue has been the relevance of the church for "the spiritual longing" of our time, and a *folkekirke* ambition is expressed in the motto that pilgrimages will bring about a church with a higher ceiling and a lower threshold (Mikaelsson 2008b; Aagedal 2010). Pilgrimages combine several topical interests in a blend that can hardly be equalled by other church efforts: religious history, cultural heritage, adventure, holistic "body and soul" spirituality as well as therapy. It can be surmised that an inclusive "pilgrim church" version of the Church of Norway would be less "life as-religion," and give more room for "subjective life-spirituality." Incidentally, one of the projects supported by Areopagos in 2008 was the establishment of the first Norwegian pilgrimage centre, Nidaros Pilegrimsgård, in Trondheim.[38]

The challenge of paranormal experience

As the above-mentioned prophecy of Heelas and Woodhead exemplifies, the transference of religious authority from church dogma to individual experience is a central issue when discussing religious change in our time. For an institution like the Church of Norway, this development invites new strategies.

---

37. His own suggestion for a possible Lutheran strategy is to distinguish between Christianity as world view and Christianity as God-given faith. The Lutheran dogma that individual faith is given by God in word and sacrament is not to be tampered with; but the world view is a human construction. In his opinion such a distinction would enable the church to reconsider its world view constructions and provide a more flexible strategy towards religious pluralism (2008, 327–328). Aadnenes's expert knowledge and suggestions made Egede Instituttet arrange a research conference in 2009, where his views were discussed and a variety of perspectives on the religious situation were presented, later published in *Nye guder for hvermann? Femti år med alternativ spiritualitet* (2011), edited by Tormod Engelsviken *et al.*

38. Cf. Stiftelsesdokument for Nidaros pilegrimsgård, stiftelsesmøte 28. januar 2008 in Erkebispegården, Trondheim.

A recent study of paranormal experiences by theologian Jan-Olav Henriksen and ethnologist Kathrin Pabst addresses this situation. The authors criticize inveterate church attitudes to such phenomena, and argue that openness would be in the best interest of church religion. Church practice has generally tended to disregard the paranormal as something irrelevant, irrational or possibly dangerous,[39] but the refusal to take such experiences seriously may, for instance, dispose people to seek accepting New Age milieus, as some of the informants in the study exemplify. The project indicates that believing Christians who have paranormal experiences disregard the negative attitudes in their Christian milieu, and rather attribute meaning and authority to what has happened to them (Henriksen and Pabst 2013, 178). Thus they exemplify the shift in authority inherent in the "subjective turn." The authors take a strategic-apologetic stand to paranormal experiences, and emphasize that "warm hands," healing, clairvoiance, meeting with angels and deceased persons are not restricted to New Age milieus, but occur in most societies; they might therefore be "christianized." Theologians should seriously consider that such phenomena give plausibility to religious belief, while the neglect of people's experiences means that theology and the church become irrelevant when people seek interpretations of what happens to them. This is a situation that not only the authors, but also Helge Hognestad and a number of critics have noticed.

One notable example demonstrates that the church has become more attentive; i.e. the assistance given by church representatives to people living in so-called "disturbed houses." Weird and allegedly true stories of ghosts afflicting people's homes have been popular entertainment for years through the television series *Åndenes makt*. In every episode a medium contacts the spirit(s) causing disturbances and learns why they have stayed behind and interfere with the residents' lives. The medium then assists the spirit to pass over to "the other side"; thereafter, peace is attained, or at least the situation improves. A new wave of spiritism is thus a notable part of today's popular religious culture (cf. Kalvig 2009 and 2012).

The spiritist dominance in this field has influenced the church to act. Thus in 2013, the Council of the Church of Norway passed a liturgy for the blessing of houses and homes.[40] The introductory comments clarify that the ritual does not imply an explanation of the disturbances people experience, a point mentioned also in the liturgy. A distance to spiritist understanding is thus underlined. Another distancing manoeuvre lies in the careful avoidance of words like spirit, seance or exorcism. The ritual, which is not restricted to disturbed houses, has to be undertaken by a priest or other church official,

---

39. Its title *Uventet og ubedt. Paranormale erfaringer i møte med tradisjonell tro* ["Unexpected and unasked. Paranormal experiences meeting traditional belief") implicitly states that the experiences described have not resulted from magic or occult practices. This is a central concern in the book addressing common prejudices in Christian milieus.

40. *Liturgi for velsignelse av hus og hjem.* KM 7/13.

and is defined as a blessing in the tradition of church religion. The introduction lays down that the liturgy is a concrete way of playing a part in people's everyday life; a majority even think that it emphasizes the Church of Norway's character as a *folkekirke*, willing to meet people's needs in this field. The liturgy thus establishes the church as a competitor on a field hitherto mostly left to the spiritists, staging the priest in a role that serves as an alternative to the medium. The ambition to become more relevant in the daily life of common people undeniably reflects a response to the criticism of irrelevance.

Final comments

The conception of religious truth as an integral part of the individual's movability, experience, and spiritual development is a serious challenge for a religious institution accustomed to thinking that it has the final answers. The Church of Norway is divided by inner tensions and worried by decline, and has proven unable to raise a bulwark against the spread of ideas and practices on the alternative religious market. Multi-religious actors swithching from church to New Age arenas contribute to maintaining both, but demonstrate an individualistic approach, ignoring the religious authority that is an integral part of the identity of the church institution. Reactions to public representatives of New Age spirituality breaking with central tenets and deep-seated convictions in church religion have, for the most part, been hostile, and still are, as princess Märtha Louise continues to demonstrate. Yet, significant sections within the institution itself call for a spiritual renewal within church religion, and have proven capable of working changes. Dialogue with alternative milieus, pilgrimages and retreats, research and academic discussions on the religious situation, and, finally, the ambition to be more relevant for the everyday life of common people—are all notable indications that the encounter between church religion and New Age spirituality has impacted that time-honoured institution. Whether a *folkekirke* freed from state intervention will be able to keep the conservative wing and the spirituality wing under its canopy is, however, an open question at this moment.

References

Aadnanes, Per M. 2008. *Gud for kvarmann. Kyrkja og den nye religiøsiteten.* Oslo: University Publishing House.

Aagedal, Olaf, 2003. "Når kyrkja brenn." In *Tallenes tale 2003. Perspektiv på statistikk og kirke*, edited by Ole Gunnar Winsnes, 141–161. Trondheim: Tapir.

Aagedal, Olaf, ed. 2010. *Kulturkyrkja og pilegrimskyrkja. Ein seminarrapport.* KIFO Notat no. 3.

Aagedal, Olaf, Pål Ketil Botvar and Ida Marie Høeg, eds. 2013. *Den offentlige sorgen. Markeringer, ritualer og religion etter 22. juli.* Oslo: University Publishing House.

Aasen, Erik Hatleli. 2015. "Metalfans er de nye turistene." *Bergens Tidende*, 21 February, 28–29.

Areopagos. Strategidokument 2002-20004. Vedtaget af Areopagos' repræsentantskab den 5. April 2002.

Aure, Astrid. 1998. "Lysbærernes ledere trenger to hustruer." *Vårt Land*, 31 October, 16.

Bertelsen, Jes. 1989. *Kristusprocessen*. Borgen.

Bjartvik. Geir Ole. 2000. "Bryter med Lysbærerne." *Vårt Land* 15 June, 11.

Botvar, Pål Ketil and Jan-Olav Henriksen. 2010. "Mot en alternativreligiøs revolusjon?" In *Religion i dagens Norge. Mellom sekularisering og sakralisering*, edited by Pål Ketil Botvar and Ulla Schmidt, 60–80. Oslo: University Publishing House.

Botvar, Pål Ketil and Ann Kristin Gresaker. 2013. *Når troen tar nye veier. En studie av pendling mellom kristne og nyåndelige miljøer*. KIFO Rapport 2013:1. Oslo: KIFO Stiftelsen Kirkeforskning.

Cumbey, Constance. 1984. *Regnbuens skjulte farer. Ny tid-bevegelsen og den kommende barbariske tidsalder*. Hovet. (Original edition: *The Hidden Dangers of the Rainbow. The New Age Movement and our Coming Age of Barbarism*. Shreveport, LA, 1983).

Davie, Grace. 2007. "Vicarious Religion: A Methodological Challenge." In *Everyday Religion. Observing Modern Religious Lives*, edited by Nancy T. Ammerman, 21–35. Oxford: Oxford University Press.

Eikeland, Jan and Johannes Morken. 1999. "Historien om lysbærerne: De tror noe stort har begynt." *Vårt Land*, 13 March, 13–17.

———. 1999. "Historien om lysbærerne: De har ventet og bedt: 'Er det nå det skal skje?'" *Vårt Land*, 15 March, 8–11.

———. 1999. "Historien om lysbærerne: For Kongen og hans Kongerike." *Vårt Land*, 16 March, 6–10.

———. 1999. "Historien om lysbærerne: Bror står mot bror. Og venn mot venn." *Vårt Land*, 18 March, 12–15.

———. 1999. "Historien om lysbærerne: To profetier på kort tid." *Vårt Land*, 19 March, 12–15.

———. 1999. "Historien om lysbærerne: Hva skal vi tro?" *Vårt Land*, 20 March, 14–17.

———. 1999. "Historien om lysbærerne: Mens det stormer omkring dem." *Vårt Land*, 22 March, 8–10.

Engedal, Leif Gunnar and Arne Tord Sveinall, eds. 2000. *Troen er løs. Bidrag til belysning av forholdet mellom folkereligiøsitet, nyreligiøsitet og kristen tro*. Trondheim: Tapir Akademisk Forlag.

Engelsviken, Tormod, Rolv Olsen and Notto R. Thelle, eds. 2011. *Nye guder for hvermann? Femti år med alternativ spiritualitet*. Trondheim: Tapir Akademisk Forlag.

Freij, Torbjörn. 1986. *New Age—de nygamle løgnene fra Eden*. Hermon Forlag. (Original edition: *New Age—de nygamla lögnerna från Eden*. Handen 1984).

Friestad, Erlend. 2015. "Tilbyr dåp og fest på 30 minutter." *Vårt Land*, 15 April, 13.

Frisk, Liselotte. 2013. *Den mediterande dalahästen. Religion på nya arenor i samtidens Sverige*. Stockholm: Dioalogos Förlag.

Garcia de Presno, Olav. 1999. "Serien om lysbærerne." *Vårt Land*, 25 Match, 21.

Gilhus, Ingvild Sælid. 2012. "Angels in Norway: Religious Border-crossers and Border-markers." In *Vernacular Religion in Everyday Life: Expressions of Belief*, edited by Marion Bowman and Ülo Valk, 230–245. Sheffield: Equinox Publishing.

Gilhus, Ingvild Sælid and Lisbeth Mikaelsson. 2000. "Multireligiøse aktører og kulturens refortrylling." *Sosiologi i dag* 2: 5–22.

Gudvangen, Stein. 1999a. "Romarheims naivitet." *Vårt Land*, 13 January, 20.

———. 1999b. "Garcia de Presnos og Svartdahls urene taklinger." *Vårt Land*, 8 April, 20.

Handberg, Inger. 1998. "Kjære Far i himmelen." *Vårt Land*, 9 November, 18.

Haavet, Thea. 1998. "Nyttige impulser." *Vårt Land*, 2 January, 3.

Heelas, Paul and Linda Woodhead. 2005. *The Spiritual Revolution. Why Religion is Giving Way to Spirituality*. Malden, MA: Blackwell Publishing.

Hegstad, Harald. 1996. *Folkekirke og trosfellesskap. Et kirkesosiologisk og ekklesiologisk grunnproblem belyst gjennom en undersøkelse av tre norske lokalmenigheter*. KIFO Perspektiv 1. Trondheim: Tapir forlag.

Henriksen, Jan-Olav and Kathrin Pabst. 2013. *Uventet og ubedt. Paranormale erfaringer i møte med tradisjonell tro*. Oslo: University Publishing House.

Hognestad, Helge. 1978a. *Forkynnelse til oppbrudd. Studier i Matteusevangeliet og kirkens bruk av det*, 1. Oslo: University Publishing House.

———. 1978b. *Forkynnelsen—kirkens forsvar? Studier i Matteusevangeliet og kirkens bruk av det*. Vol. 2. Oslo: University Publishing House.

———. 1982. *En kirke for folket*. Oslo: J. W. Cappelens Forlag.

———. 1989. *Morgendemring. En ny spiritualitet?* Oslo: J. W. Cappelens Forlag.

———. 1994. *Den indre kilde. Vår tids religiøsitet i lys av historien*. Oslo: J. W. Cappelens Forlag.

———. 2000. *Fra alter til våpenhus. På leting etter Gud bak dogmer og bastante meninger*. Oslo: Genesis Forlag.

Holberg, Sunniva E. and Ånund Brottveit. 2014. *Tilstandsrapport for Den norske kirke 2014*. KIFO Notat 2/2014.

"Jesus er den store forskjellen." 1998. *Santalen* no. 8, 21 August, 5–7.

Jordheim, Trygve W. 2010. "Hognestad fryktet at han skulle få sparken." *Vårt Land*, 23 March, 13.

Jørgensen, Jens-Petter, 1997. "New Age-folket kom til troen uten kirkens hjelp." *Vårt Land*, 31 December, 8–9.

Kalvig, Anne. 2009. "TV Norge og Kanal Fem—den nye tids budbringere." *Din* 4: 45–63.

———. 2012. "Seansar og minner om dei døde. Spirituell scrapbooking eller volva vendt tilbake?" *Kirke og kultur* 2: 128–141.

Karlsen, Jann. 1999. "Det er langt til Oslo." *Vårt land*, 27 May, 22.

Kraft, Siv Ellen. 2008. "Märthas engler: En analyse av den norske mediedebatten." *Nytt Norsk Tidsskrift* 25: 123–134.

———. 2011. *Hva er nyreligiøsitet.* Oslo: University Publishing House.

Laugerud, Tore. 1999. *Kirken i møte med den åndelige lengsel i vår tid. Betenkning til Kirkemøtet 1999.* Oslo: Egede Instituttet.

Lund, Jon Magne. 1998. "Om 'åndelige hustruer' og samtaler med døde." *Vårt Land*, 2 November 1998.

Matrisciana, Caryl. 1988. *Guder og ledere i New Age.* Hovet. (Original edition: *Gods of the New Age.* Eugene, OR, 1985)

Mikaelsson, Lisbeth. 2008a. "Regnbuens skjulte farer. Trusselen fra New Age." In *Kjetterne og kirken. Fra antikken til i dag,* edited by Tomas Hägg, 223–240. Oslo: Scandinavian Academic Press. German edition 2010: "Die Gefahren des Regenbogens: Bewachtung durch die New Age-Bewegung." In *Kirche und Ketzer: Wege und Abwege des Christentums,* edited by Tomas Hägg, 261–281. Köln: Böhlau Verlag.

———. 2008b. "Nidarosdomen og pilegrimsbølgen." *Din* 4: 41–59.

———. 2011. "Salg av spiritualitet." In *Nye guder for hvermann? Femti år med alternativ spiritualitet,* edited by Tormod Engelsviken *et al.,* 71–86. Trondheim: Tapir Akademisk Forlag.

———. 2013. "New Age and the spirit of capitalism: Energy as cognitive currency." In *New Age Spirituality: Rethinking religion,* edited by Steven J. Sutcliffe and Ingvild Sælid Gilhus, 160–173. Durham and Bristol USA: Acumen.

Nybråten, Omar. 2000. *Emmaus. Erfaringer fra et meditasjons- og dialogarbeid.* Sarpsborg.

Olsen, Harald. 1999. "Overspenthetens nettverk." *Vårt Land*, 20 April, 19.

Prinsesse Märtha Louise and Ari Behn. 2002. *Fra hjerte til hjerte.* Oslo: Forlaget Press.

Omdahl, Sven Egil *et al.* 1999. "VL har ikke brutt god presseskikk." *Vårt Land*, 23 June.

Rasmussen, Kenneth. 1998. "Vineyard-strid om 'new age' gruppe." *Dagen*, 14 October.

Redden, Guy. 2005. "The New Age Market: Toward a Market Model." *Journal of Contemporary Religion* 20(2): 231–246.

Romarheim, Arild. 1988. *Kristus i Vannmannens tegn. Nyreligiøse oppfatninger av Jesus Kristus.* Oslo: Credo Forlag. English edition: *The Aquarian Christ. Jesus Christ as Portrayed by New Religious Movements.* Hong Kong: Good Tiding, 1992.

———. 1998. "Forsøk på en nyansering." *Vårt Land*, 23 November, 19.

———. 1999. "Vårt Land til bunns." *Vårt Land*, 8 April, 21.

———. 2011. "Nyåndelig folkereligiøsitet?" In *Nye guder for hvermann? Femti år med alternativ spiritualitet,* Tormod Engelsviken, Rolv Olsen and Notto R. Thelle, 41–59. Trondheim: Tapir Akademisk Forlag.

Saliba, John A. 1999. *Christian Responses to the New Age Movement: A Critical Assessment*. London: Wellington House.

Sandsmark, Jostein. 1999. "Bryt med fortiden i new age." *Dagen*, 23 January, 5.

———. 1999. "Åpner for en demonisk dimensjon." *Dagen*, 17 April, 9.

Selberg, Torunn. 2011. *Folkelig religiøsitet. Et kulturvitenskapelig perspektiv*. Oslo: Scandinavian Academic Press/ Spartacus forlag.

Sharpe, Eric. 1984. *Karl Ludvig Reichelt. Missionary, Scholar and Pilgrim*. Hong Kong: Tao Fong Shan Ecumenical Centre.

Skaar, Kristen Edvard. 2015. "Et nytt folkekirkelig ritual." *Vårt Land* 26 January, 16–17.

Stiftelsesdokument for Nidaros pilegrimsgård, stiftelsesmøte 28. januar 2008 i Erkebispegården, Trondheim.

Smith, Jonathan Z. 2004. *Relating Religion. Essays in the Study of Religion*. Chicago, IL: The University of Chicago Press.

Stålsett, Sturla, *et al.* 2013. *Det livssynsåpne samfunn. En helhetlig tros- og livssynspolitikk*. NOU Norges offentlige utredninger 2013/1. Oslo: Departementenes servicesenter, Informasjonsforvaltning.

Sundberg, Hans and Torbjörn Freij. 1998. "Vineyard och Ljusbärarna." *Dagen*, 10 December, 2.

Sutcliffe, Steven. 2003. *Children of the New Age: A History of Spiritual Practices*. London: Routledge.

Svartdahl, Egil. "Vårt Land og Lysbærerne." *Vårt Land,* 23 March, p. 18.

Thelle, Notto R. 1991. *Hvem kan stoppe vinden? Vandringer i grenseland mellom Øst og Vest*. Oslo: University Publishing House.

———. 1993. *Ditt ansikt søker jeg. Tekster om tro*. Oslo: Oriens Forlag.

———. 2010. *Prinsessens engler: Invitasjon til en samtale om alternativ spirittualitet*. Oslo: Pax Forlag.

Warburg, Margit, Signe Engelbreth Larsen and Laura Maria Schütze, eds. 2013. *Civilreligion i Danmark. Ritualer, myter og steder*. Højbjerg: Forlaget Univers.

2

From "Network" to "Visions":
The Role of the Umbrella Organization *VisionWorks* in the Norwegian Alternative Movement

MARGRETHE LØØV

The Norwegian alternative movement[1] has been marked by a quite extraordinary feature—a national umbrella organization for alternative spirituality, therapy and lifestyle. Founded in 1992, *VisionWorks* (formerly *Alternativt Nettverk*[2]) offers common platforms of interaction for actors within the alternative field. Its core activity is the magazine *Visjon*.[3] Other important forums are the annual alternative fairs in Norway's largest cities, where individual practitioners gather and present themselves to a wider audience. The organization also arranges other events and runs a web site. By thus providing a set of common platforms for interaction, *VisionWorks* seeks to

---

1. When referring to a wide network in the Norwegian context, I have here opted to apply the term "alternative movement" instead of "New Age." The term designates a loosely cohesive cluster of actors, ideas and practices that to some extent oppose the cultural mainstream, and are connected by thematic association and/or social interaction. To a certain degree, this corresponds to what is often conceptualized as "New Age" in international research literature. There are several reasons why I find the term "alternative" more suitable in the present context. First, the "New Age" term is highly ambivalent, both in common parlance and scholarly literature. "Alternative" is less contested. Relational in nature, it highlights the relationship of the phenomena at hand to the cultural mainstream. Second, "alternative" is a more common self-designative term among the actors themselves. Third—and as will be discussed in this article—the existence of a common, national network structure has resulted in a broad and relatively organized alternative movement in Norway as compared to similar subcultures in other countries.

2. *Alternative Network*. In the following I will use the name *Alternativt Nettverk* when referring to the organization before it changed its name, and *VisionWorks* after 2013.

3. *Vision*.

coordinate actors and promote alternative thinking in the public sphere. As a common umbrella organization for alternative thought and practice, the organization is exceptional. No other countries have fostered a similarly broad and national New Age network. *VisionWorks* has also been hugely successful at gathering actors around its activities. *Visjon* is currently published four times a year with a circulation of 12,000 copies, and the alternative fair in the capital area attracts a total of approximately 12,500 people each year. By comparison, Europe's largest mind-body-spirit festival in London is visited by some 20,000 people (Roberts 2014).

This article will provide an outline of *VisionWorks'* activities, assess its ideological profile and discuss the organization's role within the Norwegian alternative movement. The analysis is based on interviews with *VisionWorks'* current and former leadership, alternative providers who participate in its activities and textual sources from actors both within and outside the network. It will be argued that *Alternativt Nettverk* was instrumental in establishing a sense of communality among those involved with alternative spirituality in Norway. The organization has also contributed to a public awareness of the existence of phenomena such as alternative therapy, new spirituality and holistic lifestyles. However, its heyday as the main agenda setter in this domain may be coming to an end. There are many indicators that *Alternativt Nettverk*'s success has also paved the way for its demise as the main node for the alternative movement in Norway. As the "alternative" has become more widespread, new and competing networks have emerged. The past few years have seen fierce debates over *VisionWorks'* regulation of its market. New media have, moreover, reduced the importance of a centralized information source. I will here address the growth and diversification of the Norwegian alternative movement and discuss the most important dynamics behind its development. Note that we are here focusing on an institutionalized network that forms a part of—but by no means represents the whole—alternative milieu or "movement" in Norway. As will be seen, *VisionWorks* today constitutes only one among several organizing forces within this field.

A web is woven: Historical background

In the spring of 1992, a leaflet was distributed to a number of groups and individuals in Norway, inviting them to become members of a national network for alternative thought and practice. The network would be held together by a bimonthly periodical that featured articles, classified ads and contact information. Behind the initiative were Øyvind Solum and Roald Pettersen, who had met at the New Age centre *Bauker* in Gausdal a few years previously. Bauker had been founded by the Bahá'í couple Harald and Benedicte Thiis in 1980. After spending their honeymoon at Findhorn in Scotland, the Thiis' wanted to create a similar centre in Norway where people could learn about new world views and practice alternative ways of living. Bauker had to wind up all activity in 1990 due to economic problems. According to Solum and Pettersen, its closure created a social vacuum among those interested in alternative spirituality in Norway (Ø. Solum 2012a; Pettersen 2012). Admittedly, there were other hubs for alternative thought, such as *Norsk Akademi for Naturmedisin,*[4] the *ILIANA* academy,[5] *Collegium Medicum,*[6] yoga and therapy centres and an emerging publishing sector for New Age literature. Nevertheless, Bauker had been an important nodal point for the alternatively minded in Norway due to its broad portfolio of courses and strategic location in the vicinity of the capital.

Solum and Pettersen moreover saw a clear lack of a large, broadly profiled alternative magazine that could provide a Norwegian counterpart to Denmark's *Nyt Aspekt* and *Guiden,*[7] which provided event and contact information in addition to editorial articles. The more commercial Swedish magazine *Energivågen*[8] also provided a point of reference insofar as it was national in scope, and displayed a wide array of offers (Pettersen 2012, 2015). Both these periodicals reached out to a nationwide audience. Existing local associations and course centres in Norway were, on the other hand, bound by geography, and had much narrower fields of impact. In short, Solum and Pettersen perceived a general lack of common platforms for people with an interest in alternative phenomena, with the result that they knew very little about each other's existence: "We had the idea that a lot of these milieus existed, but that they barely knew about each other. They did their own thing, and there was a lot of exciting stuff happening. But there was no overview. No one knew what was where, and who knew what" (Ø. Solum 2012a).

In addition to these practical considerations, the ideological convictions of its founders were driving forces behind *Alternativt Nettverk*. Solum had had mystical experiences since he was a young boy, and was passionate about environmental issues. He was also a practicing massage therapist (Ø. Solum 2012a). Pettersen had spent years at the alternative centres *Findhorn* in Scotland and *Stjärnsund* in Sweden.[9] Adhering to a worldview he himself has described as "New Age," Pettersen interpreted it as a sign of "the will of the Universe" when Solum called him to explore the possibility of future collaboration on an alternative network (Pettersen 2012). Thus aligned in their sympathies for alternative ways of thinking, Solum and Pettersen both wanted to contribute to the further proliferation of alternative thought and strengthen the alternative movement in Norway by providing platforms for interaction and a common forum for public debate. They furthermore

---

4. *Norwegian Academy for Nature Medicine*, founded in 1975.

5. Founded in 1983.

6. *Collegium Medicum—Nordic Association for Nature Therapists*, founded in 1984.

7. *New Aspect* and *The Guide*. *The Guide* is an "alternative yellow pages" published as an attachment to *Nyt Aspekt*.

8. *The Energy Wave.*

9. Both centres still exist. See https://www.stjärnsund.nu and https://www.findhorn.org.

thought that the mutual exchange of ideas and experiences would benefit the individual development of therapists and persons otherwise involved with the "alternative" (Ø. Solum 2012a).

The first practical step in the process of setting up a network was to identify prospective participants. Solum and Pettersen were able to draw upon existing, extensive registries. Solum had inherited a complete list of names from Bauker and from two rather short-lived organizations, *PSI* and *Forum 2000* (Ø. Solum 2012a). Solum and Pettersen were also able to access the membership registry of the newly-established book club *Energica* (*Alternativt Nettverk* 2012, 55). In addition to individuals, invitations were sent out to therapy centres, spiritual groups and health food stores (*Nettverk-Nytt* no. 2 1992, 14). The initiative was an immediate success. By November 1992, six hundred people had signed up as supporting members. These members would receive the journal *Nettverk-Nytt* for the slightly higher yearly fee as a way of supporting the network, and could also choose to be included in an overview of therapists and contact persons which was printed in *Nettverk-Nytt* and updated with each new issue. An additional three hundred people signed up as regular subscribers (*Nettverk-Nytt* no. 2 1992, 3; Pettersen 2013). Their recruiting success indicates that the network was a welcome and long-anticipated initiative, something which was expressed in exclamations such as "finally!," written on some of the leaflets they received (*Nettverk-Nytt* no. 1 1992, 2).

The journal *Nettverk-Nytt/Alternativt Nettverk/Visjon*

An important principle for the newly established network was that it would be user-run. The role of *Alternativt Nettverk* would primarily be to facilitate communication and interaction among its members, and the journal *Nettverk-Nytt*[10] was to be the hub in the network. The contact information for support members who signed up as contact persons or therapists were sorted according to postal zip code. In this way, they could be reached directly by other members in their vicinity. *Alternativt Nettverk* also provided a couch surfing service in which people could sign up to accommodate other members in their private homes. The bottom-up approach reflected an open profile. The network was to be independent of any particular political or religious stance, and was in principle open to all, regardless of confessional or other affiliations (*Nettverk-Nytt* no. 1 1992, 29–30). Ecumenical discussions were encouraged. The leaders wanted to promote tolerance for divergent viewpoints, and hoped that people from different alternative stances could learn from each other. They also encouraged alternative therapists to establish their own branch organizations (Ø. Solum 2012a; Pettersen 2015).

The first issues of *Nettverk-Nytt* contained only a few editorial articles. The bulk of the journal consisted of practical information, contact information and classified ads. But over the first few years, *Nettverk-Nytt* metamorphosed

---

10. *Network News.*

from a practical "yellow pages" for those interested in alternative spirituality, therapy and lifestyle into a carefully edited magazine covering the same themes. The magazine changed its name to *Alternativt Nettverk* in 1997 and to *Visjon* from 2007 onwards. Still adhering to the principle of organizational neutrality, the magazine continues to have an open profile, epitomized by the statement, "There are many answers to the same questions," printed on the spine of every issue. Additionally, an editorial declaration of intent reprinted in every issue explains the rationale behind the magazine—and network in general:

> We seek to make visible new or lesser-known activities and ways to better health, balanced life styles, personal and societal development, increased environmental awareness, and worldviews based on personal responsibility and experience. [...] VISJON considers diversity and differences to be resources. By exchanging opinions freely we may learn to appreciate the facets that others represent and challenge ourselves to progress in our own development. Groups and individuals with different experiences and views must learn to communicate in order for us to find new paths for growth. Those who write in the magazine VISJON might disagree both with the editorial board and each other. Each author is therefore accountable for his or her own articles. With this openness we hope to avoid new forms of dogmatism or fundamentalism.
>
> (*Visjon* no. 5 2014, 4)[11]

Visjon today covers a broad range of themes commonly perceived as "alternative." The magazine regularly features an astrology column, horoscopes, reviews of "spiritual" music, and—its most recent addition—a vegetarian food column. An overview of alternative therapists is also included. Each issue furthermore features a dozen or so articles written by freelance authors and the editorial team. An attempt to provide a full overview of *Visjon*'s thematic range would result in a page-long list, but a quick glance at a recent issue gives us a certain idea of what the magazine covers: the cover story was entitled "Inspired by Buddha," and featured interviews with three Norwegian Buddhists. Also figuring on the front cover was an article on Ayurveda, an article on breathing and wellbeing, and the item, "Are you highly sensitive? Test yourself!" The issue moreover included interviews with the Norwegian environmentalist Erik Dammann, a martial arts master, a mystic, the man behind a new therapy technique called "brainspotting" and another therapist promoting better-known *mindfulness* techniques to promote creativity (no. 5 2014).

Visjon thus continues to focus on religious trends, lifestyle options and therapeutic practices. At the same time, there appears to be some shifts in its thematic profile. Whereas the first issues were widely concerned with ancient

---

11. My translation, as literal as possible.

mythology and therapeutic practices, self-development and lifestyle choices became more prevalent throughout the 1990s (Øygard 1998). The trend continued into the new millennium, when self-development and psychotherapy became the dominant themes (Tampuu 2006). Mari Tampuu detected a decline in emphasis on environmentalist issues from the earliest issues to 2006, but the most recent issues break away from this trend with articles and editorials that promote green values. A do-it-yourself-approach to spiritual development and health also seems to be on the rise. The magazine has expanded tremendously over the years. From a first edition of only 32 pages, some editions since 1996 have contained 112 pages (Øygard 1998, 48–49). In recent years, 82 pages have been the norm.

Although the profile of *Visjon* remains broad, the changes over time illustrate that the "alternative" is by no means an obvious or fixed set of ideas and practices. One might argue that the magazine comes across as less "alternative" today than it did twenty years ago because of the increasing profusion of alternative spirituality and complementary medicine in the cultural mainstream. What at any given time is defined as "alternative" is relative to context. Moreover, new alternatives will always emerge. As will be explored below, the advent of new alternative magazines might also have steered *Visjon*'s thematic focus in new directions. Last but not least, no publication is untainted by the personal interests of the people who produce it. Although the intent of *Alternativt Nettverk*'s leaders was to create a broad window into the world of alternative thinking, it is beyond doubt that personal preferences have an impact on what is being showcased. Roald Pettersen says he often pursued his own interests when writing articles for the magazine, although he and Solum also had to aim at covering all of the categories expected by the readers. Occasionally humorous contributions were included, such as "Ask The Karma Office." There would be a varied "menu for a dinner or buffet, with many dishes, where there would be some of this, some of that, and something else for dessert" (Pettersen 2012, 2015). Pettersen left the network in 2000, and Øyvind Solum's half-brother Eirik Svenke Solum took over as editor-in-chief in 2009. The thematic focus remains wide, but the impact of personal tastes is still discernable. The Solum family's deep engagement with environmentalist issues is, for instance, often reflected in the magazine's content.

Ever since the network's inception, the magazine *Nettverk-Nytt/Alternativt Nettverk/Visjon* has constituted the hub in *Alternativt Nettverk*. The magazine is by far the activity with the widest outreach. The circulation of 12,000 copies is impressive in relation to Norway's modest population—a comparable distribution in the UK would amount to 150,000 copies. The magazine's primary function is to act as a channel for inspiration and information about the "alternative." Although the magazine's influence is impossible to estimate by any objective standard, it is beyond doubt that it has played a pivotal role in spreading alternative thought and practices to the Norwegian public.

Before the advent of other magazines and the internet, this magazine was one of the few channels through which people could access information on alternative spirituality, therapy and lifestyle in print. The magazine reflects broader trends and debates, and has been an important agenda setter. It has also had a key networking function through its lists of contacts and advertisements. It would also promote other sites for interaction between the alternatively-minded—magazines, fairs, websites *et cetera*—as these came into being. We will now turn to the most influential of these—the alternative fairs.

The alternative fairs

In 1993, *Alternativt Nettverk* held its first alternative fair in Oslo. Øyvind Solum and Roald Pettersen wanted to create a forum in which providers of alternative spirituality and therapy could meet in person and present themselves to a wider audience. Judging by the number of visitors, the initiative was highly welcome. The approximately 4,000 people who visited the first fair filled the premises to the brim, and long queues formed outside (*Nettverk-Nytt* no. 5 1993, 1, 10–11). This initial success was repeated in subsequent years. *Alternativt Nettverk*'s alternative fair soon became an annual event, and the number of visitors increased steadily throughout the 1990s. After a nomadic journey across Oslo—the exhibition arenas of which it eventually outgrew—the fair relocated to Lillestrøm and Norway's largest exhibition hall in 2009. The success in Oslo inspired *Alternativt Nettverk* to arrange fairs in other Norwegian cities as well. In 1997, the network arranged its first fairs in Bergen and Tromsø, and in 2001 the phenomenon arrived in Trondheim. A fair was also arranged in Kristiansand, but with limited success (Ø. Solum 2008). Today, *VisionWorks* hosts three annual fairs, in Lillestrøm, Bergen and Trondheim.

To a large extent, the profile of *VisionWorks*' fairs reflects that of the magazine *Visjon*. According to Eirik Svenke Solum, all actors promoting "alternative" ways of living, healing and thinking may in principle sign up as exhibitors (E. Svenke Solum 2012a). For a minimum fee (4,700 NOK for the Lillestrøm 2014 fair), groups and individuals may hire a stand and promote their ideas or products at the fair. Slots are advertised in *Visjon*, and there are apparently no restrictions apart from the obvious economic cost of participation. The overarching aim of the organizers is to provide an open forum for the exchange and exploration of alternative phenomena, and a necessary precondition is tolerance towards views that oppose one's personal opinions. In practice, however, *VisionWorks* exerts a considerable degree of control over what is on offer. According to Eirik Svenke Solum, the organizers strive to gather a wide scope of speakers and exhibitors in order to appeal to a large audience (E. Svenke Solum 2012a). Particularly interesting speakers are invited and paid to give lectures. It has become standard that every fair hosts at least one "New Age superstar." Famous names from recent years have included the self-proclaimed psychic Uri Geller,

Celestine Prophecy author James Redfield, the British medium Lisa Williams and *Soulspring* founders princess Märtha Louise and Elisabeth Nordeng. Considering the fact that the fair is, in itself, a commodity, which both exhibitors and visitors must pay to access, it is hardly surprising that market considerations shape what is on offer. The larger the audience, the larger the profit. *VisionWorks* is today run as a joint stock-firm that is owned predominantly by the Solum family. Hence there are obvious personal economic incentives to make the fairs as profitable as possible. But commercial interests are not the only regulating force. A certain degree of idealism is also at play inasmuch as some exhibitors are offered free stalls at the fair "because we want them there" (E. Svenke Solum 2014a). Examples include the animal welfare organization NOAH, the life-stance community *Holistisk Forbund*,[12] *Framtiden i våre hender*[13] and the Green Party (E. Svenke Solum 2015).

The regulation of the market also involves restricting access for undesired participants; that is, actors who are considered to be destructive or who challenge the alternative or holistic ethos of the fair. Øyvind Solum has especially mentioned The Church of Scientology as an "unwanted sect." Groups or persons who are known to "brainwash" or to sexually or economically abuse others have been excluded from the fair, as have actors who have aggressively proselytized or attacked other exhibitors in the past (Ø. Solum 2012a). A well-known example is the exclusion of the conspiracy theorist Per-Aslak Ertresvåg from the Lillestrøm fair in 2011. Ertresvåg was scheduled to give a talk on the background to the terrorist attack on the government headquarters in Oslo and Utøya on 22 July 2011. However, this presentation was cancelled when it came to the organizers' attention that he would be claiming that the attacks were a "false flag operation" ordered by the authorities to eradicate oppositional voices within their own ranks. *Alternativt Nettverk*'s leaders deemed such ideas utterly false and potentially dangerous, and hence did not want them to be propagated at the alternative fair. Another example is the exclusion of some Christian groups at the Trondheim fair in 2012. A relatively large number of denominations had applied to exhibit. However the organizers did not want too many such exhibitors because they feared that visitors' expectations of a truly alternative fair would not be met with them present. In the end, only some of the Christian groups were allowed to participate (E. Svenke Solum 2012a). In spite of general principles of user-dominance and tolerance, the organizers hence exert a significant control over what is on offer at the alternative fairs. As will be discussed below, their regulation might reflect some emerging fault lines within the alternative movement.

---

12. *Holistic Society.*
13. *The Future in Our Hands.*

It is difficult to underestimate the role of the alternative fairs in the Norwegian alternative milieu and the public debate concerning alternative spirituality. The fair phenomenon has gained widespread popularity. Twenty years after *Alternativt Nettverk* arranged its first fair, some 50 alternative fairs are held across the country every year, attracting a total of 100,000 visitors (Alternativopplysningen 2013). The alternative fair in Oslo/Lillestrøm has become Scandinavia's largest. In the peak years at the beginning of the millennium, the fair attracted between 17,000 and 20,000 visitors (Pettersen 2015). Since then the number of visitors has been subject to decline, but still appears impressive with approximately 9,000 paying visitors and 3,500 people acting as volunteers or exhibitors[14] (cf. Løøv 2016).

The success of the alternative fair phenomenon in Norway must be seen in relation to the general interest in alternative spirituality in the population. Much indicates that this is growing; today a relatively high percentage of Norwegians believe in phenomena like reincarnation and magical charms, for instance (Botvar and Henriksen 2010, 65). The general interest in alternative spirituality might contribute to explaining the fairs' popularity. However, this is probably a chicken-or-egg issue because the fairs have also contributed to popularising alternative spirituality. Demographic factors also play a role. In a country where any cluster of dwellings with more than 3000 inhabitants may claim the title of "city," and such places furthermore are scattered across vast geographical distances, people with interests that deviate from the mainstream need common meeting places outside their local community. Attracting visitors from far away, the alternative fairs facilitate contact between providers and clients across the restrictions of their immediate context. The lively media debate on alternative phenomena has probably also contributed to the fairs' popularity by stimulating curiosity in the general population—after all, one does not need to believe in New Age thinking to visit an alternative fair (Kraft 2001). Extensively covered by the press, the alternative fairs in Oslo, Bergen and Trondheim have been important agenda setters for the public debate on alternative spirituality in Norway.

The alternative fairs have an important role among actors who are professionally involved with alternative spirituality. According to several of the alternative providers I have interviewed, the fairs are important recruitment areas for new clients. Although the cost of participation is often higher than the income generated at the fair, the fairs offer good opportunities for promoting oneself as a therapist. The fairs also serve as a platform for contact between providers of alternative thinking, services and goods.

---

14. These numbers are based on my own survey at the alternative fair in Lillestrøm in 2011. The organizers' numbers exceed these, but are not representative of the actual number of visitors. The reason is that two- or three-day passes are counted as two or three visitors—although in reality only one person visits the fair over the span of several days.

A network on the world wide web

As will be further explored in the next section, *Alternativt Nettverk*'s position in the Norwegian alternative movement has been fundamentally affected by the advent of another network: the world wide web. The internet provides widely available access to information on alternative phenomena and social networking sites, which add to the traditional networking platforms such as the magazine and the alternative fairs. *Alternativt Nettverk* went online in 1999 with the website www.altnett.no. Here one can find information about the organization, an overview of registered therapists, a calendar with upcoming activities, selected articles from *Visjon* and news about alternative spirituality. The website primarily acts as an information channel, and as such fills a function similar to that of the magazine *Visjon*. Its main function is to provide information on events, courses, therapists and news, and to stimulate contact in the non-virtual sphere.

In 2008 *Alternativt Nettverk* decided to set up a web forum in order to provide alternatively-minded actors an opportunity for more active interaction online. The web forum *AltNett* (www.altnett.ning.com) was launched in June 2008. Looking at the numbers the initiative appears to have been a success. The number of members rose rapidly, and eventually 11,500 profiles had been registered.[15] Although two other alternative web forums, *Ildsjelen*[16] and *Esoterisk nettverk*,[17] were launched approximately at the same time, *AltNett* soon established itself as the largest alternative web forum in Norway, a status that parallels that of its mother organization offline.[18]

In terms of technical structure, *AltNett* bore a strong resemblance to Facebook. Each member created a profile and could participate in different groups and befriend other members. By far the most popular item on the web forum were the discussion or interest groups, which each featured a separate discussion wall and member list. As of March 2013, there were more than 400 such groups, featuring such themes as "Esoteric astrology," "Power animals," "We who are Doreen Virtue fans," "Distance healing," *etc.* The structure of the forum thus enabled actors to find more specific interest groups. Most of the interaction took place online, but there is also evidence that the forum initiated contact between people outside the virtual realm. As an example, the second-most popular group, "Personal meeting place," acted as a sort of lonely hearts column for people of alternative orientations,

---

15. http://altnett.ning.com/profiles/members/ [accessed 17 March 2013]. The web forum is no longer available online, but I have downloaded it on my personal computer.

16. *Soul of Fire*. This online network was administered by the same people who issued *Ildsjelen* magazine.

17. *Esoteric Network*.

18. Alternative spirituality is also subject to vibrant discussion on other, more broadly profiled web forums, notably *VG Debatt*.

where people could post personal ads in order to establish contact with new friends or the "man or woman of your dreams." On the wall of the group we can read that the post, "Alternative friends sought in Akershus/Oslo," resulted in a group named *Zunztar* which has met several times at cafés and at private homes in Oslo.[19] There were also advertisements for courses, seminars and workshops by individual therapists, and advertisements for thematically "broader" network events such as the annual alternative festival at Storefjell or *VisionWorks'* own fairs. It is impossible to estimate to what extent these made *AltNett* members seek out other sites for interaction, but it is probable that they had at least some effect.

The web forum was eventually closed in 2013. According to an explanation posted by Eirik Svenke Solum on the forum itself, the resources required to run the web site were no longer corresponding to the level of activity. After an initial period of eager interest, the number of members had levelled out, and many became passive. By early 2013, the activity level was approximately one-tenth of what it had been during the first months. Hence the economic strain and workload required to moderate the forum no longer corresponded to the output it stimulated (E. Svenke Solum 2013). In my interview with Øyvind Solum, an additional explanation surfaced; the web forum required intense monitoring to keep unwanted voices at bay, and, in the end, the task proved both extremely time-consuming and somewhat of a personal challenge. The regulations of the forum followed more or less the same premises as those of the alternative fairs. Denied expressions were: "destructive utterances of hatred, harassment, attacks on individuals, all kinds of too extreme mission—be it for alternative or non-alternative things" (Ø. Solum 2012a). As opposed to the alternative fairs, the selling and buying of services and products were unwanted on the forum on the grounds that "It shouldn't be commercial." Solum further argued that, "There needs to be an open discussion about things. It's okay to present one's viewpoints. But not to massively negate everything else."

According to Øyvind Solum, the presence of conspiracy theorists was the most challenging issue to deal with as a moderator of *AltNett*. Generally believing extreme conspiracy theories to be false and dangerous, he repeatedly had to delete posts, send warnings and even ban some members who promoted conspiracy thinking. These actions were met by severe personal attacks and threats, which were "really discomforting" (Ø. Solum 2012a). Before it went that far, however, there had indeed been some room for conspiracists on *AltNett*. Other sources state that the online conspiracy community *Nyhetsspeilet*[20] in fact sprang out of *AltNett*, and to some extent

19. http://altnett.ning.com/forum/topics/alternative-venner-nskes-starte-en-alternativsyklubb-treff-kansje?groupUrl=personligmteplass&groupId=2109341%3AGroup%3A89184&id=2109341%3ATopic%3A1505410&page=1#comments [accessed 23 February 2012]

20. *News Mirror.*

also *Ildsjelen*'s similar web forum (see Dyrendal's chapter in this book). From the autumn of 2008 onwards, there were lively discussions about the Freemasons, chemtrails and attempts to recruit *AltNett* members to the closed online community *Bakkemannskapet*. Its leader, Mike Chechanowitz, was eventually banned from *AltNett*, but conspiracy actors were allowed to operate for some time before *Alternativt Nettverk* took drastic measures (Færseth 2013, 176). Although Solum did not state this explicitly, it seems probable that one reason behind *AltNett*'s closure was that *Alternativt Nettverk*'s leaders did not want the forum to function as a catalyst for strains within the alternative field of which they personally disapproved.

Controversies, commercial interests and new clusters

VisionWorks' control of its marketplaces has engendered a great deal of controversy. In particular, there seems to be an increasingly deep fault line between the organization and the emerging conspiracy milieu in Norway. As we have seen, *VisionWorks* has increasingly distanced itself from conspiracy thinking. Until a few years ago, *Nyhetsspeilet* authors were in fact granted access to *Alternativt Nettverk*'s forums (see e.g. Ertresvåg 2006a, 2006b; Myhre 2006). Now, however, there is little talk about conspiracies in *Visjon*, and the editor has overtly denied the validity of such theories (see e.g. E. Svenke Solum 2014b). The conspiracy milieu, for its part, has responded with verbal counter-attacks on *VisionWorks*' exclusivism. The exclusion of Per-Aslak Ertresvåg from the Lillestrøm fair in 2011 was, in particular, heavily debated. Some held the opinion that conspiracy theorists should be granted access to the fair (see Johansen 2011). Others went so far as to accuse the Solum family of being part of a greater conspiracy aimed at controlling the whole world (Ø. Solum 2012a). This conflict hints at a growing diversification of the Norwegian alternative movement, and an emerging desire to selectively promote only certain aspects of the "alternative" by *VisionWorks*' leadership.

It is methodologically difficult to gain an overview of the actors who, for different reasons, stand outside the institutionalized framework provided by *VisionWorks*. Overt controversies are louder than silent opposition; large networks more visible than individual actors. Nevertheless, it is clear that *VisionWorks* exerts a considerable degree of control over what is on offer within its construction of an alternative "market." As we have seen in relation to the alternative fairs, some providers have been denied access to the network. Others fall outside of it because they do not wish, or do not have the means required, to participate. Norway's largest meditation organization *Acem*, for instance, has never taken part in *Alternativt Nettverk*/*Vision-Works*' forums. Acem is an offshoot of Maharishi Mahesh Yogi's Transcendental Meditation movement, but today promotes a secularized meditation practice and opposes any association with the alternative movement. Geographical distance and/or cost of participation might be effective hindrances for smaller entrepreneurs. The classified ads in *Visjon* and stalls at the alternative fairs come at a considerable price, and would probably not be economically viable for individual practitioners outside the large cities. Others might oppose the commercial logic of the alternative "marketplace." As an example, Norway's perhaps best-known healer, Joralf Gjerstad, has reportedly never received payment[21] for his services, unlike the vast majority of the healers at the alternative fairs. It should therefore be clear that *VisionWorks* embodies only organized activities, and that it only represents parts of the wider alternative milieu.

As the "alternative" has become more widespread, new organized clusters have emerged alongside *Alternativt Nettverk/VisionWorks*. The conspiracy milieu has been the only organized interest network with which *VisionWorks* has had a definitive fissure, but the past few years have seen the emergence of several new networking actors. These do not necessarily represent diverging views or antagonistic attitudes towards *VisionWorks*, but nevertheless constitute complementary—if not competing—platforms for interaction in addition to those provided by *VisionWorks*.

First, there are new providers of alternative fairs on the market. *Saga-forlaget*[22] was initially a publishing house, but ventured into the fair business after one of its book publications put it in touch with the alternative movement in Norway. Its first fair was arranged in 1999, and Saga today hosts alternative fairs in Haugesund, Drammen, Kristiansand, Arendal, Ålesund and Bærum (Saga Marketing 2014; Alternativopplysningen 2014b). *Kulturverkstedet i Tromsø* hosts an alternative fair in Tromsø (www.kulturverk-stedet.no). The prime mover of the alternative milieu in southwestern Norway, Christian Paaske, arranges a fair in Stavanger (www.alternativmesse.com), and there is a biannual fair at the alternative centre *Unity* in Oslo.

Second, several new alternative magazines have emerged since the turn of the millennium. The magazine *Harmoni/Ildsjelen*[23] was launched in 2000, and has a broad alternative profile. It also runs a publishing house whose primary output consists of literature written by editor Per Henrik Gullfoss, but which also translates international New Age authors for the Norwegian market. The magazine *Medium* likewise covers a relatively broad range of alternative phenomena, but—as the name indicates—has a strong emphasis on mediumship and parapsychology. Astrology is also a central theme. *Medium* was first issued in 2005. *Magic* was launched in 2008, and focuses on divination and paranormal phenomena. The last addition to the alternative magazine shelf is the health magazine *Vitenskap og Fornuft*[24] which was launched in 2010 and offers a more or less alternative angle on health and lifestyle issues.

---

21. Gjærstad however accepts unsolicited gifts.

22. *Saga Publishing.*

23. *Harmony/Soul of Fire. Ildsjelen* changed its name to *Harmoni* in April 2015.

24. *Science and Reason.*

Third, several telemarket services and web pages provide services through which people can get in touch with alternative providers. The publishers behind *Magic* run a telemarket where various divination services are sold (see http://magiccircle.no). The firm *Call AS* also provides divination services over the phone via the web sites mystisk.no, klarsynte.no, tarot.no and krystallkulen.no. These initiatives appear to be more motivated by economic profit than ideological concerns, but nevertheless constitute market platforms where alternative providers can offer their services to prospective clients. *Alternativopplysningen*[25] is another influential actor. Established as a teleservice by former *Alternativt Nettverk* employee Bertil Berg-Olsen in 1997, the firm runs several web sites with overviews of alternative fairs (alternativmesser.no), therapists (behandler.no) and news, and general information (alternativ.no) (Alternativopplysningen 2014a).

Last but not least, new media have fundamentally altered the premises for involvement in the alternative movement and the public debate about alternative religiosity (see Kraft's chapter in this book). In a process often described as mediatization, the media have to an increasing extent come to set the premises for social interaction (Hjarvard 2008, 14). The media have also been a driving force behind the emergence of the "network society," in which social relations are increasingly governed by individual choice and less dependent on physical location and local traditions (Castells 1996). The revolutionary new medium—the internet—is itself a network, and its penetration into the everyday lives of almost all Norwegians under the age of 75 has radically altered the premises by which we interact with our wider social network. Whereas a therapist twenty years ago would either depend on direct communication or transmitters such as common acquaintances, therapy centres or *Alternativt Nettverk* to get in touch with clients, making oneself known today requires nothing more than a computer and internet access. Likewise, people who seek information or providers will find a rich selection at the click of a mouse. Apart from specifically alternative web sites such as the ones covered above, alternative ideas and actors are to be found on the web forums of online newspapers, Facebook, Twitter, Instagram and other social media. Within this landscape, it is difficult to draw any clear lines of organizational demarcation, and actors flow freely between different platforms of interaction. Rather tellingly, several of the alternative providers I interviewed told me that they simply intensified their public activity on Facebook after *AltNett* was closed. Participation in the alternative "movement" or "network" has always been characterized by multiple sites for contact and information, and the internet has woven further threads and provided further nodes for interaction.

---

25. *The alternative information service.*

From *"Network"* to *"Visions"*

To a certain extent, *Alternativt Nettverk* played a formative role in consolidating this milieu into an organized network movement. Although I am hesitant to use the concept "New Age," the general distinction made by Wouter Hanegraaff between New Age *religion* and the New Age as a *movement* transfers well into the Norwegian context. Hanegraaff understands New Age religion to be a general type of culture criticism based on a foundation of secularized esotericism, whereas the New Age as a movement refers to a cultic milieu "having become conscious of itself as constituting a more or less unified 'movement'" (Hanegraaff 1998, 522). Although the ideas of the New Age have been around for a long time, those who adhered to them did not begin to perceive themselves as being part of a larger movement until the latter half of the 1970s (Hanegraaff 1998, 522). As the first wide-ranging platform gathering people interested in alternative (or—in Hanegraaff's terminology—New Age) phenomena in Norway, *Alternativt Nettverk* undoubtedly contributed to establishing a sense of "we" throughout the 1990s. The organization was also instrumental in cementing "alternative" as the leading self-designation in the Norwegian New Age milieu. This is not to say that *Alternativt Nettverk* encompassed the entire spectrum of alternative religious beliefs, political convictions, therapeutic practices and deviant lifestyles in Norway—there has always existed alternative currents outside the framework provided by *Alternativt Nettverk*. Nevertheless, the organization did gather a vast spectrum of ideas and actors under a common umbrella that promoted a common alternative identity, both amongst the actors themselves and in the greater public sphere. As such, it was a driving force in consolidating alternative actors in Norway into a relatively organized and broad national network.

One of the main features of a network is that it is not a hegemonic structure. The bonds that create a social web are woven by individual actors as they interact with each other (cf. Latour 2005, 5). There may be organising structures within this network. Authorities gather actors around them, and nodal points emerge as several actors cluster around the same person, organization, idea or practice. Hence the network lives a life of its own, and the development of *Alternativt Nettverk* testifies to this point. Whereas the organization facilitated the emergence of a large national network, the actors it gathered eventually stepped forward to establish new webs within this structure or competing networks on its fringes. As we have seen, several new platforms for interaction between people with alternative interests have emerged since the turn of the millennium. The alternative web as a whole has grown, but it has also pulled actors towards them and created new hubs and interest groups.

As a result, *Alternativt Nettverk/VisionWorks* is no longer the only networking service in the Norwegian alternative milieu. Somewhat ironically, the organization's success in making the alternative more widespread and organized has also reduced its own significance. This new role as one of several has had profound consequences for the organization's profile. In 2012, *Alternativt Nettverk* changed its name to *VisionWorks*. According to current leader Eirik Svenke Solum, the name change signalled significant changes in the organization's premises and ambitions:

> We're now changing our name to *VisionWorks* because the network is well-established and the public debate has created great changes, so that the need for *Alternativt Nettverk* as a nodal point no longer remains the same. 'The alternative' is no longer so alternative. [...] Rather than standing outside the rest of society, *VisionWorks* now wishes to contribute actively to shape our common future. We deliver visions that work! Visions that provide meaningful inspiration in life and visions that tie the personal and global together. (E. Svenke Solum 2012b)

Eirik Svenke Solum further explained the reasons for the name change in a personal interview: "*Alternativt Nettverk* was an umbrella, an interest organization for all things alternative. But because that role had become diluted, and people don't necessarily relate to *Alternativt Nettverk* as their organization any more [...] we felt that it was time to change our name" (2012a). He also mentioned another, more prosaic factor: *Alternativt Nettverk* had from time to time been approached by people who believed the firm provided IT services!

That note aside, the above citations make clear that *VisionWorks* no longer seeks to encompass the entire alternative movement. The network has acquired a dynamic of its own and no longer needs an organization to pull its strings together, according to Svenke Solum. Hence *VisionWorks* no longer sees the need to promote all things "alternative," but rather wishes to promote ideas and practices that they consider to be "positive contributions to the world, society, people living today" (E. Svenke Solum 2012a).

As we have seen, the desire to promote "positive" elements within the alternative has not resulted in a strict policy of inclusion/exclusion. The magazine continues to include a horoscope section and articles on divination and the alternative fairs still devote an entire section to mediums and fortune-tellers—albeit this is not something which *VisionWorks'* leaders personally believe in or seek to promote. The inclusion of divination and mediumship could stem from a desire to be inclusive towards different strains of alternative thought and practice. It could also reflect the fact that *VisionWorks* is a joint stock firm which necessarily needs to take into account certain commercial considerations. At the same time, the leadership has attempted to emphasize particular aspects of alternative thinking. A holistic life-stance community called *Holistisk Forbund* sprang out of *Alternativt Nettverk* in 2002. The initiative was led by Inge Ås and Øyvind

Solum, who sought to establish an alternative equivalent to traditional life stance communities such as the Church of Norway and the Humanistic Association. Its profile was to remain open and explorative, but was to rest on a holistic worldview and approach to life (see Rønnevig 2008; Ø. Solum 2012b). Holism—difficult to define as it might be—is still favoured by *VisionWorks*, especially in the form of environmentalist, responsible living (E. Svenke Solum 2012a). In recent years, many of the alternative fairs have had a specific theme on which there have been panel debates, lectures, art installations *et cetera*. As an example, the Lillestrøm fair in 2013 hosted the theme "Green Future." Likewise, *Visjon* has featured an increasing number of articles on environmentalism, vegetarianism, mindfulness and self-improvement in general in the last few years—themes with which Øyvind Solum, current editor-in-chief Eirik Svenke Solum and fair coordinator Johanne Woll are known to sympathize.

These changes mark a new direction for *VisionWorks*: from seeking to encompass all things alternative in order to consolidate and strengthen the alternative movement in Norway, the organization has become one among several networking agents within this alternative movement, and has sharpened its thematic profile. It is likely that the organization will remain the most influential networking agent for alternative thinking in Norway, and that it will continue to have a broad ethos and relatively inclusive approach to views that diverge from the personal convictions of its leaders. However, the fissures and emergence of competing networks in the Norwegian alternative landscape has radically altered the premises on which *VisionWorks* operates, and the organization is adjusting its profile accordingly. With some exceptions, the organizational umbrella still covers most colours of the alternative rainbow, but the green spectrum, focusing on ecology and sustainable living, is growing.

Concluding remarks

Alternativt Nettverk has been a key actor in the development of a Norwegian alternative "movement." The organization was instrumental in bringing about a sense of communality among actors who were involved with alternative therapy, lifestyles and new spirituality in the 1990s. By providing common platforms where alternative providers could present themselves to a larger audience, the network facilitated the dispersion of alternative thought in Norway. More than twenty years on, *VisionWorks*' magazine, alternative fairs, web sites and events are still favoured sites for marketing and interaction that draw a large audience. At the same time, new umbrellas have emerged. The target groups of magazines such as *Magic*, *Medium* and *Ildsjelen* to a large extent overlap with that of *Visjon*. Niche communities such as *Nyhetsspeilet* and online interest groups represent competing structures, and demonstrate the impact of new media on the Norwegian alternative scene. Thus, the formal network provided by *VisionWorks* today constitutes only one among several organizing forces, and there are many indicators that the organization has become relatively marginalized as the alternative landscape has expanded in size and scope. Somewhat ironically, its demise as the main agenda setter testifies to *Alternativt Nettverk*'s success in reaching its initial objectives. The "alternative" is here to stay, and the alternative network in Norway—without capital letters—has acquired a vibrant dynamic of its own.

References

Alternativopplysningen. 2013. Alternativmesser i Norge — 100.000 besøkende [Online]. Available at: http://www.alternativ.no/art/?id=75 [Accessed 25.10.2014].

———. 2014a. Alternativ.no : helse, innsikt og livsglede siden 1997 [Online]. Available at: http://www.alternativ.no/om.php [Accessed 1.11.2014].

———. 2014b. Messeoversikt [Online]. Available at: http://www.alternativmesse.no [Accessed 25.10.2014].

Alternativt Nettverk. 2012. "Alternativbevegelsens framvekst i Norge." *Visjon* 21(1): 52–59.

Botvar, Pål Ketil and Jan-Olav Henriksen. 2010. "Mot en alternativreligiøs revolusjon?" In *Religion i dagens Norge : mellom sekularisering og sakralisering,* edited by P. K. Botvar and U. Schmidt, 60–80. Oslo: University Publishing House.

Castells, Manuel. 1996. *The Rise of the Network Society: Information Age,* vol 1. Cambridge, MA: Blackwell.

Ertresvåg, Per-Aslak. 2006a. "En medisinsk mafia?." *Visjon* (4): 20–24.

———. 2006b. "Makten bak makten." *Visjon* (5) 22–25.

Færseth, John. 2013. *KonspiraNorge,* [Oslo], Humanist.

Hanegraaff, Wouter. 1998. *New Age Religion and Western Culture: Esotericism in the Mirror of Secular Thought.* Albany: State University of New York Press.

Hjarvard, Stig. 2008. "The mediatization of religion: A theory of the media as agents of religious change." *Northern Lights* 6: 9–26.

Johansen, Jarle. 2011. Per-Aslak Ertresvåg utestengt fra Alternativmessen [Online]. *Nyhetsspeilet.* Available at: http://www.nyhetsspeilet.no/2011/11/per-aslak-ertresvag-utestengt-fra-alternativmessen/ [Accessed 27.03.2013].

Kraft, Siv Ellen. 2001. "Alternativmessen. For deg som tror litt, mye, eller ingenting." *Din - tidsskrift for religion og kultur* 1: 18–24.

Latour, Bruno. 2005. *Reassembling the Social : An Introduction to Actor-Network-Theory.* Oxford: Oxford University Press.

Løøv, Margrethe. 2016. "Shoppers in the spiritual supermarket: A quantitative study of visitors at Scandinavia's largest alternative fair." *Journal of Contemporary Religion* 1: 67–84.

Myhre, Rolf Kenneth 2006. "Var 11/9-dramaet iscenesatt?" *Visjon* 5: 34–36.

Øygard, Astrid Elisabeth. 1998. *Alternativbevegelsens ideologi og strategi. En sosiologisk studie av Alternativt Nettverk/Nettverk Nytt.* Hovedfag: Universitetet i Oslo.

Pettersen, Roald. 2012. Interview by Margrethe Løøv, 12.12.2012.

———. 2013. *RE: Re: Målgrupper for Alternativt Nettverk i startfasen.* E-mail to Margrethe Løøv, 11.3.2013.

———. 2015. *RE: AN og Indre Ledelse.* E-mail to Margrethe Løøv, 28.04.2015.

Roberts, Joshua. 2014. *RE: RE: Number of visitors at the London Mind-Body-Spirit Festival.* E-mail to Margrethe Løøv, 29.10.2014.

Rønnevig, Georg 2008. "Norwegian New Age: *Alternativt Nettverk* and *Holistisk Forbund.*" *Journal of Alternative Spiritualities and New Age Studies* 5.

Saga Marketing. 2014. Om oss [Online]. Available at: http://www.sagamesser. no/om-oss/ [Accessed 22.10.2014].

Solum, Øyvind. 2008. *Alternativt Nettverk* 10 år i 2002 [Online]. Available at: http://www.altnett.no/Magasinet/9266 [Accessed 23.11.2010].

———. 2012a. Interview by Margrethe Løøv, 06.11.2012.

———. 2012b. "Holistisk Forbund og Den usynlige religionen: Indre og ytre autoritet i spennet mellom individualisme, relativisme og helhetstenkning." Master thesis, University of Oslo.

Svenke Solum, Eirik. 2012a. Interview by Margrethe Løøv, 30.11.2012.

———. 2012b. "Fra nettverk til *VisionWorks.*" *Visjon* (2): 2.

———. 2013. Svar til: Stenging? Åpent brev til Alternativ Nettverk/Magasinet Visjon [Online]. Available at: altnett.ning.com/forum/topics/stenging-pent-brev-til-alternativ-nettverk-magasinet-visjon/index.html.

———. 2014a. Interview by Margrethe Løøv, 25.11.2014.

———. 2014b. Ebola, vaksiner og konspirasjoner [Online]. Available at: http://www.altnett.no/no/artikler/nyheter/Ebola%2C+vaksiner+og+konspirasjoner.9UFRLOYU.ips [Accessed 31.10.2014].

———. 2015. *RE: Gratis stand på alternativmessen.* E-mail to Margrethe Løøv, 12.05.2015.

Tampuu, Mari. 2006. *Trender og tendenser i tidsskriftet 'Alternativt Nettverk'.* Det teologiske menighetsfakultet.

— 3 —

Bad, Banal and Basic:
New Age in the Norwegian News Press and Entertainment Media

Siv Ellen Kraft

This chapter has two, connected goals: First, to provide an overview of the presence of New Age in Norwegian news- and popular media, focusing on how much in which genres, and how it is represented in these different genres. Emphasis will—in order for this project to be manageable—be placed on secular media and the past two decades, and on the principal tendencies regarding different genres, based on my own research as well as that of other scholars.

Second, I will use the results to discuss the so-called mediatization of religion thesis, put forward by the Danish media scholar Stig Hjarvard and others. Hjarvard has paved the way for a more systematic approach to the relationship between media and religion in late modern societies. However—and this is my main focus in the latter part of this chapter—the mediatization of religion thesis has limited potential with regard to New Age-spiritualities, and its notion of "banal religion" fails to make sense of what is today the dominant religion in popular media.

New Age in news media

Henrik Reinholdt Christensen, in a quantitative study of the Scandinavian news press (2010), found hardly any signs of New Age and alternative spirituality, and concludes that they "do not play a role in public debates at all." A case-based study of religion in the Norwegian news press by myself and Alexa Døving to some extent supports this conclusion (Døving and Kraft 2013).[1] We argue that New Age representations are, on an everyday basis, lim-

---

1. The study focuses on secular news media, particularly newspapers, during the first decade of this century.

ited to advertisements for various professional entrepreneurs, and the occasional coverage of New Age superstars and happenings. New Age is normally treated as irrelevant to the understanding of public affairs—of politics, economics and societal development more broadly. It rarely makes it to the level of "hard news," and is usually left out of debates concerning that what today constitute typical religion-related topics; multiculturalism, immigration, the suppression of women, discrimination against homosexuals, terrorism, religious education in schools, the place of religion in the public sphere, etc.

However, there are examples of more significant cases, and some of these have been huge. By far the most extensive is the angel school Astarte Education, co-founded by Norwegian princess Märtha Louise and Elisabeth Samnøy in 2007. The royal ingredient makes this an unusual case, and explains the extraordinary amount of media attention given to it; the angel school ended up as one of the most profiled media stories of the year, and as probably the most profiled New Age story in Norwegian media history (Kraft 2015, 2008). It was framed from the start as a scandal, and as a media case included all the typical themes of "bad religion"— discourses "used for labelling religion as deviant and problematic" (Hjelm 2006, 63).

Titus Hjelm has, for the Finnish context, suggested a five-part typology for bad religion-discourse in contemporary news media, all of which were represented in the angel case, namely 1) *healthiness* (bad for individuals and society), 2) *heresy* (departing from true religion), 3) *rationality* (funny and foolish), 4) *ethics* (morally deviant), and finally 5) *pseudo-religion* (not fully established as "religious" (Hjelm 2006, 71). References to healthiness, rationality and pseudo-religion dominated the media coverage of Astarte Education, with concerns raised regarding the mental health of the princess, the overall status of the royal house, threats of "contagion" among "vulnerable groups" ("divination-addictions" being one suggested scenario), and numerous portrayals of the extraordinary stupidity of Her royal highness. But heresy and ethics were also represented. Conservative Christians normally keep a low profile in public debates and rarely use explicitly dogmatic language (Christensen 2010), but in this case they chose to come forth, and to do so in elaborate demonological detail. Additionally, some journalists went quite far in the direction of explicitly denouncing this New Age-style religiosity as inferior to Christianity (Kraft 2014, 2008). Coverage has not, neither in this early phase nor later, been unambiguously negative, but attempts to nuance the debate have primarily been limited to interviews and letters to the editor; most journalists have been critical.

New Age is normally categorized in the public sphere as "religion," due partly—one may assume—to the fact that the church, theologians and historians of religions have for decades spoken of it as such. However, suspicions that we are in reality dealing with cover-ups for other concerns are regularly voiced, along with notions that this *may* be religion, but of a particular kind—unlike ordinary religions, and in some ways departing from what religion really is and should be. Such suspicions tend to revolve around the possibility of economic motives, and are often—it appears—based on a notion of mutual exclusiveness: motives are *either* religious *or* economic. This, moreover, is a double standard. Christian ministers are not expected to choose between God and Mammon; they receive their monthly salaries from a state-financed church, and are neither expected to work for free nor accused of being in the religion-business solely for the money.

The unsettled and ambiguous status as "religion" (or something else) remained a feature of the angel school coverage, sometimes even in the same texts. Märtha Louise has regularly been portrayed as *both* a gullible follower of a ridiculous religion *and* a shrewd and cynical businesswoman. Estimates of the money involved have been repeated in numerous features, along with the issue of whether Märtha Louise—as a princess—should be involved in business enterprises at all. This latter issue was first raised in connection with the establishment of "Prinsesse Märtha Louises kultur-formidling" (Princess Märtha Louise's culture dissemination) in 2002,[2] but heated up dramatically with the news of the angel school. The well-known editor of *Finansavisen*, Trygve Hegnar, for instance, claimed in his editorials that Astarte Education constitutes a breach with Norwegian consumer-law, and is basically a fraud (Døving and Kraft 2013, 39, *Finansavisen* 31.07.2007). Angels, he explained, do not exist, and are accordingly not available for communication, whether through angel schools or otherwise. Märtha Louise is "neither crazy nor psychotic," but rather a shrewd businesswoman" (Døving and Kraft 2013, 39).

Their ambiguous status as "religion" may to some extent account for the overall lack of respect granted to New Age-spiritualities. The "Code of ethics of the Norwegian press" (*Vær varsom plakaten*) tells journalists to "Always respect a person's character and identity, privacy, ethnicity, nationality and belief," and to "be careful when using terms that create stigmas." Examples of disrespectful treatment of religious people are hardly limited to New Age, but few—if any— other religions can compete in terms of quantity and in terms of the repetitive themes found in such criticisms. "Proper" religions tend, moreover, to be ascribed at least some positive traits, in regard to, for instance, societal cohesion, moral guidance and ritual facilities. New Age is rarely, if ever, ascribed such traits, and is usually left out in accounts of positive and societally useful religions.

Media coverage in the wake of the massacre on Utøya, July 22, 2011, is a telling example of such tendencies. Norwegian minority religions tend to be evaluated and discussed with regard to national identity (whether they "belong here" or not), based on implicit notions of Norwegian identity and culture as connected with Christianity (Døving and Kraft 2013). During the

---

2. Märtha gave up the title Her Royal Highness in order to start this company, and during subsequent years published a children's story book and a book about pilgrimage, as well as toured the country as a story teller.

early aftermath of the massacre, a highly different set of representations were offered, with minority religions as part of Norwegian community, and important contributors to the national grief. Religious leaders, particularly Christians and Muslims, were portrayed as wise and comforting, and as coping with the tragedy together with each other and the Norwegian people—as "Together in the sorrow," to quote one of several feature stories framed along these lines (*Aftenposten* 26.7, Døving and Kraft 2013). New Age was not included in this storyline. The only example we found of newspaper coverage of new religions was one highly critical article about a group of Scientologists, whose offer of support to grievers in downtown Oslo was interpreted by the journalist as insensitive, bordering on cruel (Døving and Kraft 2013).

There are examples of the more positive implications of the status of pseudo-religion. New Age appears to have replaced "folk religiosity" as a negative version of pseudo-religion, while folk religiosity, at least in some of its forms, has moved upwards on the scale. The extraordinary career of *Snåsamannen* (literally "the man from Snåsa") is a revealing example. A locally famous healer from the countryside, *Snåsamannen* (alias Joralf Gjerstad, born 1926) became an A-list celebrity in the wake of a bestselling biography about him, written by the well-known and respected journalist Ingar Sletten Kolloen, and published in 2008. By then in his eighties, Gjerstad was the most profiled person in Norwegian media that same winter, and was announced by *Dagbladet*—one of the two major Norwegian tabloids—as "power climber of the year," and, according to the NRK[3] new year eve news cavalcade that year, "arouses interest in all parts of the population" (see Kraft 2010; Døving and Kraft 2013). Even a case involving the distance-healing by telephone of the infant son of then health minister Bjarne Håkon Hanssen received fairly sympathetic treatment. It is highly unusual that top politicians come forward with experiences that normally qualify as magical or miraculous, and equally unusual, as was the case here, that this kind of sharing is publicly supported by other politicians—without the media going crazy.

Kolloen's framing prepared the ground for this turn of events. *Snåsamannen*, according to Kolloen's portrayal of him, is a wise and humble man from the countryside, who has spent his lifetime helping others, approximately 50,000 people, all of it free of charge. His religiosity is of a minimalist kind, leaning towards the ethical and the philosophical more than the metaphysical, and he is—last but not least—an unusually pure image of traditional Norwegian-ness. Scholars have referred to "conspicuous modesty" as the chief ideal of political leadership in Norway, with sensibility, soberness and morality among the favoured ingredients (Daloz 2003). A religious version of such ideals, *Snåsamannen* is the old man next door, a version of Norwegian ideals in miniature.

This, then, was neither New Age, nor the nutty fringes of Christianity, but rather an epitome of media-style religion in Norway: old, free of cost, core-

---

3. Norwegian broadcasting.

Norwegian, and, in addition, minimalist to the point of not-necessarily-religious-at-all. Frequent references to 50,000 cases of successful healing tended to be followed by references to the possibility of future scientific documentation and explanation.

The case of Sami New Age and neo-shamanism constitutes another example of ideas and activities that tend to be exempted from bad religion discourse, and granted more positive and sympathetic treatment. Reasons for this may be partly ethical, connected with fear of offending members of a group with a recent history of suppression, discrimination and forced assimilation. They can perhaps also be connected with widespread notions of the Sami (and indigenous people more generally) as rooted in ancient spiritual traditions, of which contemporary indigenous shamans are the latest in line (Fonneland and Kraft 2013). Sami neo-shamanism is a recent phenomenon, whose articulations of Sami ideas and practices from the past have been shaped by the international movement of neo-shamanism. Journalists, however, tend to present them as old- rather than New Age, and as expressions of traditional heritage, rather than silly inventions and questionable motives.

New Age in popular media

The gap between "what people want"[4] and what the news media offer appears to be substantial, at least if presence and presentation in popular formats and channels can be taken as evidence. As early as the mid-1990s, Ingvild Sælid Gilhus and Lisbeth Mikaelsson referred to a re-enchantment of Norwegian culture, of "new religiosity," as spread thinly across culture, and of popular culture as both expression of—and contributor to—this process (Gilhus and Mikaelsson 1998). Studies focusing explicitly on popular media have further substantiated such claims. The theologian Arild Romarheim, based on a quantitative study of weekly family magazines, refers to an overall increase in religiously-framed material from 1997 to 2007 (Romarheim 2011, 54). During this same period, Christian elements declined by almost half, while alternative spiritualities tripled, with a percentage distribution of 18 to 80 percent, and only two percent on "world religions." Most popular among the alternative elements found in weekly magazines is healing, alternative therapy, divination, astrology, and what Romarheim calls "spirit beliefs" (particularly in the form of spirit helpers) and faith in spirits (åndetro)—which has increased ten-folded during the period.[5]

---

4. "What people want" (Det folk vil ha), is the first part of the title of a book by Dag Øystein Endsjø and Liv Ingeborg Lied, covering religion and popular culture (Endsjø and Lied 2011).

5. The theologian Per Magne Aadnanes, in a study of the relationship of the Norwegian folk church to New Age and new religious movements from the 1970s and onwards, focuses primarily on Christian media, but also comments on representations of New Age in the secular news media and popular and entertainment-culture (Aadnanes 2008).

Popular women's magazines (like *Stella, KK* and *Tara*) have not been subjected to similar research, but are likely to reveal similar results. Health, self-development and lifestyle issues are central features of such magazines, along with design, fashion and celebrity stuff, all of which are known from other studies as typical conveyors of New Age-ideas and concepts; feng shui for energy flow in the house, angels and Buddha statues for decoration, meditation and mindfulness for body and soul, along with coaching, yoga, martial arts, self-help techniques, pilgrimages, (super)natural remedies and alternative medicine of many sorts.

In several articles, the historian of religion Anne Kalvig has discussed the increasing presence of New Age-spiritualities on mainstream TV-channels (Kalvig 2009, 2013). "The Power of the Spirits," a program with a concept based on spiritism, mediumship and house cleaning, has for years had nearly half a million viewers weekly (in a country of five million people) (Kalvig 2009). Other nationally produced series of a spiritist or mediumship/clairvoyance-centred kind include *From Souls to Soul; The Quest for the Sixth Sense*, and the fictional drama *The deceased (Dauinger)*, representing one of the heaviest investments of the Norwegian Broadcasting systems in 2012–2013 (Kalvig forthcoming).

There are few signs of bad religion discourse in these popular cultural formats. Rather, New Age ideas and symbols tend to be presented as facts, as interesting fiction or as a combination of the two. The fact-oriented format is represented in magazine columns written by New Age-representatives of various sorts, in feature stories on gurus, self-help techniques and interviews with New Age-oriented celebrities, and in TV talk-shows like "The power of spirits." The fact-oriented tone of such media products differ little from that presented in New Age-magazines like *Visjon, Ildsjelen* and *Medium* (see Løøw's chapter, this book). They thus diverge from what Hjarvard and others have depicted as the typical development of secular media: that authority is shifted from the religions to the media. Traditional formats like Christian ceremonies *are* disappearing from mainstream media, but New Age-formats appear to be moving in, often more or less whole piece. Expert advice offered by healers in weekly magazines tend, for instance, to follow the same basic format as that of patient-client encounters in New Age businesses. The prime time mediation of house-cleansing resembles that of off-media stage projects. These are not examples of the media take over, production and control of religion, but rather of New Age-experts taking their ideas and practices to secular screens and magazines, or of wholesale use of New Age concepts; of the media—to cite Hjarvard's claim to the contrary—as "conveyors of the messages of religious institutions" (Hjarvard 2013, 102).

What the media *does* influence is the competition between different New Age-entrepreneurs, and perhaps also the favoring of certain stories, ideas and practices. New Age celebrities like Märtha Louise and Gro-Helen Tørum are media-made in the sense that the media have given them time and attention, spread their profiles to large proportions of the Norwegian population, and used them as examples, spoke-persons and commentators. Media-made celebrity status in turn promotes the careers of the persons concerned. New Age-entrepreneurs regularly refer to media coverage in their advertisements for courses and events, and increasing fame opens up novel opportunities, such as book contracts with major publishers.

The media may also help support certain New Age ideas and practices over others. There is in popular culture a tendency to downplay dogmatic correctness and doctrinal coherence (Lied 2012, 184), and "to give priority to religious expressions that are visually strong, to emotional and fascinating aspects of religion, and to aspects that accentuate atmosphere and experience" (Lied 2012, 184). The case with religions in general is also the case with New Age. It is rarely the intellectual and philosophically complex New Age-traditions that make it to prime time entertainment and popular magazines. Phenomena like UFOs and conspirituality—to name some obvious examples—are simply more suitable for mainstream entertainment than the theoretically more complex perspectives of for instance David Spangler, or—to use an example from the Norwegian context—Erik Dammann, the founder of *Fremtiden i våre hender* (The future in our hands).

The mediatization of religion thesis

The so-called mediatization of religion thesis[6] offers a frame in which to understand the relationship between media and religion in contemporary western societies, and should accordingly be able to cover and make analytical sense of the tendencies referred to above. Hjarvard defines mediatization as "the process whereby society to an increasing degree is submitted to, or become dependent on, the media and their logic" (Hjarvard 2008, 113). His main concern is long term and substantial changes following late modern media technologies, not specific cases or genres. Particular cases, genres and tendencies might nevertheless, one may assume, be used to test the general relevance and usefulness of the thesis, including its primary claims regarding what is assumed to have already taken place. One such claim is that of the media having taken over many of the functions traditionally performed by religion, and are today important agents of religious changes. Three metaphors are suggested for these developments. *Media as conduits* implies that the media "have become an important, if not the primary source of information and experiences concerning religious issues"; *media as language*

---

6. The mediatization thesis was first presented in an article in 2008 titled "The mediation of religion: A theory of media as agents of social change," and has been further refined and developed in later publications (Hjarvard 2013). It has also resulted in a lively and fruitful debate, including critical discussions of various parts of his perspective and thesis. See for instance a special edition of *Culture and religion* 12(2): 203–210), focusing on the mediatization thesis, and *Mediatization and religion. Nordic perspectives* (2012), edited by Stig Hjarvard and Mia Lövheim.

implies that the media format religion in specific ways, particularly through the genres of popular culture; *media as environments* implies that media "contribute to the production and altering of social relationships and cultural communities [...] and they have become crucial for the public celebration of major national and cultural events" (Hjarvard 2012, 27).

The mediatization of religion thesis deserves the attention granted to it, and has—particularly in regard to "organized religions"—provided important contributions. More problematic, and to a large extent left out in critical debates following his publications, is his notion of "banal religion." Hjarvard defines this as media-made representations, produced according to the logic of the media and at the same time anchored in "primal religiosity." Central to "banal religion," moreover, is a lack of or limited relationship with institutionalized religions. Banal religion consists of:

> elements usually associated with folk religion, such as trolls, vampires, and black cats crossing the street, items taken from institutionalized religion such as crosses, prayers and cowls; and representations that do not necessarily have any religious connotations, such as upturned faces, thunder and lightening, and highly emotional music. (Hjarvard 2013, 91).

Hjarvard draws upon cognitive perspectives in order to explain these elements. Banal religious representations are "primary and fundamental to the production of religious thoughts and emotions," and thus constitutive for religious imagination as well as for the secondary developments performed through (proper) religious texts and symbols. It is based on "basic cognitive skills that help ascribe anthropomorphic or animistic agency to supernatural power, usually by means of counterintuitive categories that arrest attention, support memory, and evoke emotions" (Hjarvard 2013, 92).

The choice of "banal" as the term for a particular form of mediatized religion is inspired by Michael Billig's notion of "banal nationalism"; versions of nationalism that are "unwaved" (as opposed to "waved"; that is, more noticeable national symbols), based on "low-key usage of formerly explicit national symbols," and that accordingly tend to go unnoticed. In Hjarvard's words:

> Just as the study of nationalism needs to take the banal elements of national culture into account, the study of religion must consider how both individual faith and collective religious imagination are created and maintained by a series of experiences and representations that may have no, or only a limited, relationship with the institutionalized religions. In continuation of Billig (1995) we label these as banal religious representations. (Hjarvard 2013, 91)

These representations are placed alongside "religious media" and "journalism on religion" as a distinct form; one which rarely debates religion (as in journalism on religion) or preaches a particular gospel (like religious media). Rather, banal religion constitutes "decontextualized and non-intentional religious meanings" which are there merely to entertain, amuse or help to sell other products (Hjarvard 2013, 91).

There are several problems with this construct, some of which have been dealt with by other scholars.[7] To start: the term as such is unfortunate for a discipline that aims and claims for non-confessional and non-normative studies of religion. To take seriously "banal religion" would seem to be a contradiction in terms.

Moreover, the cognitive approach, as presented by Hjarvard, adds little to our understanding of these processes and phenomena. One might, in keeping with the perspectives of cognitive theory, argue that religion is *as such* based on these types of cognitive processes. If dead people walking and talking is an example of a counterintuitive mix of categories, then so is the resurrection of Jesus and countless other examples from the world of religiosity, only some of which make it to the popular media-scapes.

Additionally, the examples referred to by Hjarvard hardly qualify as "primal," in his sense of the term—as "raw" and "spontaneous." Nor is there necessarily a lack of religious contexts and intentions. Regarding popular magazines, Hjarvard notes that personal advice columns "may occasionally feature advice by Protestant ministers," but these are "not inclined to preach a particular gospel" (2012, 35). Romarheim´s research on Norwegian magazines, as we have seen, paints a rather different picture, but one which does not limit "religion" to the world religion paradigm, and thus are able to pick up on new types of religious "gospels." It is not, for instance, "sudden strikes of lightening" and "black cats crossing the streets" that flood television series and films, but rather—to mention some of the examples referred to by Hjarvard—productions like *The Power of the Spirits*, Dan Brown's *The Da Vinci Code* and the follow up *Angels & Demons* (Hjarvard 2012, 80), all of which have been described by other scholars as typical of New Age- and occultural -logics. *The Power of the Spirits* features clairvoyants helping people with spirit problems of various sorts; dead people, ghosts, unrest in houses etc. *The Da Vinci Code* is based on what Hjarvard terms "a mixture of spiritual sensibility, conspiracy theories, and criticism of traditional orthodoxy." These mixtures, however, constitute variations of established New Age plots and storylines. As Christopher Partridge puts it in "The occultural significance of *The Da Vinci Code*," (2008):

> The popularity of books like The Da Vinci Code is interesting in that
> it would seem to support surveys indicating at least a general level of
> public interest in the spiritual and the paranormal. More specifically, an
> analysis of the dominant ideas articulated in The Da Vinci Code suggests

---

7. Lied, for instance, argues convincingly that Hjarvard reduces "religion" to the candidates included in the world religion paradigm (Lied 2012), and along with other critics describes his category of "religion" as problematic.

that it is a book reflecting key themes within Western occulture which have become central to the shift from religion to spirituality in Western societies: the sacralization of the self; the turn from transcendence to immanence; the emergence of the sacred feminine; the focus on nature and the premodern; and a conspiracist suspicion of the prevailing order and dominant institutions, particularly the church.

(Partridge 2008, abstract).

My point is not that New Age monopolizes or completely controls representations of religion in popular culture, but that it constitutes one important logic behind its discourses on *good* religion; that it to some extent structures plots and storylines, and that it provides "packages of meaning," rather than the coincidental mixing and matching of "raw" material, counter-intuitive or not. By packages of meaning, I mean cultural artifacts that "come with interpretation" or "preferred meaning attached" (Partridge 2008, 124). Partridge considers "occultural worldviews" (of which New Age constitutes the main ingredient) as an important source of the packaging provided by popular media, and popular culture—in turn—as important for the formation of occultural worldviews (Partridge 2008, 126). Popular media representations of reincarnation, for instance, usually have more in common with New Age versions than with the Indian originals, and like other popular notions from the repertoire of "the religions," tends to be formatted New Age-style—following established and recognizable codes for defining, selecting, organizing and presenting pieces of religious information. We may, in other words, speak of a New Age logic of popular media, one which intersects and interacts with media logics more generally.

We are dealing with neither "raw materials" nor the coincidental mixing and matching of religious elements from anywhere and everywhere. Rather, banal religion seems to a large extent to be based on established New Age-recipes, and to be cooked New Age style.

Different factors may explain the current popularity of New Age-concepts in the popular media. These media, first and most basically—and here I follow Hjarvard—are likely to search for what it is that people want in order to successfully compete for their attention. The popularity of New Age formats and ingredients in the media can, accordingly, be expected to reflect current interests and inclinations among the people for which they are intended. Second, New Age formats tend to combine easy recognition (for instance through the use of well-known myths and narratives) with surprising twists, and to draw upon highlights from large portions of the history of religions, rather than solely one religious tradition. The typical weekly magazine journalists have neither the time nor the qualifications to dig deeply into, for instance, the complex details of South American history. Nor is it likely that editors would allow them to. But journalists can quickly access (New Age) versions of the Maya calendar and the apocalypse connected to it, both of which can be expected (and have proven) to hold popular appeal. New Age specialists in this case, as probably in numerous others, have done the job of creating and wrapping up packages of meaning in ways more broadly appealing and easily digestible than that usually offered by orthodox theologians and historians of religion.

Last but not least: New Age formats appear to meet the mainstream media requirements of "religious neutrality." Hjarvard notes that the "unflagged" religiosity of banal religious representations allows them to "go under the radar," thus allowing for easy dissemination (Hjarvard 2013). By this he means that they are not explicitly marked as belonging to a religion or to the field of religion. This is a useful point, and one that can be further developed. New Age, one could argue, is more likely to go under the radar than the "proper" or "institutionalized religions" for at least three reasons. First, its representations tend to be not only "unflagged," but also explicitly waived as not religious. Second, key New Age terms like "the self," "self-development" and holism have secular counterparts, and the boundaries between the former and the latter tend to be fluid. Key Christian concepts, in contrast, are explicitly known and marked as religious (for instance God, salvation and resurrection). Third, the popular media context adds further to the fluidity between the religious and the secular in the case of New Age, since these formats can be perceived as entertainment, religious wisdom, and combinations of the two.

Märtha Louise's early career exemplifies the "under the radar" potential of New Age. Märtha Louise has never kept her New Age-interests a secret. It has been publicly known that she received training in Rosen Method bodywork while studying physiotherapy; in a documentary, she refers to deep-communication with horses, and in a biography claims to have "warm hands" (healing hands) and to have once healed her sister in law, Crown Princess Mette-Marit, of pyelitis (Kraft 2011). *From Heart to Heart* (2002),[8] co-written with her then newly wedded husband, Ari Behn, in the wake of a pilgrimage to Nidarosdomen, speaks of "the self" and "self-development" in ways that would, at least to scholars of religion, be recognizable as New Age. However, none of this was picked up by journalists. Reviews of *From Heart to Heart* were unusually brutal—one journalist referred to it as "lobotomized," another claimed to having become a republican out of pure fright—but none of the reviewers referred to it as New Age. Nor did any of them seem to take seriously the religious dimension. Rather, religious references were interpreted as examples of postmodern flamboyance and royal detachment from mundane reality. It was only with more established New Age markers (such as "angel school") that the religious dimension was recognized and "revealed."

---

8. The original title of the book is *Fra hjerte til hjerte*.

Concluding comments—national and global frames

The media's venues and functions have been remolded in recent years. Hjarvard speaks of a combination of homogenizing and differentiating forces, with increasing movements across borders on the one hand, and, on the other hand, the ongoing importance of "introverted" communication spaces; neighborhood radio, local newspapers, community websites, family blogs etc. He adds to this segmentation, the continued importance of the national public sphere, and the occasional ability of media events to revive the great collective "we."

This mixture of tendencies is clearly reflected in Norwegian media-scapes. On the one hand, the overwhelming proportion of media representations—particularly those found in channels of popular culture—are produced outside of Norway, and belong to media-scapes that are today global in reach. This is the case with many of the bestsellers and TV-successes referred to in this chapter—like *The Da Vinci Code* and the *Harry Potter*-series. It is the same with travelling formats, like *From Soul to Soul* and *The Quest for the Sixth Sense*. Norwegian discourses on "good" and "bad" religion similarly belong to broader international discourses (Hjelm 2006).

National frames, on the other hand, are likely to matter, and, in the Norwegian case, they certainly do. Norwegian media discourses on religion tend, as I have already mentioned, to be shaped by issues concerning national identity; of whether particular religions "belong here" or not, and Lutheran Christianity tends—implicitly or explicitly—to constitute the standard by which other religions are compared and evaluated, both with respect to the category of religion, and discourses of good and bad religions. The sharply contrasting media presentations of Märtha Louise and *Snåsamannen* depend upon this particular context to make sense; that of a country in which a Lutheran Protestant state church has until recently constituted the religious frames of the overwhelming majority of the population, and in which the church and the Royal Family are closely connected and mutually support each other. King Harald is still obliged by the Constitution to be a Lutheran Protestant, and was, until a recent constitutional reform, head of the State church. Mainstream Norwegians may no longer believe in the Christian gospel, but a sense of cultural heritage as a style of *belonging* appears to be fairly strong. New Age, the coverage of Märtha Louise's angel schools seems to indicate, is the wrong religion, an embarrassingly vulgar one, and thus highly unsuitable as our "national core."

Snåsamannen belongs to the less orthodox fringes of this constellation, but one which the Church—due in part, perhaps, to competition from New Age—has increasingly embraced. His extraordinary career indicates both the importance of media frames and representations, and the importance of specifically Norwegian discourses on national identity. Telephone healing does not normally top the news media list of *good* religion; nor is it a likely candidate for public popularity—at least not in combination with top politicians. It was in this case the framing of the media which made good of what is normally bad, albeit with the support of a religion style spin doctor (Kolloen), and dependent upon established and specifically Norwegian cultural currents and inclinations.

References

Aadnanes, Per Magne. 2008. *Gud for kvarmann. Kyrkja og den nye religiøsiteten*. Oslo: University Publishing House.

Christensen, Henrik Reintoft. 2010. "Religion and Authority in the Public Sphere. Representations of Religion in Scandinavian Parliaments and Media." Unpublished PhD thesis, Faculty of Theology, University of Aarhus.

Daloz, Jean-Pascal 2003. "Ostentation in comparative perspective: Culture and elite legitimation." *Comparative Social Research* 21: 29–62.

Døving, Cora Alexa and Siv Ellen Kraft. 2013. *Religion i pressen*. Oslo: University Publishing House.

Endsjø, Dag Øystein and Liv Ingeborg Lied 2011. *Det folk vil ha*. Oslo: University Publishing House.

Fonneland, Trude and Siv Ellen Kraft. 2013. "New Age, Sami shamanism and indigenous spirituality." In *New Age Spiritualities: Rethinking Religion*, edited by Ingvild Sælid Gilhus and Steven Sutcliffe, 132–145. Durham: Acumen.

Gilhus, Ingvild Sælid and Lisbeth Mikaelsson. 1998. *Kulturens refortrylling: Nyreligiøsitet i modern samfunn*. Oslo: Universitetsforlaget.

Hjarvard, Stig. 2008. "The mediatization of society: A theory of the media as agents of social and cultural change." *Nordicom Review* 29(2): 105–134.

———. 2012. "Three forms of mediatized religion." In *Mediatization and Religion: Nordic Perspectives*, edited by Stig Hjarvard and Mia Lövheim, 21–44. Göteborg: Nordicom.

———. 2013. *The Mediatization of Culture and Society*. London: Routledge.

Hjarvard, Stig and Mia Lövheim, eds. 2012. *Mediatization and Religion: Nordic Perspectives*. Göteborg: Nordicom.

Hjelm, Titus. 2006. "News of the unholy: Constructing religion as a social problem in the news media." In *Implications of the Sacred in (Post)Modern Media*, edited by J. Sumiala-Seppänen, K. Lundby and R. Salokangas, 63–78. Göteborg: Nordicom.

Kalvig, Anne. 2009. "TV Norge and Kanal FEM—Messengers of a New Era" (in Norwegian). In *DIN. Tidsskrift for religion og kultur* 4: 45–63.

———. 2013. "Talking to the dead in Rogaland" (in Norwegian). *Kirke og Kultur* 2: 122–135.

———. 2015. "The spiritist revival: The raising voice of popular religion." In *Handbook of Nordic New Religions*, edited by James R. Lewis and Inga Bårdsen Tøllefsen, 203–220. Leiden: Brill.

Kolloen, Ingar Sletten. 2008. *Snåsamannen: Kraften som helbreder*. Finland: Gyldendal.

Kraft, Siv Ellen. 2008. "Märthas engler." *Nytt norsk tidsskrift* 2(25): 122–134.

———. 2010. "Kjenner du varmen? Om Kolloens Snåsamann." *Nytt Norsk Tidsskrift* 3: 243–253.

———. 2011. *Hva er nyreligiøsitet*. Oslo: University Publishing House.

———. 2014. "New Age spiritualities," In *Controversial New Religions*, edited by James Lewis, 302–315. Oxford: Oxford University Press.

———. 2015. "Royal angels in the news. The case of Märtha Louise, Astarte Education and the Norwegian News Press." In *Nordic New Religions*, edited by James Lewis and Inga Bårdsen, 190–202. Leiden: Brill.

Lied, Liv Ingeborg. 2012. "Religious change and popular culture: With a nod to the mediatization of religion debate." In *Mediatization and Religion: Nordic Perspectives*, edited by Stig Hjarvard and Mia Lövheim, 183–202. Göteborg: Nordicom.

Partridge, Christopher. 2008. "The occultural significance of 'The Da Vinci Code'." *Northern Lights: Film and Media Studies Yearbook* 6(1): 107–126.

Romarheim, Arild. 2011. "Nyåndelig folkereligiøsitet." In *Nye guder for hvermann. Femti år med alternativ spiritualitet*, edited by Tormod Engelsviken, Rolv Olsen and Notto R. Thelle,41–60. Trondheim: Tapir Akademisk Forlag.

Spiritual Tourism

Torunn Selberg

In 1996, the Norwegian alternative book club *Energica* invited members on a "Magical trip to Peru."[1] The intention was to "gather spiritually seeking people for a trip of unusual experiences," a "magical journey to places with strong energies." It was emphasized that the excursion would be off the beaten track and that among other things the participants would be given the opportunity to meet with indigenous shamans. The excursion was named "Searching the light in the Andes," and was inspired by the spiritual bestseller of the time, "The Celestine Prophecy" by James Redfield, which sold 20 million copies the world over, and 30,000 in Norway. The story concerns the search for an old manuscript in Peruvian rainforests and has been described as a spiritual guidebook (see Mikaelsson 1997).

Today the Norwegian tour enterprise Gaia Travel (former *Totalhelse*) in co-operation with Energica organizes journeys to Peru and Bolivia—to "the Empire of the Incas" as told in the leaflet: "Exiting spiritual journeys."[2] This trip includes a visit to Lima, the capital of Peru, and to the world known ancient Inca capital Machu Picchu, on the UNESCO list. Inca temples, and a "magic boat trip" on the Titicaca is included in the journey. "The pilgrimage site of Copacabana in Bolivia with its holy mountain," and not least "a traditional shaman-initiation that will give a whole new experience of magic energies," is also part of the trip. In this context Peru is described as the "empire of the Incas" referring to the former high culture of the area. The two examples tell us that Peru, and especially the old culture of the Incas,

---

1. "Magisk eventyrreise til Peru." *Energica* 1996, 8.
2. Distributed on Alternativmessen, Lillestrøm 2014.

is a place attractive to seeking people and is central within spiritual tourism organized in a Norwegian context.[3]

Religion, spirituality and tourism

The relation between spirituality and tourism that is the topic of this chapter is part of long continuity and a global phenomenon. Tourism is today one of the largest and fastest growing industries in the Western world. It is also becoming steadily more segmented and specialized; we can for instance talk about religious, heritage, cultural, experience, activity and spiritually-based tourism. I will here discuss how spiritual trends and interests are becoming "touristified," packaged and popularized within the tourist industry, and also the "spiritualization" of more conventional tourist journeys. In my opinion, this is an example of how mainstream culture is being entangled with ideas from new age and alternative spiritualities (see Gilhus and Mikaelsson 1998; Heelas1996). My interests here are in tourist enterprises that package and sell journeys; individual tourism is not part of this discussion.

I will discuss how the global phenomenon of spiritual tourism is localized in a contemporary Norwegian context. This segment concerns mostly journeys *from* Norway *to* spiritual sites, or places with strong energies around the world. Thus the examples are mostly narratives, interpretations and evaluations of sites and places in the world seen from a Norwegian perspective. However, there are also—if not so many yet—examples of spiritual journeys and places in Norway. Places in the margins and the spirituality of indigenous peoples are of great interest within this kind of tourism, and thus there is a growing preoccupation with far North and Sami religion within the tourist industry in Northern Norway (Mathisen 2010, 2014; Fonneland 2011, 2012). Spiritual tourism is a growing segment within contemporary tourist industry. This, together with a renewed interest in pilgrimage, are global trends that are also interpreted and shaped in various local Norwegian contexts.

Religion has long been a vital motive for undertaking journeys, pilgrimage is usually considered the oldest form of non-economic travel (Olsen and Timothy 2006, 1; see also Gilhus and Kraft 2007, 13). The popularity of religious travel today can be seen not only in the increase of religiously-motivated travel to sacred sites tied to the great religions, but also in the relation between New Age spirituality and pilgrimage travel (Olsen and Timothy 2006, 4; Bowman 2007). Spirituality relates more to the individual than religion, and spiritual journeys are often about personal change, devel-

---

3. Also, for example, the organization Energy and Balance—whose goal it is to strengthen peoples' focus and harmony through healing, balancing of energies et cetera, offers trips to Peru. They state that their journeys are different because, in addition to visiting sights and archeological sites, they work with energies that are awoken in such places. They cooperate with the tour operator Spirit of the Condor; specialist in journeys with a spiritual content. Priests and shamans from the Andes with a direct line to the Incas will be part of this trip.

opment and self-realization. But travelling as such is also an important part of modern spirituality, and new age has provided new places in a sacred geography—and not least has given new meanings to ancient holy places (see Timothy and Conover 2006, 139ff.; Bowman 2007).

The close relation of travel and religion is demonstrated in the ways many writers on tourism employ a language related to religion—using concepts such as authenticity, sacrality, meaning and identity (Mathisen 2010; Norman 2013, x). Tourism has also been talked about as civil or implicit religion, and the Archbishop of Canterbury, Robert Runcie (1921–2000), has said that during medieval times people were tourists because of their religion, today they are tourists because tourism is their religion (Jacobsen and Viken 1999, 12). In his seminal book *The Tourist*, Dean MacCannell (1999, 44–45), talks about the sacralization of sights, and about sightseeing as a ritual, and writes: "Sightseeing is a kind of collective striving for a transcendence of the modern totality, a way of attempting to overcome the discontinuity of modernity, of incorporating its fragments into unified experience" (1999, 13). MacCannell sees "the tourist is a pilgrim in a lay world who pays homage to the attractions of modernity" (Tomasi 2002). During the past several decades, scholarly literature on the topic of religious or spiritual tourism has grown (see Vukonic 1996; Olsen and Timothy 2006; Norman 2013; Stausberg 2011; Eddy 2013), perhaps especially tied to an interest in the relation between tourism and pilgrimage (see Swatos 2006; Pazos 2014; Reader 2014).

I have chosen three examples to discuss the topic of present-day spiritual tourism in Norway. The first example is the Norwegian enterprise Gaia Travel (earlier, *Totalhelse*) organizing "exciting spiritual journeys," mainly from Norway to places in Great Britain, France, Iceland, Peru, Egypt, but also within Norway. I will then discuss two package tours, both based on spiritual themes with wide ranging connections to popular culture: a journey based on the best-selling alternative (light) novel and movie *Eat. Pray. Love.* As with *The Celestine Prophecy*, this book was a global phenomenon with a large Norwegian audience. As a third example, I have chosen a packaged and organized pilgrimage tour along the Camino de Santiago. The actual journeys exemplify the interconnection of spirituality and tourism in various ways, and demonstrate how tourism is able to package and compress the spiritual aspect of the tours with actual sites, for instance by recreating Elisabeth Gilbert's twelve months' spiritual self-realization into one week, and compressing an eleven week pilgrimage journey into the conventional duration of a tourist journey. The journeys also demonstrate how the tourist industry is able to take up and transform alternative ways of travel and destinations into a marketable and efficient product. It is said that where backpackers first went to avoid the tourists, the tourist industry followed and made a commodity of the backpackers' journeys and destinations. Constant renewal is necessary in a business dependent on offering a steadily growing variety of trips in dialogue with global trends.

Gaia Travel

Gaia Travel—earlier *Totalhelse Helse Norge AS*—is a company organising journeys to "exciting energy places all over the world" and is definitely placed within the field of alternative spirituality. John Gursli, leader of the enterprise and guide on most of the journeys, established the business in 2003 (www.gaiasenter.no). Their destinations are Mexico, Peru/Bolivia, Arizona, Egypt, England, France, Italy, Bosnia, Greece, The Azores, Iceland and Norway. The selection of destinations has been channeled down to Gursli,[4] and they are all presented and characterized as part of the "empires" of their earlier high cultures, ancient cultures that are today given spiritual associations. Mexico is the domain of the Mayas, Greece is the realm of classical antiquity, England the empire of the Celts and Druids, Egypt the kingdom of the Pharaohs, and the Azores is the sunken Atlantis. Ancient myths and mythological ideas come into play in the descriptions of the journeys. Besides being associated with spiritual ideas, these "empires" are also part of a global cultural heritage with great appeal within the modern tourist industry—a heritage in which many wish to participate. Referring to ancient myths in the marketing of tourist destinations is a common pattern within the tourist industry (see for instance Mathisen 2014), building on the idea that the past contains greater spiritual wisdom than the present, which is prominent within alternative spirituality.

Gaia Travel also offers a tour in Norway—referred to as "the empire of the Northern lights." Norway is not represented by an ancient high culture, but first and foremost by nature and landscapes full of energy places and chakra points. The journey is introduced as: "Experience Norway's unique nature and energy places." Mountains and landscapes are presented as strong energy points like the highest mountain in the surroundings of Bergen Ulriken, or the Briksdal glacier, an arm of the largest glacier in Norway; Jostedalsbreen. Well known heritage sites like the ruins of the monastery on the island of Selja off the West coast of Norway is said to be "the strongest energy place in the Western country," as are the church ruins in Hamar, or Nidarosdomen and "its significant energies in Trondheim." Both Selja and Nidarosdomen have in recent years been reinterpreted and reimagined in light of the pilgrimage renaissance. They were both medieval pilgrim destinations, silenced for many years but now revitalized. The old stories and legends tied to these sites as holy places have again come to the foreground, and their meanings as holy sites from the past have attracted new interest (Selberg 2006, 2011, 2012). Other places, like Tronsfjellet near Alvdal —not so generally well known, but familiar within the alternative field—are also part of Gaia Travel's spiritual geography of Norway.

Regarding the trip among energy and chakra points in Norway, John Gursli says: "For several years I have done a lot of travelling all over the world, but

---

4.   John Gursli in interview april 2015.

nothing of what I have seen and experienced can be compared to the fabulous nature and extraordinary energy places in Norway." He relates that the trip was channeled down already in 2004, and that every subsequent year he has tried to organize a journey in Norway. Besides providing "some of the greatest experience of nature that Mother Earth can give us," the purpose of the journey is self-development, increased spiritual insights, energy and light work. Gursli also refers to "an old legend saying that the light shall come from the North," not the northern light, he asserts, but rather that knowledge about spiritual work and the protection of Mother Earth shall come from the North, and that Scandinavia will lead the way into the new millennium. Many have channeled the notion that a Shamballa power has been established from Alta in the North to Denmark in the south, he says—a power that will be strengthened and expanded when Norway's energy and chakra places will be cleaned and enforced. Therefore, Scandinavia is in a unique position and will, to a great degree, be protected from the future climate changes and catastrophes.[5] The North has an attraction within modern tourism, perhaps because it is still considered untouched by pollution, as well as "off the beaten track." Trude Fonneland (2012) has examined how the allure of the North has acquired spiritual dimensions, and been re-defined in images and dreams about the northern region. New age ideas have been localized and wrapped in local indigenous culture and landscape in the high North. Additionally, Stein Mathisen (2014) has studied how Northern Light tourism is described and marketed in terms of references to magic and Sami mythology.

Iceland is also part of Gaia Travel's package, presented as the realm of the elves and devas, beings that have their relatives within Norwegian mythology and folk belief. Historically there have been strong bonds between Iceland and Norway; Iceland was partly populated by immigrants from Norway around 900-1000, and from the 1200s until 1536, Iceland was governed from Norway. Besides experiencing the magnificence of nature, an important part of Gaia Travel's journey is meetings with elves and devas, and also with an Icelandic shaman, Gudrun Bergmann. Well-known Icelandic sites like Thingvellir, Geysir and Gullfoss are presented as energy places.

In the magazine *Magic.no*,[6] Finn Hebbe Johnsrud tells about his "Energy journey in the realm of the elves and devas." Among other things, he relates his meeting with "the little people" (Småfolket) in a forest, and tells us that the elves were happy to come into contact with the travelling humans, and offered help when the visitors were ready for it. They also visited Dimmuborgir, "a fantastic lava landscape with towers, spears and vaults." Inside this landscape the participants meditated in a circle, and "one of the participants saw a ring of monks dressed in cloaks," a sight that makes the writer conclude that there were strong energies within Dimmu Borgir.

---

5. http://www.totalhelse.no.

6. www.magic.no.

He ends his story by relating that, at the end of the journey—when look-ing on a certain landscape—he experienced a strong feeling of déjà vu, and further that the group shared regression experiences with the guide after returning to the bus. The idea was that "we should return to earlier lives in Iceland." He ends the story by stating: "who knows, perhaps both I and the other participants have had one or several earlier lives on the island of sagas"

The various destinations in Gaia's program have in common that they relate to energies, chakra points and power lines connecting important and powerful places with each other, both in time and space. Holy sites, churches and temples are located along the energy lines, and are thus con-nected. Nidaros, for example, is, according to the manager of the enterprise, one of the most powerful places in the world—something that also has to do with the long history of this place. He claims that Olav Tryggvason had known about energy lines, and had founded churches on especially power-ful places, such as Nidaros and Moster,[7] where the Viking king, according to the sagas, first set foot in Norway when he returned from England to claim sovereignty over the kingdom of Norway.

Another core idea in Gaia Travel is the decree that, "the soul yearns for home," relating to the idea that one's immortal soul is part of a "collective soul." Our wish—or rather our need—to travel relates to the soul's desire to return to places where we lived former lifetimes. The soul longs for a place, but also for a past. As we have seen, the past has a prominent place in Gaia Travel's program in the form of various ancient high cultures—like the Mayas, the Incas, the Pharaohs or the classical antiquity, referring both to ancient wisdom as well as indicating that the past is still with us in the forms of energies and memories of former lives.

Bestselling novel, *Eat. Pray. Love.*
In the footsteps of Elisabeth Gilbert

The 2006 novel *Eat. Pray. Love.: One woman's search for everything across Italy, India and Indonesia*, by Elisabeth Gilbert, has been an international success and bestseller. It was a major film in 2010, starring Julia Roberts and Javier Bardem. The book has been translated into 40 languages, and described as "The book that changes you." It was on the top of the *New York Times* best-seller list for 57 weeks, and worldwide the book has sold 10 million copies.[8] The Norwegian edition, *Spis elsk lev. En personlig reise gjennom italia, India og Indonesia*, has sold over 100000 copies. The book is a personal narrative about the author's divorce and her subsequent search for a new meaning in life, hoping to find it during a year-long journey through Italy, India and Indo-nesia. She relates an outer journey through countries that are high on the

---

7.   intervju med John Gursli.

8.   elizabeth.gilbert.com.

list of attractive destinations within the tourist geography. Gilbert eats her way through Italy, and learns to practice yoga and to meditate at a retreat in India. At the end of the book, she meets a medicine man in Ubud on Bali who gives her insight and a new life. Her inner journey searching for meaning in her new life is fulfilled, and on Bali she also finds new love. Both the inner and outer journey is a success—through purification, a process of grief and spiritual teaching the writer is able to start on a new life.

Since the novel, in Bali has experienced a renewed tourist boom, and the film that was made in Bali further promoted the success. In 2002, Bali experienced a terrorist attack mainly aimed at tourists, and this was a heavy blow on the tourist traffic. After the success of the novel, the official tourist agency in Indonesia urged people to "Eat, pray, love and escape in Ubud," and on Indonesia's official tourism website we read: "Not even Italy or India could give her the peace she longed for. And she found it in Bali, island of gods and goddesses" (Brenhouse 2010).

Descriptions of Bali heighten spiritual and religious qualities. The description from a tourist catalogue from Ving 1994/1995, before—and separate from—the spiritual tourism trend, illustrates the ways Bali was and still is conceived:

> Explorers named Bali "The daybreak of the world." "The last Paradise of the tropics" the travelling reporters wrote. "A gift from the Gods" say the natives themselves. It will be interesting to hear what you say! Everything you have heard about Bali is true. It is a magical island that leaves deep marks on you. The whole island is a weak shimmer of sound, right through one big botanical garden. Here is a harmony between humans, nature and religion that is not to be found in any other place. It is as if everything and everybody help each other to make life beautiful [...] Look out on the soft terraced rice-fields and the lush valleys. Listen to the gekkos, the apes, the birds and the waterfalls. Enjoy the rich colours when the villagers start one of the seemingly always-ongoing ceremonies round the island."

This text paints an image of Paradise, and we are told that the lost paradise is to be found in a place on the other side of the world, characterized by abundance and harmony, and that we, the modern people of Norway, are offered the possibility of going there. This text is 20 years old, but current narratives reverberate the same visions of Paradise; "Bali is a magical island" the Norwegian journalist Vivian Songe states in an article in the magazine Elle Travel. [9]

> We are talking about picturesque green rice fields, volcanic mountains, waterfalls, banana trees and holy lakes…. Holy sculptures and innumerous temples where the locals make extensive sacrifices in colorful clothes,

---

9. viviansonge.no.

smiling people that seem to be in harmony with themselves and the surroundings.—It is not strange that the locals view their island as a goddess.... Many Westerners feel like they have returned home and are unable
to leave the island for home.... (my translation)

Luxuriant vegetation, colorful people, and ongoing rituals represent Bali,
which is described as a place where religion and magic are integral parts of
everyday life. Songe continues: "Bali has a spiritual culture with ancient religious traditions accompanied by deep involvement and colorful costumes.
According to Balinese beliefs, the world around us is full of spirits and beings
from other dimensions...." These examples demonstrate that in a Norwegian
context Bali is a tourist destination described in a spiritual and religious language within conventional tourist enterprises. Yet another current example
reflects this; the Norwegian enterprise Asiatours, for instance, characterizes
Bali as "the island of the Gods" where men and women worship the gods by
sacrificing to the gods dressed in traditional costumes and where the nature
is a miracle created by the gods."[10]

Bali is a place that for a long time has been surrounded by romantic ideas,
and where religion has been interwoven in descriptions of the place. Edward
Bruner, for instance, writes:

> Bali...is depicted in the tourist literature as a tropical paradise of haunt-
> ing beauty, an unspoiled beach, a place of mystery and enchantment, an
> exotic South Seas island of dreams, where the people live untouched by
> civilization, close to nature, with a culture that is artistic, static, harmo-
> nious and well integrated. (Bruner 2005, 191)

But he further states that such descriptions not only suppress the true
conditions of Balinese life; it also depicts a culture that has never existed,
and such descriptions are an echo of Orientalist discourse (Bruner 2005, 192).

The success of the book and film *Eat. Pray. Love.* has been transformed into
journeys to Bali packaged by tourist operators, both conventional as well
as more spiritually inspired enterprises. In 2011, the Scandinavian tourist
enterprise Star Tour organized a trip based on the book; in the presentation
of the journey, illustrated by a picture of green-terraced rice fields—a well-
known representation of Bali and "Baliness"—we read:

> Elizabeth Gilbert has written the success-novel *Eat. Pray. Love.* (*Spis, elsk,
> lev*) about travels via Italy and India to Indonesia and Bali. We were
> inspired by this journey and offer our own (one-week) variant. In Bang-
> kok we find traces of India and Italian tastes, and then we concentrate
> on Bali with its beautiful nature, colourful culture, tasty food and lovely
> climate. We start with one day in Thailand and meet a different Bang-
> kok. In Little India we go for a tour in the quarters where people in saris
> and turbans are doing their lively businesses. The aromas and tastes are

---

10. Asiatours.no.

distinctive when we are served Indian lunch. After getting to know the city on our own, we will meet for a joint dinner at an Italian restaurant where the lovely, lively kitchen that is such a great part of the Italian culture can be experienced. (my translation)[11]

Gilbert spent one year on her trip, but since very few of us have the opportunity to travel for a year to find new meaning in life, Star Tour has made the tour that Gilbert went on more effective and compressed, both in time and space. Italy and India can be experienced in Bangkok before the visit to Bali, which is the most important part of the journey. Star Tour is a travel enterprise offering trips and tours within mainstream tourism. On this trip, they do not stress the spiritual aspect of the journey, except that they promise a meeting with the medicine man Ketut Liyer known from the book, but only for those who want and ask for it. This trip was organized only once in 2011, but Bali is still on Star Tours' program—and in an introduction to the trip, Star Tour says: "Many visualize the emerald green rice terraces when they think of Bali. Others imagine the cultural capital Ubud and Julia Roberts bicycling through the rice fields in the movie 'Eat. Pray. Love.'." References to the novel and movie are still present—though not as the chief motive for a trip to Bali.

As a global phenomenon, the novel also inspires tourist enterprises in other parts of the world—for instance, *The Spirit Quest Tours*, located in Las Vegas. This is a tourist company cultivating spiritual travel, defined as "life-changing luxury travel" (Brenhouse 2010). The guests on this one-week trip will, for instance, take part in prayers in temples, dressed in the traditional Bali way, in white clothes. We are told:

> Inside the temple grounds, our guide will make a special offering of flowers and fruit to the temple, then we will pray with flowers, incense, and rice—you can follow along with our guide and the local Pedanda (Balinese priest). This is a beautiful way to honor the local traditions, and is very appreciated by the locals, especially since most tourists don't bother to learn! [12]

Elisabeth Gilbert's book is a global phenomenon, and so are the journeys in her footsteps, taking Western tourists to a destination in the Eastern part of the world, where the tourist industry in turn uses this spiritual bestseller to rebuild a tourist industry that had suffered decline, but which is again flowering, thanks partly to the novel and the film. The book, the movie and the journeys in their footsteps are communicating and perhaps reinforcing ideas about Bali as a special spiritual place in the world, where people feel they are finally *coming home,* as described in the piece cited above. Elisabeth Gilbert's tale about inner and outer journeys to find meaning in life is in dialogue with a global trend, here localized on the small island of Bali.

---

11. www.startour.no.

12. spirituquesttours.com.

Or, rather, in the (Norwegian) tales of the island infused with abundance, religious rituals, exotic nature, magic, spirituality and harmony. Such tales are in its turn packaged and sold within the spiritual segment of modern tourism, including in Norwegian contexts.

"Caminosation": The pilgrimage to Santiago de Compostela

"250,000 on their way to Santiago de Compostela" is the headline on an newspage from 2015 (abcnyheter.no/reise).[13] The pilgrimage path Camino de Santiago is well known today and is, as this headline indicates, of great interest in Norway. People from all religions walk the Camino. In 2014, there were 237,886 pilgrims who traveled along the road to Santiago—half of them from Spain, 805 from Norway. Over the period of the last ten years, about 7,000 Norwegians have received their certificate for walking at least the last 100 km into Santiago.[14] Numerous books containing personal narratives about the pilgrimage have been written and read, and Santiago de Compostela—and not least the Camino—has a prominent place in contemporary Norwegian popular culture, where, to a great extent, it represents the ideal of what pilgrimage is, or ought to be. The Camino has been the model for the restoration of the pilgrim's road to Trondheim, and narratives of walking the Nidaros way usually contain many references to the Camino (Selberg 2013, 2014). The influence of the Santiago pilgrimage in contemporary pilgrim's culture can be referred to as a caminosation (Bowman 2015) of contemporary pilgrimage, including in Norwegian contexts. Within the late modern pilgrim renaissance, the *road* to Santiago—the Camino—is far more important than the pilgrims' destination, the cathedral in Santiago. It is also important that this road should be *walked* or completed by human physical means—to be recognized as a pilgrim, one has to walk, or travel by horse or bicycle (see Frey 1998).[15]

As one of the most famous pilgrimages in our times, the Camino represents "pilgrimness" (as the Eiffel Tower represents "Frenchness," or green terraces "Baliness"). Santiago has been discovered and reinvented by spiritual seekers and lovers of cultural history and tranquility, states Peter Jan Margry (2008, 24). He also says that The Camino is the most important example of a significant change in pilgrimage culture; that the journey has become an end in itself. The Camino is well known through all sorts of media relating about experiences along the pilgrims' way. Such tales are also prominent in Norwegian contexts.[16] Santiago and the Camino also have a pronounced place in research literature about modern pilgrimage.

---

13. www.abcnews.no.
14. http//www.abcnyheter.no/reise 21032015 lest 10042015.
15. The statistics referred to here only recognize people walking, using wheelchairs or riding a biscycle or horse.
16. See for instance the Norwegian journal Pilegrimen (pilegrim.no) where Santiago is a topic in almost every issue.

Several tourist enterprises offer organized tours along the Camino, some of them just for one week, through a combination of walking and bussing. To *walk* the Camino is of importance if one wants to be counted as a pilgrim, and not least if having the pilgrim pass is a goal for the journey. I will here discuss one organized journey along the Camino, organized by Aller Travel—a tour company specializing in experience-based journeys. They offer a one-week journey. In 2013, Gaia Travel also offered one organized tour for one week along the Camino. The differences and similarities between the two are of interest here. Gaia Travel is, as noted earlier, an enterprise within the alternative field; Aller Travel is a mainstream tourist business. Aller Travel states that their journeys include cultural, gastronomic and activity-based holidays, including hiking, hunting, sports and visits to various exhibitions, all trips accompanied by dedicated Scandinavian professional guides. Hotels and meals adhering to a high standard are an important part of the package.

Let us take a closer look at Aller Travel's pilgrim's tour to Santiago, one week of walking and busing along the Camino, characterized as an "activity based holiday."[17] The introduction to this tour says:

> Walk in the footsteps of the pilgrims in a pleasant way. Few hiking roads are infused with so many myths and are so full of history. In later years, pilgrimage has seen a new renaissance, and the whole route of 1465 km is part of UNESCO's list of world heritage sites. On this trip you will experience the most beautiful landscapes, medieval towns with beautiful churches and more than one thousand years of history. All of this with our Norwegian guide, Eva.

> To walk the whole distance will take 11 weeks On this tour you will experience Spanish landscapes, medieval villages with beautiful churches—and more than 1000 years of history—and with a Norwegian guide, and within a week.

Walking the whole distance of the stretch of the selected route, Camino de Frances will take, as said, at least 11 weeks. On their trip, the agency has included some of the most interesting sights for the travelers, like impressive cathedrals and picturesque villages. Shorter walks along the route are included so that the participants can follow "the contemplative journey that pilgrims, across more than a thousand years, have accomplished with walking stick in one hand and watching for the end of the road—the holy grave of Jacob." Good hotels are included together with enjoying the good food and drink of the region. It is a tour made feasible and thus realizable for everyone, and the agency states: "If you enjoy hiking, are a social person and interested in culture—this is the journey for you. We shall enjoy the road, and the walking will be at a slow pace, the daily stages are from 2 till 5 hours." The description ends with the invitation: "An experience for life!"

---

17. www.allertravel.no.

The whole walk along the Camino towards Santiago is demanding, both when it comes to personal strain and efforts and the amount of time needed. The organization of such a tour says a lot about the enormous popularity of the Santiago pilgrimage; it also says something about the prominent place "travelling with a purpose" or spiritual travel has within modern tourism. Aller Travel's tour is a package consisting of the "real thing," walking along the Camino in the footsteps of former pilgrims, being with other ("real") pilgrims and experiencing the lovely medieval towns, and then withdraw into touristic conveniences; such as the (air-conditioned) bus and a pleasant hotel. The participants can move between being "half a pilgrim and half a tourist." The experience "field" is the Camino. The package offers the possibility of taking part in this without too much effort, but still performing the real pilgrimage—which means walking 110 kilometers, to be sure of receiving the pilgrim certificate upon arrival in Santiago.

Gaia Travel also offers a condensed pilgrimage along the Camino, where the practical aspects of the trip are the same as in Aller Travel's program. [18] As with all of Gaia Travels' tours, experiences of energies are of major importance, and along the Camino the energies are "unique" because "thousands of people walk here every day with the same goal, to find the meaning in life and to make the right life choices, (and therefore) the power on and around the road is very strong."[19] The tour leader refers to his own earlier walk where he felt that "there was a spiritual master on every stone along the road." (www.totalhelse.no). In Aller Travel's descriptions there are no references to spirituality; pilgrimage is referred to as the "meditative tour" of the former pilgrims, thus placing spirituality in the past.

The pilgrim package sold by Aller Travel and *Totalhelse* (Gaia Travel) are different, but also have things in common. Both offer the possibility of people experiencing the famous pilgrimage within a week by a combination of travelling by bus and using one's feet for the necessary 100 kilometers. They both provide possibilities for experiencing the pilgrim's roads as a real pilgrim, especially the opportunity of walking the last distance into Santiago.

Although Aller Travel invites participants to take a pilgrimage, they have a minimum of references to religion or spirituality. Rather, they characterize the tour as following "the meditative journey" pilgrims have followed across the course of a thousand years. Additionally, *Totalhelse* sees a difference between then and now. They state that pilgrimage had great religious meaning for the pilgrims of former times, but that modern pilgrims walk these roads to find meaning in life. This description of the pilgrims indicates that past pilgrimages were part of religion; today it is a question of individual spirituality. In *Totalhelse*'s conception, the Camino is full of strong

---

18. They offered this tour only in 2012.The reason why it was only one tour was simply that there was not enough interest. (Gursli in interview April 2015).

19. www.gaiatours.

energies to be experienced, energies shaped by the thousands of religious people who have walked this road in the past. Gursli says about his own walk on the Camino that he had never channeled so strongly, and further: "When thousands of people walk here every day with the same goal, to find the meaning in life and to make the right choices, the power on and around the way becomes very strong."[20]

These two journeys may be defined as staged pilgrimages. When the pilgrims leave the bus they enter a scene where other "real" pilgrims are present and a vital part of the pilgrim landscape. The participants on the tour perform a pilgrimage for a couple of hours before entering the bus again. In *Totalhelse*'s description, it is said that "the stream of pilgrims from the whole world make it lively on the road," and the pleasant greeting, "'Bon Camino,' is heard everywhere because everybody greets each other and we are part of a large fellowship." Participants are taught how to perform when on the stage, and not only to perform; they are also told how to feel. Itineraries can include descriptions of the drama; "brochures, accounts and guidebooks are 'a means of preparation and aid for tourists to perform everything in the right way by following the norms, technologies, institutional arrangements and mythologies'" (Adler 1989, 1371; Edensor 2001).

Tourism, locality, experiences

Edward Bruner claims that sites are not passive. Rather, they are given meaning and are constituted and re-constituted by the narratives that envelope them (Bruner 2005, 12). Examples of such re-constitutions in Norway are medieval pilgrim destinations like Selja and Trondheim. They have not been referred to as holy places for several hundreds of years, but today narratives about pilgrims, saints and holy sites are re-told and recreated in Norway both generally and within the alternative spiritual subculture, then often referred to as strong energy places.[21] The histories of these places are also being spiritualized when, in an interview, the leader of Gaia Travel claims that the historical figure, Olav Trygvasson, was already aware of energy lines and founded churches and sacred sites along such lines. Narratives of places and localities are created and recreated in dialogue with changing cultural climate and shifting narratives; without stories the places are empty (Bruner 2005, 12).

Tourism is very much about localizing global trends, and spiritual tourism is today such a global trend, localized into a Norwegian context. This spiritual tourism includes both packaged tours for Norwegian tourists to destinations around the world conceived of as spiritual, and the retelling and re-imagining Norwegian nature and old sacred sites in terms of magic and spirituality. Within modern tourism as a global phenomenon, places that

---

20. www.totalhelse.no.

21. www.totalhelse.no.

promise and provide experiences of locality are the most attractive. Place narratives about religious pasts and spiritual dimensions are ways of shaping authenticity and originality in a world where people may experience that places become increasingly more identical. Spirituality in late modernity is a global phenomenon that the spiritual tourist wants to experience in local or indigenous variants, often connected to ideas about stronger energies in certain places (see Bowman 2007; Kalvig 2011; Fonneland 2012). In a world where places become more and more indistinguishable, trips that take travellers "off the beaten track" are highly valued. The idea is that such places indicate experiences of something genuine and authentic.[22] Tales about Norwegian nature can provide associations with such qualities, such as when the organizer of the Gaia Travel trips states that "nothing of what I have seen and experienced can be compared to the fabulous nature and extraordinary energy places in Norway."[23]

Experiences of locality and meeting with local people are a fundamental part of the tourist journeys discussed here. On Gaia Travel's trip to Peru, Norwegian participants can experience a traditional Inca shaman initiation "which with guarantee will give you a quite new experience of such magic energies"; in Arizona, they will "experience coming home to their own spiritual roots by visiting a sweat lodge"; In Egypt, the travelers from north "will spend time with local people eating local food under the stars"; and in Iceland, they will even meet the local fairies and devas. On the two different trips along the Camino, meeting with other pilgrims is an important trait; other pilgrims taking the place of the locals and part of making up the pilgrimage landscape to be experienced on this trip.

When the tourists step outside the air-conditioned tourist bus to the pilgrim road, or when they meet indigenous people, whether in Finnmark, Peru or a Balinese temple, they enter what Bruner (2005, 17) has defined as the touristic border zone—a distinct meeting place where tourists come forth from their hotels or buses, and local performers, the "natives," leave their home to engage the tourists in structured ways in predetermined localities for defined periods of time. For the tourists, it is a zone of relaxing and experiencing; for the natives, a place and time to work. The two groups approach the scene from very different perspectives. Tourists seek peak experiences; the locals live their everyday lives (2005, 192). Although the border zone is about the local, what is performed there takes account of global influences, such as spiritual tourism. In the touristic border zone, the global is performed in local variants. On the Camino, the other people walking—"the real" pilgrims—are the locals. In Bali, the zone can consist of many things, but it seems that narratives produce a prominent scene of a spiritual and harmonious landscape where the locals are expected to do religious rituals

22. www.gaiatoours.no

23. www.gaiatoours.no

and live in harmony with nature. The tourist tries to be like the locals, look like a pilgrim or perform a prayer in the spirit of the Balinese, greeting the other pilgrims with "Buon Camino" or dressing in clothes that will make them similar to the Balinese when in the temples.

As already stated, an important point of reference in Gaia Travel's ideology is that on their journeys, the soul returns home; the essential reason for travelling is the soul's longing for home. Through meditations and regressions, travellers are encouraged to find their real home—the place they belonged to in earlier lifetimes. These ways of talking about the visit to strange places create a sense of authenticity about the journey—the travellers are not tourists in a strange place; they have travelled to where they really belong.

The journeys discussed here demonstrate how the borderline between the sacred and profane is increasingly being blurred. They are examples of how the tourist industry uses late modern spiritual trends to colour, renew and increase the number of destinations and journeys. But they are also examples of how modern spirituality is entangled with the late modern cultural currents, such as the need to travel and investigate the world.

References

Adler, J. 1989. "Travel as Performed Art." *American Journal of Sociology* 94: 1366–1391

Bowman, Marion. 2007. "Å følge strømmen. Moderne pilegrimsferd i Glastonbury." In *Religiøse reiser: Mellom gamle spor og nye mål*, edited by Ingvild Gilhus and Siv Ellen Kraft, 51–62. Oslo: University Publishing House.

Brenhouse, Hillary. 2010. "Bali's travel boom: *Eat, Pray, Love* tourism." TIME magazine July 2010. www.time.com

Bruner, Edward M. 2005. *Culture on Tour: Ethnographies of Travel*. Chicago, IL: The University of Chicago Press.

Edensor, Tim. 2001. "Performing tourism, staging tourism: (Re)producing tourist space and practice." *Tourist studies* 1: 59–81.

Eddy, Glenys. 2013: "The Kopan experience as transformative experience: An exploration of participant responses to the ten-day *Introduction to Buddhism* course at Kopan monastery, Nepal." In *Journeys and Destinations: Studies in Travel, Identity and Meaning*, edited by Alex Norman, 177–198. Newcastle-Upon-Tyne: Cambridge Scholars Publishing.

Fonneland, Trude. 2011. "Sami tour: Urfolksspiritualitet i ei samisk turistnæring." *Chaos* 55: 153–172.

———. 2012. "Spiritual entrepreneurship in a northern landscape: Spirituality, tourism and politics." *Temenos* 2012(2).

Frey, Nancy Louise. 1998. *Pilgrim Stories: On and Off the Road to Santiago*. Berkeley: Univeristy of California Press.

Gilhus, Ingvild and Lisbeth Mikaelsson. 1998: *Kulturens refortrylling*. Oslo: University Publishing House.

Gilhus, Ingvild Sælid and Siv Ellen Kraft. 2007. "Innledning." In *Religiøse reiser: Mellom gamle spor og nye mål*, edited by Ingvild Gilhus and Siv Ellen Kraft, 11–21. Oslo: University Publishing House.

Heelas, Paul. 1996. *The New Age movement: The Celebration of the Self and the Sacralization of Modernity*. London: Blackwell.

Jacobsen, Jens Kr. Steen and Arvid Viken. 1999. "Stedet i en bevegelig verden." In *Turisme: Stedet i en bevegelig verden*, edited by Jens Kr. Steen and Arvid Viken, 9–26. Oslo: Universitetsforlaget.

Johnsrud, Finn Ebbe. nd. "En energireise i alvenes og devaene rike." *Magic.no*

Kalvig, Anne. 2011. "Kornsirkler og spirituell turisme—fra åker til internet." *Aura* 2011: 1–38.

MacCannell, Dean. 1999 [1976]. *The tourist: A New Theory of the Leisure Class.* Berkeley: University of California Press

Margry, Peter Jan. 2008. "Secular Pilgrimage: A Contradiction in Terms?" In *Shrines and Pilgirmage in the Modern World: New Itineraries into the Sacred.* Edited by Peter Jan Margry, 13–48. Amsterdam: Amsterdam University Press.

Mathisen, Stein R. 2010. "Indigenous spirituality in the touristic borderzone: virtual performances of Sámi shamaism in Sápmi Park." *Temenos* 46: 53–72.

———. 2014. "Nordlys, magi og turisme." *Din— Tidsskrift for religion og kultur* 2014(1): 61–92.

Mikaelsson, Lisbeth. 1999. "Magi, fantasi og fiksjon." In *Myte, magi og mirakel I møte med det moderne,* edited by Torunn Selberg, Ingvild Sælid Gilhus, Lisbeth Mikaelsson, Bente Gullveig Alver, 104–121. Oslo: Pax Forlag.

Norman, Alex. 2013. "Preface: Both journeys and destinations." *Journeys and Destinations: Studies in Travel, Identity and Meaning*, edited by Alex Norman, x–xiv. Newcastle-Upon-Tyne: Cambridge Scholars Publishing.

Olsen, Daniel H. and Dallen J. Timothy. 2006. "Tourism and religious journeys." In *Tourism, Religion and Spiritual Journeys*, edited byDallen J. Timothy and Daniel H. Olsen, 1–21. London: Routledge.

Pazos, Anton M. 2014. *Redefining Pilgrimage: New Perspectives on Historical and Contemporary Pilgrimage*. London: Routledge.

Reader, Ian. 2014. *Pilgrimage in the Marketplace*. London: Routledge.

Selberg, Torunn. 2006. "Fortelling, festival og sted." In *Kulturelle landskap: Sted, fortelling og materiell kultur,* edited by Torunn Selberg and Nils Gilje, 132–155. Bergen: Fagbokforlaget.

———. 2011. "Pilegrimsveien som kulturarv: Den norske pilegrimsrenessansen." *DIN: Religionsvitenskapelig tidsskrift* 2011(1/2): 120–131.

———. 2012. "Om Pilegrimsleden som kulturarvsprosjekt: Fortellinger og kulturarvsprosesser." In *Å lage kulturminner—hvordan kulturarv forstås, formes og forvaltes,* 43-58. Oslo: Novus Forlag.

Songe, Vivian. "Balansert Bali-tur." www.vivansonge.

Stausberg, Michael. 2011. *Religion and Tourism: Crossroads, Destinations and Encounters.* London: Routledge.

Swatos, William, ed. 2006. *On the Road to Being There: Studies in Pilgrimage and Tourism in Late Modernity*. Leiden: Brill.

Timothy, Dallen J. and Paul J. Conover. 2006. "Nature religion, self-spirituality and New Age tourism." In *Tourism, Religion and Spiritual Journeys*, edited by Dallen J. Timothy and Daniel H. Olsen, 139–155. London: Routledge.

Tomasi, Luigi. 2002. "Homo viator: From pilgrimage to religious tourism via the journey." In *From Medieval Pilgrimage to Religious Tourism: The Social and Cultural Economics of Piety*, edited by William H Swatos and Luigi Tomasi, 2–24. Westport: Praeger Publishers.

Vukonic, Boris. 1996. *Tourism and Religion*. Oxford: Pergamon Press.

Pamphlets and Internet Resources

Magisk eventyrreise til Peru *Energica 1996:8*

Spennende spritiuelle reiser. (Pamphlet) Total Helse Norge AS

www.elixabeth.gilbert.com

www.viviansonge.com

www.asiatours.no

http//www.abcnyheter.no/reise

www.pilegrim.no

Pilgrimstur—Santiago de Compostela 19.-28. September 2012. http://www.totalhelse.no/print.asp?page=81 (lest 24032015)

Norgesturen—Total helse norge. Den store Norgesreisen 9.juni-2. Juli 2011. Opplev verdens flotteste natur og energisteder. http://www.totalhelse.no/print.asp?page=43

Aller Travel. Pilegrimsruten til Santiago de Compostela. http://www.allertravel.no/pilegrimsruten-til-santiago-de-compostela...

Eat Prey Love Bali/Spiritual Bali Tour/visit Bali. www.spirituesttours.com

www.Allertrevel.no

www.Gaiatours.no

www.energiogbalanse.no

5

New Age in Norwegian Religion Education:
An analysis of development in curricula and textbooks for RE in secondary and upper-secondary education 1996–2008

BENGT-OVE ANDREASSEN

New Age is a rather new topic in curricula for Religion Education (RE). This not only applies to Norway, but also to RE in Europe more generally. New Age has not attracted much attention from RE scholars, and for the time being remarkably little has been written about it from the vantage point of RE.[1] One reason is probably due to the fact that New Age as content (or an object for teaching) in RE is a rather new "field of manifestation." Additionally, the RE context is not something to which researchers of New Age have paid particular attention. New Age is still a small part of the curriculum (at least in Norway), which also serves as an explanation of why it has gained so little interest thus far. However, there seems to be an agreement among scholars that New Age and New Religious Movements play an important role on the contemporary religion scene. Therefore, as the legitimation of RE in public school is based on the importance of providing knowledge to pupils about the society (cf. Jensen 2008), New Age should obviously be part of a national curriculum in RE.

   The basis for this chapter is an analysis of national curricula and textbooks for RE in secondary and upper-secondary schools in Norway in the period

---

1.   Using key words as "New age," "new religious movements" and "spirituality" in a search in one of the most prestigious international scholarly journals for RE, *British Journal for Religious Education*, there are no contributions about New Age or NRM in RE curricula, textbooks or teaching. As content for teaching in RE, there seem to be very little research. However, there is new and interesting research on tendencies on the use of New Age related meditation techniques such as yoga and mindfulness in school (cf. Zetterqvist and Skeie 2014). Such techniques are usually adopted as pedagogical strategies and not as content in teaching, often accompanied by comments that this has nothing to do with religion.

from 1996 to 2008. One goal is to find out when New Age was first introduced in the national curriculum, and in what way. Secondly, the aim is to analyze how New Age has been outlined in textbooks for RE during the same period.

Curricula and textbooks as the basis for this chapter provide a clear and limited scope. This means that this contribution does not address recent trends in the educational system in the Nordic countries concerning the use of "mindfulness" and similar approaches as strategies in teaching. How New Age and "alternative spiritualities" seem to provide ideas and trends that are integrated into pedagogy and the subject's didactics (Norwegian, *fagdidaktikk*) in RE is an interesting field of research, but outside the scope of this chapter.

Curricula and textbooks

In the period since 1997—the year of a comprehensive school reform in Norway (cf. Andreassen 2013)—the curriculum for Norwegian RE in primary and secondary school has been revised three times. That means that there have been four curricula since 1997: KRL97, KRL02, KRL05 and RLE08.[2] In 1997, a compulsory RE subject labelled KRL (English, Christianity, Religion and Ethics) replaced a model in which parents could choose between "Christian knowledge" or "Ethics education" for their children. The latter was a secular alternative that was first introduced as early as 1974. KRL97 included teaching about Christianity, world religions (Judaism, Islam, Hinduism and Buddhism), secular worldviews, philosophy and ethics. All curricula since 1997 have contained these different elements, despite changes in the name of the subject.

For upper-secondary school, revisions of the curriculum have not been as rapid. Until 1976, the subject in upper-secondary was labelled "Christian knowledge." In 1976, a new curriculum also changed the name of the subject from "Christian knowledge" to "Religion" (R76). The R76 curriculum was in effect until 1996, when the name was changed to "Religion and ethics" (RE96). Ten years later, in 2006, the RE96 curriculum was again replaced by a new one (RE06). This means that there are two curricula that have been applied in the period that this chapter focuses on. Since R76, the content of the subject has been Christianity, world religions[3], secular worldviews, philosophy and ethics.

---

2. The background for all of these revisions are multiple (see Andreassen 2013 for details). In August 2015 a slightly revised curriculum for RE in primary and secondary was implemented. This revision changed the name of the subject from RLE to KRLE (Kristendom, religion, livssyn og etikk; in English, Christianity, Religion, worldviews and ethics). It also stated that at least 50% of the teaching should be about Christianity. Other than that, there were no changes compared with the RLE08 curriculum. In principle, this is the fourth revision of the curriculum since 1997.

3. The RE96 included teaching about Christianity, Islam and Judaism. Teaching in Buddhism and/or Hinduism, together with New Age, was optional. In RE06 the curriculum teaching in Christianity and Islam was mandatory. One of the main subject areas

A total of seven curricula in the period from 1996 to 2008 provides a good basis for mapping trends and developments in RE. In the Norwegian educational system, the curriculum has legal status as a regulation (Norwegian, *forskrift*) and is therefore equivalent to law. It is an official and normative document for the school system, and each revision has been a subject for political debates and decisions before it came in effect. Curricula are therefore issues of interest for politicians, and for academic disciplines providing scientific knowledge for the subject in school.

In this analysis, I can only say something about what each curriculum contains as a written text. In classical curriculum theory, this way of approaching the curriculum as text is characterized as an analysis of the formal document or the formal curriculum (Goodlad 1979, 61). In what ways New Age has been a subject for discussions in the committees of scholars revising the curricula, and how teachers have implemented the curriculum in their actual teaching, is outside the scope of this chapter. Still, curricula and developments in curricula serve as interesting documents because they reflect the public debates on religion during different time periods (cf. Copley 2008).

Textbooks for RE can be seen as a genre in which authors interpret and implement content listed in the curriculum (cf. Andreassen 2014). In addition to transmitting knowledge, textbooks are a genre that confirms the political and social norms of society, and that marks the borderline of each society under consideration (Pingel 2010, 7). Research on teaching materials has shown that the textbook plays an important role in teaching in Norwegian schools (Juuhl, Hontvedt and Skjelbred 2010). In RE, textbooks (and teaching materials designed for the specific textbook) often provide premises for the interpretation and operationalization of the curriculum (cf. Tallaksen and Hodne 2014). Textbooks are therefore a valuable source in mapping trends and developments in how New Age is defined and outlined in RE. Thus, textbooks is a genre that not only provides premises for teaching but also, to a certain degree, reflects the public debate. Importantly, it also reflects evaluations about current themes in the public debate.

It is difficult to get a complete overview of all the editions of the different textbooks that have been developed for each of the different curricula. The textbooks that I refer to are examples of how teaching goals and competencies expressed in the curricula are outlined. Due to limited space, I cannot present how every text deals with New Age in full.

Analytical difficulty: What is New Age in curricula and textbooks?

As Gilhus and Kraft write in the introduction to this volume, New Age is not a clearly defined term. When one reads curricula, and especially textbooks, one sees the difficulties authors have in choosing terminology, and in choos-

---

was named "Islam and an optional religion." Thus meaning that the teaching only had to include one other religion (eg. Judaism, Hinduism, Buddhism etc.).

ing examples. In the main subject areas of the curricula, there are no head-ings that make an explicit reference to New Age (Norwegian, *nyreligiøsitet*), New religious movements (NRMs) or similar terms. Instead, teaching goals about New Age can be found under very general headings such as "Religion in our time," or "searching for religions in our time."[4] Thus, in curricula and textbooks, New Age seems to be a wide category that includes random exam-ples on religious diversity in the Norwegian society, but also on individuals' searches for religion. Facing the traditional "world religion approach" in RE, New Age is clearly "religion on the side" of religions such as Christianity, Islam, Hinduism and so on.

Headings in curricula such as "Religion in our time" and "Religious diver-sity in our time" consequently include a range of religious groups and phenomena, including religious groups and traditions such as Jehovah's Witnesses, Mormons and Bahá'i. In the KRL97 curriculum, these actual tra-ditions appear in a separate teaching goal under the heading "Religion in our time." No overarching terms are applied to characterize or distinguish these groups from other groups or categories listed in the same subject area. Under the same heading, another teaching goal reads "new religions and religious movements that have backgrounds in Buddhism, Hinduism, Chris-tianity and Islam" (KRL97, 105). Here terms like "new religions" and "new religious movements" are used (Norwegian, *"nye religioner og religiøse bevegel-ser"*). Since curricula is a genre with a very compact text, interpretations or explanations of what is meant by "new religions" or "new religious move-ments" is not offered. This difficulty in the interpretation of categories in curricula lead to very different presentations and explanations in textbooks.

In what I will refer to as the first generation of textbooks, especially for secondary school, there are chapters on "Religion in our time" or "Religious diversity in our time" that include Jehovah's Witnesses, Mormons, Bahá'i and New Age-related phenomena such as healing and meditation. These chapters consequently include a range of rather different religious phe-nomena. In the texts, there are hardly any distinction made between the different groups. The chapters become rather complicated, and even cha-otic. As textbooks present the Jehovah's Witnesses and Baha'i in the same chapters as New Age-related phenomena such as chakras, healing, occultism and meditation, the chapters are in danger of communicating that these are similar phenomena. Another interesting tendency in the first generation of textbooks dealing with New Age and religious groups such Jehovah's Wit-nesses, the Moon family, Scientology and sometimes Hare Krishna, is that these are presented as harmful or dangerous because of their social con-trol, brainwashing and economic abuse of its members. As this is included in chapters about more general New Age ideas, this also influences the more

---

4.   The translation of the the Norwegian *i vår tid* to "in our time" is found in the official translation of the current curricula in RLE08 and RE06. "I vår tid" could alterna-tively be translated as "search for religions in contemporary society."

general presentation of New Age. The text seems to communicate that all the different groups that are examples of "Religious diversity in our time" are harmful or dangerous. In comparison, the traditional world religions are not described in these terms.

Table 6.1 New Age in RE curricula for secondary education.

Curriculum	Main subject area	Teaching goal
KRL97 (p. 105)[a]	Religion in our time (Norwegian, Religiøsitet i vår tid)	New religions and new religious movements with roots in Buddhism, Hinduism, Christianity and Islam Jehova's Witnesses, Mormons and Bahá'i Occultism and Satanism in our time
KRL02 (p. 21-22)[b]	Diversity in religions and worldviews in our time (Norwegian, Religiøst og livssynsmessig mangfold i nyere tid)	Eighth grade: Mormons and Jehovah's Witnesses, Ninth grade: Sikhism and Bahá'i Tenth grade: New religious movements and spiritual seeking in our time
KRL05 (p. 18)[c]	Judaism, Islam, Hinduism, Buddhism, other religious diversity and worldviews (Norwegian, Jødedom, islam, hinduisme, buddhisme, annet religiøst mangfold og livssyn): Religious diversity	[Enables the pupil to] give an account of new religious movements and discuss different forms of nature-religious practice of New Age, including indigenous people's nature religion
RLE08 (p. 7)[d]	Judaism, Islam, Hinduism, Buddhism, Other Diverse Religions and Philosophies of life (Norwegian, Jødedom, islam, hinduisme, buddhisme, annet religiøst mangfold og livssyn): Religious diversity	[Enables the pupil to] give an account of new religious movements and talk about the different forms of neo-religious[e] and nature-religious practices, including indigenous nature religions

a. In Norwegian: "I opplæringa skal elevene få kunnskap om, - nye religioner og religiøse bevegelser med bakgrunn i buddhisme, hinduisme, kristendommen og islam, - Jehovas vitner og mormoner, bahai, - okkultisme og satanisme i vår tid" (KRL97:105).

b. In Norwegian: "nye religiøse bevegelser og åndelig søking i vår tid" (KRL02:22).

c. This is a teaching goal that is difficult to translate into English. The original Norwegian text reads: "Gjøre rede for nye religiøse bevegelser og samtale om ulike former for nyreligiøs naturreligiøs praksis, herunder urfolks naturreligion" (KRL05:18)

d. All references to RLE08 are based on the official translation into English by the Directory of Education and Training (Utdanningsdirektoratet).

e. In the English translation, the term "neo-religious" is a translation of the Norwegian "nyreligiøs."

In reference to the very general chapters, Norwegian terminology in the curricula and textbooks is tricky to translate into English and retain their nuances. I will use the term New Age and mainly in accordance with the discussion and use of the term that Gilhus and Kraft (2017) outline in the introduction. When textbooks include religious groups such as the Jehovah's Witnesses, Mormons and Bahá'i, I will make the reader aware of that fact.

Table 6.1 illustrates the development in teaching goals about New Age. It was a topic that was first introduced in the KRL97 curriculum in the main subject area "Religion in our time" (Norwegian, *Religiøsitet i vår tid*). The three teaching goals illustrate how NRMs were listed along with other religious groups. Teaching goals only referred to special groups, and there were no distinction between organized and unorganized groups, or general tendencies. The Norwegian term "nyreligiøsitet" (New Age) was not used, yet the explicit mention of occultism and Satanism can be related to New Age, at least in a broader way than the other groups mentioned. The focus on occultism and Satanism can be explained with reference to a number of church fires in Norway, especially in the period from 1992 to 1996, and illustrates how public debate and contexts also influence what is included in the curriculum. Behind several of these fires were youth inspired by extremist environments that were labelled as Satanist or Occult. This special context significantly influenced textbooks.

In the revised curriculum KRL02 five years later, Satanism and occultism are removed from the curriculum. The teaching goals for each grade in secondary school were now divided into three subdivisions. One of these subdivisions was "Diversity in religions and worldviews in recent times" (Norwegian, *"Religiøst og livssynsmessig mangfold i nyere tid"*). In the eighth grade, it reads that pupils should learn about Mormons and Jehovah's Witnesses, in the ninth grade about Sikhism and Bahá'i, and in the tenth grade about "new religious movements and spiritual search in our time." In the KRL02 curriculum religious movements such as Mormons and Bahá'i are, in a larger extent distinguished from New Age phenomena, and consequently appear more clear. Still, New Age (Norwegian, *nyreligiøstitet*) is not used as a term.

In the KRL05 curriculum general competencies for the pupils were formulated for all the three years in secondary school, and not for each year as in the former curricula. New Age (nyreligiøsitet) is now used for the first time in the curriculum. The competencies under the heading "Religious Diversity" include several new and interesting formulations. A link between New Age, nature and indigenous "nature religions" is made. In RLE08, an almost identical formulation confirms this tendency.

There is a development in the curricula for secondary school. From the KRL02 curriculum, New Age related-phenomena are more clearly separated from Jehovah's Witnesses, the Church of Jesus Christ of Latter-day Saints and Bahá'i. After the turn of the century, one sees the terms "new religious movements" and "spiritual," and related to people's "spiritual seeking."

In the curricula from 2005 and 2008, New Age (*nyreligiøstitet*) enters the curriculum and is related to "nature-religious practices" and, further yet, to "indigenous nature religions."

After 1997, occultism and Satanism as explicit teaching goals have disappeared. After the turn of the Millennium, occultism and Satanism were more or less gone from public debate after the church fires had stopped. Less publically-visible activity made this content rather peripheral, and consequently was removed from the curriculum.

Since the mid-1990s, there have been only two curricula for upper secondary school (Table 6.2). The basis for mapping any development concerning New Age is therefore less.

Table 6.2   Curriculum/Main subject area/Teaching goal(s) in Norway.

Curriculum	Main subject area	Teaching goal(s)
RE96 (p. 4)[a]	Contemporary non-Christian religions[b]	[pupils should] know about New Age [nyreligiøsitet] as a phenomena in our time or a fourth living religion
RE06 (p. 4)[c]	Theory of religion and criticism of religion	[students should be able to] discuss and elaborate on different forms of religious seeking in our time (RE06, 4)

a. Norwegian: "Elevene skal kjenne til vår tids nyreligiøsitet som fenomen eller en fjerde levende religion" (RE96:4)

b. In Norwegian this main subject area reads: "Levende ikke-kristne religioner."

c. This is the official translation in English. The Norwegian version reads: "drøfte ulike former for religiøs søking i vår tid."

When New Age was first introduced in RE96, it was as an optional teaching goal. Teachers (and/or pupils) could choose between New Age and a "fourth living religion." Christianity, Islam and Judaism were compulsory, and the "fourth living religion" was most likely intended to be Hinduism or Buddhism. That was usually the interpretation in textbooks.

In the 2006 curriculum, New Age was not mentioned at all. The teaching goal on "different forms of searching for religions in our time" is the only place where one could think that New Age could be included. However, the formulation is rather open and does not provide any pointers to what it is referring. The formulation "in our time" indicates that it is something contemporary, but that may also include a range of different issues, and not necessarily New Age. A possible explanation as to why this formulation is so vague or open might be that it is placed in the main subject area, "Theory of religion and criticism of religion." This subject area mostly deals with theories of religion, geographical and demographical extent of religions, whereas specific religious traditions are dealt with in the other main subject areas that follow a structure based on Ninian Smart's (1989) dimension model for approaching religion. This model is based on a classical approach to religions (and ideologies), as fixed entities with clearly defined texts, doctrine, myths and rituals, and consequently not corresponding with the more dispersed nature of New Age.

Compared to curricula for RE in secondary school, New Age has gained less space in upper-secondary school. And in the current curriculum, it is not mentioned explicitly, and might consequently be completely left out. From being an optional teaching goal in RE96, to a very open aim of competency, the focus on New Age is still rather restricted in upper-secondary school. The differences in curricula for the secondary and upper secondary levels have obviously been very different starting points for textbook authors.

New Age in textbooks for RE in secondary school

Textbooks for RE in secondary school have not been revised in accordance with each revision of the curriculum. Timing for revisions has been different for each publisher. For the purpose of this chapter, it is more relevant to talk about a first generation of textbooks for RE in secondary schools, i.e. textbooks from the period from 1997 to 2005, and a second generation of textbooks in the period after 2005. I will provide examples of how textbooks have interpreted some of the teaching aims in the curricula. This means that this article will not offer an exhaustive analysis of each textbook.

In dealing with New Age, textbook authors face quite a challenge writing about a rather complex phenomenon for pupils in the age range from 13 to 16. Portraying the typical "world religions" such as Christianity, Islam, Judaism, Hinduism and Buddhism, books tend to follow a model, as in the curriculum, in which religions are approached through phenomenological categories, in terms of founders, scriptures, myths, rituals, ethics and social life. As a result, religions are often portrayed rather monolithically, which often results in an (presumably unintended) essentialism. Questions of diversity within a religious tradition are often left more or less untreated. As New Age phenomena have difficulties being approached through the same scheme, authors clearly have difficulties in finding ways to approach the New Age.

In the KRL97 curriculum, teaching goals included new religions and religious movements with roots in Buddhism, Hinduism, Christianity and Islam, Jehovah's Witnesses, Mormons, Bahá'i, occultism and Satanism. The first generation of textbooks developed for the implementation of KRL all had chapters that included all these elements. It is however interesting to see that all textbooks in the first generation use the term New Age (nyreligiøsitet) even if it is not used in the curriculum.

One of the textbooks, *Midt i vår hverdag* (*In the midst of our everyday life*) (Gilje and Gjefsen 1997), introduces the chapter with discussions on freedom of religion and secularization, and argues that the Norwegian society has become more diverse. After dealing with religious movements such as Jehovah's Witnesses, Mormons and Bahá'i, a section on "Religious traditions with roots in the East" is introduced. Here "religions of New Age" and Transcendental Meditation serve as examples of new religious movements with Eastern roots. This textbook offers a simple explanation of "New Age religions," yet struggles to explain whether it is a religion or not:

> New Age is a term we often use when old and new ideas (thinking) from several cultures are mixed and combined as a religion. New Age is not the name of a specific religion. Therefore, New Age does not have any leader or founder. Instead, there are many religious traditions and many religious leaders. Religious experience is very important. [...] The religious ideas within New Age come from different places and many religions. (Gilje and Gjefsen 1997, 150, my translation)[5]

The role of the individual, the possibilities that individuals have in New Age, are highlighted further in the text. The presentation of New Age follows the premises in the first part of the main chapter in this textbook, which is about religious freedom. New Age is generally presented very positively, for example, where it states that "The New Age movement believes that there is something true and good in all religions" (Gilje and Gjefsen 1997, 152, my translation).[6] The focus on individual freedom is related to the role of experimentation in New Age:

> New Age religions are characterized by much experimentation. Each individual must experience what the truth is for themselves. Therefore, the individual has great freedom to determine what is right for him or her. (Gilje and Gjefsen 1997, 150–151, my translation)[7]

In this quote, with the term "New Age religions," one also gets the impression that New Age can, in fact, be specific religions despite the paragraph cited above. As the next step in the textbooks is to be more specific on religious practices, i.e. the kinds of experimentation that is common within New Age, meditation serves as the core example, in particular Transcendental Meditation.

After a short paragraph on Maharishi Mahesh Yogi, Transcendental Meditation is explained as rooted in Hinduism, and "When its adherents meditate, they use a ritual that is made to worship Hindu gods. It is done in Sanskrit, the sacred language of India" (Gilje and Gjefsen 1997, 153, my translation).

---

5. In Norwegian: "New Age er en samlebetegnelse vi ofte bruker når gammel og ny tenkning fra flere kulturer blandes og settes sammen til en religion. New Age er ikke navnet på én religion. Derfor har ikke New Age noen leder eller stifter. Isteden er det mange religiøse retninger og mange religiøse ledere i miljøet. Religiøs opplevelse er veldig viktig. [...] De religiøse ideene innen New Age kommer fra mange steder og mange religioner." (Gilje and Gjefsen 1997, 150)

6. In Norwegian: "New Age-bevegelsen mener at det finnes noe sant og godt i alle religioner."

7. In Norwegian: "New Age-religioner er kjennetegnet av mye eksperimentering. Hver enkelt må oppleve sannheten for seg selv. Derfor har den enkelte stor frihet til selv å finne ut hva som er riktig for ham eller henne." (Gilje and Gjefsen 1997, 150–151).

The presentation of New Age is primarily related to Eastern religious traditions, in particular Hinduism, whereas other roots for New Age are not presented in the text. The presentation of New Age thus follows a pattern where it is related geographically to the East, in particular India, and religiously to Hinduism. It highlights individual freedom and experimentation. As the examples of religious experimentation and practices are presented, the circle is complete with its reference and link to Transcendental Meditation. This religious practice is used as an example that unites cultural roots, experimentation and individual freedom.

The presentation of New Age as having Eastern cultural and religious roots stands out as positive because it is related to individual freedom. This stands in sharp contrast is the presentation of occultism and Satanism. Dealing with the special emphasis on occultism and Satanism in the KRL97 curriculum, these are presented in a separate, yet very short, chapters with the title "The borders of religion" (Norwegian, *Religionenes grenseland*). In three pages, the text offers a short introduction that explains these "borders":

> Occult means hidden, secret. Occultism is a belief and practice about "hidden spiritual truths." These truths explain how the universe really is, the divine, the mental and the physical. Because the truths are secret, they are hidden from people that are not initiated. You can only learn these truths through special preparations and initiations. (...) Occultism is at least 2000 years old, but it is not a religion.
> (Gilje and Gjefsen 1997, 154, my translation).[8]

Despite its mystical feature, occultism is further exemplified with reference to groups that are referred to as having "difficult names" such as Gnosticism, alchemy, Theosophy, Anthroposophy and Wicca. The textbook does not offer any further explanation of these "difficult names." And it is rather odd that alchemy is mentioned as an example on par with Gnosticism, Theosophy, Anthroposophy and Wicca.

Satanism is introduced under the heading "The fantasy about Satanism" (Gilje and Gjefsen 1997, 154). It is related to "a belief in many religions," and that "some people worship evil by doing evil deeds" (Gilje and Gjefsen 1997, 154). And further, "the fantasy about a Satanic religion has led some people to try to make a Satanic religion." The example given is the Church of Satan and Anton LaVey. It is stressed that Satan is not a real being, but rather a symbol of "the power of life in human beings," and that the Church of Satan denounces illegal acts. However, in the subsequent paragraph, one

---

8. In Norwegian: "Okkult betyr skjult, hemmelig. Okkultisme er tro og praksis omkring "skjulte åndelige sannheter." Disse sannhetene forteller hvordan universet egentlig er, både det guddommelige, det mentale og det fysiske. Fordi sannhetene er hemmelige, er de skjult for mennesker som ikke er innviet. Man kan bare få lære disse sannhetene gjennom spesielle forberedelser og innvielser. [...] Okkultisme er minst 2000 år gammel, men det er ikke noen religion." (Gilje and Gjefsen 1997, 154).

can read about church fires in Norway and how youth have used Satanist symbols as a part of their rebellion. These are very powerful examples, the only ones taken from a Norwegian context, and communicate rather clearly that Satanism is something that is negative and not desirable in Norwegian society.

All in all, the chapter on New Age and occultism and Satanism has a structure and headings that lead from phenomena, beginning with Transcendental Meditation, which is clearly related to Hinduism, to vaguer phenomena. The final part of the main chapter, with the heading, "the border of religion" and its connection to youth rebellion and church fires, gives the impression that the further you move away from "true religion," i.e. Hinduism or Christianity, the sooner you meet "the borders of religions"—and beyond the borders lie criminal acts and chaos.

In another textbook, *Møte med livet* (*To meet the life*) (Kristensen *et al.* 1997) New Age, occultism and Satanism are included in an extensive chapter with the heading "Aktuelle trosretninger" (English, *Current traditions of faith*). The chapter deals with different groups within different religious traditions such as Islam, Judaism, Buddhism and Hinduism. Also, here again the Eastern roots of New Age are highlighted through Hare Krishna's relation to Hinduism. Comparatively, the presentation of Buddhism contains short descriptions about Buddha, different groups and traditions (Hinayana, Mahayana, Tibetan Buddhism, and Zen). Directly after a paragraph on Buddhism in Norway is a heading and a few paragraphs about the Mormons. This is followed by a presentation of Jehovah's Witnesses, and a very short presentation of Bahá'i. Then, at the end of the main chapter comes the heading "Occultism and Satanism" (Kristensen *et al.* 1997, 123–125). It is interesting to see that the treatment of Hinduism is much more extensive than the treatment of Buddhism, and that it is described as the background or inspiration for most new religious movements and New Age-related phenomena such as yoga and healing (Kristensen *et al.* 1997, 114).

Occultism is related to a number of different things: astrology, Spiritism, worship of the ancestor's spirits (by a shaman), the soul and the perishable body, Gnosticism, yoga and healing (Kristensen *et al.* 1997, 124–125). After briefly mentioning all these phenomena one finds the heading "Do what you will" (Norwegian, Gjør hva du vil). Here Aleister Crowley is also related to occultism, and it is stated that he "made his own perverted form of religion" (Kristensen *et al.* 1997, 125). After a short description of Crowley's revelations of the spirit Aiwass, and the assertion that Crowley's aim was to "destroy the Christian legacy," comes the heading "The Church of Satan" and a brief mention of The Church of Satan and Anton La Vey, and how La Vey further developed Crowley's ideas. The chapter concludes with the heading "Symbols and Music," where it reads that "Satanists use a whole range of symbols" (Kristensen *et al.* 1997, 126). Examples are the upside down cross, the goat, and the number 666. In the very last paragraph of this section, the importance of music for Satanists is explained:

> Music plays an important role for many modern Satanists. The music style/the genre *black metal* is often characterized by lyrics that deal with or encourages Satanism, murder, suicide, or a combination of sex and violence.
> (Kristensen *et al.* 1997, 126–127, italics in original, my translation).[9]

In this way of ending the chapter, New Age-related phenomena are once again linked to negative tendencies. When the books write about Occultism, there are only a few sentences before the texts discuss murder, suicide, sex and violence. It is the topic of occultism that seems to set in motion a chain of reasoning that ends up with negative portrayals. And as Crowley also "was very interested in the occult," and this interest made him make his own "perverted form of religion," the reader easily gets a sense that exploring your freedom, and experimenting with the Occult might well lead to harm. And this is not "real" religion.

These two examples from the first generation of RE textbooks in 1997 illustrate that descriptions of New Age were largely influenced by the teaching goals of discussing occultism and Satanism in negative terms. The quite biased and negative presentation of occultism and Satanism in both books bears the imprint of a moralizing judgement that this is something pupils must be warned against. The presentations of other examples of New Age are rather random, and there is a tendency to devalue these as not "real" religions. Whereas one textbook relates occultism to Gnosticism, alchemy, Theosophy, Anthroposophy and Wicca, the next textbook links it to astrology, Spiritism, worship of ancestor's spirits (by a shaman), the soul and the perishable body, Gnosticism, yoga and healing—so that pupils in secondary school will easily get an impression that New Age and occultism is just about anything. Yet from these different examples, one gets the impression in both books that New Age, through its unorganized systems and individual freedom, might lead to chaos and crime. Reading both books as a whole, the only chapters that mention crime and violence are those about New Age, especially the parts about occultism and Satanism.

By the turn of the millennium, and especially in the second generation of textbooks published after the KRL05 revision, the treatment of New Age has changed. There are now separate chapters about New Age that make a distinction between Mormons, Jehovah's Witnesses and New Age-related phenomena. The examples seem not quite as random as in earlier books. In the two books analyzed in this chapter, the approach and key terms are more consistent and coherent than in earlier books.

---

9. In Norwegian: "Musikken spiller en viktig rolle for mange moderne satanister. Musikkstilen *black metal* kjennetegnes ofte av tekster som omtaler eller oppfordrer til satanisme, drap, selvmord eller en kombinasjon av sex og vold." (Kristensen *et al.* 1997, 126–127, italics in original).

In the textbook *Horisonter 10* (*Horizons*) (Holth and Kallevik 2008, 80–100), New Age is outlined through a comparison with the supermarket, and a kind of "spiritual shopping." New Age-related phenomena are rooted in Madame Blavatsky and the Theosophical Society, and there are also links to Rudolph Steiner and his anthroposophy as a development of theosophy. Transcendental meditation and its roots in Hinduism, New Age and the Age of Aquarius follow as relevant examples of how it developed in the West after World War II.

Horisonter 10 is the only book that makes a distinction between "Loosely organized groups" and "Organized groups." The New Age-related alternative movement in Norway, Wicca and "Åsatro"[10] serve as examples of the first category, while Scientology and the Unification Church are examples in the second. Reference to historical and cultural roots, perspectives, organizations and terminology from scholarly research on New Age are applied throughout the chapter on New Age, to a larger extent than others in the second generation of RE textbooks.

The emphasis on nature and nature religions in the KRL05 curriculum is evident in the textbook. Shamanism, especially Sami Shamanism, serves as an example on how nature or nature elements are worshiped. Nature also forms the basis for arguing that "Nature religions" (i.e. shamanism) are synonymous with "indigenous religions": "That is why nature religions and indigenous religions often are treated as the same"[11] (Holth and Kallevik 2008, 92). In the paragraphs about Sami shamanism, the distinction between pre-Christian Sami Shamanism and current Shamanic traditions are missing in the text. This leaves the impression that Sami Shamanism has been a cohesive tradition up until present time. The connection to an earlier tradition is also present in the description of Wicca and its relation to nature. Respect for nature is especially stressed.[12] Interestingly enough, Wicca is also the only New Age-related phenomenon that provides a basis for ethics: "The Ethics—or the rules for how to live your life—can in Wicca be summarized as: Do as you wish, but do not hurt anyone."[13] (Holth and Kallevik 2008, 95).

In another book, *Under samme himmel 3* (*Under the same sky 3*) (Wiik and Waale 2007, 251–257), different topics related to New Age are listed. The headings in the chapter are: Wicca, the alternative movement and New Age, self-development, reincarnation, Yin and Yang, responsibility for the

---

10. "Åsatro" is loosely organized groups usually characterized as neo-paganism, inspired by deities and rituals in Germanic and Old Norse mythology.

11. In Norwegian: "Derfor blir det ofte satt likhetstegn mellom naturreligion og urfolks religioner."

12. "Slektskapet til gamle naturreligioner er tydelig når wiccaheksene feirer årstidene og livskraften. Wicca oppfordrer til respekt for alt levende, og legger vekt på at mennesker skal leve i harmoni med jorda og alt som lever" (Holth and Kallevik 2008, 94).

13. In Norwegian: "Etikken—eller selve levereglene—I [W]icca kan oppsummeres slik: Gjør hva du vil, men unngå å skade noen."

environment, the alternative movement and different practices. The word "practices" (in Norwegian, "ulike praksiser") refers to how people live their life inspired by the alternative movement. The examples of different practices are channeling, human personality [which is not a practice, but the heading refers to how one can find one's personality and personal qualities in astrology], personal growth [which is not a practice, but the heading refers to yoga, meditation and mantras, and alternative medicine like homeopathy, acupuncture and different forms of massage]. All in all, a range of topics are listed, which makes the text rather compact. How everything relates is not explicitly discussed, leaving the impression that New Age can be about everything.

Even if the examples for a large part are the same in *Horisonter 10* and *Under samme himmel 3*, the first seems to have adopted perspectives and analytical tools from academic research on New Age. This means that the authors are able to characterize and explain what New Religious Movements and New Age are about in a much clearer and, likely, an easily understandable way for pupils. The presentation of New Age in *Under samme himmel 3* has not integrated research on New Age and still relates "everything" to New Age in a rather unsystematic way. Interestingly, in 2013 the publisher behind *Under samme himmel* launched a new book by the same authors. In this publication, all three volumes of *Under samme himmel* are integrated and edited down into one volume that can be used for all three years of secondary school (8th–10th grade) (*RLE-boka 8–10* by Wiik and Waale 2013). In this new edition, it is pointed out that material on New Age and New Religious Movements can be found on the textbook's website. However, there is nothing on the website.

From the first to the second generation of textbooks in RE for secondary schools, there is a clear development in the presentation of New Age. In the late 1990s, New Age is related to "everything," and, even if it is not stated explicitly, through the examples given one gets the impression that this is not "real" religion. New Age-related phenomena are not "serious" in the same way as the "world religions," and following New Age phenomena, you sooner or later meet "the borders of religion" that might lead to crime. The textbooks from this period state or imply a rather clear moral judgment of New Age. This clearly has much to do with the teaching goals on Satanism and occultism which are highlighted in the KRL97 curriculum. At the turn of the millennium, perspectives and analytical approaches from study of religions are applied to a larger extent, thus providing the tools for developing an understandable, interesting and pedagogical text. The distinction between organized and unorganized activities, as well as historical background, are adopted in the texts, and communicates that it is not necessarily about anything. Additionally, explicit references to Satanism and occultism in the curriculum, and consequently also in the textbooks, are gone, thus removing the moral judgement from the 1990s that this is not "real religion."

New Age in textbooks for RE in upper-secondary school

Although the explicit references to New Age first appeared in the RE96 curriculum, upper-secondary textbooks had started to include chapters on New Age in the 1980s. At that time, the curriculum, which dated from 1976, stated that the selection of topics in teaching and textbooks should include "religious life in the world today" and "issues in the current debate about morality and worldviews."[14] Updated versions of textbooks in the late 1980s and early 1990s therefore included chapters on New Age. However, the approach and portrays of New Age from this period vary a lot, but are mostly oriented around terms such as Occultism, astrology, holism, meditation and ecology (cf. Grande and Myklebust 1992, 210–213). There are also books that relate New Age to a range of other things. Listing "some distinctive characters" of New Religious Movements and New Age, one book provides a list of characteristics for the sects that are related to brainwashing (Hellern *et al.* 1989, 298–299). And further in the text, it reads that "Sects like these [they do not provide any specific examples!] do their recruitment especially among young people searching for identity" (Hellern, Notaker and Gaarder, 299, my translation). As the text does not provide any specific examples, it can be read as a general warning against New Religious Movements and New Age because these groups brainwash people, drug their members and take their money. The same moral imprint as we saw in textbooks for secondary school from the 1990s also seems to apply to upper-secondary textbooks in the same period.

After the RE96 curriculum was introduced at upper-secondary level, all textbooks had chapters about New Age and New Religious Movements, even if it was mentioned as optional in the curriculum. Most of the textbooks in the late 1990s provide a general introduction to New Age, mostly oriented toward eclectic tendencies and experimentation, and as a kind of rebellion against society. Still, in some books, religious movements such as Jehovah's Witnesses were included in chapter about New Age (cf. Heiene *et al.* 2005). The reason for including Jehovah's Witnesses is not clear. Under the heading "Different kinds of New Age" (Norwegian, *Ulike typer nyreligiøsitet*), it instead reads that "Holistic New Age and Jehovah's Witnesses are very different religious groups"[15] (Heiene *et al.* 2005, 121). Three pages later, under the heading "The tight communities" (Norwegian, *"De tette fellesskapene"*), the argument for including Jehovah's Witnesses is:

> We have presented Jehovah's Witnesses as an example of a movement with close relationships among its members. Sociologists of religion

---

14. In the Norwegian text, it reads "problemstillingar som rår i dagens moral- og livssynsdebatt." A translation of the Norwegian term "livssyn" to "worldviews," even if one can interpret "livssyn" in a broad sense that also includes religion.

15. "Holistisk nyreligiøsitet og Jehovas vitner representerer svært ulike religiøse retninger" (Heiene *et al.* 2005, 121).

have also found the same pattern in the Church of Scientology, Unification Church and many other new religious movements.

(Heiene *et al.* 2005, 124, my translation)

The close social relationships within these movements are related to social control, followed by a section on defection and exclusion, along with a discussion of whether this is "harmful religiosity" (Norwegian, *skadelig religiøsitet*). The chapter ends with two paragraphs on "loosely organized New Age" (Norwegian, *løst organisert nyreligiøsitet*), which to a certain degree corrects the bias on organized groups such as Jehovah's Witnesses, Unification Church and Scientology. However, as New Age is included in the same chapter with groups that have strong social controls—described as "harmful religiosity"—the texts could be read as a general warning against New Age.

At present (2015), there are three textbooks on the market for RE in upper-secondary education. In general, the books seem to organize chapters and approaches to religions after Ninian Smart's dimensions, dependent on the application of Smart's model in the RE06 curriculum of religion (cf. Andreassen 2012, 91–92). As the textbooks organize the chapters about different religions in the same way, it is clear that Smart's phenomenologically-rooted model is not necessarily a good model for approaching New Age. As the RE06 curriculum does not have any explicit teaching goals on New Age, New Age is instead included as an example of the teaching goal on "different forms of searching for religion in our time."

Even if New Age is not explicitly mentioned in any teaching goal in the current curriculum, it is obvious that textbook authors find it natural to integrate it into the textbooks. Even if New Age is included in all books, it does not get as much space as in the earlier books for RE at the upper-secondary level. However, the textbooks briefly mention New Age in a few pages in chapters about religion in the Norwegian society, or in more general chapters introducing religion as a phenomenon and as an example of "searching for religion in our time." The presentation of New Age is therefore often very short, but a variety of terms and topics are usually listed. Still, it seems that the authors have struggled with the issue of where to place New Age. In an updated version of the book, *I samme verden* (Kvamme, Lindhardt and Steineger 2013, 327–328), New Age shares a section with secular humanism[16] and is very briefly mentioned as "a less noticeable, still fairly common phenomenon, partly in combination with established religions."[17] The text then refers to the introductory chapter where New Age is explained through concepts like holism, reincarnation, yoga, mindfulness, occultism, channeling,

---

16. In Norwegian the heading reads: "Livssynshumanisme og nyreligiøsitet" (Secular humanism and New Age).

17. In Norwegian: "Nyreligiøstiteten har vokst fram som et mindre markant, men nokså utbredt fenomen, til dels i kombinasjon med etablerte religioner" (Kvamme, Lindhardt and Steineger 2013, 327–328).

new paganism, Wicca and Shamanism (Kvamme, Lindhardt and Steineger 2013, 33–35).

The limited space New Age gets in the most recent generation of textbooks for upper-secondary school makes it difficult to say much about how it is treated. However, a clear development is that the current textbooks, that relates to the RE06 curriculum for upper-secondary, does not contain as much about New Age as the earlier textbooks, that related to the RE96 curriculum. Still, one could say that a general tendency in the new textbooks for upper-secondary school after 2008 is an orientation around the alternative movement in Norway, and around concepts of healing and meditation. All mention the Alternative Fair. The textbooks briefly mention that New Age can be combined with more established religions, but the main focus is on the Alternative movement (Norwegian, *Alternativbevegelsen*) and concepts of self-development.

Discussion

In the period from 1997 to 2008, one sees a tendency in curricula for RE in secondary school that New Age is more and more related to nature and indigenous nature religions. In the second generation of textbooks, this development manifests through a focus on paganism, with Shamanism and Wicca as the most-used examples. As the focus on occultism and Satanism disappears from the curriculum, and the public debate about church fires disappears, the strong moral imprint found in the first generation of textbooks concerning the warning about occultism and Satanism is reduced. The strong moral imprint in the first generation of textbook also affected the general presentation of New Age. In the second generation of textbooks, the moral imprint about New Age is more or less gone. However, in some books one can still find a tendency to portray New Age as not "real" religion when compared with religions such as Christianity and Islam.

In years between 1997 and 2008, the curriculum for RE in secondary schools has been under constant revision. The second generation of textbooks has been written with reference to curricula (KRL05 and RLE08) that emphasize impartial teaching and an equal presentation of religions and worldviews. Additionally, the emphasis on Christianity has been reduced and re-contextualized. Teaching and textbooks should no longer have Christianity as their starting point and point of reference. That has most likely also contributed to the removal of much of the moral imprint and warnings against what an individual's experimentation with New Age might lead to.

At the upper-secondary level, New Age has been a part of the curricula and textbooks for a longer period. In the first generation of textbooks from the 1980s and early 1990s, the presentation of New Age was twofold. Firstly, New Age and New Religious Movements are related to sects that do brainwashing, force young people to use drugs and exploit its members financially. Secondly, New Age is presented in a way that signals that this has more to do with entertainment than religion, and leaves the impression that this kind of "religion" is not very serious. Organized New Age (and New Religious Movements) are harmful or dangerous, and unorganized New Age is not to be taken seriously.

While in textbooks for the secondary level there is a tendency to relate New Age primarily to nature and organized New Age, the second generation of textbooks for upper-secondary schools are primarily oriented around unorganized New Age and concepts of self-development and healing, such as meditation and yoga, and the Alternative Fair. These are very general tendencies. However, as a reflection of the curriculum for each stage, textbooks for the secondary level are more oriented towards organized New Age, whereas textbooks for the upper-secondary level are more focused on unorganized New Age.

In the textbooks for both secondary and upper-secondary education, the presentation of New Age and New Religious Movements has developed and is more systematic. From an intertextual perspective, a close reading of the texts provides hints and clues that authors, for the most part have drawn on developments in academic research on New Age. The textbooks do not offer extensive references or reference lists, at least not those for secondary schools. In some of the books for the upper-secondary level, one sees that references are made in the text and in bibliographies at the end of the book. One textbook that seemingly has gained a broad reception among textbook authors is *Kulturens refortrylling* by Ingvild Gilhus and Lisbeth Mikaelsson (1998). The reception of this book can especially be traced in textbooks distinction between organized and unorganized New Age.

Concluding remarks: Can perspectives on New Age contribute in the development of RE?

New Age is still a rather new topic in RE, and compared with the emphasis on "world religions" such as Christianity, Islam, Hinduism and Buddhism, it is a rather small part of the subject in school contexts. In the textbooks from the 1980s and 1990s, the presentation of New Age implicitly bore the imprint of evaluation in terms of the "world religions" paradigm. Developments in recent decades shows that New Age is treated more as a separate area, sometimes more or less completely outside of the traditions related to "world religions," and sometimes as a part of these traditions. This applies especially for religions from Asian backgrounds.

The Swedish scholar Göran Ståhle (2014) argues that in Sweden, New Age is still often related to the term "alternative" in textbooks. That means that it is sometimes somewhat marginalized compared to "majority religions." To a certain degree this also applies in the Norwegian context. Still, textbooks, both at the secondary and upper-secondary levels, point to different quantitative research projects and argue that quite a few Norwegians have tried or are influenced by New Age. Thus, New Age is presented as a current and relevant phenomenon in Norwegian society. In general, in terms of being treated as a specific phenomenon, and through adopting concepts and terms developed within the research on New Age, the development in Norwegian RE seems to be that New Age is treated more "seriously" now than it was in the 1990s.

From the vantage point of a study of religion-based RE, New Age seems to challenge the traditional world religion approach. This might lead to a further development of RE. I will argue for two possibilities: Firstly, a theme like New Age will often elicit a question about what is "new" in New Age. Investigating New Age traditions, pupils would see that the "new" in New Age has developed not only across several decades, but also across centuries. This could also lead to a reflection on how "new" should be understood, and "new" in reference to what. In teaching, this could be an important introduction to reflections on all religions. Even the old "world religions" have at some point been new. New Age could therefore contribute by offering important reflections about how religious ideas constantly evolve and change in different contexts and in different societies. In this way, New Age is no different than Christianity, Islam and Judaism. It is constantly interpreted and re-contextualized by human beings, in new social and historical contexts. Secondly, teaching about New Age could contribute to reflections about what "religion" is. As curricula and textbooks are oriented around "world religions" and an approach to religion usually through a founder, texts, doctrine and the ethics, pupil's understanding of "religion" is often oriented about this when they are challenged to reflect about what "religion" is. New Age can serve as a challenge to a conventional understanding of religion in RE, since it can appear in different forms. This is of great value for the pupil's reflection on and understanding of religion.

As content for teaching in RE, New Age is a legitimate topic because it is an important part of the religious landscape in Norwegian society. It is therefore something that pupils should acquire knowledge about. Additionally, teaching about New Age can be of great value in developing pupils' understanding about what "religion" is.

Curricula

Kirke, utdannings-, og forskningsdepartementet. 1996. [RE96]. Læreplan for videregående opplæring. Religion og etikk. Oslo: KUF.

Kirke-, utdannings- og forskningsdepartementet. 1997. [KRL97]. Kristendomskunnskap med religions- og livssynsorientering. In Læreplanverket for grunnskolen, 89-107. Oslo: KUF.

Kyrkje- og undervisningsdepartementet. 1983 [1976]. Religion [R76]. In Læreplan for den videregående skole. Del 2. Felles allmenne fag, s. 7-15 Oslo: Gyldendal/Kyrkje- og undervisningsdepartementet.

Utdanningsdirektoratet. 2002. Læreplan i kristendoms-, religions- og livssynskunnskap. [KRL02]. Oslo: Utdanningsdirektoratet.

Utdanningsdirektoratet. 2005. Læreplan i kristendoms-, religions- og livssyn-skunnskap. [KRL05]. Oslo: Utdanningsdirektoratet.

Utdanningsdirektoratet. 2006. Religion and ethics - common core subjects in Programme for general studies. [RE06] Oslo: Utdanningsdirektoratet. [Official English translation of Religion og etikk].

Utdanningsdirektoratet. 2008. Curriculum for Religion, Philosophies of Life and Ethics. [RLE08] Oslo: Utdanningsdirektoratet. [Official English translation of Religion, livssyn og etikk (RLE)].

Textbooks

Gilje, Randi M. and Bjørn Gjefsen. 1997. *Midt i vår hverdag. 8. klasse.* Oslo: Gyldendal undervisning.

Grande, Sidsel Ø. and Jan F. Myklebust. 1992. Logos. *Religion, livssyn, etikk.* Oslo: Cappelen.

Heiene, Gunnar, Bjørn Myhre, Jan Opsal, Harald Skottene and Arna Østnor. [1997] 2005. *Mening og mangfold.* Oslo: Aschehoug.

Hellern,Victor, Henry Notaker and Jostein Gaarder. 1989. *Religionsboka.* Oslo: Gyldendal norsk forlag.

Holth, Gunnar and Kjell Arne Kallevik. 2008. *Horisonter 10.* Oslo: Gyldendal undervisning.

Kristensen, Vidar, Gunnar B. Gabrielsen and Bjørn Bolstad. 1997. *Møte med livet 8.* Oslo: Aschehoug.

Kvamme, Ole A., Eva M. Lindhardt and Agnethe Steineger. 2013. 3rd ed. *I samme verden.* Oslo: Cappelen Damm.

Wiik, Pål and Randi Bakke Waale. 2007. *Under samme himmel 3.* Oslo: Cappelen.

———. 2013. *RLE-boka 8-10.* Oslo: Cappelen Damm.

References

Andreassen, Bengt-Ove. 2012. *Religionsdidaktikk. En innføring.* Oslo: University Publishing House.

———. 2013. "Religion Education in Norway: Tension or Harmony between Human Rights and Christian Cultural Heritage?" *Temenos* 49(2): 137–164.

———. 2014. "Theoretical Perspectives on Textbooks/Textbooks in Religious studies Research." In *Textbook Gods: Genre, Text and Teaching Religious Studies,* edited by B.-O. Andreassen and J. R. Lewis, 1–15. Sheffield: Equinox Publishing.

Copley, Terence. 2008. *Teaching Religion: Sixty Years of Religious Education in England and Wales.* Exeter: University of Exeter Press.

Gilhus, Ingvild S. and Siv Ellen Kraft. 2017. "Introduction: New Age in Norway." In *New Age in Norway,* edited by Ingvild S. Gilhus and Siv Ellen Kraft, 1–19. Sheffield: Equinox.

Gilhus, Ingvild S. and Lisbeth Mikaelsson. 1998. *Kulturens refortrylling.* Oslo: University Publishing House.

Goodlad, John I. ed. 1979. *Curriculum Inquiry: The Study of Curriculum Practice.* New York: McGraw-Hill Book Company.

Jensen, Tim. 2008. "RS based RE in public schools: A must for a secular state." *Numen* 55(2–3): 123–150.

Juuhl, Gudrun K., Magnus Hontvedt and Dagrun Skjelbred. 2010. *Læremiddelforskning etter LK06. Eit kunnskapsoversyn.* Rapport 1/2010. Høgskolen i Vestfold.

Pingel, Falk. 2010. *UNESCO Guidebook on Textbook Research and Textbook.* Revision. 2nd ed. Brauschweig: Georg Eckert Institute for International textbook research.

Smart, Ninian. 1989. *The World's Religions.* Cambridge: Cambridge University Press.

Ståhle, Göran. 2014. "Går det att 'känna igen' samtida organiserad andlighet?" *Religion & livsfrågor* 3: 9–10.

Tallaksen, Inger M. and Hans Hodne. 2014. "Hvilken betydning har læremidler i RLE-faget?" *Norsk pedagogisk tidsskrift* 5: 352–363.

Zetterqvist, Kirsten G. and Geir Skeie. 2014. "Religion i skolen; her, der og hvorsom-helst?" *Norsk pedagogisk tidsskrift* 5: 304–315.

6

Alternative Medicine:
Health-Oriented, Spiritual Practices in Norway

Anne Kalvig

Alternative medicine and alternative therapy (also termed CAM, complementary and alternative medicine) is a vital part of New Age or alternative spirituality, in Norway as well as elsewhere. However, those health-oriented, spiritual practices conventionally labelled alternative medicine might be analyzed from a wide range of different perspectives. Different analytical positions give quite different answers as to "what" this is, and "why" people seek alternative medicine. In this chapter, I provide a sketchy overview of the phenomenon of alternative medicine and therapy in Norway. By presenting a few widespread and well-known—as well as a few of the more obscure—alternative, medical/health-oriented, spiritual practices, I seek to give a preliminary answer to what it means to consider such practices as *religion*.[1]

To start with, I provide a few definitions of terms and point to previous research into the field of CAM and religion. I will then use the spatial model of religion outlined by Jonathan Z. Smith (2003) and further adapted by Ingvild S. Gilhus (2013) for the purpose of categorizing and gaining a certain overview of CAM in Norway "as" religion/resembling religion or religious or spiritual practices. This categorization is not meant to be conclusive; rather, it is more of a model "to think with" and part of a further discussion of the relationship between alternative medicine and religion towards the end of the chapter. My material consists of my own fieldwork on alternative medicine and therapy in Norway since 2006 (Kalvig 2011, 2012, 2013, 2014), other studies in the field, statistics on CAM in Norway, and various media reports.

---

1. I would like to thank Prof. Geir Skeie, UiS, for valuable review of and suggestions to an early draft of this chapter.

Definitions of religion and alternative medicine

As outlined by Kraft and Gilhus in the Introduction (2017, 1–19), religion can be defined as a particular type of communication. This might be specified as communication with "superhuman beings and powers" (Gilhus and Mikaelsson 2001, 29), and in connection with health-oriented, spiritual practices, "power" is a central term, since "cosmic energy" and similar superhuman, non-anthropomorphic forces and dimensions are often considered to be involved.[2] Spiritual healing, for example, could then be defined as the ability (of a therapist/healer) to communicate with and direct/activate the spiritual energy both within and surrounding a patient's body-mind-spirit, promoting health and strength, and diminishing or healing illness. In a cosmic or holistic view, this could be understood as a process of *balancing*, since balance and harmony are often considered the "natural" or innate quality of existence. Various "disturbances" might work against this balance, though still without being "evil," since evil has no "real" or ontological place in a holist (unified) worldview central to New Age religion (Hanegraaff 1996, 119–158; Kalvig 2013, 163–197). In this respect, religion as communication with superhuman powers (energy, spirit, the Source, the Divine) translates as alternative medicine and therapy *where such forces and the communication and/or interaction with them is present in a therapeutic situation.* However, for many alternative therapists, such a categorization could easily be considered irrelevant or false. "Religion" is often thought of as dogmatic, institutionalized, manmade systems characterized by mind-control, suppression, dualisms and so forth, and not as the living, free and authentic spirituality of the New Era (cf. Heelas and Woodhead 2005, 3ff.) distinction between religion as "life-as" versus spirituality as "life from within"). Still, to fit a chapter on alternative medicine into a book on New Age in Norway, a matching of this field and phenomena with religion is required. This is not to say that everything labelled alternative medicine is relevant to the study of religion. Spirituality, religiosity or religion might be central, peripheral or irrelevant to the alternative practitioner and her/his client. These valuations might run counter to or be in accordance with the views of the historian of religions or other people analyzing the practices and the socio-cultural situation of which they are part. Various possible ways of viewing the complex relationship(s) between alternative medicine and (New Age) religion will thus be discussed throughout this chapter.

---

2. Cfr. Mikaelsson's (2013, 170–171) discussion of energy within New Age: «Energy appears as the standard explanation of why healing, therapies, and many other spiritual practices function [...] The easy, fluent, all-encompassing character of energy holism dulls the sharpness of difference between religious traditions [...] When viewed as energy the sacred becomes less sacred, less exclusivist, and less above the trivial pursuits of ordinary life."

Previous research on body, medicine and therapy within New Age

Historian of religion Wouter Hanegraaff (1996) identified "the bodily turn" as one of four main characteristics of New Age spirituality or religion in his standard work, *New Age Religion and Western Culture*. Historian of religion Christopher Partridge analyses the holistic milieu and the spiritual turn within healthcare in his *The Re-Enchantment of the West* (2005, 4–41), and sociologists of religion Linda Woodhead and Paul Heelas thematize alternative therapies and other signs of "a spiritual revolution" in their regional study of religion (Heelas and Woodhead 2005). In Norway, Siv Ellen Kraft has analyzed the field of alternative therapy and medicine in relation to New Age and public discourses in several articles (2000, 2004, 2006, 2011), and Lisbeth Mikaelsson has discussed the understanding of "the holistic energy body" within New Age (2004) and the idea of energy (within therapy and elsewhere) as a "cognitive currency" (2013). In 2013, I published my PhD-findings as a monograph entitled *Spiritual Health: Views of Life among Alternative Therapists*,[3] an in-depth study of nine alternative therapists in Norway and their worldviews and therapeutic practices. In Denmark, Lars Ahlin (2007) has headed up a sociological study of the spiritual dimension of the work of alternative therapists, based on questionnaires from 170 therapists. In Sweden, Liselotte Frisk and Peter Åkerbäck have carried out a sociological project called "The meditating Dala-horse" (2008–2011),[4] a comprehensive survey of "the religious landscape" of the Swedish region of Dalarna. Frisk and Åkerbäck focus on what they call popular religion, where "retreat centers, alternative fairs and various health institutes comprise the hub of the popular religious milieus" (Frisk and Åkerbäck 2013, 109, my translation from Swedish).

As these examples of some of the geographically and disciplinary most immediate publications show, several approaches to and investigations of the field are possible and have been conducted. But unlike the study of for example (neo) paganism, shamanism, Satanism or esotericism, the field of alternative medicine and therapy does not have its own research traditions, disciplines, or journals within religious studies (but indeed within other disciplines, like for example folkloristics, medical anthropology, nursing and various, holistic health branches). The reason why might be, among other things, the porous borders between spiritual, health-oriented practices and other health-oriented practices, as I will try to show by operationalizing the spatial model of religion on this field. This "porous situation" creates too much uncertainty perhaps, in a New Age research tradition already marked by the lack of "a clearly defined and cumulative set of research question"

---

3. Published in Norwegian: *Åndeleg helse. Livssyn og menneskesyn hos alternative terapeutar.*

4. "Den mediterande Dalahästen," my translation to English, "Dala horse" being a symbol for this region.

(cf. the introduction to this volume; Sutcliffe and Gilhus 2013, 6), thus making it difficult to establish comprehensive "schools of research" on alternative medicine within the study of religions.

A spatial model of religion adapted to alternative medicine and therapy

Smith's spatial notion of religion as here, there and anywhere has proven useful for several studies of contemporary religion, with Ingvild Gilhus adding the category of religion "everywhere" (Gilhus 2013, 43ff.) in the study of New Age spirituality. These categories described in Smith's original contribution religion in the Roman empire as the house cult and funerary rites (here), the state cult (there) and the interstitial space between the two former, characterized by entrepreneurs, astrologers, magic and associations (anywhere) (Smith 2003, 24–36). Adjusted to the contemporary, Western world, spatial categories connote private/unofficial religion (here), official religion, represented by the church (there), and the market and network based field of (alternative) spirituality (religion anywhere). Religion "everywhere" is, on the contemporary spirituality scene, closely connected with the mediatization of religion (Hjarvard 2008; Lundby 2009; Lövheim 2011)—that is, how religion is produced, spread, consumed and reproduced according to logics of media and communication technology.

As a starting point, I suggest that alternative medicine and therapy in Norway, in the form of religion here, there, anywhere and everywhere, can be translated into the categories of home and family oriented alternative medicine and therapy (here), public, institutionalized health care, education, church and monarchy (there), the variegated New Age market, entrepreneurs and products of an alternative medical and therapeutic kind (anywhere) and, finally, the overall cultural, mediatized communications revolving around the notion of body-mind-spirit and the quest for (spiritual) health (everywhere). It follows that I also see the category of "there" as characterized by spiritual, alternative medical and therapeutic practices, as with the spatiality of here, anywhere and everywhere. In the Norwegian context, the "there" spatial category has normally been left to civic national religion, Christian churches and cathedrals, and the monarchy (cf. the Introduction, pp. 5–6), implying that New Age religion/alternative (spiritual) medicine and therapy to a lesser degree is present here. This is probably so, but I would also like to point to where alternative medicine and therapy have made their way into this space—and having been able to do so exactly because of the porous, flexible and negotiable character of therapeutic religion or spiritual, health-oriented practices and because of the workings of alternative therapy "anywhere" and "everywhere." I will provide some examples of each category before further discussing the problem of demarcating and interpreting the still challenging—and enriching!—study of New Age.

Anne Kalvig

Alternative medicine as "religion there"

CAM in public hospitals

In the "there" category, alternative medicine as religion is located within the weighty institutions of public health care, education, church and monarchy. That is, alternative medical and therapeutic practices that include spirituality (in the sense of communication with superhuman entities/forces) in their basis or modus operandi may be discerned within these spaces. A relatively recent research project (Salomonsen *et al.* 2011) found that CAM is presently offered in about 50% of Norwegian hospitals and one-third of Danish hospitals. The increase in CAM use in Norwegian hospitals has been substantial, from 25% of hospitals in 2001 to the present 50%.[5] This is not to say that its use within hospitals is comprehensive. Probably more often it is marginal, but it is indeed part of what hospitals see fit to offer. Examples of alternative medicine in Norwegian public hospitals are acupuncture (by far the most common CAM offered), biofeedback, herbal medicine, tai chi, homeopathy, thought field therapy, aromatherapy, Pilates and yoga. Of these, several might be said to directly or indirectly involve communication with superhuman/spiritual forces, or being practices aligned with a kind of energy paradigm not compatible with traditional, Western medicine—like acupuncture. CAM is most frequently used in maternity wards, in departments for pain therapy/pain clinics, cancer rehabilitation, palliative care and substance abuse care, but also in emergency medicine departments, surgical/anesthetics departments and gynecological departments (only acupuncture is offered in these last three departments) (Salomonsen *et al.* 2011, 4).

Patients' rights regarding CAM is widely debated in the Norwegian public, and one response from the official side has been to initiate and finance CAM related research, as with The National Research Center in Complementary and Alternative Medicine (NAFKAM) established in 2000, located at the Fac-

---

5.   The conventional health system in Norway contains somatic and psychiatric medicine, and nursing. The health sector is to a large degree public, that is, the rule is that neither profit-making nor religious organizations run hospitals, in contrast to many other parts of the world. People educated and practicing in this sector are registered/authorized and subject to the Health Personal Act (Helsepersonelloven), regulating duties and rights for practitioners, paralleled by the Act on Patient Rights (Pasientrettighetsloven). There exist no equivalents to this in the alternative field. CAM in Norway is regulated by the CAM Act of 2003, and anyone who wants to offer health related services can do so provided he or she does not treat contagious diseases, serious illnesses, or put the patient's health at risk. CAM personnel can be charged regarding the CAM Act or other legislation if they do harm to individuals, but the possibilities for patients and clients to complain to the authorities regarding an alternative practitioner are limited, as there is no central/public licensing or registering of CAM personnel which hence can be suspended since their practice isn't part of public education and authorization. The public sector has no damage liability towards users of CAM.

ulty of Medicine at the University of Tromsø. The research of Salomonsen *et al.*, for example, is based at NAFKAM, and their intention is to monitor changes in the use of CAM in hospitals every 5th year (Salomonsen *et al.* 2011, 2). NAFKAM's mandate is to conduct multidisciplinary research on CAM, to counsel, teach and provide national and international workshops and conferences, and to register "Exceptional remission or exacerbation of diseases," which is a Scandinavian register (www.nafkam.no).[6] In addition, NAFKAM launched the public website Nifab.no ("Norwegian Information on CAM") in 2007, presented as a "website for providing the Norwegian population with evidence-based information about complementary and alternative medicine (CAM)."[7] The Salomonsen *et al.* study shows that what is meant by CAM is not clear. Even though the CAM Act in Norway defines it in specific ways, health personnel may have differing opinions as to whether the treatment they provide is alternative or not, indicating a "grey area of treatment considered neither as alternative nor as conventional—an area constantly developing and changing" (Salomonsen *et al.* 2011, 6). This disagreement is primarily related to acupuncture.

The NAFKAM researchers and the Nifab.no information site hardly discuss the possible spiritual content of CAM practices—not even when discussing healing. Spirituality and spiritual powers are, however, part of the presentation of Sami folk medicine though not in the presentation of other folk medical practices.[8] An example of folk medicine integrated into public hospitals, is health personnel at the University hospital in Nordland (Northern Norway) who for decades have sent for or telephoned both Sami and Norwegian folk healers when they themselves have been unable to stop severe hemorrhages (Henriksen 2010). Then rituals have been performed, often in the form of so-called 'reading'—the use of religious texts and prayer to stop blood, with positive results, according to the newspaper *Nordlys*.[9] Most of the time, the calling for folk healers is requested by the patient, but contact has also been made by health personnel independently.

CAM education—in health sector and public school

In 2011, in a research dissemination article, a professor of psychology at NTNU (The Norwegian University of Science and Technology), Ingunn

---

6. Since 2008, NAFKAM has been a WHO Collaborating Center on Traditional Medicine, of which there are 17 globally, though only two in Europe, NAFKAM and the other in Milan, Italy.

7. The role and responsibilities of nifab.no are to "neither hinder nor promote the use of CAM. Nifab.no is tasked with creating greater clarity in a complex field, by offering unbiased information as a decision-helper for the public to make informed choices about health and treatment" (http://nifab.no/om_nifab_no/information_in_english).

8. http://nifab.no/behandlingsformer/samisk_folkemedisin. See also Kraft 2006.

9. http://www.nordlys.no/nyheter/article4092395.ece.

Hagen, promoted the idea of yoga and meditation as part of Norwegian schooling, by referring to the view that "In India children learn this from young age, among other things from yoga and Hindu philosophy. In India they are better at strengthening children's self-worth and teach them techniques for self-connection." She is supported by Hindu-emic views offered by a Hindu visiting professor at NTNU, Usha Sidana Nayar, who claims that Hindus are particularly concerned about living in "bliss," and are particularly good at it, too. Promoting Hindu views, Hagen is perhaps atypical regarding the general trend in the educational sector, where Buddhist views in the form of Mindfulness are in vogue—though not to the same extent in Norway as in Sweden (Grønlien Zetterqvist and Skeie 2014). Mindfulness is perceived as a "diluted" or non-religious version of Buddhist practice, and has proven attractive to the educated classes of the medical, church and business sectors—an increasing number of physicians (GP) and Christian priests now offer courses in Mindfulness.[10] The psychological health sector, however, has shown a greater interest into this than the medical education milieus, who generally have been more critical. An example of a psychological embracing of Mindfulness is the conference "Mindfulness. Nærvær i liv og helse" ("Mindfulness. Presence in Life and Health") in Tromsø in 2014, hosted by two university hospitals, in Nordland and Tromsø, as well as by a network called *NFON—Norsk forening for oppmerksomt nærvær i helse, utdanning og forskning* (Norwegian Union for Mindfulness in Health, Education, and Research).[11] Attendance at the conference program, which was presented as "an explorative, practice oriented and opening introduction to Mindfulness as phenomenon and method," served as a certification maintenance course for The Norwegian Psychological Association, and as a specialist course for The Norwegian Nurses Organisation and for the Norwegian Union of Occupational Therapists. The present leader of *NFON*, Anne Sælebakke, is a teacher and physiotherapist now working full time with Mindfulness. She has for the last three decades regularly taught at the Danish Vækstcenteret, a spiritual center founded and headed by famous New Age spirituality leader Jes Bertelsen.

In Bergen, Mindfulness is also offered as a further qualification course for nurses, and includes yoga and meditation, at Haraldsplass Deaconess University College, a private, academic institution founded in 1918 and based on Christian values.[12] In an article called "Mindfulness on the curriculum"

---

10. Cfr, GP Tonje Talberg and her defense of the medical use of Mindfulness: http://www.aftenbladet.no/meninger/Mindfulness-trening-et-godt-alternativ-3650900.html

11. http://uit.no/om/enhet/aktuelt/arrangement?p_document_id=376291&p_dimension_id=88120.

12. Course presented here: http://www.haraldsplass.no/hogskole/studier/mindfulness-tverrfaglig-videreutdanning.

in the newspaper *Bergens Tidende,* one of the students, Dorthe Neu Hatland, says: "We had an exercise where we did a body scan by reviewing our own bodies, part by part. If I manage to transfer this to patients, it could be used as analgesia and other things. It becomes a sort of alternative therapy."[13] A psychologist not associated with the institution, Katharina Cecilia Williams, is also interviewed and claims that "in reality, it is a Buddhist meditation practice," not sufficiently researched as to its effects on anxiety or depression.

CAM in The Norwegian Church

The Norwegian Lutheran Church was a state church until 2012, when a constitutional amendment ended 500 years of exclusive relationship (cf. Mikaelsson, Chapter 2 in this book). Still, the Norwegian Church continues to have privileges in society; its basic values are part of the constitution and 75% of the population are members—one of the church's names in Norwegian is "The People's Church" (*Folkekirken*).[14] Could this national, official church also be a provider of CAM practices, then unfolding as "religion there"? To some extent, yes: The Norwegian Church takes "the spiritual longing" (understood as the embracing of New Age practices) of people seriously and tries to meet this in various ways. One initiative is the churchly Dialogue Centers, addressing both "traditional" religious dialogue work between different confessions and religions, as well as having a special focus on the New Age or alternative spirituality, and offering practices meant to "open up" the church to groups of people perhaps unfamiliar or uncomfortable with traditional Lutheran liturgy and rituals.

Christian meditation is one of the priorities of the Dialogue Centers, and in this they might be said to come close to CAM practices flourishing elsewhere in society. This is how the Dialogue Center explains what Christian meditation is about: "God is not far away. God lives in your innermost core. In the midst of the silence. Centering prayer is a form of meditation in which we can experience God's presence in us."[15] In the subgroup of the Dialogue Center in Oslo, called "The Breathing Space" ("Pusterommet"), meditation is also presented in a more "health-oriented" way by explicit relating the meditation practice they offer to stress reduction and coping, as well as contact

---

13. http://www.bt.no/nyheter/lokalt/Har-meditasjon-og-mindfulness-pa-pensum-3233054.html (for subscribers only).

14. Outside of this dominant Lutheran church, there exists a multitude of various Christian congregations, movements and sects, not part of "official religion" as "religion there." Thus, they are not part of this discussion, but worth mentioning as vital sites for CAM practices in the form of healing and prayer, not least in charismatic congregations like those inspired by American K. E. Hagin and his Faith Movement/ Word of Faith Movement. For a discussion of a Norwegian example, see Lavik 2015.

15. http://www.kirkeligdialogsenter.no/stavanger/kristen-meditasjon.

with God.[16] Furthermore, the Dialogue Center in Stavanger offers a monthly "Dialogue Mass." In this alternative mass, crystal bowl healing[17] (by an alternative therapist, Siw Torill Rugland, also widely known in this region as a medium) has been one of the ritual forms, as well as healing given as blessing from the dialogue priest herself, Silje Trym Mathiassen. Trym Mathiassen was an alternative therapist for 20 years before she received the calling to become a Christian priest. In 2014, Trym Mathiassen was the initiator of a seminar called "Faith and therapy," with an advertisement framing the subject in the following manner:

> Has God become a therapist? Is God a feminine therapist who is supposed to listen to our problems and help us solve them? Have health and wellbeing become the new ways of worship of today? Has the church become a place we turn to in order to feel more at ease with ourselves? Is going to church healthy? This and more will perhaps be answered in our seminary March 29 at Sola Health Farm.[18]

Organizations arranging this seminar, in addition to the Dialogue Center, were Areopagos (another Christian dialogue organization), Stavanger diocese, The National Council for Faith Communities and the Theosophical Society.

The Royal family and alternative medicine

In Norway, the royal family is popularly known for being associated with religion anywhere in the form of princess Märtha Louise and her former enterprise "The Angel School" (see Gilhus' chapter in this book). Currently, her spiritual business is called "Soulspring," offering courses and education in healing, reading and "light touch," thus more clearly an alternative therapeutic enterprise. However, the royal family is predominantly and in terms of royal authority connected to the national church.[19] CAM is not thematized to a great extent by the members of the monarchy besides Princess Märtha Louise, but Crown princess Mette-Marit has publicly announced that the

---

16. http://pauluskirke.org/voksne/pusterom.

17. Crystal bowl healing is a kind of sound healing, with deep sounds and vibrations produced when the practitioner "plays" the crystal bowls of various sizes with a wooden stick. See Trym Mathiassen 2015.

18. The seminar material is no longer available on the internet. Translation by the author. See Kalvig 2015.

19. Princess Märtha Louise renounced the title «Her Royal Highness» in 2002, when she entered the Norwegian work market by establishing her own enterprise, "Princess Märtha Louise Cultural Communication." King Harald interfered with the parliamentary process on dividing church and state in 2008 by asking the responsible minister not to remove the "Duty on Confession" (to the Norwegian Lutheran Church) for the King. See Døving and Kraft 2013, 27–28).

former healed her pyelitis by a laying on of hands.[20] Mette-Marit is known as a pious Christian who has, among other things, issued a CD with psalms that have a special meaning to her.[21] By publicly praising the healing hands of Princess Märtha Louise, she might be said to contribute to a (royal, Christian) legitimizing of both the CAM practice of healing, as well as the natural talents of her sister-in-law. Another example is Queen Sonja, who invited the national icon of folk medicine (in the form of healing with a Christian basis), the *Snåsamannen*, to the Royal Palace in 2010. In this way, the mutual acknowledgement of the healer and the royal family was conveyed to the public.[22]

Inasmuch as the monarchy can be said to represent CAM as religion there, it is in a complex relationship with religion everywhere as mediatized communication: In 2012, the newspaper *Dagbladet* revealed that the king and queen had for years used CAM, in the form of acupuncturist and homeopath Tony Venbakken. The news covered the larger part of the front page, and was a two-page main article inside the paper where the editors as a side story reminded their readers that royal family members also talk to angels (Märtha Louise) and travel to India "in search of the meaning of life" together with meditation guru Sharon Myoshin Kelley (Mette-Marit). "The royal family is known for having liberal views on CAM and alternative lifestyles," the newspaper stated. The mentioned trip by the Crown princess to India in 2012 generated a stir when it reached the public. However, after the Low Church representatives had had their fling, the stir faded, Buddhist meditation generally being considered too respectable and noble, perhaps, to function as a "safe target" for the critics.[23]

Religion here—CAM as "cult of the family"

Gilhus (2013, 42) holds that there is little research on domestic religion ("religion here") in Norway, except on death and rituals in the graveyards. She adds that saying grace and evening prayers are examples of contemporary domestic religion, but this spatial category of religion is viewed as rather unexplored. However, returning to Smith's original "framing" of the category of "religion here," we could loosen the ties between the official religion of "there" (civic, imperial religion in antique Rome, turned national church in contemporary Norway) and the religion of the "here" as church-related in Norway, as Smith (2003, 24) holds that this form of religion is "concerned with the endurance of the family as a social and biological entity, as

---

20. http://www.aftenposten.no/nyheter/kongelige/Mette-Marit---Jeg-ble-helbredet-av-Mrtha-Louise-6475376.html.

21. http://www.vl.no/kultur/her-er-mette-marits-salmer-1.46918.

22. http://www.dagbladet.no/2010/09/17/nyheter/snasamannen/overtro/healing/13432592/.

23. See also Døving and Kraft 2013, 31.

a community, as well as with the relations of that community." CAM practices, of varying spiritual relevance, can indeed be seen as domestic religion
and as part of a "cult of the family."

Family Constellations and Spiritualist, domestic therapies

In Norway, more women than men use CAM (49.2 % versus 32.2 %).[24]
Traditionally, women are the ones taking care of the health and well-being of
the family. When a parent, especially a mother, uses CAM, one could expect
such use to be transferred to the children as well, if the adults believe the
treatment to be effective and/or existentially meaningful. Comprehensive
numbers are difficult to find, but various, limited studies show that parents
do seek CAM for their children,[25] and these practices may have a spiritual
dimension. There are, also, CAM practices that to some extent "sanctify"
the family and family ties (including former generations and generations
to come), as with the specific CAM therapy called "Family Constellation"
therapy. In Kalvig 2013[26] I discuss this therapy as a systemic perspective on
suffering, closely connected to the notion of original sin (the creator of Family Constellations, Bert Hellinger (1925–) is an ordained Catholic priest and
former missionary, in addition to being a psychotherapist). To a greater or
lesser extent, various techniques following Hellinger identify a kind of "love
energy" or "Movements of the Spirit-Mind" manifesting itself throughout
a family (past, present and future), a kind of energy that it is important to
identify and address in order to understand the dynamics of the family and
its challenges. The Hellinger Institute presents its teaching today as highly
"cosmic" and transcendental,[27] whereas Family Constellation in its Norwegian variant is presented like this by one provider (author's questions in
italics):

> A child may take on disease out of blind love—a disease that perhaps its
> grandfather died from. *Why so?* Yes, why? Out of love, but it is blind love,
> bad conscience for the suffering of others; children do that: "if only
> mum will be happy," it is something hovering in the ethers, in the space.
> *Children are, you say, able to take on disease out of a childish, naïve desire to
> help?* It is unconscious; it is something that hovers in a family system.[28]

---

24. http://nifab.no/hva_er_alternativ_behandling/tall_og_fakta/nafkam_under-
soekelsen_2014.

25. See for example http://www.medicalnewstoday.com/releases/271108.php, and
http://www.bt.no/familie-og-oppvekst-old/Desperate-smabarnsforeldre-soker-til-
det-alternative-3121432.html.

26. Kalvig 2013, 205–211.

27. See for example: http://www2.hellinger.com/en/home/cosmic-power/family-con-
stellation-and-cosmic-powerr/.

28. Kalvig 2013, 205, my translation from Norwegian.

In Family Constellation therapy, the domestic sphere and the unit of the family is given deep, existential, cosmic and spiritual relevance. Another "domestic" variant of CAM fulfilling the criteria for "religion here" might be spiritist-oriented therapy; that is, spiritualism in its family—in-house—and dwelling-focused variants (see also Kalvig's chapter in this book). Spiritualist practices and products easily bring us over to the "religion anywhere" and "religion everywhere" categories. However, "religion here" seems appropriate, when spiritualism tends towards ancestor worship and "women's work" (Day 2012)—when revolving around the healing of family wounds beyond death (the therapeutic outcome of mediumistic communication), and when it is something done in solitarily and/or with family members along, mentioned or prayed for. This is the case in the Facebook distant healing and communication with the dead site provided by medium Anita-Helen Rasmussen, where participants write the names of family members they want to be included in the healing and greetings from the dead.[29] House cleansing as mediumistic and spiritualist practice also borders on CAM as "religion here," inasmuch as it deals with the health and well-being of those dwelling in a haunted house.

Spiritual items and arrangements with therapeutic effect on house and family

Finally, I will add a few examples of a more inert kind of CAM *qua* "religion here," namely the use of various, religious-spiritual items and the arrangement of these in people's houses, believed to promote good health, balance, harmony with the universe and so forth. One such "material" or concrete variant of CAM as religion here are crystals and semiprecious stones placed and arranged in a home. Within the alternative therapeutic tradition and New Age, stones are considered to have healing qualities. As one Norwegian crystal healer puts it:

> Stones and crystals are part of the light or energy of the universe [...] The energy waves from the stones and crystals influence our energy field [...] The frequencies create balance in our bodies, and when we have reached perfect balance, we are healed. Some stones and crystals contain frequencies and colors that connect with spiritual areas, and through them we increase our sensitivity to the supernatural and strengthen our contact with our spiritual guides.[30]

Simple examples of domestic uses of crystals might be: Rose quartz on or by television sets, computers and decoders in order to neutralize unhealthy radiation affecting those dwelling in the house; rock crystals anywhere to channel pure energy into the home; moonstone under a woman's sleeping pillow to help her conceive; citrine on a young student's desk to promote

---

29. See Kalvig 2014 for a mediatization theory-informed analysis of Facebook healing and spiritualism as "transgressive belonging."

30. http://www.larsrolle.net/Steinbeskrivelser/krystallerinformasjon.htm, my translation from Norwegian.

concentration and learning. Additionally, perhaps, stones arranged in small "altars" or displays to attract whatever positive, cosmic qualities they are thought to represent—as well as beautifying the home. Also, crystals and stones may be part of more elaborate ritual performances in the home intended for health and healing, as is also the case with a great variety of other therapeutic techniques available for people to perform privately, for example with the guidance from oracle cards or spiritual self-help literature. The enormous number of books available and present in many homes, of the DIY spirituality and CAM kind, represent a vital, lasting "input" of "religion here." In Norway, the New Age book club *Energica* has existed for 25 years and is still a success, in spite of the harsh competition that traditional book clubs have experienced from online bookstores.

Another, more widely known CAM in the house decoration area and hence "religion here" is, of course, Feng Shui. Feng Shui is a Chinese tradition of "how to balance the energies of any given space to assure health and good fortune for people inhabiting it," as explained by Feng Shui expert Rodika Tchi.[31] In the Norwegian fengshuiforum.no one underscores the spiritual content of the practice: "Feng Shui is like a flower, which in our materialist era has started unfolding its petals, one by one, formed and supported by spiritual impulses all over our planet."[32] Feng Shui is a good example of CAM as domestic religion, with, as in many of the phenomena hitherto presented, connections to other fields and areas, for example "religion anywhere" and "religion everywhere." One last magical item illustrate the "religion here" kind of CAM, namely a piece of cloth for purchase by the aforementioned healer and medium Anita Helen Rasmussen. This cloth, nothing but a piece of fabric, is called "healing cloth," and is meant to be used by an individual or a family to extract pain and disease, and to attract good health in the body part where the cloth is placed. The cloth has been "invested" with Rasmussen's healing energy, channeled into it before being sold and given, or mailed, to a recipient. The cloth has a special family story to it; Rasmussen as a child learnt from her father that what saved him from a bleeding ulcer as a young man was a similar cloth, sent from the U.S. to Norway. Knowledge about the American cloth was obtained during a visit in the U.S., where Rasmussen's family had met a Christian, charismatic preacher, who provided such healing or prayer cloths.[33] They had him send one of them when Rasmussen's father had his health crisis back in Norway.

---

31. http://fengshui.about.com/od/thebasics/qt/fengshui.htm.

32. http://www.fengshuiforum.no/, my translation from Norwegian.

33. Such cloths seem common within Pentecostal congregations (and, earlier, Mormons as well) in the USA, see http://www.materialreligion.org/journal/handkerchief. html. As one website providing such cloths states: "Prayer cloths originated as an old practice of spreading prayers that can be found throughout Christian history and in the Bible. Traditionally prayer cloths were taken from the clothing of the

CAM as religion anywhere

"Religion anywhere"—the spatial category characterized by "small-scale entrepreneurs and by client and audience cults" (Gilhus 2013, 42) is of course the most commonly known and obvious "place" for CAM practices and practitioners of more or less spiritual relevance. CAM enterprises comprise a flourishing field in Norway. However, figures for exactly *how many* who offer CAM, their background, gender, age, religious/spiritual adherence etc., are not available. The reason why is that there is no obligation to register one's CAM enterprise, no obligation of membership in CAM practitioner organizations, and no need for specific education or certification to practice within the CAM field.[34] Approximately 3100 practitioners are registered in the "CAM Practitioner Register" of the Brønnøysund Register Centre (a government body consisting of several different national computerized registers), but this is voluntary and not representative of the number of actual practitioners.[35] Estimates on numbers of alternative therapists and CAM practitioners are therefore highly suggestive, and range between 15000 and 3500 in 2011 (Kalvig 2011, 47). Considering the fact that a large number of therapists might be working in many different non-CAM professions in addition to being CAM providers part-time, it is not possible to reach a conclusion on numbers. Also, as we have seen with the examples of practices thus far placed in the various spatial categories, what is meant by alternative medicine and therapy is diverse. Instead, the general interest in the public is more of a clue, and nearly half the population has used some form of CAM.

An example of a spiritual therapist and of authorized health personnel in the same (New Age) market

Thus far, I have wanted to show that New Age as CAM has found its way into the "religion there" and "religion here" categories, as well as in the form of "religion anywhere" and "religion everywhere" (see below). Since the CAM of the "religion anywhere" is such a large and highly varied category, I will only give a short presentation of one alternative therapist from my study of views of life among alternative therapists in Norway (Kalvig 2013), as a characterization of an actor in this spatial category of "religion anywhere." I will also provide a couple of examples of how authorized health personnel have

---

and apostles, even Jesus Christ Himself. These prayer cloths or "handkerchiefs" were believed to have the power of Jesus flowing through them": http://sending-troopsprayers.bravehost.com/. See e.g. http://www.doveministries.com/content/how-receive-healing-using-prayer-cloth; http://orders.rodparsley.com/Order_First.aspx?ostr=ZC%2F1DobEHtQ%3D.

34. http://www.nifab.no/hva_er_alternativ_behandling/om_bransjen. Note that nifab. no does not mention religion/spirituality in their discussion of the CAM industry and practitioners.

35. http://www.nifab.no/lov_og_rett/utoeverregisteret_i_broennoeysund.

entered the same space, contributing to a sense of intricate webs in the field of CAM and religion, rather than a clear-cut, fourfold spatiality.

This alternative therapist—we will call her Tora—is now in her sixties. Born and raised in a little industrial village in Norway, she decided to study to become a teacher, in the mid-Norwegian city of Trondheim. One of her earliest encounters with the field of alternative spirituality and therapy was the pioneering couple Benedicte and Harald Thiis and their New Age center, the Mandala Center, in Trondheim in the 1970s—a contact initially established via mutual friends in the Bahá'í movement. Later on, Tora travelled to stay in the New Age community Findhorn, Scotland, for a period, in addition to several trips to and retreats in India, Nepal and Tibet. Having profound spiritual experiences during these travels, Tora decided to postpone her teacher education to start studying at a *Naturheilschule* in Germany; that is, to become a naturopath and acupuncturist. She started practicing as such in Norway in the 1980s. Tora later discovered regression therapy, and felt it to be spiritually rewarding in a more profound sense than those more physically-oriented practices from her German education. She started a regression therapist education held by Lisbeth Lyngaas, a woman who herself had gotten to know regression therapy by taking part in a tv program (TV Norge) called "A Soul's Travel," in which psychologist Rune Amundsen (who lost his psychologist authorization) led people to alleged former lives via hypnosis. Tora now offers regression therapy, acupuncture, mineral and vitamin therapy, healing and dream reading as a solitary practitioner in a building that houses several CAM providers and therapists—some of them authorized health personnel, some of them not. Tora has thus been an actor on the CAM-oriented scene of "religion anywhere" for nearly forty years.

Quite a few authorized health practitioners—mainly nurses and midwives, but physicians as well—also offer various alternative therapies and medicine outside of the public sector. This contributes to blurred lines between conventional and alternative medicine, in Norway as elsewhere in the Western world (see also Partridge 2005, 22ff), as does the offering of CAM within hospitals and the public health service. An example of authorized health personnel gone alternative are a team of three midwives who are behind the enterprise "Mamastork," which gives private pregnancy checkups and classes in the city of Stavanger in southwestern Norway. The three work part-time as midwives at the University hospital of Stavanger, and part-time in Mamastork, where they offer acupuncture and hypnotherapy as well as conventional obstetric procedures. On their web pages, they list various collaborators, among them an acupuncturist, a massage clinic and a "childbirth educator," who provides a whole range of alternative therapies.[36] As registered health personnel, the women behind Mamastork provide (medical) legitimacy to these wider circles of alternative therapy enterprises.

---

36. http://www.mamastork.no/samarbeid.htm.

Two medical doctors illustrate how this trend is not limited to the feminine area of midwifery and nursing: Well-known general practitioner, specialist, author and teacher of medicine at University of Oslo, Stig Bruset, heads up the private clinic "The Rainbow Health Center" (Regnbuen Helsesenter) outside the city of Drammen. It has become highly popular, and focuses on preventive medicine in addition to acupuncture, massage, various forms of training in yoga, pilates and Qi Gong. Bruset and his team's vision is to run a "health center focusing on integrated health, interdisciplinary cooperation and prevention of life style illnesses," and to rent out premises for private practitioners within the fields of psychotherapy, massage, and coaching. Chief physician Audun Myskja is perhaps even more renowned, and leads the private "Center for Life Help" (Senter for livshjelp) in Ski, a small town. He has been one of the central characters on the alternative spirituality scene in Norway for decades, and on his center's web pages, the famous Irish healer Bob Moore is listed as a mentor. Myskja has published a wide range of books within the alternative health and self-development field; his latest book is entitled *The Art of Dying* (*Kunsten å dø*, Myskja 2012), with the telling subtitle: "Life before and after death in a new light." In 2013, I participated in a spiritualist medium congress where Myskja was invited, and spoke of his experiences with patients' deaths and dying processes, as well as his own (NDE, Near-Death-Experience, that is), with emphasis on spiritual, metaphysical and existential connections and consequences. Bruset and Myskja thus epitomize and expand the tendency of identifying with holistic health and mind-body-spirit-practices, widely held in the field of nursing (Johannessen 2006), within the medical profession. They are fewer in numbers, but all the more famous.

Religion everywhere—holistic health and "energy-paradigm" as mediatized, cultural ideas

"Religion everywhere" as communication about religion (cf. Gilhus and Kraft's Introduction in this book) and as the flow of information on and within religious and spiritual communities and fields, are closely connected to the "religion anywhere" category. A lot of what takes place within the "religion anywhere" category—and the other two categories as well—is intertwined with changes in communication technology over the past several decades, and the globalized, freer floating ideas, practices and persons. "Religion everywhere" as mediatized religion (Gilhus 2013, 40) is an interesting category in relation to CAM. The former categories I have exemplified with concrete people and practices. Discussing alternative medicine as religion via spatial categories, I have chosen to focus on the empirical field instead of on media debates on and theorizing of CAM in culture—all of which might be said to belong to CAM as "religion everywhere."

We may identify CAM and its various, related worldviews as cultural communication and as media use, with mutual influence and formation.

Alternative, medical and therapeutic communication is far from esoteric; it is "shouted out loud" on every corner of the internet, from the (online) bookstore shelves, in advertising, and within entertainment industry— though often more implicitly in the latter arena. Consider, e.g., what spiritual/ideal views on health, body-mind-spirit, medical possibilities, civilization criticism and visions of a sustainable future are conveyed in a global blockbuster like the movie *Avatar* by James Cameron (2009); how healing by elves are the preferred way of saving the main characters in the *Lord of the Rings* (2001–2003) and *Hobbit* (2012–2014) trilogies, both by Peter Jackson; or how health and the possibilities of new technology and transgression into other dimensions are communicated to children through an animation success like *Big Hero 6* by Don Hell and Chris Williams (2014), to name only a few.

The communicated ideas and practices about CAM influence how media remediates the subject, and influences how the field further develops. As the Salomonsen *et al.* (2011) study put it, when explaining the relatively rapid increase in the use of CAM at hospitals:

> This could indicate that the health personnel's main motives for introducing the modalities—"interest from the employees, treatment without side effects, interest from patients" are stronger than arguments based on evidence/no evidence and arguments based on lack of knowledge about safety. These arguments follow the societal tendencies among patients toward an extensive demand for more natural-based therapies [...][37]

Analyzing CAM as "religion everywhere," I believe the last few words from the NAFKAM report quote to be central: "extensive demand for more natural-based therapies." The idea of good health as something natural, and the "natural" as inherently good, harmonic and progressive, connects with wider circles of contemporary spirituality as well as the contemporary eco-movement and various counter-cultural trends and social movements— perhaps with conspirituality at the (right wing) end of a spectrum here (see Dyrendal's chapter). The relative success of mediatized CAM as "religion everywhere" depends on the solid foothold of the notion(s) of holism in Norwegian culture and society—as in many places elsewhere—understood as something more natural, ecologically sustainable and future-oriented concerning health. If the "canopy" of CAM in this respect is *holism*, its various manifestations may be bundled together with the notion of *energy*. Holism and energy, when mediated, are flexible enough to contain both spirituality and materiality, religion and science, and provide clues to their success as a New Age key symbol (cf. Mikaelsson 2004, 2013), also permeating cultural communications outside of core CAM areas.

---

37. Salomonsen *et al.* 2011, 7.

Alternative medicine as religion in different places

Summing up, where does a modelling of CAM in terms of the spatial religion-notion lead us? It has made possible a more general portrayal of how CAM can be discerned as religion (when involving spiritual aspects) in various places of Norwegian socio-cultural reality, whereas other perspectives easily would have led to more limited sketches. With respect to religion there, here, anywhere and everywhere in the field of CAM, both CAM *as* (or resembling) religion, and its various *spheres of activities* (as religion or religion-like), have been possible to thematize. At the beginning of this chapter, I asked whether it was meaningful to categorize CAM as religion, and by using Gilhus and Mikaelsson's (2001) definition of religion as communication with and about superhuman beings and forces, I continued with a programmatic notion of CAM practices involving such communication as being relevant and legitimate to include in this overview.

The spatiality of religion, following Smith/Gilhus, makes possible an "explicit and comprehensive model of religion" (Gilhus 2013, 47), better suited, I believe, to covering shifting empirical realities than metaphorical notions of implicit religion, invisible religion, absorbed religion, etc.. Medicine and therapy involving spiritual communication may well be labelled religion—or New Age religion—and via categories of space, we may find it in far more places than we might have expected in the beginning. CAM is in many ways a difficult field to grasp for the historian of religion, being as it is, at times, quite concrete, "magical," concerned with hopes and objectives for the here and now, and for bodily functions and familial affairs. As such, CAM as religion often comes very close to the "lived religion" notion (McGuire 2008, Ammerman 2014) of people's everyday experience, a mixture of many things, (spiritually) meaningful according to one's experiencing, practicing and relating. Therefore, CAM "as religion" as outlined in this chapter may well come close to "non-religion" *also*, for example to those seeking even the most "spiritually" solemn CAM—and not "believing" in it, but seeking it only for the physical effect one expects, experiences or hopes for.

References

Ahlin, Lars. 2007. *Krop, sind—eller ånd? Alternative behandlere og spiritualitet i Danmark.* Gylling: Forlaget Univers.

Ammerman, Nancy T. 2014. *Sacred Stories, Spiritual Tribes: Finding Religion in Everyday Life.* Oxford: Oxford University Press.

Børtnes, Jostein, S. E. Kraft and L. Mikaelsson, eds. 2004. *Kampen om kroppen: Kulturanalytiske blikk på kropp, helse, kjønn og seksualitet.* Kristiansand: Høyskoleforlaget.

Day, Abby. 2012. "Extraordinary relationality: Ancestor veneration in late Euro-American society." In *Nordic Journal of Religion and Society* 25(2): 169–181.

Dyrendal, Asbjørn, O. Pettersen and D. Søderlind, eds. 2006. *Åpent sinn eller høl i huet?* Oslo: Humanist forlag.

Døving, Cora A. and S. E. Kraft. 2013. *Religion i pressen.* Oslo: University Publishing House.

Engedal, Leif Gunnar and T. A. Sveinall, eds. 2000. *Troen er løs: Bidrag til belysning av forholdet mellom folkereligiøsitet, nyreligiøsitet og kristen tro.* Trondheim: Egede Institutt Tapir.

Frisk, Liselotte and P. Åkerbäck. 2013. *Den mediterande dalahästen.* Stockholm: Dialogos.

Gilhus, Ingvild S. 2013. "'All over the place': The contribution of New Age to a spatial model of religion." In *New Age Spirituality: Rethinking Religion,* edited by Steven J. Sutcliffe and Ingvild Sælid Gilhus, 35–49. Durham: Acumen.

Gilhus, Ingvild S. and L. Mikaelsson. 2001. *Nytt blikk på religion: Studiet av religion i dag.* Oslo: Pax Forlag.

Grønlien Zetterqvist, Kirsten and G. Skeie. 2014. "Religion i skolen; her, der og hvor-som-helst?" In *Norsk pedagogisk tidsskrift* 5: 305–315.

Hanegraaff, Wouter J. 1996. *New Age Religion and Western Culture: Esotericism in the Mirror of Secular Thought.* Leiden: Brill.

Heelas, Paul and L. Woodhead. 2005. *The Spiritual Revolution: Why Religion Is Giving Way to Spirituality.* Malden, MA: Blackwell Publishing.

Henriksen, Anni M. 2010. *Å stoppe blod: Fortellinger om læsing, helbredelse, varsler og hjelpere.* Oslo: Cappelen Damm.

Hjarvard, Stig. 2008. "The mediatization of religion. A theory of the media as agents of religious change." *Northern Lights* 6: 9–26.

Johannessen, Berit. 2006. "Sykepleiere i alternativ behandling: Hvorfor velger offentlig godkjente sykepleiere å tilby alternativ behandling?" Unpublished PhD thesis, University of Bergen.

Kalvig, Anne. 2011. "Åndeleg helse: Ein kulturanalytisk studie av menneske- og livssyn hos alternative terapeutar." Unpublished PhD thesis, University of Bergen.

———. 2012. "Alternativ folkemedisin? Om røter og nye skot på det sørvestlandske, holistiske helsefeltet." *Tidsskrift for kulturforskning* 11(2): 45–62.

———. 2013. *Åndeleg helse: Livssyn og menneskesyn hos alternative terapeutar.* Kristiansand: Cappelen Damm Akademisk.

———. 2014. "Overskridande tilhøyrsle: healing og dødekontakt via Facebook." *Aura. Tidskrift för akademiska studier av nyreligiositet* 6: 113–144.

———. 2015. "Frå New Age til nyåndelegheit: Praktisert nyreligiøsitet gjennom seksti år." In *Levende Religion: Globalt Perspektiv, Lokal Praksis,* edited by Anne Kalvig and A. R. Solevåg, 154–173. Stavanger: Hertervig Akademisk.

Kalvig, Anne and A. R. Solevåg, eds. 2015. *Levende religion: Globalt perspektiv, lokal praksis.* Stavanger: Hertervig Akademisk.

Kraft, Siv Ellen. 2000. "New Age, sykdom og kroppsbilder i endring" In *Troen er løs: Bidrag til belysning av forholdet mellom folkereligiøsitet, nyreligiøsitet og kris ten tro*, edited by Leif Gunnar Engedal and T. A. Sveinall, 41–54. Trondheim: Egede Institutt Tapir.

————. 2004. "Alternativ medisin i Norge: Et kritisk blikk på nyere forskning og offentlige strategier." *Din. Tidsskrift for religion og kultur* 4: 3–11.

————. 2006. "Medisin eller religion? Nafkam og det nyreligiøse landskapet." In *Åpent sinn eller høl i huet?*, edited by Asbjørn Dyrendal, O. Pettersen and D. Søderlind, 175–200. Oslo: Humanist forlag.

————. 2011. *Hva er nyreligiøsitet?* Oslo: University Publishing House.

Lavik, Marta Høyland. 2015. "'Forsvinn i Jesu namn!' Om sjukdom, bibelbruk og impulsar frå global trusteologi." In *Levende Religion: Globalt Perspektiv, Lokal Praksis*, edited by Anne Kalvig and A. R. Solevåg, 192–211. Stavanger: Hertervig Akademisk.

Lövheim, Mia. 2011. "Mediatisation of religion: A critical appraisal." *Culture and Religion*,12 (2).153–166.

Lundby, Knut, ed. 2009. *Mediatization: Concepts, Changes, Consequences*. New York: Peter Lang.

McGuire, Meredith. 2008. *Lived Religion: Faith and Practice in Everyday Life*. Oxford University Press.

Mikaelsson, Lisbeth. 2004. "Den holistiske energikroppen." In *Kampen om kroppen: Kulturanalytiske blikk på kropp, helse, kjønn og seksualitet*, edited by Jostein Børtnes, S. E. Kraft and L. Mikaelsson, 365–396. Kristiansand: Høyskoleforlaget.

————. 2013. "New Age and the spirit of capitalism: energy as cognitive currency." In *New Age Spirituality: Rethinking Religion*, edited by Steven J. Sutcliffe and Ingvild Sælid Gilhus, 160–173. Durham: Acumen.

Myskja, Audun. 2012. *Kunsten å dø: Livet før og etter døden i et nytt lys*. Oslo: Stenersen Forlag.

Noegel, Scott, J. Walker and B. Wheeler, eds. 2003. *Prayer, Magic, and the Stars in the Ancient and Late Antique World*. University Park: The Pennsylvania State University Press.

Partridge, Christopher. 2005. *The Re-Enchantment of the West, Vol 2*. London: T&T Clark International.

Salomonsen, Laila J., *et al.* 2011. "Use of complementary and alternative medicine at Norwegian and Danish hospitals." *BMC Complementary & Alternative Medicine* 11(4): 1–8.

Smith, Jonathan Z. 2003. "Here, there, and anywhere." In *Prayer, Magic, and the Stars in the Ancient and Late Antique World*, edited by Scott Noegel, J. Walker and B. Wheeler, 21–36. University Park: The Pennsylvania State University Press.

Sutcliffe, Steven and I. S. Gilhus, eds. 2013. *New Age Spirituality: Rethinking Religion*. Durham: Acumen .

Trym Mathiassen, Silje. 2015. "Det er i møtet vi lever, beveger oss og er til: dialogarbeid som religiøs praksis." In *Levende Religion: Globalt Perspektiv, Lokal Praksis*, edited by Anne Kalvig and A. R. Solevåg, 276–295. Stavanger: Hertervig Akademisk.

— 7 —

Angels:
Between Secularization and Re-enchantment

INGVILD SÆLID GILHUS

Introduction

Angels travel light. They seldom bring with them more luggage than that they can slip through the masks of the cultural net. Angels are cultural constructions that are continually reimagined and "easily transformed into vehicles for present-day concerns" (Hobson 2011, 180). Appearing in a secular context, their religious origin contributes to making them attractive (Hobson 2011, 9). When, for instance, angels are used to promote Christmas sales, they tap into the Season's spirit of love and willingness to give, both of which have strong Christian connotations.

The notion of angels has undergone several cultural transformations across time. In Christian theology, they are subordinate to god and appear as his messengers, as they did in the ancient Near East.[1] But the different spectacular and hybrid varieties known from the bible and the ancient world long ago left their monstrosities behind and are now appearing visually as beautiful humans with wings. When people have angel experiences, the wings are frequently lacking, and the apparitions they describe look like humans (cf. Muehlberger 2013, 18).

The biblical and globalized world of angels reached Norway during the Christianization of the country more than thousand years ago. In the later part of the twentieth century, a second wave of globalized angels settled. This new wave has strong roots in the so-called "American angel craze" where ideas from several Christian denominations were mixed (Gardella

---

1. The term for messenger is *malakh* in Hebrew, which is translated in the Septuagint as *aggelos* (Greek).

2007).[2] While angels are usually tied to a specific religious universe and get their richness and depth from this universe, they may also operate independently and change from being intermediate and subordinate—messengers between the world of god/gods and the world of humans, to become agents in their own right. In the contemporary New Age, angels tend to appear more like companions to humans than messengers from gods.

Versatility clearly belongs to the *modus operandi* of angels and it works in many directions—geographically, historically, linguistically, and across the religious/secular divide,[3] contributing to making these cultural constructs successful and useful. This also implies that angels are part of several spaces and are often thought of in spatial categories. In times of religious change, their versatility sometimes gets them into trouble. In Norway, a traditional Lutheran angel discourse today opposes a corresponding New Age discourse. These discourses influence each other and have in their turn given rise to a discourse of contestation. In this chapter we will identify and map the discourses and spaces of angels in a historical perspective and as they are currently developing in Norway.

Spaces for angels

Norwegian church buildings have not been stripped as ruthlessly of their images as churches in some other countries, so there are still pictures of angels in many of them.[4] Some of the post-Reformation angels in Norway consist of head and wings; they appear as children or look like women (Wang 1986, 84). Angels are further depicted on monuments in churchyards, and they are abundantly present in hymns used during the liturgical year.

The most important area for angels is probably childhood, where these beings have been able to live on relatively undisturbed. The angels of childhood exist in pictures and prayers, children's scrapbooks, and Christmas celebrations where they appear in hymns and decorations. Their rootedness in childhood is also expressed in the special connection between dead children and angels, shown in epitaphs and funeral announcements.

The Church of Norway has upheld the traditional connection between angels and children, especially through Sunday schools, and primary schools have also employed angels as pedagogical instruments. These are institu-

---

2. The esoteric use of intermediary beings in Norway is not treated in this article (cf. Asprem 2014).

3. Terhi Utriainen stresses that "angels" is a complex and unstable category (Utriainen 2013, 244).

4. According to Peter Marshall and Alexandra Walsham, there "is an evident contrast to be drawn here between Lutheran Germany and Scandinavia, which generally tolerated the continued presence of their churches of medieval Catholic imagery and the more iconoclastic impulses which prevailed in the Reformed territories of Switzerland, England or the Netherlands" (Marshall and Walsham 2006, 16).

tional spaces for religion.[5] Through personal information I have learnt how angels were used as pedagogical instruments in the fifties to teach Christian faith. One example is a school-class which was asked to draw pictures of two angels, each of them carrying a basket up to God, one with prayers of thanksgivings, the other filled with prayers for getting something. The first basket was light, the second quite heavy. In this lesson, the angels did what they were meant to do, acted as messengers between humans and God and functioned in line with the Scriptures.[6] One of the boys drew the basket of thanksgiving much bigger than the other, which, of course, immediately made the drawing into a failure. He had internalized the theological message correctly, that god was good and humans were ungrateful, but it came out quite wrong in the drawing.

In homes, angels have especially been connected to children's bedrooms, to evening prayers and to pictures over the beds with angels who watch over children so that they do not fall down from a cliff or a bridge. The connection between children and angels in the home has found new expressions today on personal blogs, for instance as pictures of sleeping children cast as angels (cf. Endsjø and Lied 2011, 145–146). Angels are intimately connected to childhood and combine the roles of caretakers and watchers over the morals of children.

We will pause for a moment and introduce a spatial model of religion and consider the conceptions and practices related to angels in accordance with the model. It is based on Jonathan Z. Smith's model of religion in the Roman Empire with religion "here," "there" and "anywhere" (Smith 2003). "Religion here" is domestic religion found in homes and burial sites; "religion there" is national and imperial religion in temples; and "religion anywhere" is religion between these spaces in the form of religious entrepreneurs, cults and associations. In this chapter, the model is transferred to contemporary religion and one space is added, "religion everywhere." Today this space is strong and takes the form of "mediatization" of religion (Hjarvard 2008, cf. Gilhus 2013, 38–40, and the Introduction to this book).

Angels are part of the religious spaces of "here" (homes) and "there" (institutional spaces of church/Sunday schools and primary schools). When angels appear in the spaces of "there" and "here," they are confined to the church-room, the churchyard and the bedroom of children. They are mediated by the texts of the bible, the hymns of the congregation, children's prayers as well as by statues and pictures.

---

5. In Norway, the angelology of anthroposophy may have had an influence on the general conception of angels (cf. Steiner 2008; Walther 2002). There are 34 Steiner schools and 35 Steiner kindergartens in the country, which means that the Norwegian Steiner school movement is the biggest in the world, relative to population density. The connection between children and angels is important in anthroposophy (cf. Gilhus 2012, 238; 243, n.5).

6. The angels in the *Revelation of John* carried prayers from humans to God (5:8; 8:3).

During the last decades of the last century, angels broke loose from their allocated spaces of "here" and "there" to occur abundantly in the spaces of "anywhere" and "everywhere," which means that they currently, to a greater degree than before, appear in various media ("everywhere") and among religious entrepreneurs who use them to set up business ("anywhere"). The connection between the spaces of "everywhere" (media) and "anywhere" (religious entrepreneurs) is strong, and interacts with the two other spaces as is suggested below.

This also implies that angels changed, as superhuman constructs always do, because they are dependent on historical circumstances and cultural context. Angels have been part of several discourses. In Norway today, there is, as mentioned, an international New Age discourse about angels as companions and helpers, and a Christian discourse about angels as messengers and guardians. There is further a theological angel discourse of contestation. In this last discourse, theological positions are developed in relation to contemporary concerns and in opposition to the New Age discourse, and brought into alignmnent with the Scriptures.[7] These three discourses are described below.

The New Age discourse on angels as companions and helpers

Ideas and practices focussing on angels and self-development are distributed worldwide in popular culture, religion and commerce. In religions, angels are part of therapies where healing is dependent on communication with them. Norwegian spiritual entrepreneurs contribute to this distribution as well. A typical advertisement for a seminar states (my translation):

> Meet your Angels. Communication and healing with your angels. A seminar that gives you powerful tools to communicate and heal with your angels. Everyone can learn it in a weekend, thanks to comprehensive magical initiations, which give you immediate and powerful results![8]

The expression "your angels" is used three times in this advertisement. It underlines the closeness to and ownership of angels which the seminar promises to the participants. The idea that everyone has her/his personal angel is also found in the most famous application of angels in recent years in Norway. In 2007, Princess Märtha Louise and Elisabeth Nordeng (formerly Samnøy) founded Astarte Education (later Astarte Inspiration, now

---

7. The idea of angels and theological contestation is borrowed from Muehlberger, who has recently written about angels in late antiquity (cf. Muehlberger 2013, 9, 23, 213–214).

8. "Møt dine Engler. Kommunikasjon og healing med dine Engler. Et seminar som gir deg kraftfulle verktøy for å kommunisere og helbrede med dine engler. Alle kan lære dette på en weekend takket være omfattende magiske innvielser som gir deg umiddelbare og kraftfulle resultater!" (www.wanvig.no/engler 8.09.2014).

Soulspring Education), often called "the angel school" (cf. Kraft's chapter).[9] The two entrepreneurs offer courses on angels, publish books about angels, participate in international angel-conferences and in Norwegian alternative belief fairs, and appear in interviews. The angels function in this case as an emblem for several central New Age ideas, for instance holism, healing and the power of thought.

In 2009, the Princess and Elisabeth Nordeng published their first book, *Møt din skytsengel: En innføring i å møte din unike kraft* ("Meet your guardian angel: An introduction in meeting your unique power," my translation).[10] The cover of the book is a blue sky with some clouds and a huge white wing. In the upper right corner is printed *Engleskolen* ("the angel school"). The book is about spirituality and the universal power of love. It offers "spiritual tools" which can be used across religions; chief among them are meditations, and it encourages everyone to find their unique spiritual way (2009, 9). The book's message is that one should be present in one's body, keep the aura at appropriate distance from it, not be invaded by the energies of others, be connected with the earth and the universe and invite angels into one's life. According to the authors, angels can be sensed in several ways, in terms of sound, light, taste, smell, feeling and colour (2009, 164).[11] This flexibility also corresponds very well with the space of "anywhere," which this and similar approaches to angels contribute to producing.

At the same time as these angels function as condensed symbols for New Age ideas and practices, they are also grounded in the traditional close association between angels and childhood. Elisabeth Nordeng connects angels to her childhood experience of a fantasy-friend (2009, 169); the illustrations in the chapter about angels are mainly of angels as material objects somehow connected to children and childhood (an angel scrap, an angel in the snow, a gingerbread tin in the shape of an angel) (160–181), and there are references to childhood prayers with angels (181). In other words, these angels are, for all their obvious New Age associations, also firmly anchored in the emotional landscape of childhood and in the "here" dimension of religion. The picture on the cover reflects that the sky/heaven is still the place of angels.

The two authors' conception of angels further illustrates a general tendency of New Age spirituality, which is to synonymize. Angels are described as universal beings that exist in almost all religions. In addition to angels in Christian, Jewish and Islamic traditions, devas in India, *amesha spentas*,

---

9. The school offers a three-year educational program, but also shorter courses and seminars.

10. The book has been published in English with the title *The Spiritual Password: Learn to Unlock Your Spiritual Power* (2014).

11. In their second book about angels, *Englenes hemmeligheter: Deres natur, språk og hvordan du åpner opp for dem* ("The secrets of the angels: their nature, language and how you open up to them") (2012), seven angels, each with its personal name, are described.

yazatas and *fravashis* in ancient Iranian religion are described as the same as angels (Märtha Louise and Samnøy 2009, 160).[12] Another tendency is to translate the concept of "angel" into a higher-level abstraction, and to speak of angels as energies or powers (cf. Mikaelsson 2013). The two authors describe a guardian angel as "an aspect of the universal power of love" (Märtha Louise and Samnøy 2009, 161, my translation).[13] The synonymization and the abstraction facilitate the use of angels and angel therapies across religions, and helps integrate basic New Age ideas and practices with conceptions of angels.[14] The authors open up the panorama of angel conceptions in New Age spirituality since they are seen as guides and helpers, as actual beings with wings, and as abstractions.

The international character of New Age ideas and angel practices was clearly seen on June 6th 2012, when the Princess and Elisabeth Nordeng arranged "A Night with the Angels" in Oslo Concert Hall, together with Doreen Virtue. Virtue is an American author and spiritual entrepreneur, famous for her books on angels, angel cards and angel therapy. She is one of a handful of international experts on angels who travel between countries and teach and sell items connected to angels (cf. Utriainen 2014, 237). Several of Virtue's books are translated into Norwegian (cf. Virtue 2008, as an example). This type of co-operation underlines the international dimension of late modern angels. The international character of angels also made it possible for the bestselling English writer, Emma Heathcote-James, to give the Norwegian translation of her book *Seeing Angels*, the title *Märthas engler* ("Märtha's Angels")—and use a photo of the Princess on the cover. However, the Princess took her to court, with the result that Heathcote-James was allowed to keep the title, but not the photo.

The transmission of ideas of New Age angels in films, books and newspapers ensures that these creatures become part of a common field of communication which is open for individual interpretation. Even if everyone is allowed to and even encouraged to develop their own perception of angels, there is a tendency toward unity in the different experiences of angels. In November 2010, the television program "Den andre siden" (The other side) (TV Norge) had invited five people prominent on the New Age scene in Norway, among them the Princess and Elisabeth Nordeng, to a talk about angels.[15] The agreement of the participants on the conception of angels was striking, even if they made a point out of having experienced different things.

---

12. This is a universal trait of New Age spirituality, one of the Findhorn founders, Dorothy Maclean, received a message from an angelic being in 1963, and she refers to that being both as "angel" and as "deva."

13. In Norwegian, "et aspekt av den universelle kjærlighetskraften."

14. New Age magazines in Norway sometimes include articles about angels in different cultures, which is also part of the contemporary "synonymization" tendency.

15. https://www.youtube.com/watch?v=uXpzCvRb0N0 (visited 19.02.2015).

What characterizes these angels? They are elements in a re-enchantment of the secular world and part of a shared aesthetics. Different from biblical angels, they are used in a therapeutic approach to humans and address challenges to the individual such as mastering life, personal relations and the need for safety. These challenges are basic to human life, but also closely connected to women. Terhi Utriainen has recently made an analysis of angels in Finland, based on interviews, questionnaires and participant observation. According to her analysis, angels and practices related to angels "construct emotions and relations as particularly a woman's realm" (Utriainen 2014, 250). Even when the androgynous character of angels is stressed, they seem to be conceived of more like females and to be part of a feminine world-view. At "A night with the angels" in Oslo Concert Hall, the audience were in the main women. Generally, metaphorical use of angels refers to women and children rather than to men.

The churchly discourse of angels as messengers and guardians

The church's construction of angels is based on its dependence on Scripture on the one hand and on its theological categorization on the other.[16] The late ancient flowering of angels in Christianity was both restricted and continued during the medieval ages. Protestantism made a new change: In 1537, Norway became part of the Lutheran domain, and from that time on angels had in principle a more marginal existence than they had in the Catholic Church. Martin Luther wrote about angels in many of his works, and showed much more interest in these beings than did Calvin (Soergel 2006).[17] In his later works, where his attitude became more critical, Luther is, to a greater degree than in earlier years, preoccupied with defining the role angels should play within an evangelical Christianity. He never ruled out the possibility of visions and apparitions of angels, but he thought that in the main their work took place in unseen fashion (Soergel 2006). This also became the view of the Lutheran churches: "For its theologians and officialdom, trained in the tradition of Luther's mature evangelical theology and in the razor-like accuracy of the orthodoxy that emerged after his death, apparitions of angels became an increasingly remote possibility" (Soergel 2006, 80).

---

16. Angels constitute an important group of superhuman beings in the Christian religious universe, and are mentioned a little less than 300 times in the bible. Two angels are named here—Michael and Gabriel. Raphael appears in the *Book of Tobit*, which is part of the Catholic canon. In late antiquity bishops and theologians tidied up the world of angels, both excluding Pagan ones and those that functioned more like ancient gods (cf. Cline 2011), and included in lists and hierarchies those that were left.

17. According to Philip M. Soergel, a search in the Weimar edition of Luther's works, revealed 4.691 uses of the world angel in singular (*Engel*), 849 uses of the plural form and 1431 occurrences of the Latin word, *angelus*. In addition, there are a host of references to seraphim, cherubim and to the specific archangels (Soergel 2006, 67).

In the theology of the Lutheran churches, including the Church of Norway, angels are seen as God's helpers and part of the providential worldview of Protestantism (cf. Marshall and Walsham 2006, 14–15). They fight on God's side against evil, provide protection, but are not independent spiritual beings and should not be objects of worship in their own right. The notion of personal guardian angels had not been developed (Marshall and Walsham 2006, 15–16). The Protestant view of angels is basically restrictive.[18]

In addition, there is a problem with discerning between good and evil angels. One thing is that, according to Luther and the stand of the Church, angels were more visible in the time of the Scriptures than they are today; another thing is that people who claim that they have seen angels, may in reality have encountered evil powers. Fallen angels and demons, known from Scripture, are explicitly or implicitly part of the churchly discourse on angels.

Arne Bugge Amundsen has analysed visions of angels among Norwegians after the Reformation (Amundsen 1995). One of his examples is the bell-ringer Samuel Christensen in Fjellberg, Sunnhordland, who in 1669 said that he had seen a man in white clothes with a white beard. The message of the apparition was that the bell-ringer should go to the local priest and tell him to continue to preach against sin and evil because the day of judgement was very close. After that the white man was lifted up into the air (Amundsen 2008, 24). The vision was reported to the local priest. Rumours of doomsday were spread, and the superior of the local priest reported the incident to the bishop in Bergen, Niels Randulff (Amundsen 2008, cf. also Henriksen and Pabst 2013). After five weeks, the bishop made his decision. The crucial thing turned out to be the beard. Randulff had consulted theological books and found that none of them described bearded angels (Amundsen 2008, 23). Consequently the vision could not have been an angel. The bishop did not doubt the bell-ringer's vision, but doubted the categorization. Instead, he saw the apparition as a messenger from Satan. The bell-ringer was told to stay home, and that if he had more visions, he should not tell anyone about them except the local priest. In this way a rumour of doomsday was nipped in the bud. Such rumours usually implied a criticism of elites and authorities, so the bishop had a strong interest in not promoting them (cf. Amundsen 2008). This narrative illustrates very well that while it was in principle possible for people to have visions of angels, it was difficult to have that type of experiences accepted as genuine by church authorities.

In the nineteenth century, the development of science and secularization forced angels further into the margins. In the book, *Om Aanderne eller Englene efter Den hellige Skrifts lære* ("About spirits or angels after the teaching of Holy Scripture"), the Norwegian dean, J. L. Qvisling, struggled with the problems

---

18. Laura Sangha points out that "the ambiguities in the status of angels were to give them a contested place in Protestant theology" (Sangha 2012, 9).

that angels posed to Lutheran theology at the turn of the twentieth century (Qvisling 1889). The book combines learned theology with homespun philosophy, and is in many ways a curiosity. Qvisling believed that angels existed, but saw them as no longer belonging to the daylight. According to him, they are, metaphorically speaking, part of the night from which all existence arises (Qvisling 1889, 36–37). In other words, the angels are moved backstage.

Lutheran theology has in the main treated angels in accordance with the frequently quoted words of Karl Barth, as "essentially marginal figures."[19] These constructs are messengers and guardians, and seen more as divine drones than independent actors (Muehlberger 2013, 5). In line with this view, the theological faculties in Norway have traditionally paid little attention to them (Garlid 2005; Gilhus 2012).

The theological angel discourse of contestation

So far we have briefly presented two contemporary discourses on angels, the international New Age discourse and the traditional angel discourse of Lutheran theology. There is a more recent theological discourse of contestation, where these intermediate beings have become border markers between Lutheran Christianity and the New Age Movement. In this discourse, angels promote the Church and its theology in opposition to New Age spirituality. In newspaper discussion about the angels of the Princess, belief in angels was also used as border markers between the elite and people in general (cf. Kraft 2008).

Creating borders

In 1994, Øystein Bjørdal and Olav Skjevesland, both from MF, Norwegian School of Theology, wrote a book about the church's view of angels, *Engelen ved din side* ("The Angel at your side") (cf. Gilhus 2012). It was reissued in a slightly expanded version in 2009. In line with Karl Barth's thesis, Bjørdal and Skjevesland ascertain that angels are "at the outskirts of our theology and on the edge of the divine service" (Bjørdal and Skjevesland 1994, 26).[20] The book was written in an attempt to make angels into a genuine Christian concern, and Bjørdal and Skjevesland warn about the real danger, namely that New Age spiritualities have captured the interest in angels (1994, 23).

The church met the general renewal of interest in angels with a re-introduction of Michaelmas as a trial project in 1999 to celebrate Michael and all the angels, and, we might add, to reclaim the angels for Christianity and for the Church (Garlid 2005; Gilhus 2012). Michael's traditional function as a defender of the faith and a marker of boundaries was evoked. The prayer

---

19. Karl Barth, *Church Dogmatics: The Doctrine of Creation*, III, 3 § 50–51, p. 81. London: T.&T. Clark, 2010.

20. In Norwegian: "Englene lever i ytterkanten av vår teologi og i randen av vår gudstjeneste."

on this Michaelmas Sunday included thanks to God because he sent the holy angels to protect and guard against the powers of evil.

The first edition of the book by Bjørdal and Skjevesland was published before Astarte Education, "the angel-school," was established. The establishing of Astarte Inspiration in 2007 led to a huge media-debate, and afterwards popular opinion largely associated angels with the two spiritual entrepreneurs, Princess Märtha Louise and Elisabeth Nordeng. According to Siv Ellen Kraft, the debate in the newspapers included three main arguments; a secular argument about the irrationality of a belief in angels, a Christian argument about the offensiveness of deviant and heretical beliefs, and arguments about the potentially negative effects on the constitutional monarchy of Norway (Kraft 2008).[21] The arguments were repeated two years later when the first book by the Princess and Nordeng was published (2009). One of the newspapers labelled the book "spiritual quackery" (åndelig kvakksalveri, *Dagbladet* 23.10.2009).

The religious argument has several aspects from mild criticism to heavier opposition, and has further been elaborated in recent books. Notto Thelle from the Theological Faculty at the University of Oslo discusses the relationship between Christianity and New Age beliefs in a book with the title *Prinsessens engler: Invitasjon til en samtale om alternative spiritualitet* ("The Angels of the Princess: An Invitation to a conversation about alternative spirituality") (2010). The cover of the book alludes to the cover of the book by the Princess and Elisabeth Nordeng, which, similar to their book, has a picture on the cover of the wing of an angel in a context of the sky and uses similar colours. The first chapter deals with the angels of the Princess and what the Church and the New Age has in common, at the same time as Thelle attempts to show what is different. According to him, New Age angels differ from Christian angels by being idyllic, an extension of what goes on in people's minds and available for humans when they ask (Thelle 2010, 17–21). The other chapters in the book treat New Age in general. The title and the cover signal that the angels of the Princess function as a condensed symbol of popular New Age ideas and practices.

A similar tendency is reflected in the establishment of *Engleskolen* ("the Angel School") by the Christian organization Areopagos.[22] *Engleskolen* is

---

21. The Princess and Elisabeth Nordeng have recently commented on the reactions they have been met with on The Huffington Post website where they run a blog: "We angel-institute-entrepreneurs know what it is like sticking our necks out founding our spiritual institute, Astarte Inspiration, here in Norway. Many people with new and slightly outside-the-box-kind-of-ideas know it too. If you flag that you are different, odds are good you will be chastised, ridiculed, criticized and humiliated by family, friends, co-workers and in the media. People will say your ideas won't work; they will call you a megalomaniac!" (*huffington.post.com.* 26.02. 2014) http://www.huffingtonpost.com/princess-martha-louise-and-elisabeth-nordeng/changing-the-world_1_b_4845896.html)

22. For Areopagos, see Mikaelsson's chapter.

obviously a Christian answer to the "angel school" of the Princess and Nordeng.[23] The purpose of the school is to help participants find answers to how they as Christians should react to phenomena such as healing, reincarnation, spiritualism and karma. The Seventh Day Adventist Church in Norway runs a correspondence course and an internet-course called *Angels*. A flyer asks, "Angels, more than scraps?" The course illumines "the fight between light and darkness, good and evil, in the incredible drama which is played out behind the scenes" (my translation).[24] One of the themes is "What the angels are not." In these cases, angels are used as border markers against the angels of New Age, and especially against the angels of the Princess, and as an emblematic sign for an opposition against a broader complex of New Age ideas and practices. While angels seem to have led a quiet existence in churchly life and in the main been restricted to certain spaces, genres and times (childhood, psalms and Christmas), the popular and New Age focus on angels has forced the Church to give them more space.

Angels as a religious resource

In his classical article "The Cult, the Cultic Milieu and Secularism," Colin Campbell asked how the cultic milieu survives "in the face of the continuous disapproval and even outright hostility of the organizations representing cultural orthodoxy?" (Campbell 1972, 129). Among his hypotheses are that the cultic milieu "functions as a cultural 'gene pool' for society," a "source of renewal for ailing orthodox belief systems," but also that the cultic milieu is used as a "negative reference group" for the advocates of cultural orthodoxy and "facilitating adherence to dominant scientific paradigms by practising scientists and associated practitioners" (Campbell 1972, 130). As we have seen, Princess Märtha Louise and Elisabeth Nordeng's communication with angels has clearly been a negative reference for what lies outside Lutheran orthodoxy, but it has also inspired attempts to reclaim angels for the Church, activate them and define their proper Christian and churchly space.

People still have experiences of angels (Amundsen 1995, 2008; Garlid 2005; Arnesen 2007; Henriksen and Pabst 2013), but, as already seen, traditionally people's experiences of angels have been more difficult for the Church to accommodate than childhood angels and angels in the Scriptures, dogmas and pictures. This now seems to be changing.

One indication of this change is the recent book, *Uventet og ubedt*, ("Unexpected and Uninvited"), by Jan-Olav Henriksen (MF, Norwegian School of Theology) and Kathrin Pabst (Vestagdermuseet), who have interviewed men and women with paranormal experiences. The criteria for the selection of

---

23. Areopagos works on dialogue between religions, studies contemporary religion and spreads Christian spirituality. It hosts Substans, a network for asceticism and activism, which also contributes to the Christian "Engleskolen."

24. http://www.norskbibelinstitutt.no/bibelkurs/englene/ (visited 25.01.17)

the informants were that they should have a background in Christian belief and practice and more than one exceptional experience (Henriksen and Pabst 2013, 23). The title of the book describes its content, which are unexpected paranormal or exceptional experiences. They are presented as what the authors discovered in their material. However, the title also refers to an ideal for how Christian paranormal experiences should happen. They should be "unexpected and uninvited," which implies that they should occur spontaneously and not be sought. In some of the examples, however, the angels do not seem to be quite as uninvited as they ideally should have been, and tend to partake in both a Christian and a New Age discourse. In a chapter entitled, "Rumours of angels and a more 'porous' world"—which refers simultaneously to a book by Peter Berger and a concept used by Charles Taylor in *A Secular Age*, the book discusses experiences of angels (Henriksen and Pabst 2013, 80–117). Characteristic for the angels in this book is that they protect and give comfort.

Henriksen and Pabst stress that, different from the older Christian visions of angels in Norway, the function of the angels has changed. Angels no longer bring messages, which the receiver in his or her turn is expected to give to others (Henriksen and Pabst 2013, 91). Instead, the message is directed at one person and is meant to protect or give comfort to that person or someone else close to him or her. The last chapter in Henriksen and Pabst's book discusses the role of the church in society versus the religious experiences of individuals. The two authors point out that the Church of Norway is more open to such experiences than people usually think (Henriksen and Pabst 2013, 176). They propose that the Church should be more accepting when it comes to subjective and mystical experiences, and to undertake theological rethinking of the status of such experiences (Henriksen and Pabst 2013, 184–185). Henriksen and Pabst ask rhetorically if theology and Church should leave those who have such experiences to the interpretative resources in alternative milieus or accept that these resources also exist in Christian milieus and try to develop or supplement them (Henriksen and Pabst 2013, 160). The book is an attempt to expand the Church's borders and include some of the individual experiences of angels into Lutheran orthodoxy.

The category of angels

Angels are part of language and are often used in metaphorical expression, for instance, when one asks someone to do something with the phrase "be an angel." Angels thus fluctuate easily between reality and metaphor, and it is open to interpretation whether they are somewhat real or just part of a turn of phrase. When a dead child is described as an angel, does it mean that the child has turned into a superhuman being or is it just a figure of speech? In many cases it remains undetermined exactly what such a phrase indicates (cf. Alver 1999).

An angel is "the meta-empirical other" (Utriainen 2013, 242). What sort of meta-empirical other is an angel? Or put in another way, how does the super-human species of angels relate to other species—natural as well as supernatural? This is a classical theological problem, at least from the time of Origen in the third century when the similarities and differences between angels, demons, humans and the dead were negotiated. In this chapter, however, we are interested in how angels are used in contemporary discourses and folk taxonomies. The point of departure is the Great Chain of Being, or in this case the extended Great Chain, which includes both the relation of human beings to other species and to inanimate objects and their relation to "society, God, and the universe" (Lakoff and Turner 1989, 166–167). The extended Great Chain of Being is a cultural model or folk theory of the hierarchical relationship of the things in the world. The system becomes metaphorical when one level of the chain—animal, human or superhuman being—is used to describe another level. In this system, humans can be understood as angels or angels can be understood as animals. When we are invited to understand human behaviour in terms of angels or angels in terms of animals, it implies that angels are mapped onto humans or animals onto angels (cf. Lakoff and Turner 1989, 196). In some cases, this is about allegedly quintessential properties, which lead to essential behaviour (Lakoff and Turner 1989, 170); in other cases it is about something more diffuse. In religious discourses, the distinction between "metaphorisity" and reality is frequently blurred or deliberately fused.

The connections between humans and angels are strong. The interpretation of contemporary experiences of angels sometimes leaves open the possibility of whether the encounter has been with a spiritual being or with an extraordinary human. Angels can be mistaken for humans, and humans can be described as angels, especially in relation to the quintessential property of kindness. The gender of angels has varied through history. It has been suggested that because angels today are taken less seriously and command less cultural respect, they are portrayed as females (Jones 2010, 36). This might be part of the explanation, but more important is probably that they are conceived of as female because their functions today are closer to what are conceived of as female tasks (see above).

The relation between angels and children escapes, in the main, the secular and theological criticisms that have been the lot of New Age angels. Children are not yet quite domesticated, which is perhaps one reason why they are sometimes associated with angels—as they are with animals (Ehn and Löfgren 1996, 30). When they are associated with angels, it is the innocence and kindness of children that is stressed, though it might also be their strangeness as guests from another world. These ideas are combined in death notices when a deceased child is spoken of as an angel: "A small angel to us came, smiled sweetly and turned around."[25]

---

25. The status of angels versus the status of the dead has been discussed for nearly 2000

There has always been a connection between animals and angels, especially between birds and angels, because of the wings, which are the angels' most common visual characteristic and their airborne manner of locomotion. Today, other animals are drawn in as well. In the presentation of Astarte Education on the web (2007), the Princess says, "through horses I learnt to communicate with animals on a deeper level. It was while I was taking care of the horses that I took up contact with the angels."[26] When the values assigned to a category change, this might lead to changes in the relative value allotted to the other categories as well—also in the values of supernatural categories. The status of some animals is rising, at the same time as the status of the angels has been lowered, and these changes influence how animals and angels are combined. For instance, in a puppet play for children about death, which has been played in churches at the end of the Divine Service, a guinea pig is the leading character. When it dies, it is described as a guinea-pig-angel ("A little guinea-pig-angel to us came, sweetly smiled and turned around").[27]

The connection to birds is still there. A tangible sign of angels is sometimes a feather (Märtha Louise and Samnøy 2009, 167). According to the Princess, feathers found in unusual places are signs of the presence of angels.[28] Even if it is realized that the feathers come from birds,[29] the feathers are perceived as an index of angels and as part of a sign-reading approach to reality.[30]

In these examples animals or animal characteristics are gates into the enchanted world of angels. Of a different kind is the award-winning Norwegian author, Karl Ove Knausgård's, harsh description of the fate of angels in a secularized world. Knausgård writes in *A Time to Every Purpose under Heaven* about the sixteenth century polymath, Antinous Ballori, who experiences angels and describes in a treatise how they changed over the centuries (Knausgård 2008). When God died with Christ on the Cross, the depressed and marginalized angels finally became seagulls on the Norwegian coast: "They got smaller, their legs became thinner, and the feathers which previ-

---

years with participants ranging from Origen to one of the leading theosophists, Charles Webster Leadbeater. While angels and the dead are often treated as functional equivalents (the same people allegedly have experiences of both categories) and sometimes as overlapping (dead people become angels), the official teaching in the Lutheran Church is that they are different groups.

26. "Gjennom hestene lærte jeg å kommunisere med dyrene på et dypere nivå. Det var mens jeg holdt på med hestene at jeg tok opp kontakten med englene" (Astarte Education 2007).

27. The play is based on a book by Ulf Nilsson, *Goodby Mr. Muffin*. London: Hawthorn Press, 2010 [2002].

28. www.magasinetvisjon.no/no/artikler/spiritualitet/Englenes+hemmeligheter.9UFR nGXx.ips (visited 19.02.15).

29. In the critical debate in the newspapers one professor offered to read the DNA of the feathers.

30. I am grateful to my colleague Lisbeth Mikaelsson for this observation.

ously had covered only their wings began to sprout on other parts of their bodies." (Knausgård 2008, 469). Few of these creatures remember their former glory. Secularization is per definition a religious process, because its point of departure is religion, and Knausgård's description of the angels' fall into bestiality can be read as a religious narrative of secularization.

Large numbers of angels are fabricated and sold in the form of women or children with wings, small as well as large. They are material things, which have a commercial potential and are used to sell stuff, especially at Christmas. These material angels are bridges between a secular and a religious world, between Lutheran Christianity and other varieties of religion. They are prominently present in the "everywhere" dimension in which religion and secularity meet and fuse—in Norway from the middle of November to January—the long season of Christmas. They even give name to a Christmas dessert, *Englelapskaus*—"angel stew"—made of fruit, which refers to the sweet taste of paradise where the angels in Christian thinking ultimately belong, and to a cake, *Englekake*—"angel food cake."

Gordon Lynch says that in general it is "more useful to think about religion as a form of 'cultural tool-kit' rather than a world-view—a set of conceptual, social and material resources that can be drawn on for different purposes" (Lynch 2007, 41). Angels are part of that toolkit with their grounding in Christianity and childhood emotions, which make them attractive and also plausible—at least to a certain degree and in certain contexts (cf. Meyer 2013, 9).

Conclusion

In this chapter, angels have been related to three discourses and to four spatial categories. Angels appear in places, cross between places and appear on the margins, and they can be included in or kept out of a specific religious space. The chapter has applied a spatial model to describe the localization and distribution of angels in contemporary religion in Norway.[31]

Gregor Ahn labelled an angel "religiöse Grenzgänger" (Ahn 1999, 275) or "border crosser." Contemporary angels cross the borders between Lutheran Christianity, popular religion and New Age. In historical perspective, angels always seem to have easily crossed borders. One reason is that these superhuman beings are minimally counter-intuitive, which is part of their attractiveness and applicability. Sometimes their only superhuman characteristic is the wings, though it might also be light, and they usually have an ability to appear and disappear without notice. In addition to their minimal counter-intuitiveness, another characteristic that facilitates their movement between religions and between the religious and the secular is that they are usually not theologically very well defined.

---

31. Angels could also have been studied from the perspective of a chronological model and in relation to how they appear as "momentary gods" in the present, but as fixed in a textual past.

As shown in the spatial model, angels cross between the four spaces of "here," "there," "everywhere" and "anywhere." Sometimes they connect these spaces; sometimes they keep them apart. Their border-marking function is especially evident in the churchly use of them (cf. Gilhus 2012).

New Age discourse allocates more space to angels than they have normally been allotted in the traditional angel discourse of the Lutheran Church. This has recently made the Church give angels more attention. In spite of the angels' close connection with a Norwegian Princess, they do not at first glance seem to have a national dimension.[32] However, the theological discourse of contestation where angels are border-makers between the Christianity of the Church and New Age spiritualities is dependent on the special status which the Norwegian Constitution gives to the Evangelical-Lutheran Church. Finally, there is the question of whether the contemporary growth of practices related to communication with angels and other intermediary beings such as the spirits of the dead implies that a monotheistic religious approach is giving way to a more polytheistic approach.

References

Ahn, Gregor. 1999. "Engel." In *Metzler Lexikon Religion*, vol. 1, 273–275. Stuttgart: J.B. Metzler.

Alver, Bente Gullveig. 1999. "Fra englevagt til englevinger. Den mirakuløse hverdag og det hverdagslige mirakel." In *Myte, magi og mirakel i møte med det moderne*, edited by Bente Gullveig Alver, Ingvild Sælid Gilhus, Lisbeth Mikaelsson and Torunn Selberg, 183–199. Oslo: Pax.

Amundsen, Arne Bugge. 1995. "'Mig Engelen tiltalte saa...' Folkelige visjoner som kulturell kommunikasjon." In *Sæt ikke vantro i min overtroes stæd: studier i folketro og folkelig religiøsitet. Festskrift til Ørnulf Hodne på 60-årsdagen 28. September 1995*, edited by Arne Bugge Amundsen and Anne Eriksen, 21–59. Oslo: Novus forlag.

———. 2008. "Himmelens eller helvetes budbringere. Hvordan har vi snakket med engler og demoner gjennom tidene." In *P2-akademiet*, vol. 40, edited by Annette Hobson, 20–29. Oslo: Transit.

Arnesen, Hege Kristin. 2007. "Engler: guddommelige skapninger eller folketro." Unpublished MA thesis, Oslo University.

Asprem, Egil. 2014. "Intermediary beings." In *The Occult World*, edited by Christopher Partridge, 646–658. New York: Routledge.

Barth, Karl. 2010. *Church Dogmatics: The Doctrine of Creation*. London: T.&T. Clark.

Bjørdal, Øystein and Olav Skjevesland. 2009 [1994]. *Engelen ved din side*. Oslo: Verbum.

Campbell, Colin. 1972. "The cult, the cultic milieu and secularization." In *A Sociological Yearbook of Religion in Britain*, 5, edited by Michael Hill, 119–136. London: SCM Press.

---

32. I am grateful to Siv Ellen Kaft who pointed this out to me.

Cline, Rangar. 2011. *Ancient Angels: Conceptualizing Angels in the Roman Empire.* Leiden: Brill.

Ehn, Billy and Orvar Löfgren. 1994. *Kulturanalys: Et etnologiskt perspektiv.* Malmö: Gleerups forlag.

Endsjø, Dag Øistein and Liv Ingeborg Lied. 2011. *Det folk vil ha: Religion og populærkultur.* Oslo: University Publishing House.

Gardella, Peter. 2007. *American Angels: Useful Spirits in the Material World.* Lawrence: University Press of Kansas.

Garlid, Line Sæther. 2005. *Engleforestillinger i Den norske kirke*, masteroppgave. Bergen: University of Bergen.

Gilhus, Ingvild Sælid. 2012. "Angels in Norway: Religious border-crossers and border-markers." In *Vernacular Religion in Everyday Life: Expressions of Belief*, edited by Marion Bowman and Ûlo Valk, 230–245. London: Equinox.

———. 2013. "'All over the place': The contribution of New Age to a spatial model of religion." In *New Age Spirituality: Rethinking Religion*, edited by Steven J. Sutcliffe and Ingvild Sælid Gilhus, 35–49. Durham: Acumen.

Heathcote-James, Emma. 2007. *"Märthas engler": Om folk som har møtt engler.* Oslo: Publicom.

Heelas, Paul and Linda Woodhead. 2005. *The Spiritual Revolution: Why Religion Is Giving Way to Spirituality.* Oxford: Blackwell Publishing.

Henriksen Jan-Olav and Kathrin Pabst. 2013. *Uventet og ubedt: paranormale erfaringer i møte med tradisjonell tro.* Oslo: University Publishing House.

Hjarvard, Stig. 2008. "The mediatisation of religion: A theory of media as agents of religious change." *Northern Lights* 6: 9–26.

Hobson, Suzanne. 2011. *Angels of Modernism: Religion, Culture, Aesthetics 1910–1960.* New York: Pallgrave Macmillan.

Jones, David Albert. 2010. *Angels: A History.* Oxford: Oxford University Press.

Knausgård, Karl Ove. 2008 [2004]. *A Time to Every Purpose Under Heaven.* London: Portobello Books.

Kraft, Siv Ellen. 2008. "Märthas engler: En analyse av den norske mediedebatten." *Nytt Norsk Tidsskrift* 25: 123–134.

Lakoff, George and Mark Turner. 1989. *More than Cool Reason: A Field Guide to Poetic Metaphor.* Chicago, IL: The University of Chicago Press.

Lynch, Gordon. 2007. *The New Spirituality: An Introduction to Belief Beyond Religion.* London: I.B. Tauris.

Märtha Louise and Elisabeth Samnøy. 2009. *Møt din skytsengel: En innføring i å møte din unike kraft.* Oslo: Cappelen Damm.

Märtha Louise and Elisabeth Nordeng. 2012. *Englenes hemmeligheter: deres natur, språk og hvordan du åpner opp for dem.* Oslo: Cappelen Damm.

Marshall, Peter and Alexandra Walsham. 2006. "Migration of angels in the early modern world." In *Angels in the Early Modern World,* edited by : Peter Marshall and Alexandra Walsham, 1–18. Cambridge: Cambridge University Press.

Meyer, Birgit. 2013. "Material mediations and religious practices of world-making." In *Religion Across Media: From Early Antiquity to Late Modernity,* edited by Knut Lundby, 1–19. New York: Peter Lang.

Mikaelsson, Lisbeth. 2013. "New Age and the spirit of capitalism: Energy as cognitive currency." In *New Age Spirituality: Rethinking Religion,* edited by Steven J. Sutcliffe and Ingvild Sælid Gilhus, 160–173. Durham: Acumen.

Muehlberger, Ellen. 2013. *Angels in Late Ancient Christianity.* Oxford: Oxford University Press.

Nilsson, Ulf. 2010 [2002]. *Goodby Mr. Muffin.* London: Hawthorn Press.

Qvisling, J. L. 1889. *Om Aanderne eller Englene efter Den hellige Skrifts Lære.* Kristiania: Alb. Cammermeyer.

Sangha, Laura. 2012. *Angels and Belief in England 1480-1700.* Abingdon and New York: Pickering and Chatto.

Smith, Jonathan Z. 2003. "Here, there and anywhere." In *Prayer, Magic, and the Stars in the Ancient and Late Antique World,* edited by S. Noegel, J. Walker and B. Wheeler, 21–36. Pennsylvania: Pennsylvania State University.

Soergel, Philip M. 2006. "Luther on the angels." In *Angels in the Early Modern World,* edited by Peter Marshall and Alexandra Walsham, 64–82. Cambridge: Cambridge University Press.

Steiner, Rudolf. 2008 [2000]. *Engler: vesen og virke: ti foredrag 1912-1924* (utvalgt og redigert av Wolf-Ulrich Klünker, oversatt av Arne Møller). Oslo: Antropos.

Thelle, Notto. 2010. *Prinsessens engler: Invitasjon til en samtale om alternatv spiritualitet.* Oslo: Pax.

Utriainen, Terhi. 2013. "Doing things with angels: Agency, alterity and practices of enchantment." In *Angels in the Early Modern World,* edited by Peter Marshall and Alexandra Walsham, 242–255. Cambridge: Cambridge University Press.

———. 2014. "Angels, agency, and emotions: Global religion for women in Finland." In *Finnish Women making Religion: Between Ancestors and Angels,* edited by Terhi Utriainen and Päivi Salmesvuari, 237–254. New York: Palgrave Macmillian.

Virtue, Doreen. 2008 [2005]. *Englemedisin: la kjærlighetsfylte lysvesener helbrede kropp og sinn.* Oslo: Damm.

Walther, Winfried. 2002: "Engleerfaringer i vår tid. Hvordan å komme i forbindelse med skytsengelen?" *Libra* 1-2: 51–54.

Wang, Marit. 1986: *Engler i Norge.* Oslo: C. Huitfeldt forlag.

— 8 —

New Age and Norwegian "Conspirituality"

Asbjørn Dyrendal

During the early 2000s, a surprising new phenomenon occurred: the fusion of New Age spirituality and conspiracy culture into "conspirituality." This is the argument of Charlotte Ward and David Voas (2011). Contrary to Ward and Voas, this paper takes as its starting point the view that theories of conspiracy are not really surprising anywhere. The current conspiritual scene is but the continuation of older traditions, arising out of the dynamics of "the cultic milieu" (Asprem and Dyrendal 2015). Esoteric discourses on secrecy and concealment have also always encompassed the attribution of both to hidden, *evil* actors. Narratives about such actors and their deeds perform, among other things, the work of theodicy.

The current actors have their acknowledged "foremothers" in earlier conspiritualities, and this also holds true for Norway (Dyrendal 2015). But the visibility and prominence of conspirituality within both international and local scenes varies widely over time—possibly in contrast to conspiracy discourse in general society: While social conspiracy talk in general seems to show a stable and downward trend (Uscinski and Parent 2014), Ward and Voas (2011, 109) quite rightly insist that the particular international trend they discuss, from meager beginnings in the 1990s, gained prominence after September 11th 2001.

This holds, from my own observations, true for Norway as well. During the period in question, we see the rise (and partial fall) of a scene within the New Age milieu where conspiracy discourses took center stage. The scene investigated here is the Norwegian group blog *Nyhetsspeilet*, in that the blog and its rise and "fall" serves as the primary material. The blog was chosen as the central, most important Norwegian example of international conspirituality. It was also, for a time, the hub where Norwegian conspiracy culture met "New Age" interests. What did this scene look like? Why did it rise, and why did it "fall"? I shall argue that part of the answer lies in trends that include heightened millennial expectations in parts of the New Age milieu: it was, partially, a manifestation of Norwegian New Age entering "apocalyptic time," with its decline following the downside of the apocalyptic wave (Landes 2011, 52–61).

Before we can get to the material, however, we need to delve a bit into some of the terms that are less familiar to religious studies scholars, and place them into the context of the study of "New Age." Then I shall introduce *Nyhetsspeilet* in its Norwegian and international context, before moving on to its constructions of enemies, with particular emphasis on the central role of epistemic authority. In closing, I examine the "apocalyptic wave" of its rise and fall.

Conspiracy theory and conspirituality

I stated above that the attribution of conspiracy to others is not to be treated as surprising. The general reasons for this are intertwined. First, humans are social animals with communicative capacity. We have the ability to plan, communicate and co-operate with each other to further our own causes. Sometimes, the causes in which we co-operate are ones that others find to be to their own disadvantage, or unlikeable. When strategies for furthering such goals are made in secret, they are deemed to be a "conspiracy." Second, being social animals with a "theory of mind," humans *recognize* the capacities for planned behavior in others. Since we meaning-making humans are overly good at finding patterns, we also find patterns in what is actually random: it may be costly not to see dangerous patterns when they are there, thus false positives abound.

A tendency towards false positives in identifying conspiracy, often by routes of certain (bad) habits of thought (e.g. Bruder *et al.* 2013), is one marker for "conspiracy belief," and what commonly passes for "conspiracy theory" in everyday language. It is, however, merely one of them. While there is evidence of personality playing a role (e.g. Swami *et al.* 2011), there is no particular reason to choose between *either* "innate" *or* "historically developed" when explaining or analyzing conspiracy discourse. It is necessarily both. Particular rhetorical patterns, *topoi* etc. clearly reflect historical processes, both global and local. Patterns of reasoning and discursive activity are permeated by *learned* behavior. Thus we should not be surprised that although the *capacity* for conspiracy thinking is innate, and the *tendency* to engage in it is partially influenced by personality, the strongest predictor for partaking in conspiracy discourse of specific types is participation in a social group where this kind of discourse is prevalent (e.g. Byford 2011).

The promotion of conspiracy theories thus has multiple causes and/or motives. The theories may be involved in a variety of context-based and sometimes strategic uses. Beliefs may be held with any degree of sincerity, and both promotion and belief are guided by multiple possible dynamics (e.g. Fenster 2008; Gray 2010). Top-down, elites may use conspiracy discourse to distract and derail criticism, mobilize the public around ethno-nationalist causes, or a host of other concerns. Bottom-up, interest groups may mobilize conspiracy discourse as, e.g., explanation of misfortune, as claims to knowledge that demand reallocation of power, or as critique of political and other powers-that-be. Conspiracy theory claims a form of esoteric knowledge, and it may also be used explicitly as such by religious movements (e.g. Dyrendal 2013).

Conspiracy discourse may be embraced in different forms and at different levels of commitment. It is common to differentiate between belief in small-scale, event-oriented theories of conspiracy, and theories that conspiracy is more ubiquitous (e.g. Pipes 1997; Gray 2010; Barkun 2003). The latter kind of theories makes use of the former, and the most ubiquitous sense of conspiracy is often termed "conspiracism." It is this type of conspiracy discourse that permeates *conspirituality*.

In their original formulation of the concept, Ward and Voas (2011, 104) describe conspirituality as a hybrid "politico-spiritual philosophy," manifesting in two core "convictions": that "a secret group covertly controls, or is trying to control, the political and social order," and that "[h]umanity is undergoing a "paradigm shift" in consciousness." Conspiracy culture presents a problem in the form of a worldly evil to be overcome, while (New Age) spirituality provides the soteriological solution: to act in accordance with an awakened "new paradigm" worldview and usher in a global change in consciousness. To Ward and Voas, conspirituality was a new phenomenon anchored in the marriage of conspiracy culture and a segment of the New Age movement through the world wide web. While Asprem and I (Dyrendal and Asprem 2013; Asprem and Dyrendal 2015) would redefine the concept to take into consideration a much older and more pervasive involvement of conspiracism in esoteric discourse, the area delineated in the original formulation is very much the one with which this article is concerned. Nevertheless: to understand the phenomenon slightly deeper in terms of history and social dynamics, I will briefly sketch the underlying dynamics whereby the discourses of "New Age" and conspiracism are intertwined more generally.[1]

If we, as Wouter Hanegraaff (1996) suggests, see New Age as a phase in the history of the cultic milieu (Campbell 1972), we should take a brief look at the description of the latter. What we find is that Campbell insisted that deviance from "dominant cultural orthodoxies" (1972, 122) is one of two central features (the other being "mystical religion") of this "cultural underground." Moreover, secularization, science and its institutions are more and more taking the place of theology and the institutions of the church as the space from which the relevant cultural orthodoxies are being promoted.

---

1. For deeper discussions, see the references above.

Thus the alternative treatments, history, physics, economics etc. of the milieu become more important for its defining characteristic of "deviance" than its alternative theology. Stressing the aspects of deviance, Michael Barkun (2003) suggested that a new type of conspiracy culture, "improvised millennialism," was based on dynamics relating to the embrace of what he called "stigmatized knowledge-claims."

Stigma is a crucial factor. If something has a stigma, somebody is (perceived to be) doing the work of stigmatization. In this case, the knowledge-insiders, the institutions of authorized knowledge, belong with the culprits, since they refuse to recognize the legitimacy of the claims which thus receive stigma. Since the field of "New Age" continues the tradition of counter-knowledge, from astrology and numerology to crystal healing and ufology, there is never any dearth of knowledge-claims to be dismissed. This is no superficial and new trend: the search for hidden knowledge in the past, among outsiders, and from higher sources, partly stems from traditions of esoteric knowledge-claims generally (Hammer 2001; cf. Hanegraaff 2012). Their history and their attraction lie partially with precisely their status as hidden, rejected, and forbidden. The implication, spoken or not, is that this knowledge is being actively suppressed by forces that know better (cf. Barkun 2003). The tradition thus partly takes for granted, and partly provides an impetus for, conspiracy thinking.

This picture includes a utopian, "millennial" dimension. The observation of Olav Hammer (2001) about New Age history as a U-shaped curve, with a long fall from a high position and a long climb back upwards, also applies to claims of knowledge being lost and then recovered. The knowledge-claims of the cultic milieu are filled not only with "lost" and "hidden" knowledge, but also with promises of how the light of *gnosis* will at one point—soon—shine through, with e.g. "the paradigm shift." When this time comes, the "epistemically dispossessed," their claims, and their counter-epistemology (cf. Robertson 2014) will be recognized, and the agency lost by the stigma of non-recognition will be recovered. With the paradigm shift looming, scenes within the milieu (or the milieu more broadly) at times become "semiotically aroused" (cf. Landes 2011), seeing current events as evidence of forthcoming changes. However, like the millennium, the paradigm shifts tend not to appear. This sets the scene for conspiracy theory; e.g., as a strategy to deal with cognitive dissonance, but also for larger scale disappointment that may lead to disaffiliation.

How did this play out in the ongoing saga of modern Norwegian conspirituality as seen on *Nyhetsspeilet*?

Introducing *Nyhetsspeilet*

Nyhetsspeilet published its first blog post—about *Zeitgeist: The Movie*—in January 2009. The topic was fitting, in that it addressed several central concerns of the blog, which began on a wave of Norwegian conspiracy interest following events like 9/11, an important part of *Zeitgeist*. The increased globalization of American conspiracy culture also shows, in that the interest in conspiracy theories about finance and the money system—important both to the movie and the blog—tended to center on the Federal Reserve system.

The group venture had its background in a convergence of interest among some of the Norwegian proponents of alternative history and spirituality. The instigators found each other mainly through the alternative forum altnett.ning, the official forum for the Norwegian *"Alternativt Nettverk."* An important factor in drawing them together was—over and against the mainly spiritual interests of most other users—their shared desire to address larger social and political issues, and to do so through conspiracist convictions.

They were by no means alone: the interest in wide-ranging conspiracy theories had exploded in the "New Age" milieu during the first decade of the new century. Conspiracy theories had, of course, bloomed in the past, as part of alternative history, and as explanation for the lack of recognition of the alternative physics, treatment modalities, and spirituality of the "cultic milieu." Conspiracy theories were alluded to in articles and talks on the dangers of vaccination, and they were explicit in articles and talks on the suppression of UFO-evidence. Both "big pharma" and "the military-industrial complex" were recognized as villains capable of, and probably guilty of, almost anything in general, and numerous crimes in particular (cf. Dyrendal, 2015; Lie 2009; Færseth 2013a). These theories, at their abstract level, may be seen as generalized expressions of political and spiritual dissent (cf. Imhoff and Bruder 2014). They tended to be expressed as part of a generalized suspicion of "negative forces" in society. Sometimes presenting the dark forces of conspiracy was part of a wider, more positive vision for spirituality-based change. The latter, anecdotally, seemed to play the central role in the milieu.

As in the international scene described by Ward and Voas (2011), conspiracism gradually came more to the forefront. This process accelerated after the events of September 11th 2001, or to be more precise: American foreign policy adventures *following* September 11th. Earlier, central adopters of international conspiracism in the New Age milieu had met with harsh internal criticism (see Heilund 2003), but in the years after 2001, grand conspiracy theories became more mainstreamed. By 2006, the audience for conspiracist speculation had grown big enough to sustain a more-or-less self-published conspiracy book, Per-Aslak Ertresvåg's *Makten bak makten*, at the top of the best-seller lists for "non-fiction" several months running.

The book recapped many of the most important conspiracy theories of the American far right, with a small dose of others; e.g. "green leftist" theories, thrown in for good measure. The villains were thus the usual ones: the Illuminati, the bankers, globalization, popular music, big pharma et cetera, and they were behind all the usual plots, from JFK, 9/11 and the world wars to "chemtrails," Ebola and HIV. Alternative history vied with alternative medicine and alternative economics for space. The book was a typical case of narrating a nested "superconspiracy" (Barkun 2003), with a wide variety of specific targets, and underlying antagonism against globalized society, capitalism, and the medical, cultural, and academic establishments. It appealed to a wide readership, and not least the Norwegian alternative spiritual community in which Ertresvåg was a veteran. Parts of his book were reprinted in *Alternativt Nettverk*'s flagship journal *Visjon*, and Ertresvåg joined other speakers at fairs, talking about the global conspiracy. He also participated in one of the competing Norwegian "911 Truth"-groups, "911 PK-gruppen," with one of those behind *Nyhetsspeilet*.

Conspiracy theories about September 11th were important in the promotion of broader conspiracy claims to the Norwegian public. They also played a part in getting an active readership and a community of commenters for *Nyhetsspeilet*, where 9/11 joined other conspiracy topics in its section on "society." "Society" was one of three sections, related to the blog's goal of a "triple awakening" for its readers in three areas: "consciousness" (spirituality), "extra-terrestrial contacts" ("cosmos"), and "society." The three were interrelated. Extra-terrestrial contacts were seen as supplying spiritual messages, while their very existence, and all the evidence for their existence, was seen as suppressed by epistemic and political power. "Consciousness" involved prophetic messages of both spiritual and political transformation, including the fall of reigning powers and epistemic paradigms. While not present in every single article, conspiracism permeated presentations regardless of topic.[2]

Conspiracism was most dominant in the blog posts tagged with "society," which tabulated at 714 of 1085 posts by December 2014. The extra-terrestrial topic (the "cosmos"-tag) was, in line with general developments in the alternative movement, least used, including only 95 posts. Spirituality does not quite make up the rest, as some posts are untagged and some are also (double-)tagged as "video," but considering that these topics could flow over into each other, we get an impression of the relative interest. All of the categories could include apocalyptic messages of forewarning, including forewarnings about very tumultuous times, related to the 2012-apocalypse.

One of the reasons for the dominance of spirituality and conspiracy theory as topics was that they could *also* be driven by events. Constructing conspiracy *theory* in a manner that delineates the complex relations of postmodern "superconspiracies" is time consuming, and can make for dry reading. Conspiracist *interpretations of events* is less difficult, continually actualizes itself as "news," and can draw on an international community of interpreters. At the height of activities, relevant events could be anything from a prophesied collapse of the financial system, forthcoming or recent alien visitations (and the lack of media interest), to earthquakes, terrorism, or international

---

2. There was a gradual change here, with one of the more prominent contributors gradually (and only partially) breaking with the conspiracist paradigm, relegating it to a lower grade of importance, most clearly from 2012.

conflicts; all were construed as acts of the conspiracy. There will thus always be numerous international events that can be interpreted and integrated into a larger ideological framework, especially when millennial expectations have driven semiotic arousal to the level of promiscuity (cf. Landes 2011). So while the theories presented were often related to a global conspiracy—in the earliest formulations of triple awakening, the "New World Order" was an important area of interest—the superconspiracy was often constructed through its alleged influence on specific events.

This use of events and interpretation made it easier to accommodate a community of partially conflicting voices, via multiple interpretations that often involved both internal and external contradictions. As noted by Wood, Douglas, and Sutton (2012), the contradictions are not central as long as they each appeal to higher order beliefs that cohere with the worldview. The antagonisms raised and the higher order enemies tend to be the central points, rather than the details. This contributes to a general characteristic of conspiracism.

Enemies as populist cultural work

It is commonly accepted that conspiracy theories constitute a form of populist discourse. They do cultural work Michael Butter (2014, 18–20) pointedly summarizes as *distortion* and *deflection* in specific areas of conflicting interests.[3] Everything associated with the conflicts becomes, in line with the logic of populist dualism, associated with either friends or enemies, and the conflict gets similarly simplified into black and white. If we take this as our starting point: who were the culprits, or, more interestingly, which areas of antagonism were delineated and what were the primary solutions offered during the height of *Nyhetsspeilet*s activities?

If we start with the broadest picture, "enemies" could be almost anyone outside the conspiritual milieu, as the theories create *potential* conflicts that cover almost all sectors. This follows from the superconspiracist New World Order-theories. Obviously, the "could" was not always realized in explicit accusation. Choices were made, they form a pattern, and "internal," or local, enemies were notoriously related to "external" enemies as acting on behalf of the latter as agents or dupes. For the most part, they signaled the same areas of conflict. (I shall return to a subsection related to knowledge below.)

In good conspiracist tradition, everything was interrelated, the big with the small, the issues with each other, and the internal enemies with

---

3. Conspiracy theories by Butter's definition necessarily distort ("misrepresent") matters of fact. He uses the paired concepts distortion-deflection (mostly) to dissociate between conspiracy theories where "scapegoating" (deflection) is the central part of blaming, and those where the reasons for conflict are "merely" distorted, and blame is still delivered within society or group. I have adapted the terms here, so distortion is a necessary relation with regard to "facts," while "deflection" is a scale of degree regarding blame.

the external ones. One such area of entanglement may be seen when The Norwegian Institute of Public Health was tied to the larger global conspiracy like this:

> Former [foreign] minister Thorvald Stoltenberg has for many years been in league with the "godfather" of big pharma, David Rockefeller, among other things through his membership in the Rockefeller-led secret societies, *The Trilateral Commision* and *The Bilderberg Group*. The Norwegian Institute of Public Health—FHI (publicly known as the Norwegian Institute of Public Poisoning after the swineflu vaccine scandal) has a key role in the hidden co-operation between Rockefeller/Stoltenberg.[4]
>
> (Gaarder 2010)

The father was tied to the son (then prime minister) and daughter (then director of the institute), implicating a whole order of government and public health. Through activities (vaccine campaigns), both levels and people were tied to money-making schemes for Rockefeller, secret plots to decimate the world's population, and to schemes for enslaving the remaining world population. The latter was achieved through their connections to the wider "Rockefeller scheme" of Bilderberg and other "New World Order" organizations, which include a satanized Roman Catholic Church.

The internal enemies had, necessarily, local faces, but the vitally important ones were the external enemies running the show. The *external* enemy could be divided into the (semi)hidden power at the top of the conspiratorial pyramid, and its executive arms. The latter shows the antagonisms and parts of the ideological heritage. At the top of the list, we may summarize the enemies as financial elites and global, military power. Geopolitically, the United States, its institutions, government, and elites were at the center of theories. This is also the case if one excludes articles on 9/11. More locally, but still partially geopolitical, institutions, laws, and regulations related to the European Union were also among the popular targets. In line with the logic of superconspiracy theory, the "real" power behind the scenes was opaque. This created an opening for participants, either as contributors or as commenters, who blamed the Jews, the Vatican, the Illuminati, global bankers, the military-industrial complex, the Communists, evil aliens, or any combination of these and more. *Religion* was both a topic on its own and a way of uniting and demonizing "the enemy" as, when e.g. the Catholic Church, Judaism and esoteric societies were tied to an occult, Satanic conspiracy.

The multiplicity of possible villains was, in Norwegian as international conspirituality, tied to a more limited range of overarching topics. Most relate to knowledge, power, and freedom, with power at the center: power limits freedom and dominates what passes for knowledge. Still from a bird's eye perspective, but a little closer to particulars, many of the more popular

---

4. All translations from original sources in Norwegian are my own.

themes relate to globalization, in the shape of imperial, *martial* dominance over nation states and the *financial* dominance of a global elite. Conspiracy theories about prophesied or current events related to the "war on terror"—theories about "false flag"-terrorism—tended to present the events as caused by authorities hungry for further limits to personal and political freedom. When used to interpret what is commonly accepted as natural disasters (earthquakes, hurricanes etc), the conspiracy theories could vacillate between *politically* instrumental interpretations and interpretations fixed on the hidden *knowledge*. The political interpretations could present the "natural disaster" as e.g. *punishment* for some political transgression against the globalist agenda, or as *warning* to others. For instance:

> The Japanese finance minister told Benjamin Fulford in a video interview last year that Japan was threatened with earthquakes by New World Order (NWO) agents if they did not hand over [control of] the Japanese monetary system to American oligarchs. And shortly afterwards, two earthquakes [hit Japan] with epicenter directly under a nuclear power plant. (Karlstad 2011)

When "knowledge" came into focus, the events could be seen as *experiments* with e.g. the reach of new weapons. One such "weapon" was frequently thought to be Alaska's High Frequency Active Auroral Research Programme (HAARP), and its alleged underlings in the European Incoherent SCATter (EISCAT). These were, among many other things, speculated as behind the Haiti earthquakes of 2010, a host of disasters in 2002, as well as hurricanes through weather control (e.g. Hanssen 2010, 2013). The fact of HAARP being closed down since 2013 has not done any harm to its secret powers of destruction.

In either case, misuse of power or misuse of knowledge, the disasters—especially when we include diseases—were also made to thematize corrupt and evil expertise, showing the hidden reach of science and technology in the service of the conspiracy. (I shall defer further treatments of this side until the next section.)

The range of specific theories, as mentioned above, shows American theorists as the primary center from which ideas flow to the European and Norwegian periphery.[5] Hypertext linking habits and the textual focus on American topics and American governance all attest to this. This is not only the case for topics relating to international politics and local ramifications. Looking merely at *economic* conspiracy theories, we may note that although the alleged Jewishness of certain bankers could be viewed as relevant, common knowledge, the primary interest has more often been directed towards the Federal Reserve system. This interest is more than passing; theories of "the Fed" are, especially when tied to the Rockefeller and/or Rothschild family, linchpins integrating the concerns expressed in networks of partially over-

---

5. Theories from *Russia Today* and other anti-American propaganda sites dealing in conspiracy theory were also frequently used by some.

lapping theories. Again, even when the focus is Norway and local cases, the alternative history of the Federal Reserve is often prominent. Moreover, this history mostly follows something approaching a John Birch Society-version or a Sovereign Citizen-movement (more on this below) version, with explicit references to the same.

It is probably no coincidence that some of the primary concerns we see reflected in *Nyhetsspeilets* articles are about power in the form of imperialism in foreign policy and the financial dominance of elites. These are, albeit mostly "leftish," not only populist but also mainstream political topics of debate. The handling of 9/11 and the international banking crisis did not make them any less central. In the populist, conspiracist version, they serve as prime areas of conflict, with analyses projecting a dualist worldview onto the actors and extending their range of evil. There is a partial "deflection" of blame. It is quite clear that the assumption of guilt follows, not deflects from, the main line of conflict when political and financial power are at the center. However, when the tales of evil's course and causes center on invisible actors (e.g. an esoteric, satanic-globalist elite), particular family lines, or specific ethnicities, the distortion of fact necessarily also deflects blame. One example of this is when those following the Sovereign Citizen version of economic history, with its background in Christian Identity, even while disclaiming anti-Semitism, evoke and make use of old-school anti-Semitic theories.

The evocation of such theories seems to have been an important contributing factor to the site extending its reach to a more narrowly politically interested, right-wing audience. Since most of the writers shared neither the political allegiance nor the narrower interest, what kinds of solutions did they see for the problems they presented? The "easy" answer points towards that of an apocalyptic millennium, but that is only part of a more complex tale.

We may start with the catastrophic millennium that, during the height of the blog, was often connected to the wider expectation of the "2012 milieu" (see Gelfer 2011). Rarely directly related to the "old" date of December 21st, the multiple apocalypses of the 2012 milieu involved everything from a disaster related to a "pole shift" following the coming of "planet X" (Nibiru), to a spiritual renewal that would turn everything upside-down and right every wrong. Gradually. Participants but rarely foresaw a *passive* millennium. A few certainly did, but in the conspiritual scene, Norway included, most seem to have followed countercultural forerunners[6] and saw any coming cataclysm as an opportunity for more long-running cultural work in alternative economics, agriculture, medicine et cetera to take center stage in rebuilding a better world. The spiritual renewal of the cataclysm was not *always* presented as "heightening vibrations" with the spiritual manifesting more clearly in the material world, but it generally was expected to lend a hand.

---

6.   E.g. Reality Sandwich and its related activities, such as Evolver.

There were two elements here important to how the conspirituals saw a solution to the power of conspiracy. On the one hand, the current situation with the domination of current regimes of power-knowledge was not primarily presented as something to reform, step-by-step. Still, the step-by-step method *outside* and as *alternative* to the system was the primary answer when change was the topic. It did, however, on the other hand, seem to have to wait for the system to collapse before the new culture could take over. It was no revolutionary (or even "evolutionary," as with Reality Sandwich's *Evolver*) measure; at best, it was a protest and a way to prepare.

The most "revolutionary" protest came later, with the adoption of Sovereign Citizen-ideas to the European conspiritual scene. What is this? Very briefly, the "movement" developed as extreme versions of protests against U.S. federalism, and it denies legitimacy to authorities above the local level. An idea essential to the theory of Sovereign Citizens (or "Freemen," which is another label for theories that overlap) is a division between the "legal person" ("strawman") and the physical self. Individuals are, in their physical selves, "sovereign citizens," and not answerable to laws passed by what are deemed illegal authorities. The ideas have served to legitimize tax denial, and, indeed, to deny authority to any law outside its own, peculiar understanding of common law. An idea basic to the Freeman-variety is that governments have taken illegal ownership of individuals through their name, birth certificate, or other official documents, but that this is a contract that can be revoked by relinquishing surname and documents. Freeman ideology furthermore includes an idea that money (as token of value—"fiat money" as opposed to e.g. gold) is issued by taking the "legal person" as guarantee for value, effectively giving authorities ownership of the "strawman."[7] This idea is sometimes used to ground a particular set of actions: it is claimed that by the right juridical formulae one may not only free oneself of the state's claims, but also of any financial claims from banks et cetera, and instead *claim* large sums from the bank (see e.g. Wessinger 2000; Barkun 1994).

This alternative theory of money and jurisprudence has taken hold of Freemen-on-the-land to the degree that its practice tends to be viewed as a financial scam (e.g. Rooke 2012). From a legal point of view, this is probably correct. Catherine Wessinger (2000) has a sociologically more astute observation when she compares the byzantine, pseudo-legal and -financial theories to traditional nativist movements' magical rites and remedies to counter the Europeans' bullets. The slings and arrows of modernity take the shape of incomprehensible power, and integrated global economies may take turns that affect private incomes in a similarly incomprehensible manner. Thus remedies take the form of Richard Feynman's "cargo cult science,"

---

7. Accordingly, one of the sometime writers at Nyhetsspeilet has recently tried to raise a court case against the prime minister for enslaving the Norwegian people through such means. (http://www.ta.no/Ingunn_truer_nye_eiere_av__Niceland_-5-50-32758.html)

mimicking the shapes, sounds, and sights of the legal and financial language, institutions et cetera that are seen as suppressive.

The following piece of writing from *Nyhetsspeilet* gives an example of the kind of reasoning involved:

> To become a freewoman I first did three things:
> 1. Announced to the state that there is no contract or anything enforceable between us, referring to my natural right to live in the country because I was born here. ...
>   In this letter I specify that I refrain from provision of state benefits and that I will not be contributing to this community. ...
> 2. In the letter above, I asked the government to inform all their agents via its registers that there is no contract between us ... I ... also sent a legal document to some public agencies ... and informed that there exists no authority to act, sign, negotiate or anything else on my behalf. ...
> 3. Then, most importantly: I am in the process of establishing a company through a private process (no registration in public registers) and then pledge my birth certificate in a holding company. My birth certificate is a security that I rightfully own. (Sigurdsdatter 2013)

Among the declarations we find statements that the author's house was an independent state, that the mortgage with the bank was invalid, and, of course, that there would be no taxes paid. There are multiple examples of this particular pseudo-legal language[8], but these are mainly reserved as legal documents and prescriptions for others who want to follow the same road.

Unsurprisingly, neither the bank nor the government took heed. The author was expelled from her state, and the house foreclosed. Her remedial acts are perhaps, as Wessinger argues, best seen as "magical," but this is a matter of degree, with Norwegian conspirituals ranging close to the pure type. In the U.S., by contrast, movements proposing the theory and acting accordingly are defending "their" property and their interpretations with guns. They have shot police officers and tax collectors, and sometimes they rally a group of armed believers in hope of a revolutionary uprising. Acting along the lines of ideology provokes governments and banks to retaliate, and so it guarantees a further radicalization among some of the believers. In Norway, and as covered by *Nyhetsspeilet*, "freemen" may write about the ideology, lecture on it, and, in some cases, adhere to it to the extent that they become homeless—but in the three cases nationally to date, believers have gathered and sung "Kumbaya." They have become angered, but they have not taken up arms, nor appealed for such. The protest is thus resolved—so far—as a purely ideological struggle. It has a high personal cost, but the "solution," when protests and attempts at withdrawal from the corruption

---

8. See http://www.sigurdsdatter.com/juridisk-hoveddokument-edssvoren-erklaeligring.html

of society have been tried to the end, is still the conspiritual "love and light" (cf. Eggen 2014).

The conflict over epistemic authority

The generalized overview above gives a vague impression of some superordinate areas of conflict. It does not attempt to give full insight into the multiform theories and their multitude of specific pictures of enemies internal and external. Nor have I yet done more than mention an important, specific area of conflict—that over what gets to count as knowledge. This was and is a central topic for conspiracy culture, both in the conspiritual sense and outside, and for *Nyhetsspeilet* as a modern day venue for a wider "cultic milieu."[9]

The problem is a general one. Within a fully conspiracist worldview, the complicity of knowledge workers becomes central to the explanation of how truth is hidden. One of the early ways this was written into *Nyhetsspeilet* was a list of the "taboos" of mainstream media (e.g. Gaarder 2009, 2010). The early version was relatively brief, and centered on foreign policy, recent history and current events. Later, it filled out, and areas where science and scientists were explicitly presented as part of the conspiracy became more numerous. The audience expanded, and the articles expanded both in territory and in reach.

This creates its own set of dynamics. With relative success in attracting an audience, writers, and a high public profile, come countering voices. The social elite previously attacked for hiding masonic, Jewish, or other identities deemed problematic did not answer, but certain academics did.[10] Obviously, the response engendered (heightened) conflict.

There were two general, topical responses from the conspiracy scene, sometimes from the same people: the individual, activist academics were dismissed and tied to a conspiracy against the truth-tellers, or the whole enterprise of institutionalized science was dismissed as corrupt. When tied to current events or particular lines of history, the local enemies could be particular individuals representing institutions, the whole institution (e.g. Norwegian Institute of Public Health) or both. The first line, especially the one where the critics were dismissed as skeptics (or "septics") is the one I have followed most closely. Since some of the publicly profiled critics (such as myself) were organized skeptics, the conclusion tended to be that any kind of critic—including those from alternative religion forums—was also a hidden skeptic, sent out by the Skeptics society. These were often, but not

---

9. I will not address criticism of Campbell's theory here, but I will note that the evocation of the theory is highly instrumental and focused on Campbell's interest in science as the new orthodoxy from which "alternatives" are being cast as heterodox (and wrong). See Asprem and Dyrendal 2015.

10. Disclosure: I was among the earliest, as an established public voice on and against conspiracism. Thus other critics were, for a time, seen as my dupes, while I was construed as a dupe of, complicit with, or small-time, paid lackey of "Them."

always, then tied to external enemies in the larger conspiracy: the established truth of the government being run by alien forces (e.g. the Bilderberg-group, NWO, etc) was temporarily forgotten as some wanted to appeal to authorities, local and national, to stop all this critical attention.

As more skeptics at the grassroots level started blogging critically, the attention shifted again. When the Humanist society started a campaign for critical thinking[11] directed specifically against alternative business forms, alternative treatment modalities, conspiracy theory, vaccine denial, etc., these became proof of a many-headed, local conspiracy (Humanist-Skeptics) against e.g. health freedom and religious freedom. This particular constellation was again, of course, tied to a broader conspiracy: a socialist (Fabian society), satanic-pedophile, occult, and/or Catholic-Jewish one. The latter designations were optional, and seemed less important, other than as integrating the local enemy within a total worldview. The *important* enemies were the local, visible individuals and groups, and while conspiracist discourse certainly *distorted* the scientific evidence and the position of its critics, it is more difficult to dismiss completely the blame as *deflection* (cf. Butter 2014). The skeptical voices did become scapegoats for the grand conspiracy, and by protesting the distortion of history or facts of natural science, served as opposition in in epistemic claims even where they may have shared concern about *issues*. But protesting claims to truth is central on its own.

The question of what gets to count as knowledge is obviously not wholly removed from the question of economy and power. It is, rather, related at many levels. At the level of daily life and daily bread, it is related when we look at the part of the alternative scene where many make their living from "holistic" medicine and its multitude of services and products.[12] To conspiracy *theorists* it is even more important. Counter-knowledge is their coin *and* often their way of salvation (e.g. Dyrendal 2013). David Robertson (2014) notes that while conspiracy theory is a theodicy of the dispossessed, the the-

---

11. The campaign was called "Ingen Liker Å Bli Lurt"—nobody likes to be fooled, and manifested primarily as a web page and a Facebook group. It engendered debate and conflict so intense that the controversy was enough to spill over in both media and court rooms. (I should mention that although I've had no part in the campaign after it started, I was commissioned to write part of the campaign's original "manifesto" on critical thinking, possibly contributed some ideas on direction, and played in one of the campaign YouTube-videos—on conspiracy theories. All this is well-known to interested parties, and has contributed to some interesting varieties of predictable hostilities: Starring in homoerotic "anti-fan fiction" is a long step up from death threats, and this kind of satire certainly puts its own twist on "love" as the solution to all problems. (For a brief review, see Eggen 2012; Færseth 2013b.)

12. Theorists, practitioners, and/or vendors were a minority among *Nyhetsspeilets* authors, but theories of conspiracy against "health freedom" (another American, Bircher-based import) were among those broadening the appeal of *Nyhetsspeilet*. This became most clearly visible with the implosion of the milieu as *Nyhetsspeilet* lost traction.

orists generally present themselves as an epistemic counter-elite:

> Whether aligned with left or right political values, metaphysical con-
> spiracist narratives reframe Marxist critiques in terms of epistemic
> rather than economic capital. The liberation of the oppressed is re-con-
> structed as being realised through a revolution in knowledge, a seizing
> not of the means of production, but of the means of cognition. Knowl-
> edge is power. (Robertson 2014, 196)

The conspiracy theorists in question have little other cultural capital *qua* theorists. What they *can* claim is special insight. The claims to special knowledge, "epistemic capital," stand at the center of the whole venture. It is therefore unsurprising that those who publicly argue that the coin is counterfeit and that the "counter-epistemic elite" should generally be seen as epistemically dispossessed come high on the list of specific, local ene-mies. Academics, journalists, newspaper editors and other knowledge work-ers who perform a role of gate-keepers, by closing them from conspiritual claims, naturally become part of the bigger scheme.

Skeptical voices are, therefore, central to the conflict. They may or may not reflect the conflict over *values* or *issues*, but they are vital, and real, oppo-nents in the antagonism over facts, epistemology, and the complexities of power and knowledge. But the antagonism serves as deflection at another level: when some go out of their way to counter the conspiracy claims, they become an identifiable, hostile, local out-group. Focusing on such enemies contributes to communal identity and to keeping internal tensions under the carpet.

This may have become more important over time, as conspiritual dis-course had its own set of fault lines. It may, perhaps, have had more of them than most, as the scene attracted people with widely different primary interests and differing primary religious and political identities. Internal tensions were always visible, so what kept the "community" together and what split it apart? Could its rise and fall be seen as part of the rise and fall of apocalyptic expectations?

Growth and decline of an apocalyptic wave

When *Nyhetsspeilet* started out in 2009, they had the Norwegian scene mostly to themselves (cf. Dyrendal 2015). The flagship of the alternative movement, *Visjon*, may have printed similar material (cf. Lie 2009), and older actors in the scene had also become more interested in conspiracy theory. Neither put conspiracy at the center, and neither focused on web presence. One of the central actors behind *Nyhetsspeilet* had long experience in IT and online publishing. Others had long experience in writing for the alternative scene, and they reached out to a crowd that had gotten familiar with "web 2.0," that is: online comments, blogs, and other interactive, "alternative media." But there was, as yet, no one filling this niche. *Nyhetsspeilet* had a reach broader than they may have planned, and since it was the place where things were happening, people with more single-issue interests also frequented the pages as commenters or even (often one-shot) writers.

Creating and maintaining an audience online demands visibility, and regular activity along lines of public interest. *Nyhetsspeilet* presented a slick, well-designed page from the start, and posted frequently, often relating their theories to current events. Already during the first year, in 2009, they published 282 blog posts (Figure 8.1). Next year saw even more activity. They built a following, with at times a lot of activity in the comment fields from a varied mass of commenters. Sometimes the posts consisted of little more than embedded video links with short (or no) text between, but, more often, they were more essayistic. Since they wanted to be an alternative *magazine*, the blog posts could be feature-length or longer.

As we have seen above, and in line with the original concept of conspirituality, *Nyhetsspeilet* embodied a millennial vision. To be precise, they were carried by and promoted several varieties of millennial ideas, some more explicit and focused in time than others. With the general ideological and semiotic promiscuity of the milieu, the explicitly millennial visions derived from many different sources. The 2012 prophecies were given wide play, and accordingly many drew on ideas current in the broader 2012-milieu. They did so without, in general, identifying with the particular date or a very specific stance (e.g. Aune 2010, 2011, 2012). To the degree some did, it was typically *not* December 21st 2012 or the main theorists of 2012: when upheavals were expected, they were typically expected *in advance* of the key date (e.g. Myhre 2010).

This is one of several things that also fit the pattern of activity over time, as we can see in the table opposite. Looking at the levels of activity over time, we note a high of 303 posts in 2010, with a low of 37 by mid-December 2014. Comments behave in a corresponding (but not identical[13]) pattern, and the forum, a late addition, has had very little activity.

There are many reasons for the fervor in the early period and the drop off since 2011. We can take the obvious first. Both one-person and group blogs tend to be temporary ventures, with more enthusiasm and energy at the beginning. As with movements, they are dependent on someone to carry the venture, and the fewer who are able and willing, the more strain on those who do. Eventually, most tire. Group blogs have another source of strain that will eventually turn up almost anywhere: internal, personal conflicts, and dissent over ideology, authority or both. In cases of defection or schism, such dissent tends to become ideologized.

---

13. I have also broken down the publications on a monthly basis. While doing so, I anecdotally got the impression of a possible trend: a drop in comments, combined with a more hostile tone towards some of the writers, seemed to presage less activity on behalf of the writers.

Figure 8.1   Annual blog posts *Nyhetsspeilet.*

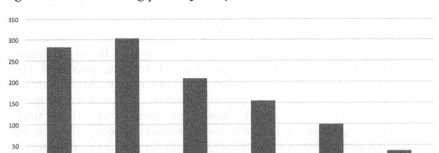

With the exception of the last part, we may observe all this in the brief history of *Nyhetsspeilet* (cf. Færseth 2013a). While there were more writers joining than leaving at the beginning, the opposite happened later. Some were, according to gossip, "forced" out, others dropped out. One of those who left was one of the most active writers. When he moved back to his own solo venture (*Riksavisen*), he seems to have taken most of the others inclined towards Nordic Israelism, or his highly esoteric version of it, along with him. Since these were, at the time, among the most active commenters, both posting and comments became more rare. Others had already left, some to start group blogs or Facebook groups, focusing on topics and theories closer to their own particular interests. The fission created a differentiated conspiritual landscape, but apart from *Riksavisen*, none of the others put as much *emphasis* on the combined topics of spirituality and conspiracy as *Nyhetsspeilet.*

It is thus anything but surprising that we see a sharp decline after a highly active start. Judging from both social activity and social media, the conspiritual scene does not, at the same time, seem to have become smaller. It has become more diverse, but, with few exceptions, the millennial aspects have been toned down severely. This is one of the reasons why I want to present "millennial fervor" as another possible factor. Another indicator leading to this interpretation was the varied reception of prophecies in the comments over time.

Nyhetsspeilet started their movie links with *Zeitgeist* and later moved on to *Thrive*, both combining conspiracy theory and alternative culture with a sharper apocalyptic twist in the latter. Ward and Voas (2011, 109) note the importance of *Zeitgeist* for the international trend, but the "zeitgeist" of the period and scene also quite clearly related apocalypticism to the "Maya calendar"-prophecies. The presentation and reception of such prophecies on the international scene could be quite contentious.[14] The range of com-

---

14.   Brief note on background: I followed the 2012 scene online for many years, system-

ments varied from highly positive and strong belief, to doubt, cynicism, and harsh criticism. That is *before* I take visiting skeptics into account; parts of the 2012-culture were sophisticated and jaded users of prophecy. We see something similar with *Nyhetsspeilet* as well, but as in other online settings, there was a development. Part of the early criticism came from loosely interested participants, whose interest in conspiracy was more selectively political, parts from participants whose particular take on conspirituality excluded their specific version of millennialist prophecy. Many more of the comments engaged in their own prophecies, or related "signs" or prophecies from other sources.

Two of the regular writers were more interested in specific time periods for apocalyptic expectations than others. One in particular tied date-setting to catastrophic coming events (e.g. Myhre 2010; cf. Aune 2010). Both showed a high level of interest in millennial dreams, with clear, albeit different specific expectations. One gradually dropped activities to nearly nil after prophecies had failed. The other shifted his blogging to other topics. This did not, initially, help. Hostile reactions followed, and his posts tended to be voted down to a lower level than others. Commenters positive to the mayanist prophecies dropped out, or stopped commenting. The tone and content of comments shifted. A sharper, Biblicist language suggested that the "Nordic Israelites" had taken over comments. Then they dropped out as well.

Certainly not all of this was related to the end of 2012 prophecies, or even jaded attitudes towards prophecy. First, conspiritual activities elsewhere continued. Secondly, the trend started earlier, in the first months of 2011. There is no clearly visible drop in activity immediately after the bombing of government buildings in Oslo and mass murders at Utøya on July 22nd. Rather, the events revitalized the scene at a part of the year when activities are low on almost all blogs, group or otherwise. But the conspiracism of Breivik combined with the slaughter of children led to a more explicitly critical attention towards, and action against, conspiracy theory. This happened broadly in society, and it also happened specifically within the broader New Age scene. Conspiracists had antagonized and alienated others at alt-nett.ning earlier. Now many of them were banned. The flagship journal and organizers of the alternative fairs took issue, and conspiracist contributors were shut out—including Ertresvåg, a previously popular speaker. The alternative mainstream asserted itself, and it restigmatized the most aggressively conspiritual scene from "inside" New Age as being morally beyond the pale.

The shock of the terror attack and group pressure from inside the alternative scene may have added to the lack of activity, and the increasingly sharper drop in activity. When "hangers-on" saw no bonus in using *Nyhetsspeilet* as a venue, but a possible gain in doing it on their own, the scene was set for exodus.

---

atically with students in a related course each Fall term from 2009 through 2012, and had three master's students writing about the varied scene.

All the above is also consistent with, and may be seen as the expression of, the passing crest of an "apocalyptic wave."

The "anatomy of an apocalyptic wave," Richard Landes (2011, 52–61) explains, forms a bell-shaped curve, with a curve of activity from the onset of apocalyptic time to people re-entering normal time. He describes two relevant sets of perception of time, normal and apocalyptic, with the first a flat (time-)line, where people expect the future to be a continuation of the past. Apocalyptic time presents the possibility for (or inevitability of) a *break* with the past. With the growing perception of a crisis about to be resolved through such a break with the past, the flat line curves upwards with rising expectations and activity. On the rising crest, apocalyptic expectations enter the public sphere, more people are recruited to belief, and current events are turned into signs of the coming resolution ("semiotic arousal"). As expectations rise further, semiotic arousal is turned into full-scale promiscuity, with any- and everything becoming a sign of what, when, who, and why.

While believers need not set particular dates, the waveform comes from the tendency (or inevitability) of millennial expectations to fail, even or especially when they grow to their most intense levels. Cognitive dissonance sets in, certainty fails, adherents are lost, activity drops, and, with the re-emergence of "normal time," there is a tendency to retreat to the private sphere.

We may now return to the "curve" of publications, and their relation to apocalyptic expectations. As noted, two of the central writers were highly involved in presenting interpretations of apocalyptic prophecies, and at their height, many more of the commentators were similarly engaged in giving their own—"intuitive," channeled, prophetic or other—takes on the coming turnabout. However, far from all of the writers, and a smaller percentage of commenters, were actively engaged in *this* kind of revealed knowledge, or from a similar stance. Engaging in "rolling prophecy" (Robertson 2013) is a risky venture. When successful, one may take credit for whatever happens or has happened, but this often means adhering to the rhetorical strategies of the psychic trade: vagueness, ambiguity, semantic forks, shotgunning, etc. One should have established enough authority to make the audience *want* to interpret you as correct in the aftermath of events. With *Nyhetsspeilet*, the apocalyptic prophecies were fairly straightforward and relatively unambiguous; they were delivered in writing (thus easy to check); and to a diverse audience where the writers had not established sufficient authority. Thus, they contributed to making a possible fault line an actual one when the prophecies inevitably and quite clearly failed.

We can add to this that other believers also clearly seem to have become disappointed in the lack of progress. Some floated back to the alternative mainstream less affected with millennial fervor. Others may have become disappointed with the internal mainstreaming of *Nyhetsspeilet*: posts gradually changed focus as it re-entered "normal time." They became longer, many became more "theoretical," more academic, and, when not, the spiritual message was more mainstream, inspired by e.g. late Theosophy. Current events played a much lesser role in the increasingly smaller output of posts. There may be signs of revitalization, particularly with events relating to "Freemen"-ideology playing out, but, effectively, the (first) crest has passed. Norwegian conspirituality has diversified, but for the moment seems less intense.

Final remarks

Conspiracy theory is rarely a stranger to any human scene. This is also true for "New Age" in both the broad and narrow sense. The wider New Age scene tends to be less enamored of the dualism, harsh language, and antagonism-driven activism of the conspirituals. A version of e.g. the conspiracy theory of ignorance is nonetheless a natural side effect of the ideas of hidden knowledge that dominate the same scene. Whether addressing history, health, economics, self-development, channeling revelations or other activities, alternative routes to alternative knowledge are unavoidable. So is the, at best, disinterest of science. When the knowledge elites disrupt claims of "counter-knowledge elites," conspiracy theory is close at hand.

This does not mean explicit conspiracy theory is equally important to, or welcome in, all alternative circles at all times. Norwegian conspirituality may have a long history (Dyrendal 2015), but it blossomed in millennial fervor during a few, short years during the final years of the "noughties," then cooled off. But while the fervor may be less intense, the phenomenon looks unlikely to go away anytime soon. The first scene to set conspirituality at its center took its inspiration from a US-dominated, international conspiracy scene. New Age millennialism, with a dream of a kinder, more spiritual world, was one part of the background, but writers borrowed frequently from more militant sources as well. While the specific theories may have seemed strange to outsiders, the *general concerns* were common ones. They ranged from agency loss to health issues, to religious, cultural, political, military, and economic power. With semiotic promiscuity, they could see evidence anywhere, and their enemies could be everywhere and anyone. The enemies were powerful, but the tone was often optimistic. Certainly, there were clear tendencies towards presenting Western democracies as hidden dictatorships ruled by a global oligarchy, but the attempts at "raising awareness" showed implicit or explicit ideas that an informed populace can still prevent a full take-over. At the most pessimistic, they could still shake off their chains, albeit mainly by magical means or after apocalyptic events. Helpful aliens or other spiritual forces could be invoked as help, but still, the important thing was to handle both the current and the forthcoming situation by developing oneself spiritually and building good alternatives on the side of a culture ruled by greed.

The example addressed here rose to prominence as an "early adopter" of international trends, and served to present "rolling prophecy" (Robertson

2013) that predicted and presented events in the light of conspiracy and millennial change. It thus served to generate and maintain a state of "semiotic arousal" in a diverse audience, drawing on the 2012 milieu (e.g. Gelfer 2011). The weight of failed expectations, internal dissent, and reactions to events contributed to the "fall," with the temporary amalgamation of people and interests dissolving and new unions establishing new, related ventures. The rise to dominance of Facebook (especially its group function) did nothing to help older online media. Following the implosion of the first scene, there has also been a change in focus. The new websites and groups center their attention on more specialized, smaller spectrum of issues. Their conspiracy theories are rarely as wide-ranging, the issue of spiritual development has become less important, and the extra-terrestrials are rarely addressed at all. None of the topics are dead, but at the present time, others are more important.

But although many of the current sites read almost like secular conspiracy theorists, and the mainstream New Age has distanced itself even more clearly from conspiracism, conspirituality is still a vital discourse and a living milieu. It shapes Norwegian (as well as European) "Freemen-on-the-land"-ideas, and many of the original concerns are addressed in both lectures and texts, committed by more people than the original entrepreneurs. Dreams of the millennium may have currently passed for most, but social critique in a conspiracist manner has not.

References

Asprem, Egil and Asbjørn Dyrendal. 2015. "Conspirituality reconsidered: How surprising and how new is the confluence of spirituality and conspiracy theory?" *Journal of Contemporary Religion* 30(3): 367–382.

Aune, Frank. 2010. 2012: Det store dimensjonsskiftet. *Nyhetsspeilet* June 21st 2010. http://www.nyhetsspeilet.no/2010/06/2012-det-store-dimensjonsskiftet/

———. 2011. NB: Oppstigning pågår! *Nyhetsspeilet* August 6th 2011. http://www.nyhetsspeilet.no/2011/08/nb-oppstigning-pagar/

———. 2012. Enden er nær. *Nyhetsspeilet* June 21st 2012. http://www.nyhetsspeilet.no/2012/06/enden-er-naer/

Barkun, Michael. 1994. *Religion and the Racist Right.* Chapel Hill: The University of North Carolina Press.

———. 2003. *A Culture of Conspiracy.* Berkeley: University of California Press.

Bruder, Martin, Peter Haffke, Nick Neave, Nina Nouripanha and Roland Imhoff. 2013. "Measuring individual differences in generic beliefs in conspiracy theories across cultures: Conspiracy mentality questionnaire." *Frontiers in Psychology.* doi: 10.3389/fpsyg.2013.00225

Butter, Michael. 2014. *Plots, Designs, and Schemes. American Conspiracy Theories from the Puritans to the Present.* Berlin: Walter de Gruyter.

Byford, Jovan. 2011. *Conspiracy Theories. A Critical Introduction.* New York: Palgrave Macmillan.

Campbell, Colin. 1972. "The cult, the cultic milieu and secularization." *A Sociological Yearbook of Religion in Britain* 5: 119–136.

Dyrendal, Asbjørn. 2013. "Hidden knowledge, hidden powers: Esotericism and conspiracy culture." In *Contemporary Esotericism*, edited by Egil Asprem and Kennet Granholm, 200–225. Sheffield: Equinox.

———. 2015. "Conspirituality in Norway: A brief sketch." In *Handbook of Nordic New Religions*, edited by James R. Lewis and Inga B. Tøllefsen, 268–290. Leiden: Brill Academic.

Dyrendal, Asbjørn and Egil Asprem. 2013. "Sorte brorskap, mørke korrespondanser og frelsende avsløringer. Konspirasjonsteori som esoterisk diskurs. Din." *Tidsskrift for religion og kultur* 2: 32–61.

Eggen, Torgrim. 2012. "I skitstormen." *Humanist* 2012(2): 4–25.

———. 2014. De som hater staten. *Humanist* 2014(3): 5–24

Færseth, John. 2013a. *KonspiraNorge*. Oslo: Humanist forlag.

———. 2013b. "Med Human-Etisk Forbund som skyteskive." *Humanist* 2013(4): 48–71.

Fenster, Mark. 2008. *Conspiracy Theories. Secrecy and Power in American Culture.* Minneapolis: University of Minnesota Press.

Feynman, Richard P. 1985. "Cargo Cult Science." In *Surely You're Joking Mr. Feynman*, 338–346. London: Random House.

Gaarder, Hans. 2009. Tabu-oversikten for norske redaktører. *Nyhetsspeilet*, March 10th 2009. http://www.nyhetsspeilet.no/2009/03/tabu-oversikten-for-norske-redaktorer/

———. 2010. Norske mediers samlede tabo-oversikt. *Nyhetsspeilet*, March 21st 2010. http://www.nyhetsspeilet.no/2010/03/norske-mediers-samlede-tabu-oversikt/

Gelfer, Joseph. 2011. *2012. Decoding the Countercultural Apocalypse.* Sheffield: Equinox.

Gray, Matthew. 2010. *Conspiracy Theories in the Arab World.* New York: Routledge

Hammer, Olav. 2001. *Claiming Knowledge. Strategies of Epistemology from Theosophy to the New Age.* Leiden: Brill.

Hanegraaff, Wouter J. 1996. *New Age Religion and Western Culture: Esotericism in the Mirror of Secular Thought.* Leiden: Brill.

———. 2012. *Esotericism and the Academy: Rejected Knowledge in Western Culture.* Cambridge: Cambridge University Press.

Hanssen, Maarit M. 2010. HAARP et geofysisk våpen. *Nyhetsspeilet* Jan.18, 2010. http://www.nyhetsspeilet.no/2010/01/haarp-et-geofysisk-vapen/

———. 2013. EISCAT og HAARP er ferdigstilt som våpen i 2013. *Nyhetsspeilet* Jan.4, 2013. http://www.nyhetsspeilet.no/2013/01/eiscat-og-haarp-er-ferdigstilt-som-vapen-i-2013/

Heilund, J.B. 2003. "Konspiratører og det ytre rom. Konspirasjonsteorier i norske ufo-miljøer." In *Konspiranoia. Konspirasjonsteorier fra 666 til WTC.* edited by A. Pettersen and T. Emberland, 262–294. Oslo: Humanist forlag.

Imhoff, Roland, and Martin Bruder. 2014. "Speaking (un-)truth to power: Conspiracy mentality as a generalised political attitude." *European Journal of Personality* 28: 25–43.

Karlstad, Tor. 2011. Japan truet med jordskjelv av NWO. *Nyhetsspeilet* March 13, 2011. http://www.nyhetsspeilet.no/2011/03/japan-truet-med-jordskjelv-av-nwo/

Landes, Richard. 2011. *Heaven on Earth: The Varieties of the Millennial Experience.* New York: Oxford University Press.

Lie, Jørgen. 2009. "Ondskapsforståelse i New Age. En diskursanalyse av magasinet Visjon." Unpublished MA thesis, Department of Archaeology and Religious Studies, Norwegian University of Science and Technology.

Myhre, Rolf Kenneth. 2010. Mens vi venter på Nivå 7-kataklysmene. *Nyhetsspeilet* July 23rd 2010. http://www.nyhetsspeilet.no/2010/07/mens-vi-venter-pa-niva-7-kataklysmen/

Pipes. Daniel. 1997. *Conspiracy.* New York: Free Press.

Robertson, David G. 2013. "(Always) Living in the end times: The 'rolling prophecy' of the conspiracy milieu." In *Prophecy in the New Millennium: When Prophecies Persist,* edited by Sarah Harvey and Suzanne Newcombe, 207-219. Farnham: Ashgate.

———. 2014. Metaphysical conspiracism: UFOs as discursive objects between popular millennial and conspiracist fields." Unpublished PhD Thesis, University of Edinburgh.

Rooke, J. D. 2012. *Meads v. Meads, 2012 ABQB 571. Reasons for the Decision of the Associate Chief Justice J.D. Rooke.* Edmonton, Canada: Court of Queen's Bench of Alberta.

Sigurdsdatter, Ingunn. 2013. Så hvorfor bli frikvinne og hvordan gå fram? *Nyhetsspeilet* May 30, 2013 http://www.nyhetsspeilet.no/2013/05/sa-hvor-for-bli-frikvinne-og-hvordan-ga-fram-artikkel-1-av-to/

Swami, Viren, Rebecca Coles, Stefan Stieger, Jakob Pietschnig, Adrian Furnham, Sherry Rehim and Martin Voracek. 2011. "Conspiracist ideation in Britain and Austria: Evidence of a monological belief system and associations between individual psychological differences and real-world and fictitious conspiracy theories." *British Journal of Psychology* 102: 443–463.

Uscinski, Joseph E. and Joseph Parent. *American Conspiracy Theories.* Oxford: Oxford University Press

Ward, Charlotte, and David Voas. 2011. "The emergence of conspirituality." *Journal of Contemporary Religion* 26(1): 103–121.

Wessinger, Catherine. 2000. *How the Millennium Comes Violently.* New York: Seven Bridges Press

Wood, Michael J., Karen Douglas and Robert Sutton. 2012. Dead and alive: Belief in contradictory conspiracy theories." *Social Psychology and Personality Science* 3: 767–773.

9

Contemporary Spiritualism in Norway:
Faith Assemblies and Market Products

ANNE KALVIG

Communication with spirits of the deceased has been one of the major themes of the New Age movement. It was an important current prior to and in the days of the Theosophical Society and similar innovations in the nineteenth century, and has been a lasting component of and impulse within modern New Age and alternative spirituality.

In this chapter, I present spiritualism in contemporary Norway, offering an overview over a wide field that has not received much scholarly attention. I outline organizations with spiritualist content, as well as provide examples of actors and practices of spiritualism within a more loosely organized, market-oriented field. I thus consider how spiritualism is lived out in Norway today, and how the variegated forms, actors and organizations influence each other and contribute to a varied, yet identifiable, thematic field of transgressive communication—with the dead and with other entities in "the spirit world." In my concluding remarks, I explore whether and how spiritualism in Norway today might be seen as religion here, there, anywhere and everywhere.

My material consists of fieldwork data, and written and online sources.[1] I present the larger organizations more thoroughly, and then look into psychic telephone lines and other examples of mediumistic enterprises. I choose to focus on these manifestations of contemporary spiritualism in Norway

---

1. As a project involving data collection of information regarding persons, this is registered in the Norwegian Social Science Data Services (NSD). People within the spiritualist/ mediumship field with official roles, spokespersons, or people of considerable fame, are not anonymized, neither those who have explicitly asked for identification.

as they clearly involve and engage people and represent somewhat more "active" spiritist-mediumistic practices than does for example watching the popular house cleansing program "The Power of the Spirits" on TV Norge (attracting around half a million viewers each week). I also focus on Norwegian spiritualists, spiritists and mediums (people residing in Norway) and not on international personalities like mediums Lisa Williams or Colin Fry.[2] Although they are highly popular in Norway, my aim is to outline national actors and practices. However, it is important to bear in mind both that contemporary spiritualism in Norway is obviously part of a global phenomenon, and that mediums of who present themselves in a "global format," like Willams, are part of a national discourse on spiritualism and mediumship.[3]

In its classical heyday of the nineteenth and early twentieth century, spiritualism was marked by a great variety, and the same holds true for what we might call the present spiritualist revival. Considering its various traits and modes, the characteristics of spiritualism are occultist, neo-spiritual and folk religious. Within these wide frames, it is possible to analyze further forms, actors and organizations of spiritualism, and gain a better insight into the practitioners' own understandings and motivations. Communication with the dead in the form of a psychic telephone line or as a meeting in the evening in a village hall are obviously quite different, but the common denominator is the central meaning given to communication with spirits of the dead, and possibly other kinds of spirits. As a parallel, we might point to the great variety of religion in general, in Norway and elsewhere: What is, for example, the similarity between a High Mass in a Cathedral and a Free-Church revival meeting, or between a solitary evening prayer and a prayer in a morning service? All of these forms belong to (Lutheran) Christianity's modes in today's Norway, even though they are quite variegated. Similarly, spiritualism has its complex existence, and the variation probably serves to strengthen, not weaken, the phenomenon.

Spiritualism or spiritism?

Historically and in the present, spiritualism and spiritism have been designations for different traditions, spiritualism being the Anglo-American variant introduced by the Fox sisters, whereas Spiritism originated in France with Allan Kardec, eventually spreading to South America, especially Brazil.[4]

---

2. Colin Fry passed away in August 2015.

3. I have in this chapter chosen to focus on the field of spiritualist practices, and, for the sake of clarity, not on the Norwegian, public discourse on spiritualism and mediumship.

4. The three Fox sisters are generally acknowledged as the spiritualist movement's first mediums. The sisters heard and later interpreted mysterious raps as spirit communication in their house in Hydesville, New York, starting in 1848 (Braude 2001, 10–11). Allan Kardec, the pen name of French author Hippolyte Léon Denizard Rivail (1804–1869), is the founder of the organized spiritist movement, commencing with the publication of his *Le Livre des esprits* in 1857, four years after the first events

These designations may hold for the Norwegian situation today, spiritualism being the spiritualist actors and activities organized within the "Norwegian Spiritualist Union" (NSU)[5] with its subgroups, in addition to a few other, independent spiritualist groupings, such as "Mediumship in Drammen"[6] (a town in the southeastern parts of the country). There is also a network of spiritist groups in the tradition of Allan Kardec, primarily GEEAK Norway—The Group for Spiritist Studies Allan Kardec.[7] These organizations will be presented below. The more loosely organized field might also be called spiritism, or the spiritist field. However, in English spiritualism is more commonly understood as the denominator for a wider spectrum of concepts and practices of communication with spirits and the dead, not necessarily organized in spiritualist churches, and hence is used as such in this chapter. This wider field has composite traits and modes other than the traditional ones that we associate with an organization/church involving membership, meetings, certain forms of executive committees and the like. I will investigate the field, roughly distinguishing the more traditionally organized forms of spiritualism/spiritism such as NSU and GEEAK from a more generalized spiritualism that has other composite traits such as, for example (and to a greater extent), products on a market.

Norwegian Spiritualist Union: An umbrella organization for a religious community and practitioners' unions

The Norwegian Spiritualist Union, present online as spiritualist.no, has over 1100 members and consists of a religious community and two unions for practitioners within healing and mediumship, in addition to the umbrella organization, or union, itself. NSU has chosen a star-shaped symbol as a logo; symbols often used by spiritualists include the sun, stars, and/or an open book. NSU leader André Kirsebom explains the Norwegian design:

> In the beginning of 2007, when the Norwegian Spiritualist Union was founded, it was important to create a logo that could represent the union and be easily recognized. After a few hours of intense, creative work and channeled help from the spirit world, our logo was formed. It consists of the colors blue, green and white/yellow light, symbolizing spirituality, love and healing. There are 7 outer triangles pointing out to the universe and forming a shining star. Each triangle represents one of the seven principles and simultaneously means coming together and creating a space. [...] The inner circle symbolizes a spiritual circle, medi-

of table turning in France (Brower 2010, 11).

5. Norwegian: Norsk Spiritualist Forening, NSF. In this chapter, all references to web sites, personal communications, books and other material were originally in Norwegian; I have translated these into English.

6. Norwegian: Mediumskap i Drammen.

7. Norwegian: GEEAK—Gruppen for spiritistiske studier Allan Kardec.

umship and contact with the spirit world. Inside the circle is a heart that represents our faith and a place for love, whereas the green color symbolizes healing. The logo conveys a powerful message and is a gift to our members and a message saying that we belong together, and that it is important to create room for understanding, love and happiness.[8]

On NSU's internet pages, one reads that NSU is "A union for those interested in the spiritual in Norway. Included in this are mediums, clairvoyants, healers and everybody with an interest in these. NSU is a purely special interest organization, and has nothing to do with anybody's faith. All members may believe whatever they want."[9] Membership costs about 28 EUR (250 NOK) a year, whereas NSU's subgroups Medium Union and Healer Union cost 40 EUR (350 NOK). These unions are related neither to "faith" nor anything religious, but NSU's religious community, Norwegian Spiritualist Community, NSC, is a faith-based community for which one has to register separately. Membership in NSC is free, and automatically gives one membership in NSU.

So what does one believe in as a member of NSC, and does this fundamentally diverge from what is described as the founding principles for the umbrella organization NSU? This is how the spiritualist faith's "core" is presented under the description of NSC on their web pages:

> I believe in God, a Universal Force, which resides in everything and in all.
> In an eternal life in light and love.
> Reincarnation and eternal development of all souls.
> In angels, guides and helpers, who assist us in our learning.
> That we must take responsibility for our lives, our fellow human beings, animals and nature.
> And that we must take responsibility for our thoughts, speech and actions,
> for what is sent out will mark our souls.

The word God may also mean The Universal Force, The Source, Allah or The Creator. This can be left to each person to define.[10]

This "core of faith" concurs with the seven principles of spiritualism, with which both NSU and NSC are associated. Spiritualists understand these principles as having been channeled from the spirit world by "the mother of spiritualism," Emma Hardinge Britten (1823–1899), who obtained them from the English social reformer Robert Owen (1771–1858) a few years following his death. The principles are not to be taken as authoritative in the same way as other religions' dogmas are codified in holy scriptures, but they

---

8. Personal communication, May 2014. Kirsebom names the woman Taban Lak as designator of the logo.

9. http://www.spiritualist.no/organiasjonskart-hvordan-er-vi-organisert2.

10. http://www.spiritualist.no/om-oss.

are still presented as principles "ruling everything." An understanding of them might be based on the individual's own interpretation, characterized by time and place. The seven principles, which, as we saw, are also pointed to by NSU's logo are 1: God residing in everything and everybody, 2: Human loyalty and love, 3: Acceptance of the spirit world and of angels, 4: The eternal life of the soul, 5: Personal responsibility, 6: Your choices influence your life and your development, 7: Eternal development for all souls.

Spiritualism and the seven principles are presented the same way for both NSU and NSC, but the difference is that the members of NSC have registered themselves in a community of faith, and accordingly cannot be members of other such communities, such as The Norwegian Church. The foundation remains the same, and the easing of "dogmas" and the stress on each human being's right to define what "God" means to them, contribute in making a gliding transition from NSU to NSC. Traditionally, spiritualism is presented as a unity composed of three parts, namely as philosophy, religion and science. Kirsebom, the leader of NSU, wrote in a textbook on mediumship and clairvoyance (Kirsebom 2012, 26) that NSU suits those who welcome spiritualism as their life philosophy, whereas NSC is for those who (also) identify spiritualism as their faith. The scientific aspect is understood as systematic, independent investigations of mediums and séances to obtain evidence that the information from the medium is from the deceased and not from any other sources, and that physical mediumship, in those cases where it occurs, is real. Such investigations were highly popular in the classical period of spiritualism. This part of spiritualism gradually became parapsychology, a part of psychology that resides on the fringes of established science.[11]

Spiritualist ceremonies and practices

As a community of belief, NSC offers ceremonies at the points of life's transitions, meaning namings, confirmations, weddings and funerals. Adults who would like to have a "name day" where they receive a "spiritual name" are included as well. Spiritualist priests, or priestesses as the women are called, conduct spiritualist ceremonies. To become a priest, one participates in a

---

11. The Norwegian Parapsychological Society, NPS (Norsk Parapsykologisk Selskap), founded in 1917 and modelled after the British Society for Psychical Research (SPR) (founded in 1882), focuses on ESP phenomena, as well as (physical) mediumship. I attended a meeting arranged by NPS in January 2015, at which the Swedish author and physical medium Camilla Elfving was presented. In addition to a lecture on physical mediumship, she held a séance for a select group from the audience in which I also participated. See http://www.parapsykologi.no/hvaskjer.shtml#januar. NPS can thus be viewed as a facilitator of mediumship in Norway, but the organization itself does not take an official stand on the existence and nature of ESP phenomena, but rather "encourages independent, critical thinking on such phenomena and the research on them," see http://www.parapsykologi.no/nps.shtml. See below for a presentation of physical mediumship by spiritualist organizations.

part-time study program for four years; after the first two years, one may practice leading ceremonies. In 2014–2015, eight persons were involved in this education, seven women and one man. The ceremonies of NSC can be held all over the country, although local branches for the time being are limited to Oslo (the location of the main office, both for NSU and NSC), Bergen, Stavanger, Drammen and in the county of Østfold.

Flowers are an important part of the naming ceremony, and parents and all participants in the ceremony bring flowers that are gathered together for the little one: the parents give several flowers whereas the guests provide one each, and these are handed over to the child with a few words. The flowers symbolize life and purity. Lighting candles is also a part of the ceremony. Also, in addition to the name the parents have chosen for the child, the leader of the ceremony or the priest might convey a spiritual name from the spirit world. The parents can choose to use this name, and possibly include it in the national registration of the child. On NSC's web pages the following story of a naming ceremony for a mother and her child appears:

> On the 9th of July 2011 my son and I had our naming ceremony in The Spiritualist Community. It was by coincidence, or with some help from my Guides, that I last year found information about such a community in Norway. I had read several books on such communities in Denmark and England, and was a bit upset it didn't exist here. So when I understood that it was to be found here in Norway, I quickly went to Bolteløkka [school in Oslo were meetings are held] to find out more. [...]
>
> The 9th of July 2011 was set for "party" with André, Hege, Jan and Monica attending from the community. Many of those invited were a bit skeptical, but also curious as to how this would be carried out. I myself was mostly excited and happy. [...] The ceremony was incredibly beautiful, with speeches, songs and a lovely story about God, the Light and flowers. What everybody waited for (not least myself!) but also the invited guests was the names. Several people had asked me what spiritual name I would be given, but I had to answer, "I won't know before you know!"
>
> So when Hege gave my son the name MAWU, and André gave me the name OCEANIA, I was convinced this was a proper name for me to use [...]
>
> What's been funny after the change in names is that the name Oceania is unknown to everyone, so I think it's great to be able to tell my story about why that is now my name [...][12]

Spiritualist confirmation is an option that finds its parallel in Norway to churchly, humanist or holist confirmation. The spiritualist confirmation is held on a weekend so that youth from different parts of the country can attend. Attendance at two spiritual evenings and two healing evenings

12. http://www.spiritualist.no/nst.

(see below) at one of NSC's local branches is recommended but not compulsory. The eight main themes of the confirmation are a mix of typical ethical themes directed towards youth at confirmation, and more specific, spiritualist themes: community and communication, spiritualism and spirituality, individual development and identity, mediumship and science, group identity including problems concerning intoxication, healing and ethics, love and responsibility for the world. Spiritualist confirmation was conducted for the first time in 2010, but the number of confirmands has been low, with four in 2012 and two in 2013. The ceremony of confirmation itself takes place in the youth's hometown, with text reading, prayers and flowers for the youngster.

Spiritualist weddings are more in demand, perhaps because the members of NSC are more adults and young adults than children and youth. What characterizes a spiritualist wedding is that one promises to be together as long as love binds one together, not till "death do you part," as spiritualism teaches that existence continues after death. NSC has published parts of the wedding wows on their web pages:

> The priest to the bride: In union with [...] in marriage, and in light of our personal responsibility, will you love, honor and support him through life's joys and sorrows, - and be honest and faithful to him as long as love lasts? [...]
>
> Priest to both: (priest holding his hand over the couple)
>
> Since you now before God and before witnesses, both the physical ones and the spirits, have promised to live together in matrimony, I am pleased to pronounce you an officially married couple.

Here we note that the spirits are not only thought of as communicating with people, they are also considered to take an active part as witnesses in a life phase ceremony. In a spiritualist wedding, there is room for individual adjustments, and in one case the NSC includes photos of a "Star Wars"-themed wedding, in which Darth Vader and four clone warriors escort the bride![13] In 2014, NSC held its first marriage for a homosexual couple, presented on their web page with the following text:

> For us in NSC, the eternal soul or spirit is the most important part of a human being. The soul is here on earth to gain learning and experience. Two people may find each other on a soul level and then wish to spend life together. Then gender is not important. What is important is to find peace and harmony together. That is why we think it is great to have been able to help Talla and Silje with a wonderful ceremony.[14]

Spiritualist funerals are held in chapels, as the Norwegian state is obliged to provide all denominations ceremonial rooms for burials. The NSC pro-

---

13. http://www.spiritualist.no/bryllup.
14. http://www.spiritualist.no/bryllup.

vides priest, ceremony and speeches, whereas a funeral parlor takes care of the practicalities. There is a focus on the eternal life of the soul in the spiritualist ceremony, and instead of a cross as a symbol in the death notice or on the tombstone, an infinity symbol is preferred and/or stars for both the date of birth and the date of death. Kirsebom (2012, 37) writes that the atmosphere in a spiritualist funeral is somewhat different from a Christian one, since the emphasis on eternal life and rebirth in another dimension makes the transition more "marked by something good, and it is a festive ceremony." Grief is still a natural part of it when one commemorates the one who has passed over, but "It is more as if the person has set out on a long journey—the person is gone, but present still" (Kirsebom 2012, 37).

Spiritualist meetings, called spiritual evenings and healing evenings, are assemblies in schools and town halls where the primary activity is contact with "the other side" (that is, with the dead). This is perceived as proof for their beliefs, and through this concrete contact, the border between religion and faith as traditionally understood is transcended. The evening meetings are called the "services" of spiritualism, and they last about one and a half hour, with song, speech and "demonstration"—that is, channeling messages from the deceased, or a healing demonstration. A successful evening meeting is presented in the following way on NSC's web pages:

> A wonderful night at Bolteløkka!
>
> With the scent of freshly baked buns, cakes and coffee, the attendees came to the last evening meeting this season [...]. It seemed as if the audience enjoyed well-performed stage mediumship, with accurate descriptions of those coming through. The ones who had a visit this summer evening probably went away touched, with a verification that we do live on... the day our life on earth is over.
>
> We do not speak of the large and smaller healing demonstrations in the same way, even though the principle is quite similar. We are happy the ones who received help this evening felt that something happened there and then. [...] To combine healing and mediumship in an evening such as this one shows that both the audience and the practitioners appreciate this kind of arrangement [...].
>
> A joyful summer from us at NSU/NSHU/NSC/NSMU in Oslo.[15]

I attended the same kind of meeting in Stavanger, though instead of a healing, a lecture was held after the spirit demonstration. The meeting leader opened the session with a short welcome and introduced the two mediums of the night, Signe Sandvig from Oslo and Anne Kahn from Stavanger. Forty-five persons attended that evening, with great diversity in age, though dom-

---

15. http://www.spiritualist.no/47-nsf/nyheter-nsf/338-en-fantastisk-kveld. NSHU and NSMU stands for Norwegian Spiritualist Healing Union and Norwegian Spiritualist Medium Union.

inated by females. "Often, we are many more than this, too," the organizers told me when I expressed some surprise at the relatively large number of attendees. To begin with, we sang the popular ballad "The Rose," and then Sandvig presented the spiritualist philosophy of the evening, inspired, she said, by her guides.[16] This was a discussion of what the second principle of spiritualism might mean in our daily life: with the words, "What my guides finally wish to convey is that love is the greatest word of all, the development of the principle of love is the greatest," Sandvig concluded her spirit-inspired speech—this was presented as a spirit message to all of us attending, as each and every one of us could not expect our dead ones to come through. Thereafter, we sang the Abba hit "I have a dream," and Khan explained that the point of singing is to raise the energy in the room so that spirit communication is facilitated, as well as singing for the joy of it, as a community. In the following three quarters of an hour, the two mediums channeled the deceased coming through to the audience. Most impressive, perhaps, was the spirit of a young man, described as dressed in jeans and T-shirt, rushing in on his motorcycle, with a big smile and wind blowing through his hair. "A gorgeous guy!," Khan exclaimed. The motorcycle had been his death. A relative recognizing the man, received his greeting: "Cut all those thoughts off, just *do* it!" (and then there was more to his message, "though inappropriate to convey in plenary," as Khan said, keeping it to herself until she could transmit it directly to the sitter). After seven spirit messages it was coffee break time, followed by Sandvig's lecture on one of Norway's most famous psychics of all time, Marcello Haugen.

In addition to meeting activities, NSU offers a whole range of courses and seminars throughout the year, with themes of mediumship and healing, including the priestly education courses. NSU do not have a building of their own for their activities, but hopes to eventually obtain such facilities so that renting schools and town halls will be unnecessary. The premises at Bolteløkka School is, for example, often occupied by the school's own events in June and December. Lately, a youth hostel has been the preferred premises in Oslo. They also want to establish a spiritualist library. Fund-raising is done for a "building-account," and there are plans for a proper "Spiritualist Center" in due time.

Other organized spiritualist and spiritist actors

"Mediumship in Drammen" was established in 2011 as a joint venture between this group and NSU in Oslo. They offer monthly spiritualist evenings and courses in mediumship, but are not a membership-based group. Their goal is to "offer common people a meeting place where they can get in

---

16. Guides are considered spirits of higher energy frequencies, of persons oneself has not known in life, or spirits that have not lived on earth at all, but in other dimensions. Angels might be a sub category of guides (cf. Kirsebom 2012, 262).

touch with their beloved ones in the spirit world."[17] Leading voices here are Adele Leyha and Naomi Sol, both with their own practices and web sites, a situation that also holds for many of NSU's and NSC's members who have a high profile. "Mediumship in Drammen" also invites mediums and lecturers from England.

Further north in Norway, in Trondheim, is a network called *Spiritus Omni*, Latin for "All is Spirit." This network was originally an assembly with subtitle "Spiritist Union Mid-Norway," established in 2006. In 2011, they chose to reintroduce their activities as community and network based. On their web pages, the two permanent volunteers of the network, Line Anita Osen and Monica Agentha Haugen, explain that, "We found that we did not need those organizational frames (which were also demanding in terms of time and resources), and neither did we want to limit our work and offerings to a fixed, geographical area."[18] *Spiritus Omni* distinguishes itself from other actors by underscoring its independence from English and American traditions, and by focusing on physical mediumship, which Osen and Haugen call "The Crème de la Crème of Spiritism."[19] The dominant form of spiritualism (and spiritism) today is mental mediumship, transmitting channeled messages from the spirit world. In its classical period, physical mediumship was popular. Physical mediumship involves bringing sounds, items, moving and levitating objects, ectoplasm and materializations (spirits manifesting in partial or full material form). Like other forms of mediumship, the purpose of these activities is providing proof for our existence beyond death. *Spiritus Omni* invites physical mediums such as the famous German Kai Muegge—who offers traditional cabinet séances and levitations—to their community. The well-known Danish-Norwegian medium, Marion Dampier-Jeans, is both a mental and a physical medium, and is associated with *Spiritus Omni* both by being friend of Osen and Haugen, and by being Haugen's mentor. On *Spiritus Omni*'s web pages, one sees Dampier-Jeans in the new cabinet of the network (then assembly), draped in black cloth.[20] In the report, "Course in physical mediumship, Trondheim, August 27–28, 2010," we read that Dampier-Jeans demonstrated transfiguration; that is, the shape of her face changed according to which spirit "came through," and that four different spirits were identified—among them, a spirit who turned out to be one of the sitters' (participants') grandmother.[21]

"Mediumship in Drammen" and *Spiritus Omni* have chosen very varied presentations. The first has a picture of a white silhouette on a blue background; the silhouette is of a woman dressed in old-fashioned clothes next to

17. http://drammen.aandekommunikasjon.com/#category4.

18. http://www.spiritusomni.com/Spiritus-Omni.html.

19. http://www.spiritusomni.com/Fysisk-mediumskap.html.

20. http://www.spiritusomni.com/Marion-Dampier-Jeans.html.

21. http://www.spiritusomni.com/Marion-Dampier-Jeans.html.

a chair with a heart carved on the back of it. The press contact for the group, Naomi Sol, tells in an email that the logo symbolizes a spirit, and is designed as a friendly and comforting picture to underscore the spiritual character of mediumship. Group leader Adele Leyha, who also practices psychic drawing, has drawn the logo. *Spiritus Omni* is represented by a purple circle with a purple rhombus in it, where the corners of the rhombus are stretched out into four triangles with peaks turned inwards. This sign is supposedly an antique symbol of reincarnation, whereas the circle symbolizes the spirit. Former board member Laila Leonhardsen designed this logo.

In Eiker, located in the Drammen region, there was in the period in 2011–2013 activities of a membership-based assembly called "The Assembly of the Spiritual." Online, they presented themselves as: "AoS—The Assembly of the Spiritual—Eiker/Drammen, is a meeting place for people interested in spirituality, and includes such activities: Drop-in workshops, circles of medium-healing-personal development, Clairvoyance/Psychic abilities/ the 6th sense, healing, lectures/ discussions and demonstrations within the alternative." The assembly documented substantial activities through photos and articles on their web page, in a blog and on Facebook, with meetings held every Monday and Thursday. However, in April 2013, it was announced that the assembly will be closed down, due to lack of response.[22] By this time, the assembly had an offshoot in Åmot, geographically quite a distance north of the Drammen region. This assembly is not online. Spiritualists and spiritists say that this is a common situation: some groups and assemblies choose a more public profile, while others remain more private, made up of people with a joint interest in practicing mediumship and communicating with spirits. The forming and closing down of spiritualist and similar groups and assemblies is a sign of interest, engagement and a will to organize, regardless of the durability of the congregations. It adds to the dynamic character of the spiritualist field, also to the more organized part of it. In addition, there are often no sharp boundaries between what appear to be collective enterprises, and what seem more like individual, spiritual businesses, as we shall see.

Spiritist organization in Norway—GEEAK Norway

GEEAK is short for the Portuguese name Grupo de Estudos Espíritas Allan Kardec—The Group for Spiritist Studies Allan Kardec. GEEAK Norway has a Brazilian origin, where spiritist groups and faith communities based on the teachings of Allan Kardec constitute a considerable part of that huge country's religious profile. In Europe, GEEAK is found in Portugal and Germany in addition to Norway, but GEEAK Norway keeps in touch with spiritist groups all over the world. The Norwegian branch was established at the beginning of the 1990s, as board member (of 2014) Claudio Latini explains. He and his

---

22. http://dsfblogg.com/2013/04/17/dsf-status-17-april-2013/.

wife Cristina came to Norway from Brazil in the mid-1980s, and felt the need for a spiritist organization, as customary in their homeland.

In 2015, the board of GEEAK Norway consisted of five women, all of Brazilian descent, including Cristina Latini. GEEAK Norway has branches in Bergen, Trondheim and Stavanger, but these are small groups that stay in touch with the community in Oslo via Skype. The primary goal of GEEAK Norway as formulated on their web pages is to: "arrange studies and practice and convey the three most important aspects of Spiritism: The Science, Philosophy—and Ethical and Religious Consequences of—Spiritism."[23] GEEAK Norway emphasizes that they are a Christian organization, and that the teachings of Kardec is in accordance with the gospel: "Jesus Christ taught us love, and Kardec followed the gospel, but he particularly investigated the philosophical side of it through his mediumship," Claudio Latini tells.[24] GEEAK Norway rents their premises, situated in the central parts of Oslo. Here members meet for spiritist studies in Norwegian each Tuesday, with similar meetings in Portuguese every Wednesday. The meetings in Portuguese are specified as studies in *The Book of Spirits* (by Allan Kardec), with voluntary participation in "energy transfer at the end of the meetings."[25] Mediumship is practiced every Monday as a continuation of the study circle. This is for closed groups only, whereas the study circles or groups are open to all, and are free of charge. Claudio Latini says that GEEAK Norway is about to register as a belief community, having up until now been a special interest organization. So far, they do not offer ceremonies for life transitions, but, as typical for spiritist organizations, GEEAK Norway provides activities for children, a "Saturday school" (as in Catholic catechesis) called "Meimei—for children and family." The children and family group's name is in honor of the shining spirit Meimei. This was the pet name given to the young Brazilian woman, Irma de Castro Rocha (1922–1946), who died only 24 years old from complications after a tonsillectomy. The legendary, Brazilian medium Chico Xavier (1910-2002) later channeled her. Meimei/Irma de Castro Rocha is known as a noble person/spirit with particular affection for children, and many spiritist children's groups are dedicated to and named after Meimei.[26]

Another, newer spiritist organization in Norway with ties to GEEAK is the student organization, The Norwegian Spiritist Student Union (NSSU), which was established in 2013 at the University in Oslo. The union initially held weekly meetings on campus. In the summer of 2014, the union held a summer seminar together with "The Spiritist Federation of Maranhão in Brazil," aiming at unifying all of the spiritist assemblies in Norway. So far, this has not happened. It also turned out to be difficult to get students involved in

---

23. http://geeaknorge.com/.

24. Personal communication, June 2014.

25. http://geeaknorge.com/aktiviteter/.

26. http://spiritualisticschoolforchildren.blogspot.no/2011/03/meimei.html.

NSSU on a more binding basis, leading one of the founders of NSSU to express doubts about the future of the organization by the beginning of 2015.[27]

The spiritist, Brazilian-characterized Norwegian groupings are probably, to a notable degree, limited to people with some kind of connection with Brazil, whereas the spiritualist groups like NSU and NSC have a broader impact. However, in 2012 GEEAK Norway was properly presented in an article in the alternative magazine *Medium* under the heading: "The fundamentals of Spiritism: BELIEVE IN THE ETERNAL LIFE OF THE SPIRIT without hell, the devil or eternal punishment" (Hægeland 2012, 10).[28] The article seemed to anticipate the readers of the magazine would be interested in the difference between spiritism and spiritualism: "Spiritism and spiritualism have much more in common than what makes them different. One difference is that spiritism is clearly inspired by Christianity and the teachings of the Christ, except that they do not believe in hell, the devil or eternal punishment." In four pages, GEEAK Norway and kardecian spiritism were presented and compared to spiritualism and the broader, spiritualist aspect of culture. *Medium*, an alternative magazine with a special focus on mediumship, psychic practices and folk religiosity, here succinctly illustrates the loose boundaries between organized spiritism and spiritualism, and the wider spiritualist field.

The Spiritualist field: Psychic telephone lines

In the more loosely organized spiritualist field, transgressive communication appears more complex and varied than within the more organized frames of NSU and GEEAK, at least when considering the belief community's self-representations. If one flicks through a publication like *Medium: The Magazine for Insight and Outlook*,[29] one finds reports, interviews, an activities calendar and psychic telephone line offerings with mediumistic and spiritualist content, in addition to "common" neo-spiritual material ranging from horoscopes to holistic health. In *Medium* 1/2015, for example, there is an interview with former florist Britt-Helene Johansen Hestetun, part of the stable of clairvoyants offering their services by phone via the magazine—in Johansen Hestetun's case, healing and help with finding lost items (Høie 2015, 6–9). Johansen Hestetun says her abilities are innate, and that she is clairaudient like her mother. Among other things, she could "hear" the neighbor girl screaming as she died from meningitis even though she was not present in her home at the time.

The psychic telephone lines announced in alternative magazines may be said to reside both in the middle and on the outskirts of spiritualism—they concern mediumship, channeling and healing, and are often related

---

27. Personal communication, January 2015. The Norwegian name of the organization is "Den Norske Spiritistiske Studentforening," DNSSF.

28. NSU and NSC were presented in the same magazine a few years earlier.

29. Norwegian: *Medium. Magasinet for innsikt og utsikt.*

to "energy," "a force," "helpers," "angels" or to psychic remedies like tarot cards where communication with the dead is peripheral. However, to a significant degree, psychic lines involve contact with "the other side," understood as deceased ones "coming through" and giving advice, as well as souls "brought over" when callers ask for information on or help for their beloved dead ones. Many mediums with telephone services (often referred to as "operators") also convey an underlying understanding of an energetic, multidimensional universe where the division between life and death is reinterpreted; energy as such cannot disappear, only assume new forms, is a fundamental idea here. The psychic lines thus represent a complex field where the therapeutic effect of the transgressive communication is central, and where the "transgression" may be expressed in a variety of ways within a broad spectrum: As the "operator's" knowledge of where a key ring is misplaced, as (distant) healing of physical and psychological pain, as channeling of messages from the dead, as removal of ghosts from a house or as guidance in relational matters without consulting extrasensory entities. As a couple of the advertisements read: "International seer: From a family line with innate abilities. Finds lost items and animals. All aspects of life. Distant healing. Dream reading. Animal interpreter [phone number]" and

> Psychic Alva. Started predicting and healing early as a 10-year-old.
> I grew up in a family practicing reading and healing through several generations. I can tell fortune in cards, angel cards, tarot, runes, pendulum, and in coffee grounds. Also have knowledge in astrology, color- and crystal healing, feng shui and palmistry. Can easily take in energies and messages from the dead [phone number]."[30]

In *Medium*, the last 10 pages of the magazine constitute a regular catalogue called "Medium Psychic Catalogue." A full page introducing the advertising pages conveys guidelines and a warning:

> Read the advertisements thoroughly and use your intuition in choosing with whom to talk. If you are in an acute life situation and feel an urgent and prevalent need to talk to professionals, it might also be a good idea to contact one of these: HELP TELEPHONE MENTAL HEALTH [phone number], The Church's SOS [phone number].

Magic Magasin is constituted the same way, with an associated telephone line market called "Magic Circle," with advertisements for the operators collected in several full pages throughout the magazine. Both the magazine and the tele-market are products from magic.no, described as "Norway's largest portal into the alternative market where our daily 20,000 readers find an extensive offering."[31] At magic.no there is also information on various pub-

---

30. In *Medium* 1/2015, 99 and *Magic Magasin* 4/2014, 57, respectively.

31. http://magic.no/om-oss?tlf=79000404.

lic help lines; the "Anxiety line" and an "Information line on forced marriage" in addition to the two listed in *Medium*.[32] Brita Furulund is the manager
of Magic Circle, and she says that both the switchboard operators and the
psychic operators constantly evaluate whether the callers should use their
services or should be referred to others. At the beginning of 2015, Magic
Circle had approximately 40 operators handling 50-100 calls a day. This means
this tele-market alone had 350–700 callers a week, or 27,000 calls a year, on
average—and several such markets exist. Previously, Magic Circle was open
24 hours a day, but today the psychic lines are open between 9 in the morning
and 1 at night—the late night callers were few and tended to have problems
in need of other solutions than psychic advice, according to Furulund. Furulund has been a manager in this field for twelve years, and she talks about an
ever more niche-like development: From companies in the home decoration
business, there are calls for help in feng shui-related questions on behalf of
their clients. Animal interpretation is in increasing demand, and, in addition
to specialization and niches, Furulund says that a greater seriousness and
existential depth now characterize the questions and needs of the callers.
This stands in contrast to when Magic Circle started in 2003, when callers
seemed to purchase the services more for entertainment and fun.[33]

"Psychic Alva" says that fortune telling or reading is about contact and
communication with forces greater than ourselves.[34] She had worked as an
operator for a year when I talked with her, but the abilities she uses in this
service are abilities she has had all her life—refer to her advertisement cited
above. "Everyone with innate abilities that I know of, has at some point in
life wished to not have them," she says. "It is also a burden to have such
abilities, especially for children; it is heavy, they are often misunderstood."
In Alva's understanding, death has several phases and appears to be as individual of a process as our different lives. Life is not incidental, and soul mates
are examples of this—strong human meetings that perhaps have been pre-
destined in another dimension. She offers contact with "the other side,"
with souls who have "passed over" or are "stuck" because they were not
prepared to go when death struck. Alva comes into contact with these, and
senses their sorrow and despair, and, she says, often cries herself. However,
she has the capacity to release them and bring them forth, via the telephone
contact with the caller, or in her other work, as a medium and psychic outside of the tele market.

The telephone service is a visible and accessible part of the more loosely
organized, spiritualist-like field. Many of those associated with a tele-market
also have their own practices, and often provide a web address in the psy-

---

32. In Norwegian: "Angstringen" and "Informasjonstelefon om tvangsekteskap."

33. Personal communication, January 2015.

34. Personal communication, January 2015. Alva may be found under this name as a
psychic line operator, and does not want anonymity.

chic line advertisement.[35] Individual web sites are not given in the advertisements from Magic Circle, appearing somewhat more rigid in its regime as tele-market, whereas *Medium's* psychic catalogue is a more varied collection of advertisements. Quite a few of the advertisers provide, in addition to a phone number, the web address www.a-heavenly-voice.com, which is yet another variant of a tele-market, with a separate department for clairvoyance and contact with the dead (spirits). Social media such as Facebook also comprise a mediumistic, spiritualist and healing-oriented "field of practice," where practitioners can create "events"—virtual happenings—and invite people in to receive healing and messages from the dead. Medium and healer Anita-Helen Rasmussen from Sandnes, Norway, has specialized in this kind of transgressive, Facebook-based communication. She weekly gathers around 1000 participants to her event, participants who are given distant healing and can read greetings from the dead who "came through" on the event's "wall" after Rasmussen's healing and channeling sessions. The participants take part by receiving the healing energies wherever they are, and by writing their wishes and thanksgivings on the event's Facebook page—as well as their memories of and greetings to their beloved deceased ones (Kalvig 2014).

Other mediumistic or spiritualist practices

One of the advertisers in *Medium's* psychic line catalogue, who also runs her own business, is Linda Thorstensen. She won the first season of the popular competition, "The Quest for the 6th Sense," on the television channel TV Norge, which she also uses promotionally in her telephone advertisement. The web page given in the advertisement is called "Medium development: Start your development today!" Here she describes how tough it was to "relive" the so-called Asker disaster from 1972 doing the television filming; a plane crash occurred that year in which 40 out of 45 persons onboard were killed.[36] Thorstensen works as clairvoyant, medium and healer; and offers private consultations, lectures, courses and a medium school. In 2014, she participated in seven alternative fairs. Her Medium school is in the small town of Tønsberg, Eastern Norway, where students attend with a binding registration for half a year at a time, with meetings of 4–5 hours every fifth week. The educational themes at her school resemble the varied offers of the tele-market advertisements:

> Mediumship proper—readings—clairvoyance, intuition—healing—communication, your conduct—your personal spiritual development—psychometrics—your capacities and talents—how to develop your skills

---

35. The operators decide themselves when and to what extent they will be available for calls by handing in weekly "list of wants," and so they may combine this kind of work with other kinds of work and with family life, even though they receive the calls in their private homes.

36. http://www.linda-thorstensen.no/6-sans.html.

in the best way—practical training—the various techniques—personal feedback—information from animals.[37]

As with many a medium, Thorstensen is a middle-aged woman who has found a way to employ her perceived mediumistic capacities in an individual enterprise. She describes how her talents work: "Things come to me like a good thought I have not yet started to think myself."[38] She describes her path into this practice on her web site:

I worked in kindergarten for 30 years [...] It was not until I reached adulthood that I became aware of my abilities. I ran "The Angel Corner" in Kongsberg for a few years. Here I held courses and led séances. For several years now, I've led what I call big séances, where 10 to 20 persons are present to get in touch with the Spirit world. There is nothing spooky in my séances [...] There are no candle lights or darkened room. It may well be sunshine on a weekday. Those from the other side still come to me. And the strange thing is that there is always someone coming through! There is no queue, exactly, but it seems as if most of them are very happy to come through.[39]

"The Siwi Center" in the small village of Figgjo in the South-West of Norway is another kind of practice in the spiritualist field.[40] Unlike Thorstensen, who largely travels about offering her services, the center in Figgjo is a large, well-established alternative center that has been run by the married couple, Siw Torill and Kennet Østensen, since 2001. The couple's background is varied; he has experience as a sailor, mechanic, business manager and home aid, she as a worker in various caring professions and institutions—before they both devoted themselves fulltime to the field of alternative therapy. Siw Østensen also has health personnel authorization.[41] The Østensens offer a whole range of courses and education in reiki healing, meditation, rebirthing and mediumship,[42] and list 20 different "therapies and products" available, among them "Clairvoyant reading," "Contact with the dead" and "House cleansing."[43] In the folder "Clairvoyance—Counselling for a New Era," the Siwi Centre describes its practice:

A person with clairvoyant talents can communicate with the spirit world where angels, guides, deceased ones and various other spirits and energies reside. Sometimes, all of us need help in making choices, when

---

37. http://www.linda-thorstensen.no/mediumskole.html.
38. http://www.linda-thorstensen.no/mediumskole.html.
39. http://www.linda-thorstensen.no/6-sans.html.
40. In Norwegian: "Siwi Senteret," Figgjo in Rogaland.
41. http://www.siwi.no/om-oss/.
42. http://www.siwi.no/kurs-og-utdanning/kurs-og-aktiviteter-vaar-2015/.
43. http://www.siwi.no/terapi/.

we are at crossroads, life changing situations and more [...] the Clair-voyant person works as a channel for your guides in the spirit world. The advice brought via the clairvoyant will most likely show you your challenges and describe your possible choices, and explain what conse-quences they may have.

The theme "House cleansing (Exorcism)"[44] is quite straightforwardly pre-sented:

At the Siwi Center, we use a "medium" who travels to the place where the phenomenon occurs. The medium establishes contact with the "ghosts" or "spirits" and try to make these enter "the light," that is to say, "the other side" or "home" to "the spirit world." The medium might use remedies like salt, sage, incense or the like in his/her cleansing. Quite similar to what is shown in such TV series as "The power of the spirits" and the like.

Various kinds of spirits, such as ghosts, poltergeists and knocking spirits are then described, followed by a prosaic discussion of guarantee, prices and mileage allowance. Siw Østensen gained fame from a wider audience than the alternatively interested in this region of the country when she contrib-uted as a medium in an art project to which she had been invited by the Stavanger Museum in 2014. The project turned out to be controversial due to the mediumship part of it, and was relocated from the cultural histori-cal department to the Art Museum.[45] Additionally, she has contributed with crystal bowl healing (sound healing by playing on crystal bowls) in a dia-logue service at the St. Petri Church in Stavanger (Trym Mathiassen 2015), thus representing transgressive practices in established fields of faith and culture, not just transgressive communication "between the dimensions."[46]

---

44. http://www.siwi.no/terapi/rensing-av-hus/.

45. http://www.nrk.no/rogaland/lot-klarsynt-tolke-utstilling-1.11566861; http://for-skning.no/content/kven-eig-historia.

46. Spiritualism and mediumship are of growing interest within The Norwegian Church. Theologians and church-based researchers are discussing how to meet the popular interest in conversations with the dead and other mediumistic phenomena, and also how to handle this concerning churchly tasks of spiritual guidance in times of grief (Henriksen and Pabst 2013, Austad 2015). A seminar at the MHS School of Mission and Theology in Stavanger in April, 2015, focused on these issues: http://www.mhs. no/?606. The Norwegian Church's representatives attending the seminar, reported of active parish members who seek advice from the priest, on how to use their mediumistic skills in service of God and the church. Many mediums are Christians, defined as one's childhood faith, as a positive relating to Jesus as Christ, as alignment of spiritualism with Christianity, or otherwise. Since 2013, The Norwegian Church also offers a "mediumistic" kind of liturgy meant to cleanse houses from what people experience as ghosts or spirits, called "Liturgy for the blessing of house and home."

A discussion of the alternative fairs will conclude this examination of forms, practitioners and organizations in the spiritualist field. The alternative fairs in Norway have grown considerably in terms of numbers and size since the alternative network, "VisionWork," held their first fair in Oslo in 1993, which initially attracted 4000–5000 visitors. This fair has grown to be one of the largest in Europe—with 15,000 visitors each year, 300 exhibitors and 350 lectures, workshops and concerts—and is now held in the large trade exhibition facilities in Lillestrøm outside of Oslo. Today, alternative fairs are held from Arendal at the southernmost tip of Norway to Alta in farthest north. They are the swarming squares and meeting places of the self-development, health and neo-spirituality field, usually held from Friday to Sunday, and spread throughout the year, with estimates of 100,000 visitors a year.[47] In both the larger and smaller fairs, mediumship and spiritualism have claimed increasing space. In the program of the Stavanger alternative fair in 2014, 25 out of 90 lectures/demonstrations were mediumistic/spiritualist; that is, nearly one-third. This is paralleled by the program for the Fagernes (Mid-Norway) alternative fair in 2015, with 11 out of 30 lectures/demonstrations of the same kind, and the same tendency goes for the other alternative fairs.[48] From the Fagernes fair, the following presentation of a lecture may illustrate this:

Lecture/workshop:
The Invisible Ones among Us
Held by: Astrid Olsen
Astrid was born with psychic capacities and will report from a world invisible to most of us (her meetings with UFOs, elemental beings, spirits and ghosts). Astrid can see hundreds of years back in time, see houses that were once on a property, see the people who lived there and past events. She can tell the story of an item, its owner and where it has been. She can see your helper, if it chooses to reveal itself to her.

At the grand fair of Lillestrøm, we also find mediums with greatest fame, such as Lilli Bendriss and Anne Kristine Augestad, renowned as mediums in the TV series "The Power of the Spirits" and bestselling authors. Bendriss also attended the Alta fair for the first time in 2015, as did the medium Anita-Helen Rasmussen (the one who also offers Facebook healing and mediumship). Rasmussen has Sami family lines, and calls herself shaman as well as a medium, and Bendriss has strong affiliations to shamanism, without referring to herself as a shaman.[49] NSU and NSC also participate in the larger

---

47. http://www.alternativ.no/messer/nyheter/alternativmesser.php.

48. The program for the Stavanger alternative fair of 2014 is no longer available online, whereas Fagernes is found here: http://www.sagamesser.no/wp-content/uploads/Fagernes-Messeprogram-2015-LowRes.pdf.

49. For a discussion of the relationship between spiritualism and Nordic (Sami) shamanism, see Kalvig 2015.

alternative fairs, with stands, lectures and séances. In addition to mediumistic/spiritualist-like demonstrations, séances and lectures, many individual mediums present themselves with stands in the fairs without being part of the program of lectures and events, providing their counselling throughout the weekend of the fair, and perhaps making appointments for consultations later on. Several mediums participate in many fairs during a year. Clairvoyance, mediumship and spiritualism thus comprise a solid part of the alternative fairs, and these in turn, are important "vortexes" considering the spiritualist impact of culture, paralleled in the wider parts of culture by the spiritualist themes seen in the entertainment area and in mass media.

A vibrant field of practices and concepts

We have seen how spiritualism is lived out in Norway today through various forms, actors and organizations. Seen as parts of contemporary culture, we note that spiritualistically and mediumistically inclined persons and practices fluctuate and move more or less unrestrained between various areas and sectors. The activists within the organizational expressions of spiritualism—such as NSC—participate in alternative fairs and may run individual enterprises where spiritualist practices are offered as products. Alternative magazines convey information on organized spiritism to a reading audience, primarily offering the entrepreneur kind of spiritualism—that is, individual consultants and operators of psychic telephone lines. Spiritualist real life meetings and conversations on a wide range of arenas parallel online healing and mediumship, and communications *with* spiritual entities are indeed supported by communication *about* these entities, in the case of spiritualism and mediumship. A reservoir of ideas and practices on transgressive communication with the dead and with other entities in "the spirit world" has become available, and has attracted large groups of people. There are also porous boundaries between spiritualism and both shamanism and alternative therapy in general (see Kalvig 2015 and in this book).

A central perspective on religion in the present volume is religion viewed spatially as present here, there, anywhere (Smith 2003) and everywhere (Gilhus 2013, Kraft and Gilhus in the introduction to this book). With spiritualism, we easily recognize it in its various forms as finding and taking place in all of these categories. As religion here, it can be seen (in an ideal type way) as domestic religion focused on family ties and dead relatives, and on maintenance of a peaceful (as opposed to haunted) house/ home. As Smith puts it, in practices of contact with the dead as religion here, "The appropriate form of the presence of the dead is expressed, as well, in general categories such as 'blessing,' as well as in their oracular or intercessory roles within familial settings" (Smith 2003, 27).

As religion anywhere, spiritualism takes place in the interstitial spaces between the organized forms of, e.g., NSC and GEEAK and family ties-focused religion here-spiritualism. What the rich variety of entrepreneurial forms manifesting in a market situation—be that of a tele-market, an alternative fair, or a therapeutic/ spiritual consultant market—have in common is, in Smith's words (2003, 30), "that it is tied to no particular place." Spiritualism by telephone or social media, in a fair or in a medium's/consultant's hired premises or private home, is characterized by offering "means of access to, or avoidance of, modes of culturally imagined divine [spiritual] power (Smith 2003, 30).

Spiritualism as religion everywhere is the category of communication *about* communication with the dead and other spirit entities, a category that was not the focus of this chapter. However, it points to that wide field of spiritualism trickling into or permeating popular culture and its products, and cultural discourse on spiritualism, mediumship and its value or dangers constitute an important place for religion in a society like contemporary Norway.

The last category, of religion there, might seem the least applicable for spiritualism in Norway. As noted, spiritualism and mediumship is finding its way into The Norwegian Church ("religion there"), though obviously in new ways defined by the church itself, as in the "Liturgy for blessing of house and home." Still, one might think of one modality of spiritualism resembling religion there more on its own terms. This modality is not present in Norway, but many Norwegian spiritualist groups and individuals positively relate to it. I have in mind the magnificent construction of Stansted Hall, The Arthur Findlay College (AFC), in Stansted, England, "The World's Foremost College for the Advancement of Spiritualism and Psychic Sciences," as its self-designation goes. Stansted Hall is a large, Victorian block of buildings from 1871, gifted to the Spiritualists' National Union in the UK by J. Arthur Findlay, a former Honorary President of the Union. Describing religion there, Smith says it is what we think of (in his case, concerning ancient religion) as:

> [...] the impressive constructions associated with temple, court, and public square. Wherever one's domicile, these latter locales are someplace else, are "over there" in relation to one's homeplace. To some degree, access to such constructions is difficult, as expressed in the architectural language of walls and gates, of zones and nested interiors.
>
> (Smith 2003, 27)

The religion of there has to do with power (Smith 2003, 28), and AFC, its teachers and teachings, are "revered" by many spiritualists in Norway. Most teachers within NSC received some of their education from AFC, and being able to follow the costly courses at AFC is "auspicious" and rewarding.

There is no simple "dynamics of spatiality" saying those religious or spiritual practices that can be discerned in more of the categories of the spatial model of religion are stronger or more lasting. For example, friction and conflict might also be the result of different religious/spiritual expressions taking place in different modalities while referring to (some of) the same spiritualist and mediumistic notions. However, my impression is that those variegated forms and practices of spiritualism are less of a problem for spiritualists. What represents more of a problem is secularism and skepticism. At a medium congress in which I participated in 2013, a wide range of spiritualists and mediums with different "locations" seemingly had a fruitful gathering, where even the Old Norse practice of "galdr" (magical chanting) was a unifying activity (see Kalvig 2015, 92). What was discussed at this congress as a threat was the media's critical coverage of mediumship, exemplified by an historian of religions cited in one of Norway's largest newspapers on the first day of the congress, claiming contact with the dead to be impossible and hence the practice of mediums unethical.

The ability of contemporary spiritualism to "take place" in those various spaces of here, there, anywhere and everywhere probably points to flexibility and strength as modern religious expressions. The teachings and buildings of AFC may remain permanent and solid and continue to be a point of reference for Norwegian spiritualists, just as Kardec's teachings are the spiritists' permanent basis, but the mediums of the market and business area must be flexible and respond to demand. The persons practicing in these various fields, in organized and market-based forms, might be one and the same. Spiritualism and mediumship, with its accompanying worldviews of the possibilities and positive effects of transgressive communication, seem to have become an ever more integrated part of Norwegian culture and society. It gives deep or partial meaning to people, for a lifetime or for a short period of time, and is often practiced—as with many aspects of the wide New Age area—in combinations with other spiritual traditions and worldviews as the medium or spiritualist sees fit.

References

Austad, Anne. 2015. "'Passing Away—Passing By': A Qualitative Study of Experiences and Meaning Making of Post Death Presence." Unpublished PhD Thesis, MF Norwegian School of Theology, Oslo.

Braude, Ann. 2001. *Radical Spirits: Spiritualism and Women's Rights in Nineteenth Century America*. 2nd ed. Bloomingtown: Indiania University Press.

Brower, M. Brady. 2010. *Unruly Spirits: The Science of Psychic Phenomena in Modern France*. Urbana: University of Illinois Press.

Gilhus, Ingvild S. 2013. ""All over the place": The contribution of New Age to a spatial model of religion." In *New Age Spirituality: Rethinking Religion*, edited by Steven J. Sutcliffe and Ingvild Sælid Gilhus, 35–49. Durham: Acumen.

Henriksen, Jan-Olav and K. Pabst. 2013. *Uventet og ubedt. Paranormale erfaringer i møte med tradisjonell tro*. Oslo: University Publishing House.

Hægeland, Elisabeth. 2012. "Tror på åndens evige liv." I *Medium* 10: 10–13.

Høie, Julie C. 2015. "Magi i de synske hender!." I *Medium* 1: 6–9.

Kalvig, Anne. 2014. "Overskridande tilhøyrsle: healing og dødekontakt via Facebook." In *Aura. Tidskrift för akademiska studier av nyreligiositet* 6: 113–144.

————. 2015. "Shared facilities: The fabric of shamanism, spiritualism, and therapy in a Nordic setting." In *Nordic Neoshamanisms*, edited by Siv-Ellen Kraft, Trude Fonneland and James R Lewis, 67–88. Palgrave Macmillan, New York.

Kalvig, Anne and A. R. Solevåg, eds. 2015. *Levende religion: Globalt perspektiv, lokal praksis.* Stavanger: Hertervig Akademisk.

Kirsebom, André. 2012. *Mediumskap og klarsyn—i teori og praksis.* Oslo: Kolofon.

Kraft, Siv Ellen, Trude Fonneland and James R. Lewis, eds. 2015. *Nordic Neoshamanisms.* New York: Palgrave Macmillan.

Noegel, Scott, J. Walker and B. Wheeler, eds. 2003. *Prayer, Magic, and the Stars in the Ancient and Late Antique World.* University Park: Pennsylvania State University Press.

Smith, Jonathan Z. 2003. "Here, there, and anywhere." In *Prayer, Magic, and the Stars in the Ancient and Late Antique World,* edited by Scott Noegel, J. Walker and B. Wheeler, 21–36. University Park: Pennsylvania State University Press.

Sutcliffe, Steven and I. S. Gilhus, eds. 2013. *New Age Spirituality: Rethinking Religion.* Durham: Acumen.

Trym Mathiassen, Silje. 2015. "Det er i møtet vi lever, beveger oss og er til." In *Levende religion: Globalt perspektiv, lokal praksis,* edited by Anne Kalvig and Anna Rebecca Solevåg, 276–295. Stavanger: Hertervig Akademisk.

10

Contemporary Sami-shamanism in Norway:
A Patchwork of Traditions and Organizations

TRUDE FONNELAND

"They call us a new religion, but actually we are the oldest." [1]

This chapter deals with contemporary shamanism in Norway. Beginning in the late 1980s, I will show how shamanism gained a foothold and slowly developed into one of the largest and most multifaceted of the New Age spiritualties in Norway. Shamanism in a contemporary Norwegian context is expressed through New Age courses and events, as well as through various secular or semi-secular activities. It influences cultural life and has been established as a religious denomination performing religious ceremonies like baptism, weddings, and funerals—additionally, obtaining financial support relative to membership.

This chapter is based on interviews with central persons in the shamanic environment in Norway from 2005–2014, as well as on fieldwork at courses, ceremonies and festivals.[2] Information about shamanism presented on shamans' home pages and Facebook pages is also a key part of my analysis.

Three different cases are in focus. First, the pioneer of Sami shamanism Ailo Gaup's life story serves to highlight the rise and establishment of Sami shamanism in Norway. Further, the chapter addresses the shaman festival Isogaisa, and portrays how festival life and religious life merge and create a venue for a global neo-religious movement, and where negotiations and resistance regarding the merging of local and global religious expressions are a central concern. Finally, the newly established Shamanic Association

---

1. Lone Ebeltoft, the leader of Shamanistic Association in the County of Troms, northern Norway interviewed by the local paper *Itromsø* 25.10.2014.

2. With their consent, I have chosen to use the shamans' real names.

provides an insight into the processes involved in converting shamanism into an authorized denomination.[3]

This chapter can also be described as a study of cultural border zones in which the production of meaning takes shape through the encounter between religious actors, religions, myths and stories, laws and regulations as well as through the interaction between the local and the global.

Death of a shaman

On twenty-fourth of September 2014 the Sami poet, journalist and shaman Ailo Gaup died at 70 years old. In the following weeks, newspapers all across the country published tributes and words of memory from his friends and colleagues describing Gaup as a person who dedicated his life to the continuation of a Sami cultural heritage through his work as a writer, poet, theater pioneer, cultural mediator, advisor and not least shaman. The tributes highlight that he met and exchanged knowledge with shamans and tradition bearers from all corners of the world and presented shamanism as "the ancient culture course."[4]

I met Gaup in 2005 in his home at Hovseter, a 30 minutes' drive from the capital of Oslo when, as a PhD-student, I interviewed people central to the shamanic environment in Norway. Not knowing that I was about to face my most challenging interview ever, I approached the address he had sent me. The block building in the suburb at Hovseter did not resemble the home of a stereotypical shaman and, dressed in slippers, jeans and sweatshirt, Gaup did not look like the shaman I had imagined when reading his books. Gaup immediately indicated that he was skeptical of my project, and encouraged me to read his books all over again and come back at some later point. He also advised me to focus on a subject that he found much more interesting and relevant, namely the abilities of the shaman drum and the drum's vibrations. Having travelled over 700 miles from Tromsø, I was not particularly set to come back later and the vibrations of the drum was way beyond my field of knowledge (as well as interests). Disappointed, I switched off my recorder and went to get my coat. He must have realized that I was upset and, in the hallway, he stopped me and asked me to return to his living room. We sat down and started talking.

Gaup was born at Mount Rávdooaivi on the Finnmark plateau 18 June 1944. As a baby, he was cared for by the Sami Mission and at age 7 he was adopted and send south to a foster family in southeastern Norway, far from Sami cul-

---

3. This chapter is based partially on two previously published articles; "Approval of the Shamanistic Association: A local Construct with Trans-local Dynamics" in Lewis and Tøllefsen, eds., *Nordic New Religions* (2015) and "The Rise of Neoshamanism in Norway: Local Structures—Global Currents" in Kraft, Fonneland and Lewis, eds., *Nordic Neoshamanisms* (2015), but it also adds new aspects to the analysis of shamanism in the local Norwegian context.

4. *Helgeland Arbeiderblad* 17.10.2014, *Klassekampen* 10.10.2014, *Nordlys* 2.10.2014.

ture and the land of his birth. In his semiautobiographical *The Shamanic Zone*, Gaup describes this period in his life as a dark chapter where he both physically and mentally faced the negative impacts of the assimilation of the Sami (2005).

As a young adult, Gaup began studying to become a journalist, but due to strong interests and curiosity, he also studied scholarly literature on the pre-Christian Sami religion. What he found these studies lacked was the practicalities, in terms of how to initiate a trance and embark upon spirit journeys. Searching for his Sami roots, not the least for traces of Sami shamanism, in 1975 Gaup traveled back to northern Norway where he stayed for ten years. Among other things, he engaged with the Sami political environment by participating in the founding of Beaivváš Sami National Theatre, and by fighting for Sami rights in the demonstrations against the damming of the Alta Kautokeino River. The early phase of the Sami ethno-political movement was concerned with rights and politics, as well as identity issues. But for Gaup, they also served as a spark for religious revival (see Fonneland 2010).

The "Alta affair" was triggered by the Norwegian Parliament's decision in November 1978 to approve a hydroelectric project that involved the damming of the Alta-Kautokeino River, which flows through central parts of Finnmark, Norway's northernmost county. After a prolonged period of acts of civil disobedience as well as hunger strikes, the decision was effected in January 1981, despite massive protests. These demonstrations sparked a Sami ethnic revival, and are generally regarded as the beginning of the Sami cultural revival movement (Hætta 2002). They also served as premises for what Gaup has referred to as the 78 generation—the Sami version of the 1968 generation (*Klassekampen* March 11–12, 2006).

At the same time as these protests and demonstrations played out, new cross-Atlantic religious ideas and trends were introduced into Norwegian society. Just a decade earlier, anthropologists Carlos Castaneda and Michael Harner had published books based on their fieldwork among Indians in Mexico, Peru, and Ecuador that provided the groundwork for a neo-shamanic movement with an international scope. As Bente Gullveig Alver describes in the article "More or Less Shamans," (2015) Harner also visited Finnmark to gain knowledge about Sami culture and religion. Searching for traces of Sami shamanism, he visited Gaup's uncle, the Sami Mikkel Gaup, a well-known "wise man" both in Norway as well as in a broader Scandinavian context, bearing the nicknames "Miracle Mikkel" and "Healing Fox." Until the early 1990s, Mikkel Gaup described himself, as did those around him, as a "reader" or healer (Fonneland 2010, 156).[5] Later he was called a shaman. Inspired by the neo-shamanic movement, the term "shaman" came to be used more commonly through the 1980s and beyond. Harner's focus on a core shamanism free from all cultural and social contexts made his reli-

---

5. The term reader indicates that Mikkel Gaup used Christian words and formulas in his practice and was involved in a Laestadian milieu. Laestadianism is a conservative Christian movement which spread among the Sami during the nineteenth century.

gious practices easy to integrate into almost every symbolic language of the sacred (see Harner 1980). His presence, courses, and writings also came to influence the development of Ailo Gaup.

Sami shamanism in its infancy

In 1986, Gaup literally decided to step onto the path of the shaman and moved to California to take part in the shamanic courses that Harner had organized at his Foundation for Shamanic Studies in Esalen. Besides Gaup, another shaman from Norway was a student of Harner, namely Arthur Sørenssen.[6] After their stays at Esalen, both Gaup and Sørenssen wrote books about their experiences. These books, *Shaman. A Ritual Initiation* (*Shaman: En rituell innvielse*) (Sørenssen 1988) and *The Shamanic Zone* (*Sjamansonen*) (Gaup 2005), are central in terms of the development of shamanism in Norway. Gaup was the one who gained the most attention and publicity for his shamanic courses and writing, something that could be due to his indigenous affiliation and his promotion of Sami shamanism.

Having been trained in the practice of core shamanism, Gaup settled in Oslo and established himself as a professional shaman. He developed his own shaman school based upon his newly acquired knowledge. This school is known as the *Saivo Shaman School* (*Saivo* being a Sami name for the underworld). Saivo Shaman School was organized as a series of courses consisting of six gatherings that extended over three years. The school was arranged throughout the country, and it is these shaman courses that have had the broadest resonance in Norway. All the established shamans I interviewed for my doctoral thesis in 2010 had been trained by Gaup and had participated in one or more of his shaman gatherings. This means that Gaup played a crucial role in designing the shamanic milieu in Norway. This is also, as Galina Lindquist argues, what is striking in the world of shamanic performances: "an important condition of its existence, its performative expressions, hinges entirely on certain individuals" (1997, 189).

The first ten years, the Norwegian shamanic movement was more or less a copy of the system developed by Harner in the United States. Similarly, the broader New Age scene differed little from its equivalent in the United States (Andreassen and Fonneland 2002). However, over the course of the first five years of the new millennium, the situation gradually changed (Fonneland and Kraft 2013). From this period forward, professional shamans were depicted as representing an ancient Sami shamanic tradition (Christensen 2007), and the Norwegian New Age scene was increasingly filled with Sami shamans, symbols, and traditions, along with a new focus on local- and place-specific characteristics unique to the northern region, particularly in terms of domestic geography (Fonneland 2010).

---

6. Sørenssen is now the leader of Shamanistic Association's local branch in Hordaland, western Norway.

Contemporary Sami shamanism has become a core subject within the field of shamanism in Norway. The most profiled shamans—Gaup, Eirik Myrhaug, Kyrre Gram Franck, and Ronald Kvernmo—teach courses and/or hold ritual and ceremonies marketed as inspired by Sami shamanism. Except for Franck, they have all also published books on the subject (see Gaup 2005, 2007; Kvernmo 2011; Brunvoll and Brynn 2011). Additionally, guided vision quests in the northern Norwegian region, as well as courses on the making of ritual drums (*goavddis* [northern-Sami], *goabdes* [Lule-Sami] or *gievrie* [southern-Sami]) and ceremonies profiled as rooted in Sami traditions, have been added to the shamanistic offerings. A wide variety of products, courses and services are marketed and available through shamans' home pages on the Internet, local media coverage, Facebook groups, alternative fairs, and through local shops. A variety of Sami ritual drums are, for instance, today offered both in tourist shops, at the annual New Age market, as well as on the Internet home pages of Sami shamans (see Fonneland 2012). Sami shamanism is expressed and has found its way into various sectors of the Norwegian society. It caters to spiritual needs, but also to the more mundane needs of the tourist trade, place branding and entertainment, as well as for Sami nation building and the ethno-political field of indigenous revival.

The Isogaisa festival

Sami shamanism is also celebrated and developed through a distinct festival, Isogaisa. This festival is an annual happening held in the county of Lavangen, in northern Norway, and was arranged for the first time on 3–5 September 2010.[7] Isogaisa is an innovative festival concept. On the basis of Sami pre-Christian religion and neo-shamanic philosophy, the festival uses symbols, rituals, and ideas to enrich the experience of the audience. In this way, Isogaisa also exemplifies cultural production through reinterpreting and redefining the past. One of the products that take shape in this way is a Sami spiritual and cultural heritage. This type of heritage can be seen not only as part of one's personal negotiation of identity (see Lowenthal 1998), but also as part of the marketing of the local, which is conveyed as being beyond—and thus of interest to—postmodern society (see Kirshenblatt-Gimblett 1998: 149–153). The Isogaisa festival is presented as a celebration of the new local scene of Sami shamanism. In this way, Isogaisa can be viewed as a significant contributor to the growing and evolving Sami shamanic scene and is a key arena for the further development of Sami shamanism in a specifically northern Norwegian environment.

---

7. For the first two years, 2010 and 2011, Isogaisa was held at Heggelia, a county north of its present location. In the long term, the organizers of the festival want Isogaisa to evolve into a spiritual center focusing on indigenous culture. I conducted fieldwork at Isogaisa in 2010, 2012 and 2014, and interviewed festival leader Ronald Kvernmo.

Sami pre-Christian religious expressions, symbols, and narratives serve as inspirational sources for the program and for the products on offer. At the same time, festival organizers say they want to communicate these expressions in a modern language and adapt them to contemporary life. The program of the festival changes from year to year, with different shamans taking part and different artists and musicians responsible for the entertainment. Thus, some program posts are stable. Among these is an alternative fair, which operates in parallel with the other festival activities. Compared with other alternative fairs, arranged annually in small and big Norwegian cities, this festival fair is a "mini alternative fair" with about 20 exhibitors. Whereas the traditional alternative fairs gather a wide range of exhibitors, the focus of the Isogaisa fair revolves around shamanism—selling drums, brass rings, *duodji* (Sami artwork) and other products related to the practice of shamanism. Additionally, a course in drum making is held yearly. Here participants are trained by a professional *duodji* artist to create their own drums to be used at the festival. Another stable program post is a mountain hike to a Sami *sieidi* (Sami pre-Christian sacrificial stone) where participants take part in a ritual and a sacrifice under the guidance of Sami shaman Eirik Myrhaug.

Through the various program posts, Isogaisa offers festival participants an access to the Sami past, and thus forms a bond between past and present. The festival generates a feeling of how it all happened *here*; and that here it is all happening *now*. It is loaded with powerful symbols, which not only bring us back in time, presenting tales of the past, but also conveys information about which values we regard as important in the present (see Eriksen 1999, 87ff.). The past, which is revived during the festival, is not the past we know from history books and the discourses of scholars. At Isogaisa, it is a link between memory and the imaginary world that is being staged (Lowenthal 1985). Here, the past is not a closed chapter; rather, it is a process that extends into the present and reaches into the future.

Festival organizer and shaman Ronald Kvernmo has been apprenticed to Ailo Gaup and became part of the shamanic movement at a time when Sami shamanism was in its infancy. Like Gaup, he was eager to revive and recreate bits and parts of the Sami pre-Christian religious past, and, in 2008, he arranged his first workshop on Sami shamanism at a Sami school in Målselv municipality, Nord-Troms.[8]

In order to create room for growth and development, Isogaisa allows for the gathering and uniting of Sami religious traditions from all of Sápmi, the Fennoscandian Sami region. Each year, a specially selected group of Sami people is invited to take part in the event. In 2010 as well as in 2014, eight shamans from the Murmansk region in Russia participated. The purpose of these invitations, which are financially supported by the Barents Secretariat

---

8. This was also the first shamanic course in Norway that explicitly use the wording "Sami-shamanism" in its heading and promotions.

and the Sami Parliament, is to establish a bond between Sami shamans in Norway and Russia. "Mini Isogaisa" festivals also take place throughout the year in both Norway and Russia, and the objective is the same, that is, to spread information about the festival and to link different Sami cultures. The program of the "Mini Isogaisas" spans the course of one day and focuses on socializing and on the performing of rituals, and usually concludes with a concert featuring Sami performers.

In the aftermath of Isogaisa 2013, media announced that some Sami communities criticized the festival because of its promotions of parts of Sami culture that, in ancient times, were not to be made public, such as the practices surrounding healing and the contact with spiritual powers.[9] The Barents Secretariat thus ordered an independent review of the ethical aspects to support the event, and in February 2014 Camilla Brattland and Marit Myrvoll, both researchers at the Norwegian Institute for Cultural Heritage Research (NIKU), drew up a report.

The questions that were highlighted in the report were as follows; "does Isogaisa help to support and enhance the Sami culture, or does the festival go against traditional ethical principles connected to the practice of spirituality and healing? Furthermore, what does Isogaisa mean for the Sami people and society in general? Is it important and useful to have such events?" (Brattland and Myrvoll 2014, 1). The report's concluding remarks examined every aspect of the problem. The report highlights that the festival's marketing of shamanism violates the traditional principle of secrecy of spiritual and healing powers or abilities, but it also further points out that this is how Sami shamanism generally is practiced. Brattland and Myrvoll underline:

> The festival is based upon a global concept that has been given a local anchoring [...]. We [will] say that the differences between old and new practices are greater than the similarities and they should be considered as different practices. There is no evidence that Sami neo-shamans represent a threat for practitioners of healing in today's Sami Christian tradition. [...] Based on our impressions, the festival reaches out to an audience that would not otherwise be affiliated with Sami cultural offers. It supports local culture, but at the same time it connects to a global movement where Sami spirituality already circulates as part of multifaceted offerings. That Sami people actively participate in this movement with their own offerings and on their own terms is a strength for the Sami community and indigenous peoples in general. The fact that Sami people can represent themselves in the religious field can counteract the global tendency for others to present indigenous spirituality separate from its historical and local context.
> (Brattland and Myrvoll 2014, 5–6 my translation).

---

9. http://www.salangen-nyheter.com/noeytral-vurdering.5547021-28288.html, Accessed 29.10.2014.

The report's conclusion is that Isogaisa's activities do not contribute to ethical concerns for the Barents Secretariat and similar institutions that provide financial support, and further that the festival should be welcomed as a resource for local Sami communities and the global indigenous movement (Brattland and Myrvoll 2014, 5–6). Notions of traditions and authenticity, of what is new and what is old, global or local, differ according to the viewers' standpoints and contexts. While the authors of the report present indigenous spirituality as a global phenomenon, Kvernmo sees it otherwise and takes the local as a starting point, referring to the religious traditions of Sápmi as a cradle for contemporary Sami shamanism. In our interview, he emphasizes:

> [...] things that are coming from the US via Michael Harner, that is a lot of stuff; that is where the main beacon is. But we don't have to go further than just past Murmansk, to the Komi and Nenets peoples—and then there's the Sami; that's three different people in a small geographical area just over the border, and they [...] at least the Nenets people, many of them haven't had contact with the Russians, so shamanism is a living culture. (my translation)

This desire to connect to local and trans-local traditions, which are understood as close both geographically and spiritually, can be seen in the context of a growing reaction against Harner's core shamanism. As early as the 1980s, the Swedish shaman Jørgen I. Eriksson, a proponent of northern and especially Sami shamanism, was already writing extensively in the Swedish shamanistic magazine, *Gimle*, pointing out that Harner's core shamanism stripped shamanic traditions of their cultural uniqueness (see Svanberg 1994, 30). His main issue was to develop or "retrieve" the northern roots and ground shamanism in a Nordic landscape and culture, and thus make "Northern Shamanism live and have an independent life again without any need of crutches form the Turtle Island" (Eriksson in Lindquist 1997, 42).

In the practice of contemporary shamanism, various religious entrepreneurs obtain legitimacy through adaptation to the local environment and local culture. Featured cultural expressions are enrolled in discourses connected to tradition and continuity that legitimate the entrepreneurs' products and services, and reaffirm a certain quality of life. By underscoring their connection to "local" religious traditions, some of the practitioners of Sami shamanism wish to distance themselves from their American origins and present their practices not as "core," but as locally inspired.

Shamanistic Association

Negotiations and resistance regarding the merging of local and global religious expressions are also a central concern within the Shamanistic Association. SA is a religious innovation created by a key person in the local shamanic community in Tromsø, northern Norway, approved as a religious denomination by the County Governor of Troms 13.03.2012. In Norway, this was the first time a neo-shamanic body was able to obtain the status of an official religious community with the right to offer and perform life cycle ceremonies and gain financial support relative to its membership.[10]

According to Kyrre Gram Franck, the leader of SA on a national level, the intention behind the establishment of SA is that the association will develop into a unifying force with the ability to strengthen individuals' and groups' rights to practice shamanism. Not least, he hopes that the association will develop into a true alternative for those who adhere to shamanistic belief systems, and that the construction of life cycle ceremonies like baptisms, confirmations, weddings and funerals will help to increase people's interest in shamanism.

Franck can be seen as the founding father of the Shamanistic Association in Norway. It was he who received a vision about SA's creation and this vision may also be considered as SA's "myth of origin." Franck's central position is also reflected in the organization of SA where, in addition to being a leader, he also has the status of vision keeper. According to the board protocol, in cases where decisions might lead to significant changes of the vision, the vision keeper retains veto power. The position of vision keeper will follow Franck for life, and makes him a central catalyst in terms of how the Shamanistic Association is profiled, and what is to be emphasized and possibly omitted in the creation of the group's identity and community.

At the same time as an interaction between the board and individual members is highlighted as central to the development of SA, the external forces of Norwegian governmental laws and regulations have also been playing a role in shaping the Association. In the application process, governmental regulations had to be dealt with in many arenas. Governmental regulations also influence the design of the ceremonies. For a wedding to be considered legally binding, for instance, certain formulations need to be included. SA, then, is a construct designed to meet the requirements for the recognition of religious communities, highlighting how religious practices are adapted, transformed and changed to fit governmental regulations (see also Taira 2010).

Even though the Shamanistic Association emphasizes shamanism as a universal phenomenon and embraces shamanism in its many variations, at the same time it promotes an agenda emphasizing local roots and a local connection. The focus on local traditions and a local past is also highlighted in SA's official statement where it is emphasized that their goal is to develop the organization into a tradition keeper for northern shamanic traditions. Northern shamanism, according the association's Facebook page, refers to both Sami and Norse traditions as well as related religious traditions from all Nordic countries.

---

10. This was not, however, the first time a pagan association was granted status as a religious denomination in Norway. In 1996, the Norse community, *Bifrost*, was provided the same status. The dissolution of the Nordic Paganism Association (NPA) in 2013 may create ripple effects for SA. It is conceivable that some of those who were active in NPA will join SA

The term Nordic shamanism creates a common Nordic approach and a focus on shared traditions across a restricted geographical area and across different ethnic groups and cultures. To include both Norse and Sami traditions in their theological foundation can thus be seen as a strategy for reaching a larger number of potential members. It is a strategy of inclusion that dissolves the taxonomies of insider and outsider, and of who has access to the traditions of the past. By adopting traditions that can be presented as domestic, the management of SA also wish to avoid characterizations such as "fake shamans" wannabe-shamans" and "plastic shamans," which has been key charges against practitioners of Harner's core shamanism.

In our conversation, Franck emphasized that the goal is to restore the original roots of northern shamanism, preferably back to 5,000 to 10,000 years ago when the differences between the "nature religion practices" of the various local tribes were minimal. This is clearly a strategy for identifying a common origin and common roots. Drawing inspiration from a time when the boundary between Sami and Norse traditions was—according to Franck, invisible—may be seen as an attempt to avoid tensions. It allows for an access to the past and for an abolition of the boundaries between "their" traditions and "ours."

In the process of developing what is considered the roots of northern neo-shamanism into a source for SA's members' shared community and identity, key figures in SA are doing research to get closer to what they experience as a shared Nordic shamanic community. To embark on this work both Franck and others in the management read literature on the Norse and Sami religions, and interview researchers and other people with knowledge about the subject. Additionally, inspiration from popular culture and from various practitioners in the field of shamanism are included in this search, illustrating the creativity that characterizes this type of historiography. Research results are distributed, popularized, commented upon and embellished on the Association's homepages on the Internet and on Facebook.

To invoke "tradition" in order to legitimize one's religious beliefs and practices is central to Western religious history, from antiquity to the present. When seeking to restore the roots of northern shamanism back to 5,000 to 10,000, one deals with a past so distant that there are no living memories to challenge or support its images. This then is a past far away in the mists of time, which can be touched only indirectly, through narratives, popular culture, myths, legends, and sagas, as well as through shamans' own religious experiences. The quest for a Nordic shamanic heritage involves liberation from established discourses about the past, and opens the past for individual approaches and interpretations. These types of "invented" traditions that take form in the shamanic milieu also first achieve meaning through an interaction with the present and through an anchoring in people's current social concerns. As folklorist, Anne Eriksen underlines: "The past ceases to be a bygone age; it can be perceived as a now because it is related to a here—a here that is also part of contemporary man's own direct experiences" (1999, 92, my translation).

The *here* that SA highlights to bring local forms of shamanism to life is the Nordic landscape with its mountains, plains, fjords, light and climate. There is an attitude that shamanism is a religious tradition grounded in our nature and in our bloodlines. It is a tradition retained in the Nordic landscape, among our ancestors, in old burial places and archeological sites, and thus it is a tradition available to everyone inhabiting the northern latitudes. Embedded in this is also the idea that the landscape has the ability to "release" ancient energy and knowledge, and can serve as a magic doorway into the world of ancient religious ideas and practices. Being present in and using this landscape, past and present melt together and allow for a crossover where the past can be retrieved as a resource for shamanic practitioners in the present.

Concluding remarks

The religious denomination SA is but one of many examples of how shamanism is expressed and organized in Norway at present. Contemporary shamanism is a highly diverse venue and the intent of this chapter has been to throw light on some active and profiled personalities, organizations and tendencies.

Developing the field of shamanism in Norway, practitioners also draw on a variety of different sources. As mentioned, practitioners look for inspiration through literature on pre-Christian religions and Norse religion as well as through core shamanism, popular culture, meditation, and various New Age courses. In terms of this juggling of different sources and the transparency toward traditions from various cultures, how then does Nordic shamanism differ from its US origins? In the article "Sami Neo Shamanism and Indigenous Spirituality" (2013), Fonneland and Kraft claim that Gaup, as well as his colleagues in the Norwegian shamanic milieu, have followed a route discussed in Harner's teachings. There is, according to Harner, a core content in the multitude traditions that together constitute "world shamanism." Having identified what he considered to be the key ingredients of indigenous people's religious notions and practices, Harner urged indigenous people to trace their own roots, and thereby to contribute to the reservoir of shamanic resources. This, one might claim, is precisely what Gaup and his colleagues have set out to achieve (2013, 136). This does not mean, however, that the products developed have a unilateral character.

An indication of the complexity of the shamanic environment in Norway, Gaup´s, Isogaisa's and SA's stories speak of global influences, local traditions, as well as encounters between cultural and religious revival. Being "home grown," referring to local traditions and being on local lands, shamanism in Norway has also become part of the international scene—constantly evolving, with ongoing reciprocal impacts between regional and international developments.

References

Alver, B. G. 2015. "More or less genuine shamans!: The believer in an exchange between antiquity and modernity, between the local and the global. In *Nordic Neoshamanisms,* edited by S. E. Kraft, T. Fonneland and J. Lewis, 141–171. New York: Palgrave Macmillan.

Andreassen, B. O. and T. Fonneland. 2002/2003. "Mellom healing og blå energi. Nyreligiøsitet i Tromsø." *Din. Tidsskrift for religion og kultur* 4/2002, 1/2003: 30–36.

Brattland, C. and M. Myrvoll. 2014. *Etiske problemstillinger ved støtte til samisk nyreligiøsitet.* Rapport NIKU. Tromsø: Barents Secretariat.

Brunvoll, B. and G. Brynn. 2011. *Eirik Myrhaug: Sjaman for livet.* Oslo: Nova Forlag.

Castaneda, C. 1968. *The Teachings of Don Juan: A Yaqui Way of Knowledge.* Los Angeles: University of California Press.

Christensen, C. 2007. "Urfolksspiritualitet på det nyreligiøse markedet. En analyse av tidsskriftet Visjon/Alternativt Nettverk." *Din. Tidsskrift for religion og kultur* 1: 63–78.

Eriksen, A. 1999. *Historie, Minne og Myte.* Oslo: Pax Forlag AS.

Fonneland, T. 2010. "Samisk nysjamanisme: i dialog med (for)tid og stad." Unpublished PhD thesis, University of Bergen.

———. 2012. "Spiritual entrepreneurship in a northern landscape: Spirituality, tourism and politics." *Temenos: Nordic Journal of Comparative Religion* 48(2): 155–178.

Fonneland, T. and S. E. Kraft. 2013. "New Age, Sami shamanism and indigenous spirituality." In *New Age Spirituality: Rethinking Religion,* edited by I. Gilhus and S. Sutcliffe, 132–145. Sheffield: Equinox Publishing.

Gaup, A. 2005. *The Shamanic Zone.* Oslo: Three Bear Company.

———. 2007. *Inn I naturen. Utsyn fra sjamansonen.* Oslo: Three Bear Company.

Hætta, O. M. 2002. *Samene: Nordkalottens urfolk.* Kritiansand: Høyskoleforlaget.

Harner, M. 1980. *The Way of the Shaman: A Guide to Power and Healing.* San Francisco: Harper & Row.

Kirshehnblatt-Gimblett, B. 1998. *Destination Culture. Tourism, Museums, and Heritage* Berkeley, CA: University of California Press.

Kvernmo, R. 2011. *Sjamanens hemmeligheter.* Own Imprint.

Lindquist, G. 1997. *Shamanic performances on the urban scene: Neo-Shamanism in contemporary Sweden.* Studies in Social Anthropology, 39. Stockholm: Gotab.

Lowenthal, D. 1998. *The Heritage Crusade and the Spoils of History.* Cambridge: Cambridge University Press.

Sørenssen, A. 1988. *Shaman. En rituell innvielse.* Oslo: Ex Libris.

Svanberg, J. 1994. *Den skandinaviska nyschamanismen: En revitaliserande rörelse.* Unpublished MA thesis in Comparative Religion, Åbo, Akademi University.

Taira, T. 2010. "Religion as a discursive technique: The politics of classifying wicca." *Journal of Contemporary Religion* 25(3): 279–394.

11

Hindu-inspired Meditation Movements in Norway:

TM, Acem and the Art of Living Foundation

INGA BÅRDSEN TØLLEFSEN

"All that we need to do and achieve in our life is: purity in our heart, clarity in our mind and skill or dexterity in our actions."

Sri Sri Ravi Shankar

Introduction

This chapter aims to present select global Hindu-inspired Meditation Movements (HIMMs)[1] in Norway, by means of a short historical introduction, an examination of media relations, and a closer look at practitioner demographics and motivational data. The primary example is the Art of Living Foundation (AoL[2]), where data from the 2011/2012 AoL online questionnaire will be used to illuminate certain aspects of religion *here*, that is, Norwegian Hindu-inspired meditation and breathing practices. There will also be examples from two older movements in the same "guru lineage," Transcendental Meditation and Acem.

Art of Living is one of the largest New Religious Movements in the world. According to the organization itself, it operates in over 150 countries.[3] Art of Living was founded in India in 1981 by Sri Sri Ravi Shankar, and has its headquarters in the organization's Bangalore *ashram*. In 1989, following a schism with its parent organization, Transcendental Meditation (TM), AoL started sending its first "missions" abroad, to Germany and to the United

---

1. A definition borrowed from Lola Williamson (2010).

2. Some of the data and some parts of this chapter are previously published, see Tøllefsen 2011, 2012

3. http://www.artofliving.org/no-no/om-art-living-foundation (accessed 30.10.14)

States[4]. The Art of Living Foundation first appeared on the Norwegian spiritual scene in 1999, about ten years after the organization had branched out of India and established itself in other parts of the world. In a Norwegian context, the Art of Living movement can be viewed as a New Religious Movement (NRM) within a wider New Age[5]/ holistic health culture. AoL is not an authoritarian, strict-boundary, deviant, communal-living type movement; quite the opposite. Rather it functions as what Roy Wallis (1984), following Weber, calls a *world-affirming* organization. With a clear this-worldly orientation, the organization aims to increase practitioners' well-being through breathing techniques, meditation and yoga, and to nurture world peace and human unity through peace work, education, development, social work and *seva*[6]—spreading its guru-leader-founder's message of a "violence-free, stress-free society." The AoL movement requires no official membership; rather it is up to the practitioner herself to determine how much time and resources she devotes to the organization and to her practice of its techniques. AoL Norway now offers several types of courses, retreats and follow-up programs. Most of the organization's activities are located in the south of Norway (the most densely populated area), particularly around the capital Oslo. Compared to movements like its "parent," Transcendental Meditation, and the Norwegian-founded meditation organization Acem, the AoL organization is quite young. However, it seems to function in its "new" cultural landscapes much like its older counterpart TM in both its American and Norwegian contexts—by simultaneously adapting to the local culture and by retaining its distinct Indian "flavor."

The mainstreaming and popularization of yoga (and, to some extent, meditation practices, *pranayama* and chanting) says something about contemporary Norwegian culture. Practices like these, which used to be alternative in the Norwegian cultural and spiritual "climate," have become rather commonplace. One illuminating example can be found in the small North Norwegian town of Tromsø, with a current population of about 73,000. At the time of this writing, there is about ten dedicated yoga studios or cent-

---

4. (see http://www.artofliving.org/art-living-overview, accessed 30.10.14).

5. New Age is in Norway commonly referred to as *nyreligiøsitet* (new religiosity), a quite unorganized and individualistic form of spirituality. Eileen Barker points out that new religiosity includes "ways of thinking and acting that are associated with new religions in the cultural rather than the structural or organizational sense" (1998, 16), thus highlighting an open, undogmatic and extremely diverse field. Generally, New Ager practice possesses "some kind of religious or spiritual rituals or assumptions" (Barker 1998, 16). Siv Ellen Kraft highlights this diversity, saying that New Age-"believers" take on everything from crop circles, angels, magic, energy and healing—assuming thereby that everything is connected, that the "self" is constantly evolving and that it is only the individual that can affect any changes (2011, 36) [my translation].

6. Selfless service, work offered to god/ the guru/ the organization

ers, where only a few years ago there were just a few. Most gyms offer yoga as part of their group training classes. Some of the yoga studios also offer mediation sessions, and there are both Acem and mindfulness meditation courses on offer. This small town example is a case on point: in the Norwegian context, there seems to be a fast-growing market for some Indian-inspired practices like *asana* yoga, where the focus (in varying degrees) seems to be on yoga as a physical exercise and health-promoting practice. This exercise, if not understood as fundamentally *spiritual*, at least has an esthetic veneer of glossy "Indianness." Ganesha-printed yoga tops, statues, incense and candlelight, and the occasional *mantra* singing are all what can be seen as signs of a new age-inspired practice that is decidedly India-inspired, but which has taken on a unique Western flavor. The "alternative" somehow seeps into the surrounding culture, informing it of what is new and cool, or reinterpreting activities in a new light. It seems that the current axis of interpretation is health and self-development, which long have been core tenets of the new age field (see Kalvig in this volume). As Siv Ellen Kraft (2011) notes, it is the individualized self that is the focal point of activity, that can always be developed and improved, and there is no reason why even secular activities (see for example Campbell 2007), cannot be approached with a more or less defined spiritual point of view. It matters less whether people *believe*. What matters is the actors' confidence that the practices (or therapies or rituals) actually *work*. In that sense, Art of Living seems to hit the cultural nail on the head as their Norwegian website subheading states, "Making Life a Celebration. Art of Living personal development combine the mystical and the modern to help you create a life of purpose, joy and confidence."[7]

Hindu-inspiration in Western spirituality

The appropriation of non-Western and/ or indigenous ideas and practices is a mainstay in New Age culture. Native American ideas and practices are (and have over many decades been) ubiquitous, and across the world indigenous practices are reinterpreted and adapted to new global-local contexts, from sweat lodges to enthenogenics (see for example Hanegraaff 2013). In the Nordic countries, particular forms of global-local neoshamanisms have developed over the last four decades, as indicated in both this volume and in Siv Ellen Kraft, Trude Fonneland and James R. Lewis' 2015 volume, *Nordic Neoshamanisms*. However, it can be argued that the single most significant influence on the New Age has come from the East, and particularly from India, bringing pervading philosophical ideas like reincarnation, and practices such as yoga and meditation to the West. Andrea Diem and James Lewis (1992) have traced the history of the influence of Hindu spirituality on the West, particularly in North America. They state that historically South Asian religions, among them Hinduism, entered the US in three waves—each with

---

7. http://www.artofliving.org/no-en (accessed 22.05.15)

a different emphasis. The first, dating to the early or mid-1800s, was overwhelmingly textual, resulting from the translation of Hindu religious scriptures into English. These texts became available particularly to members of the literary, academic elite, many of whom were enthusiastic about the texts being produced by the Bengal Asiatic Society. The Society had translated both the *Bhagavad Gita* and *Shakuntala* (a classic play from the Gupta period) into English in the late 1700s. Henry David Thoreau used materials from the translated *Bhagavad Gita* in his *Walden* (1854). Several other of his contemporaries, such as Ralph Waldo Emerson and Walt Whitman, used Indian imagery and ideas in their works, for example in their respective poems "Brahma" (1856) and "A Passage to India" (1871). A similar cultural wave took place in Europe, for example among noted academics such as the philologist and Sanskrit scholar Friedrich Max Müller (1823–1900), whose translations of Vedic literature had a significant impact on the popularization of Eastern religion in the West. Enlightenment-inspired scholar-officials were open to discovering a Hindu golden age in the past, in part because of a "cosmopolitanism engendered by the universalism of rationalism, and in part by the desire to find societies other than classical Western civilization to use as an element of critique of eighteen-century Europe" (Diem and Lewis 1992, 52). Their focus was not on the India of their contemporaries, but on an idealized notion of a great classical Indian culture in the past to serve as a civilized, admirable ideal for what Western culture *should* be. "Idealized stereotypes" of India, her religion and philosophy may well have been a factor in the growth of Hinduism in the West, and for its incorporation into new age spirituality.

Translated Indian scriptures also influenced the Theosophical Society (TS), a movement which has been formative for the New Age field (Kraft 2011; Hammer and Rothstein 2013). From the mid-nineteenth century until after the First World War, TS and its "competitor," Rudolf Steiner's Anthroposophy, embodied "modern occultism" *par excellence.* These movements, in different fashions but in similarly distinct eclectic and syncretic ways, both aimed for a higher synthesis of religious and scientific knowledge. The Russian-born medium and founder of TS, Helena Petrovna Blavatsky, saw herself as the channel for the "ancient masters," spiritually superior beings of ancient wisdom. Blavatsky (along with Henry Steel Olcott, her partner in crime, so to speak) traveled to India in 1879, and there enjoyed great success with their characteristic mix of spiritism, reformed Hinduism and Buddhism (Aadnanes 2008, 107). From the 1890s, spiritism and these modern occult movements gained some traction in Norway (see Gilhus and Mikaelsson 1998), which undoubtedly was helped along by visits from both Theosophical Society's Annie Besant and Anthroposophy's Rudolf Steiner. Although these visits and the growth of "occultism" in Norwegian intellectual and artistic circles was well-known at the time, Per M. Aadnanes points out that these NRMs were not perceived as a much of a threat by the church or the media. The reason for this may be the intellectualist and elitist nature of these movements, as perceived by "Christians dominated by anti-intellectual attitudes" (2008, 108, my translation).

In the late 1800s and early 1900s, a second phase of Indian influence on the West begins (Diem and Lewis 1992). Hindu *swamis* increasingly started visiting the U.S., lecturing to audiences on their particular forms of Hindu spirituality. Most famous of these was Swami Vivekananda, whose Vedanta Society became enormously influential despite its relatively small membership. The interest this first of many Western-oriented gurus created for his particular brand of neo-Hindu spirituality in the US and in Europe is not to be underestimated (Aadnanes 2008, 82), and Vivekananda may be viewed as the "blueprint" for many later efforts in the "Easternization" of the West.

The empire strikes (back): Transcendental Meditation and Acem meditation in Norway since 1960

The third and lasting phase of Indian influence on Western spirituality began around 1965—or, for some gurus, even earlier. In the U.S. laws restricting immigration from Asia were lifted and "a new wave of Indian gurus found a receptive audience among young Americans seeking religious inspiration from nontraditional sources [...] Indian spiritual teachers were the most numerous (as well as, in the long run, the most influential)" (Diem and Lewis 1992, 49). Among these was Maharishi Mahesh Yogi, the founder of Transcendental Meditation, an organization which quickly become one of the most famous and most controversial.

The history of Transcendental Meditation and its "offshoots" Acem and the Art of Living Foundation is a telling example of how a HIMM arrives, expands, localizes (and globalizes), diversifies, and (in the course of time), schisms. Transcendental Meditation began as the "Spiritual Regeneration Movement" in Madras, India, in 1957. Cynthia Humes and Dana Sawyer call TM an *intentional* international movement (2013, 18, my emphasis), which makes it clear that the organization intended, from the very beginning, to "go global." The movement quickly grew, and as early as 1959 the movement's guru/ leader/ founder Maharishi Mahesh Yogi had set up operations in Los Angeles. The Maharishi visited Oslo as early as 1960, and started teaching his meditation technique there; subsequently, a "chapter" of the Spiritual Regeneration Movement was founded in Norway in 1961. Since then, some sources claim the organization has taught meditation to 40,000 people in Norway[8]. The organization itself says little about its impact with respect to numbers reached. In its early days, the movement taught what at the time was called "Transcendental Deep Meditation," a form of mantra meditation said to bring bliss and prosperity not only to the meditators, but also to the entire world. The organization seems to have been readily absorbed

---

8. https://snl.no/Transcendental_Meditasjon#menuitem0 (accessed 07.04.14)

into both the American and Norwegian culture of the time, as the early sixties brought tangible change to most Western societies. With the rise of the
counterculture, Transcendental Meditation found its niche operating in the
intersection between spirituality, science and self-development, in what has
become commonly known as the "spiritual supermarket." This process was
certainly not without controversy, but in the US the Maharishi and the TM
organization managed to balance counter-cultural draw and psychedelic
romanticism on the one hand, with mainstreaming and "scientific" legitimation on the other (Tøllefsen 2014). Maharishi's visit to Norway, the founding of the first Norwegian TM "chapter" and the subsequent founding of the
Norwegian TM offshoot AMS (Academic Meditation Society, later known as
Acem) in 1966 did create a few waves—both within State Church circles and
in the public press. These controversies will be treated briefly below, after a
short overview of the Norwegian Acem organization.

Then psychology student Are Hoem founded the AMS as an organization under the umbrella of Maharishi Mahesh Yogi's Spiritual Regeneration
Movement. According to Margrethe Løøv (2010, 2012), AMS co-operated
closely with the international TM movement during the first five years, but
in 1972 internal conflicts led to a parting of ways, and an "excommunica-
tion" of Hoem and the AMS group. AMS changed its name to Acem in 1974,
the same year it was sued by its parent organization over the use of the name
of the meditation technique. The two organizations came to a settlement,
and to this day Acem's technique is simply called Acem meditation. The
organization clearly found a niche in the spiritual marketplace, both in Norway and abroad—professing what Løøv (2010) calls a strictly non-religious,
rational and empirical worldview. Currently, in addition to teaching the
meditation technique through courses and retreats, running a radio station
and publishing the *Dyade* journal (Løøv 2010), Acem runs Norsk Yoga-skole
(The Norwegian School of Yoga), which teaches *asana* yoga with a focus on
Acem meditation. This school was founded in 1968, also by Are Hoem, which
makes it the oldest yoga school in the country. Norsk Yoga-skole seems
to keep with the Acem organization's rational worldview, as their website
states that their teaching holds a "solid professional level, and is completely
devoid of nonsense and Indian romanticism" [my translation].[9] Acem is a
growing organization, in Norway and particularly outside the Nordic countries. According to Løøv (2010), around 60,000 Norwegians have attended
the organization's introductory meditation course. The organization's
international website[10] lists courses and retreats in countries ranging from
the Netherlands, the US and Taiwan, and Acem meditation has even made
it "back" to India. There the organization has a center in New Delhi, and

---

9. "Vår undervisning har solid faglig nivå, og er blottet for fjas og indisk svermeri,"
   http://www.yoga.no/norsk-yoga-skole/ (accessed 08.04.15)

10. http://www.acem.com/ (accessed 07.04.15)

holds beginner courses in Acem meditation in Delhi, Madurai, Tiruchirapalli and Chennai, as well as the occasional meditation retreat. The movement's (at the time of writing) under-construction website's sub-headline states, "Non-religious meditation. No guru cult,"[11] emphasizing the rationalist aims of the organization, thus setting it apart from the many other (often more guru-oriented) HIMMs in India. The re-globalization of an Indian-origin meditation technique, and not to mention its re-introduction into India as a scientifically oriented, psychologized and non-religious technique, certainly calls for a closer investigation that is unfortunately beyond the scope of the present chapter.

The conflict, schism and competition between TM and Acem in Norway is not, by far, the only such incident within this particular family/ guru lineage; in addition to Acem, Transcendental Meditation has "fathered" several other gurus and movements. In the seventies and early eighties, the TM movement changed its orientation (Tøllefsen 2014) and went into decline. The schism in Norway seems to have been an early incident in a pattern of schisms from the TM organization, as new and charismatic potential leaders surfaced from within the organization.[12] In the early nineties, TM publically broke with both Deepak Chopra[13] and The Art of Living Foundation's guru Sri Sri Ravi Shankar, likely based on competition for customers and the need for "product differentiation" (Humes 2009, 386). The risk of TM adherents leaving the movement and spending money on the less costly programs offered by Ravi Shankar and Deepak Chopra seems to have become too large. Humes (2009) has also noted an interesting development among TM defectors; instead of staying within the TM milieu (as individual practitioners), they subsequently become involved with other neo-Hindu groups, such as the Art of Living Foundation—which share certain basic beliefs with TM.

HIMMs and mass media

TM and its many offshoots have quite successfully accomplished the processes of both globalization and localization. TM hit the West on the cusp of a cultural shift, and was integral to much of the religious innovation in the field of new age—both creating and adapting to cultural change. The organization has since its beginning been quite shrewd in its PR efforts; the very public relationship in the late sixties between the Maharishi and the

---

11. http://www.acem.in/ (accessed 07.04.15)

12. One good example is Robin Carlsen and his World Teacher Seminar Teacher Training Programs, which were in the limelight for a while. However, after a legal battle with the parent organization, Carlsen was "excommunicated" from TM, and was compelled to inform participants that his program and that of TM were incompatible.

13. For another ex-TM devotee and "rival Indian leader" to become a religious entrepreneur in his own right (Humes 2009), now running his own highly successful meditation and well-being "empire," see https://www.deepakchopra.com/ (accessed 07.04.15)

world-famous pop group the Beatles was undoubtedly significant for TM's countercultural legitimacy (Tøllefsen 2014). This marketing success also impacted Norway. Aadnanes (2008) notes that Norwegian media quite frequently reported on TM and Acem from the mid-sixties onwards, much of it with a wait-and-see attitude or even favorably, until the media interest in meditation and meditation organizations went into decline in the nineties. In these thirty years, however, the Christian public debate on meditation, meditation organizations and their relationship to the Norwegian Church became critical and polarized.[14] Using mass media to its advantage (and, sometimes, detriment), the movements have managed to keep going until today—even as diversification and competition in the "spiritual supermarket" continues to grow.

In the almost fifty years since TM came to the West and Acem was founded, similar mechanisms of integration into a wider framework of new age (or, in Acem's case, probably recruiting from the same pool but with a strictly secular viewpoint), attentiveness to physical and mental wellbeing, and use of scientific legitimation strategies and social media can be observed in another of TM's "children," the Art of Living Foundation. Before going into the particulars of AoL in Norway and the movement's Norwegian practitioners, it is worth taking a look at how AoL has been treated in the media, in comparison to its older "family members."

James Beckford emphasizes in his analysis of NRMs and media that NRMs are generally mentioned in the media only when conflict is involved, as "(a) the main occasion for the portrayal and (b) as the principal means of structuring the account. Even those accounts which aspire towards a balanced, i.e. two-sided, presentation of the issues tend nevertheless to allow the conflictual aspects to predominate" (1994, 4). This analysis seems to fit well with Norwegian discourse around TM and Acem (Aadnanes 2008). However, in the case of AoL, media coverage seems to be the opposite—the accounts are positive or neutral, rather than negative. An internet search for AoL and media[15] turned up fairly scant results, both in Norway and abroad. There may be a discrepancy between what is accessible in printed media and in online news, but still Art of Living is infrequently mentioned. The most comprehensive source for AoL PR is actually AoL webpages[16] themselves, and in their press report pages archives of AoL media relations, which go back a few years.

International press reports are naturally positive, sporting headlines like "Global Humanitarian and Spiritual Leader Sri Sri Ravi Shankar Embarks on

---

14. For an overview of the media coverage, focusing especially on TM's reception in Norwegian Christian media debate, see Aadnanes 2008, 83–95.

15. Accessed 15.03.12, in both English and Norwegian.

16. See for example http://www.artofliving.org/latest-news and http://www.artofliving.org/no-no/press-archives (accessed 15.03.12).

a Peace Mission to Pakistan"[17] and "Karnataka lawyers boycott courts; spiritual guru Sri Sri offers to mediate."[18] The Norwegian AoL organization press reports website currently has six entries, three from August 2011 and three from May 2012.[19] Both periods coincide with Sri Sri Ravi Shankar's visits to Norway, one in the aftermath of the 22 July incident[20] and one in which the guru led a course in Sarpsborg which about 200 people attended.[21] These reports are positive as well, as it is rather unlikely that any organization would openly publicize negative press. However, AoL press coverage is still conflict-oriented. Although Beckford's emphasis on the importance of the theme of conflict regarding NRMs and the media fits well with earlier TM and Acem press, with respect to AoL the conflict does not revolve around the organization or the guru in conflict with the wider society. Rather, the press coverage revolves around AoL and Ravi Shankar entering areas of conflict in *society*, in an attempt to spread a message of peace and facilitate an environment for communication. Thus conflict can be interpreted as a leitmotiv even in the AoL media coverage, but with a different root cause and meaning than Beckford intended.

The advent of the internet has probably changed the way the public views NRMs—especially because of the possibility of gathering information that is more diverse. Of course, internet presence can be a double-edged sword: anyone is free to post whatever he or she wants about a movement. Many movements have a staunch community of critics in the blogosphere—Scientology is the most obvious example, but there also is a large number of webpages and blogs critical towards the organizations and practices of TM, AoL (and to some extent Acem) that can be found with a simple internet search. However, it is interesting to observe that over the last few years, a variety of social media, notably Facebook, seem to have become *the* way of movements keeping in touch with a wider audience. At the time of this writing, the official TM Facebook page has 223,500 likes. Acem meditation's international page (and its various country-specific sub-pages) does not clock in quite as high, currently at almost seven hundred (while sub-pages range between fifty and three hundred likes). Likewise, The Norwegian Art of Living page

---

17. http://www.sfgate.com/cgi-bin/article.cgi?f=/g/a/2012/03/12/prweb9273590. DTL#ixzz1pBwOlye7 (accessed 15.03.12).

18. http://www.ndtv.com/article/karnataka/karnataka-lawyers-boycott-courts-spiritual-guru-sri-sri-offers-to-mediate-18287 (accessed 15.03.12).

19. http://www.artofliving.org/no-no/press-reports (29.05.15).

20. 22. July 2011 the right-wing extremist Anders Behring Breivik set off a bomb outside the Norwegian Parliament building, and subsequently went on a shooting spree at the small island Utøya, where the Norwegian Labour Party Youth Camp was held. 77 people lost their lives.

21. http://www.artofliving.org/no-no/verdenskjent-inder-p%C3%A5-sarpsborg-bes%C3%B8k (29.05.15).

has 485 likes, The Art of Living global Facebook page sports about 748,000 likes, and Sri Sri Ravi Shankar's public figure page is liked by 1.9 million people. Of course, likes are not necessarily indicators of a movement's popularity "on the ground," but a presence in social media is useful both for PR and for directly connecting the movement and practitioners—as well as practitioners with each other. One can almost say that unless an organization has a presence on the internet it hardly exists—and more so for an organization like AoL that aims to create a global community. On the internet, organizations have much more control over PR, image and (self) presentation than earlier, which lessens the potential for conflict with media (and society).

In a Scandinavian context, it is hard to say much about public reception of NRMs without a proper analysis of media. But generally, having been spared such public dramas as those seen in the United States, views of NRMs may be more positive in this part of the world—or perhaps NRMs are just less visible. The "invisibility" of NRMs may allude to the relative secularization of Scandinavia, or to a relative homogeneity of Scandinavian society. Too much publicity either way causes an organization to be viewed as extravagantly deviant, thus leaving it in tension with or in opposition to mainstream society. However, this also depends on the nature of the NRM. In the Scandinavian context, it seems like it is the "homegrown" NRMs that have been viewed as most controversial. Certain neo-pagan belief systems, particularly Satanism, have been met with what borders on extreme opposition.[22] However, traditions like Hinduism and especially Buddhism are received very differently. For example, David Thurfjell notes—regarding the extremely positive reception of Buddhism among Swedes—that this tradition is not seen as "equally political, hierarchical, violent and unscientific as other religions, but is rather often presented as a purer and less problematic form of spirituality than one can find in other religions" (2013, 124, my translation). There is reason to believe that Hinduism, or at least Hindu-inspired movements such as AoL, are perceived similarly; tapping into a representation or reputation as peace-loving, health-oriented and eminently suited for the modern, individualized Scandinavian "looking eastward for something more moving, authentic and interesting" (2013, 137, my translation).

James Beckford mentions that traditionally "the movements which drew on Asian philosophies and cultures tended to arouse suspicions merely for being foreign and therefore perceived as threatening" (1994, 2). Historically, and especially in an American context (Tøllefsen 2014; Humes 2012), this may be true. In modern-day Scandinavia, however, these NRMs do not seem to pose a problem—probably also because Indian-oriented beliefs and practices have become an integrated part of a common and seemingly legitimate New Age mindset in this part of the world.

---

22. Especially in the US, but also in Scandinavia, see for example Hjelm (2006) and Lewis and Aagaard Petersen eds. (2008).

The Art of Living Foundation

The AoLF Questionnaire

This balance between the global, the local and "Indianness" was one of the many aspects that came to my attention as a consequence of the Art of Living questionnaire, which collected data from 2011 to 2012. Norwegian AoL practitioners were contacted through an online survey, using a convenience sampling method that was constructed in cooperation with the Norwegian Art of Living board of directors. Members of the board provided input on questionnaire items, made themselves available for questions and queries, and sent out the survey twice through their electronic mailing list. The AoLF Questionnaire was based on several earlier NRM questionnaires developed by James R. Lewis and Helen Berger, and was hosted on the questionnaire website surveymonkey.com. The extensive survey asked 50 questions, which ranged from participant demographics, levels of education and income, political and social activism, religious background and "conversion careers," to questions specifically regarding AoL and *Sudarshan Kriya*. In addition to multiple-choice questions, a number of open-ended items were included, allowing for more nuanced responses. The questionnaire was completely anonymous, and did not collect IP-addresses or any other identifying information. Due to the length and complexity of the questionnaire, the majority of responses came from serious SKY practitioners/AoL affiliates.

The logic behind an online questionnaire is summarized by Stenbjerre and Laugesen (2005), where they state that "To contain costs as much as possible, we rely on internet surveys. When conducted properly on carefully selected samples, research has shown these to be highly representative." By April 2012, the survey had received 100 responses from Norwegian residents, which represented a reasonable percentage (about 50%) of Norwegians then *active* in Art of Living. AoL Norway leaders estimated that the number of active participants was close to 200 at the time, indicating that the survey had collected a reasonably representative sample, considering that it was a convenience sample. Thus, based on questionnaire responses, it should be possible to draw some cautious conclusions about Norwegian AoL members—especially where the data supports both field observations and data from Art of Living literature and online presence.

Norwegian Art of Living practitioners

Liselotte Frisk (1998) notes that, generally speaking, more women than men are engaged in any measurable form of religious activity, and the prevalence of females in New Religious Movements has long been a "known fact." The general pattern in most NRMs (as well as in Christian sects and denominations) is that women are in the majority,[23] and this seems to be the case in the

---

23. See tables in Lewis and Tøllefsen (2013). For overviews of women/ gender in NRMs, see Palmer (2008), Goodwin (2014), or Tøllefsen (2016)

wider New Age as well. There is no real consensus among observers as to why female overrepresentation is the case in so much of the New Age field and in so many NRMs. Some writers have pointed out that women are socialized to be more religious than men (e.g., Trzebiatowska and Bruce 2012; Walter and Davie 1988); other explanations vary from those based on the sexual stereotyping of women's attributed greater emotionality, to their physical vulnerability, to their lower social status than men—stereotypes that point to why women should be more attracted to the appeal of religion. Stuart Rose (1998) notes that although New Age practitioners are a very diverse group, they tend to share three defining characteristics: at least half are middle-aged and middle class, and almost three-quarters are women. In the questionnaire measuring participant demographics and attitudes of Art of Living Foundation members, AoL practitioners were found to be approaching middle age, and the male to female ratio was 29.6 percent to 70.4 percent—tallying with Rose's observations (Tøllefsen 2012). These figures also dovetail with the author's observations from an AoL course and a *satsang*[24] at the AoL Centre in Oslo, Norway. In the course, almost all attendees were women. In the *satsang* the genders were more balanced, but still female-dominated. The age of Norwegian AoL survey respondents averaged in their mid-forties, reflecting a general age change in the NRM demographics (Lewis 2014). Norwegian respondents generally affiliate with the organization in their mid-thirties, and have on average been practicing eight years. They are almost exclusively heterosexual, have a response average of 1.36 children, and almost sixty percent are married, living with a life partner, or are in a committed relationship. Almost a quarter were single at the time of the questionnaire.

Because the organization is still small, Art of Living in Norway does not have a live-in center or *ashram* like the Bangalore headquarter or other international hubs. This means that the majority of Norwegian respondents tend to have quite infrequent/sporadic social contact with others (non-family members) involved with the AoL movement. A little over a third of the respondents meet other practitioners daily or almost daily/ weekly, while the rest meet others ranging from monthly to yearly, or almost never/never. A factor preventing greater participation seems to be distance from an Art of Living center, and respondents' family situation. Two respondents noted this in almost the same words: "I don't attend the weekly follow-ups often due to the distance to the location. Also because the time of the follow ups are difficult in combination with family life with small children." And, "Unable to do so as much as before because the kids are a priority; money, time and proximity to centre in that order." Ališauskienė (2009), describing levels of involvement among AoL practitioners in Lithuania and Denmark, sees a

---

24. *Satsang* comes from Sanskrit: *sat* (true) and *sanga* (company). According to Frisk a *satsang* is "a traditional activity in the Indian spiritual context, meaning "being with good/righteous companions." Satsang is a sitting together with an enlightened person who usually gives a short speech and then answers questions" (2002, 67).

clear distinction between practitioners that are devotees (*swamis* and teachers) and those who are adepts-clients (permanent visitors). Ališauskienė's analysis also seems to fit the Norwegian data where she says that

> Swamis commit their life to the organization, they live and work in the ashrams, while teachers give most of their time to the purposes of the organization in the society in which they live. Adepts-clients are the permanent visitors of Art of Living Foundation activities, they attend courses and participate in satsangs, and they are distinguished from other clients in their loyalty to the organization." (2009, 20)

Similar patterns of involvement can be found in AoL around the world, and also in Norway, where a few key actors are strongly involved with running the organization and with teaching activities. Some practitioners are loyal adept-clients with a relatively high level of involvement, while the majority of respondents are somewhat less frequently, or infrequently, involved. This situation seems to fit with what Eileen Barker notes when describing the lifestyles of NRM practitioners which tend to vary, both between organizations and within them; "from community living with members working full-time for the organization to members leading perfectly "ordinary" lives but joining with other members for special gatherings once a week or so" (Barker 1998, 19).

In their chapter in the present volume, James R. Lewis and Oscar-Torjus Utaaker have analyzed select questionnaire data (among them the AoLF Questionnaire) from members of different NRMs and readers of the alternative Norwegian magazine *Visjon*, examining the respondents' spiritual interests, both at present and previously. Findings from this study shows that participants tend to go through "seekership" processes, and are rarely exclusive in their selection of groups and practices. Rather, Lewis and Utaaker find that "most members also have a variety of other spiritual, divinatory, therapeutic, healing and alternative lifestyle interests that they simultaneously pursue—supplementary interests and practices that they nevertheless regard as being an integral part to their spiritual quest." About forty percent of the Art of Living respondents have been involved in other groups, ranging from just one group to three or more. Interestingly, Eastern traditions were the most popular alternative for all groups involved, not only AoL. But it seems that many AoL practitioners have had an affinity for Indian groups and practices throughout their "conversion career." Eighteen respondents had been involved with some form of Buddhism or Buddhist meditation, and sixteen AoL members had previously been involved with Hinduism, another Hindu guru or Hindu-inspired meditation. Transcendental Meditation was frequently mentioned by respondents (and Acem once or twice)—which may suggest there is some foundation to TM's worries about competition and product differentiation before the AoL schism. This also correlates with Humes' (2009) "spiritual career" findings mentioned above.

Art of Living practices

AoL (like TM and Acem, and almost every meditation movement out there) seeks to alleviate stress and increase practitioners' wellbeing in their everyday lives. The questionnaire respondents were mainly oriented towards health and self-development issues, and indicate that they have chosen AoL and its practices to help them deal with various physical and mental ailments, stress and worry.

Several of the AoLF questionnaire items were aimed specifically at *Sudarshan Kriya*, the cornerstone practice of the movement. The technique itself is a cycle of breath in three rhythms. The practitioner sits on his/her knees, relaxing the body in the yoga position known as *vajrasana*, while breathing through the nose. At the end of the cycle, the practitioner takes a few long breaths, and then relaxes, lays down for a while, and enters a state of meditation where the mind and body are aware but deeply rested. The technique is taught in two varieties; the long guided *Kriya* (where practitioners often listen to a tape of Ravi Shankar's instructions) which is meant to be practiced in a group, for example once a week. The short *Kriya* is meant to be practiced every day, following two other breathing techniques used as "warm up" exercises. By controlling the rhythm of breath, Art of Living teachings say that people can also control their emotions, their bodies and their minds. For example, when one is sad, the breath is long and deep. Likewise, when angry, the breath becomes short and quick. Because the rhythm of the breath responds to emotions, the organization's teachings assert that this process can be reversed; the breath can be used to *change* emotions and states of mind, and to relieve stress. "It [*Sudarshan Kriya*] flushes our anger, anxiety and worry; leaving the mind completely relaxed and energized."[25] AoLF Questionnaire respondents (of both genders) who practice[26] the *Kriya* frequently report similar effects.

> "Have felt I have been in touch with the self; absolute peace and bliss"

> "Stress relief -Experience of a "broader view""

> "My body gets peaceful and calm. I feel clean inside"

> "I discovered breath as an essential tool for health, balance and energy and it's a gift. I am not very well disciplined, but I talk about it to others, and recommend it especially to those who might need it. Through the course, I learned the knowledge that I find beautiful and essential too. My psychic health and understanding of life, dealing with problems, other people etc., has improved immensely. Thank you."

---

25. See http://www.artofliving.org/in-en/sri-sri-sudarshan-kriya (accessed 26.09.11).

26. Norwegian respondents' frequency of SKY practice: 19.4 % practice every day, 34.7 % practice regularly, 23.5 % practice sometimes, 17.3 % practice rarely, and 5.1 % never practice the *Kriya*, although they usually have regularly in the past.

Almost every respondent mentioned feelings and emotions in connection with their SKY practice, and the words "stress" and "relaxation" were extremely common in the responses. According to Ališauskienė, "the majority of her [Danish and Lithuanian] informants were brought to the Art of Living Foundation by stress, increased speed of life and the problems it creates, and a search for the answers to modern existential questions" (2009, 20). This seems to be a theme among the informants of the Norwegian study as well: the attitudes toward the practice and the results the informants experienced from practicing the technique were positive. When asked to if they have had any particularly meaningful experiences as a result of practicing SKY, Norwegian respondents basically fell into two categories: those who perceived *Kriya* as relaxing and harmonizing, and those who have (had) health issues and felt that the practice helped them overcome these issues. Two questionnaire respondents described their experiences with the *Kriya:*

> "My experiences come from regular practice rather than "during" the SK. After 5-6 months of practicing, I had reduced my allergy problems (food and animals) to a mini-minimum. I have not had chronic sinus problems after my very first AoL course, and I used to have infections about 5–7 times a year! I am in a better shape/ increased lung capacity and have a better immune system with practicing the SK—stopped for a period some years ago, and got worse/ sick more often again. I have better capacity during the day, and the quality of my work is better when I do the practice. My communication skills are better when my energy level is higher, and the practice brings up the energy very fast! Tolerance and temper is improved when I to the practice, I am more relaxed and handle situations a lot better in general."

> "I suffer from Chronic Fatigue Syndrom / Myalgic Encephalopati. The yoga and breathing exercises have absolutely a positive influence on my health :))"

Based on questionnaire responses like those above it makes sense to interpret *pranayama*/ SKY (and to some extent yoga) practice as a form of therapy. According to Kraft (2011), the therapeutic/health-related aspect of new age is strong in Norway; its very core revolves around health-related strategies and products. Kraft quotes numbers from 2010 which indicate that one of two Norwegians have tried so-called "alternative" medicine (2011, 86).[27] However, it is important to note that users of alternative medicine do not necessarily have to define themselves as "new age" or even "believe" in any of the associated ideas. Belief, according to Kraft, is irrelevant for the

---

27. Kraft mentions similar numbers from Denmark and Canada, where up to 70% of Canadians had tried alternative medicine. However, she also mentions that the Norwegian survey has been criticized for defining alternative medicine too broadly—for example including massage—and that the numbers may therefore be too high.

social significance of new religiosity. Rather, there is an inherent willingness to "try everything" (especially in the context of chronic illnesses or pain), and thus it may be that "*offerings from alternative medicine overlap with the New Age view of reality, and many of the therapists stand on New Age ground*" (Kraft 2011, 87, my translation). In "Bumper Car Ride Through a Maze of Spiritual Trips…" Lewis and Utaaker analyzed not only previous group affiliation, but also divinatory systems and body-mind therapies common in the new religiosity milieu. Art of Living respondents scored high on the use of astrology (as did respondents from other groups)—about 40 percent found it to "really be of help." Looking at mind-body therapies, it turns out that AoL respondents have tried out a wide variety of activities. Some seventy percent have tried acupuncture, aromatherapy, homeopathy and healing/ spiritual healing, while a little above forty percent have tried acupressure and Reiki[28]. These numbers indicate that while AoL affiliation and SKY practice may be primary, it is one among many—or a "stop-over" on the journey of spiritual seekership.

AoL practitioners seem to interpret SKY as a useful technique for enhanced wellbeing, and their experiences are generally positive. At the same time, they do use other therapies and practices as complimentary those of AoL, which may indicate a quite instrumental and rational approach to their own health and wellbeing—similar to what Kraft points out above regarding new age. This perspective on practitioner attitudes seems to fit respondents' experiences regarding other, more *religious* aspects of AoL. As will be discussed below, practitioners exhibit quite ambivalent attitudes towards some of the more "typically" Indian characteristics of the movement, most retaining a fundamentally pragmatic approach to their involvement.

Indian—or not so Indian after all?

Indian-derived beliefs and practices are integral to Art of Living Foundation, as it is in the wider new religiosity field. Apart from *Sudarshan Kriya*, the organization offers several other practices, either "directly" borrowed from, or inspired by, TM. Both TM and AoL teach a simple *mantra*-style form of meditation. The form of meditation the Maharishi taught in TM's early years in the West was relatively easy, based upon words selected for the meditator by a TM teacher, derived from *mantras* from Indian tantric traditions (Lowe 2011). Tailored to the Western mind, TM insisted that their particular style of meditation should be natural, modest and uncomplicated. The meditation techniques taught in AoL are quite similar, a "graceful, natural and effortless" meditation technique called Sahaj Samadhi Meditation (or Art of Meditation). Also, both TM and AoL teach a set of simplified hatha yoga postures as the core of their yoga endeavors. The *Kriya*, meditation technique and *asana* yoga are decidedly of Indian origin and tradition, but are also practices that are easily incorporated into an everyday "secular" framework—because

---

28. For a full list of therapies, see Lewis and Utaaker in this volume.

they have a definite positive experiential dimension (the authority of the self), and (partially) because they are understood equally as *scientific* and *spiritual* techniques (Tøllefsen 2011). However, one aspect of AoL life seems to give Norwegian respondents pause—it seems that serious devotion to a guru is just not a very *Norwegian* thing to do.

The guru

Other forms of authority and of legitimization of the techniques will be discussed below, but first an aspect of AoL experience that seems to be particularly Norwegian will be analyzed—namely the relationship to the guru. Sri Sri Ravi Shankar is presented as a figurehead, and as the founder he has great importance to the movement—especially in India. In the Bangalore *ashram*, Shankar can be understood in terms of a Hindu mode of legitimacy, and his "godlike" presence makes him a popular choice in guru for some Indians. Expressions of love and attachment to the guru are most visible in weekend satsangs (gatherings of holy people) devoted to Sri Sri, where, unlike in TM circles, traditional *bhajans* [hymns] are sung (Humes 2009, 384). Humes' observations are similar to the author's own from the Bangalore ashram, where guru worship is frequent and important to practitioners. When Ravi Shankar is in attendance, large gatherings (*darshans*) are held, where the devotees meet the guru. These are enormously popular, and the large prayer/ meditation hall fills to the brim every night. Guru devotion is prominent and highly emotional, expressed through *bhajans* as well as individual songs, poetry recital, and testimonials in open-mike sessions (Tøllefsen 2011). In the *ashram* (when the author visited, which coincided with the guru in attendance), the whole atmosphere felt loaded with his presence; his figure seemed central to most activity at the ashram. An attempt was made to distribute the questionnaire described above at the Indian *ashram*, but with little success. However, the few answers to questionnaire items regarding the guru from Indian respondents were all extremely positive towards Ravi Shankar.

The AoL organization in Norway is definitely Indian-oriented, much like other guru-led meditation movements. It retains the particular Indian flavor of the movement, as well as some of its parent religion, Hinduism. There are guru photographs and paraphernalia, and especially in the *darshan* sessions, the Norwegian AoL "chapter" comes across as "Indian." These sessions contain meditation, *bhajan* singing and a knowledge session, generally watching a videotaped speech of Sri Sri Ravi Shankar. However, it seems that only a small fraction of practitioners actually attend the *darshans*—which fits withAlišauskiene's (2009) observations of levels of involvement from *swamis* to adept-clients and occasional/ infrequent visitors. As noted above, most Norwegian respondents seem rather ambivalent, not so much to the guru himself, but to the idea of *devotion*. As one respondent put it:

I came from the AoL courses with a feeling that AoL is more "Indian" in the sense that the role of the guru is strongly emphasized. Being a typically scientifically minded Westerner, I prefer a more individualistic approach. [...] I found the philosophical part of the AoL course annoying. I also find that in AoL the guru gets a bit hyped as very intelligent and the kriya presented as something extremely unique, but in fact there are many powerful practices available in different yoga traditions/ styles, as there are many deeply wise people in the history of yoga and meditation. Which practice suits you depends on your temperament and body type, not a particular guru.

Another respondent expressed similar sentiments:

Kissing guru pictures and talking about souls and the afterlife is religious. I think resting one's sense of security and meaning on imaginary, vague notions of immortality and transcendence is risky, and I think teaching and encouraging irrational thinking is immoral, but for being religious AOL does comparatively little damage. The practices are healthy, but I've seen people dedicating almost their whole lives to this organization and being completely obsessive about the ideas of purity and rules. I guess it's better that they ended up in AOL than some cult.

The *darshan* sessions may be instrumental in keeping the "Indian essence" and portraying the movement as exotic enough to appeal to people drawn to the "alternative" lifestyle of a certain new religiosity framework. However, the importance of/focus on the guru seems to be consciously toned down in the Norwegian context. This may be a strategic choice pertaining to Norwegian culture, which can be interpreted as more individualistic than Indian culture (if viewed through a lens of new religiosity and the authority of the self). Some opposition and skepticism towards external authority in the form of a guru can be expected, at least among new members and practitioners. The Norwegian focus in the AoL is more on self-development and personal spirituality, as opposed to the stronger community-oriented and guru-driven atmosphere in India. While Indian practitioners tend to, as noted above, be what Ališauskienė calls spiritualistic in their relation to the guru, most Norwegian respondents are what she refers to as pragmatists: "informants maintain a pragmatic relationship to the leader of the group; he is understood as the one who provides "useful" information" (2009, 21). In this sense, the Norwegian style of AoL involvement seems similar to the findings from Ališauskienė's research in Lithuania, where the popularity of AoL seems to rely on the "strategy of providing spirituality and the means of coping with everyday stresses" (2009, 6).

Sri Sri Ravi Shankar has visited Norway a couple of times over the last couple of years.[29] Sentiments may have changed or been reinforced by the gen-

---

29. Once attending a public meeting in the aftermath of the terrorist attack in July 2011,

erally positive media attention Shankar and the AoL organization received in Norway after his visit.[30] Practitioners who otherwise would not have had an opportunity to meet the guru may have be able to, but without longitudinal data, it is impossible to know if attitudes towards the guru have changed after his visits to Norway.

Authority of tradition, of science, and of the self

While teaching SKY, meditation techniques and yoga (and even combining *Sudarshan Kriya* practice with tango dancing), the Norwegian Art of Living "chapter" seems to have found a middle way between Indian impulses and the pragmatic, health-oriented application of the movement's practices. This balancing act is even spelled out, as the organization makes sure to emphasize the universality of their philosophy and practices:

> Many of the techniques used in our programs are indeed based on yoga, and it is also true to say that "the East" in general has a long tradition of ways of dealing with stress. You might say that eastern cultures in some way have specialized in knowledge about stress, personal development and handling various emotions. And the founder of the International Art of Living Foundation, Sri Sri Ravi Shankar, is from India as well. However, the techniques taught and the human values we promote are completely universal. For example, breathing techniques are a key to stress release—and we all breathe, whether we were born in the so-called "West" or so-called "East'![31]

That is not to say that Indian tradition is without value—it clearly has. For the advanced practitioner there is opportunity to study the "Wisdom Series,"[32] in which Sri Sri Ravi Shankar comments on the ancient Hindu sacred texts, *Ashtavakra Gita, Narada Bhakti Sutras* and the *Patanjali Yoga Sutras*, and attempts to make these traditional teachings relevant in the modern world.

Science

That the movement's practices are scientifically proven to work is an important legitimizer on an organizational level—not only for AoL, but also for movements like TM and Acem (Tøllefsen 2011, 2014). Is scientific legitimation of the practices also relevant for individual Norwegian AoL practitioners? For the Lithuanian practitioners from Ališauskienė's 2009 AoL study, science

---

and most recently being present at a huge course weekend in Sarpsborg between 27th April and May 1st 2012.

30. See for example the interview in A-magasinet (Aftenposten) 04.05.12, and in Sarpsborg Arbeiderblad 02.05.12

31. http://www.artofliving.org/no-en/about-us-faq (accessed 24.09.12)

32. http://www.artofliving.org/no-en/wisdom-series (accessed 09.04.15)

is an important legitimizing factor for the movement's techniques, which may have a background in a particular Lithuanian post-communist "ethos" of scientific atheism. However, the Danish respondents in the same study did not emphasize the scientific aspects of the practices as particularly important—a pattern that also holds for the Norwegian AoLF Questionnaire respondents. Almost half of the respondents interpreted SKY as a mind-body therapy (as opposed to a purely spiritual path, or a combination of the two), and almost ninety percent highlighted physical and psychological benefits of the practice as especially important to them. Some of the Norwegian respondents even seem rather skeptical toward the way science is portrayed in the organization—perhaps deeming it "new agey" and not sufficiently orthodox.

It seems that many Norwegian respondents emphasize their personal experience of SKY as being much more important than a rational, scientific explanation. One respondent noted: "When I personally experienced the difference it made to my life, why should I bother with scientific support?" Attitudes like these align with one of the basic tenets of new age thought, namely that the authority of a practice ultimately comes from the self, not from an outside agency (Kraft 2011). I would at this point argue that, for most practitioners, direct personal experience combined with the physical and psychological benefits that seem to accrue from the practice is the key to understanding participants' ongoing relationship with SKY rather than the appeal of SKY as a "scientific" technique. In Norwegian AoL, it seems that the authority of science has taken a backseat to the new age ethics of the "authority of the self"—the "authority" derived from personal experience of the practices—and a backseat to the therapeutic (not necessarily in the orthodox medical sense of therapeutic) aspects of the practice.

However, a scientific mindset/worldview may be difficult to "escape." What if the questionnaire had contained, for example, a question asking "Would you have joined the Art of Living movement if you knew its practices were entirely unscientific?" Particularly in the West, people live in societies and with mindsets that are fundamentally scientific—science has become inseparable from how most of us interpret the world. There is no doubt that science is an important legitimation strategy in Art of Living—perhaps so fundamental to practitioners that it is "taken for granted." With that perspective, most answers to the hypothetical question above would probably have been negative.

Without the joint effects of Indian-oriented new age spirituality on one hand, and the legitimating power of science on the other, Art of Living as a NRM would have lost a large part of its meaningfulness. Much of the success of this type of movement lies in offering *useful* practices in line with the *zeitgeist*. In that sense, Art of Living manages to balance tradition and modernity, spirituality and science in a way that is understandable in a globalized world. The structure of the movement and the basic teachings are the same in every country, but it seems that the various "chapters" attend to aspects like

Indian-orientation and the science question differently. However, no matter how varied beliefs and motivations may be, the AoLF Questionnaire indicates the they share a common goal: the most important purpose of SKY practice is to help them to help themselves, towards a better, less stressful life.

Conclusion

AoL Norway's website subheading reads: "Art of Living personal development programs combine the mystical and the modern to help you create a life of purpose, joy and confidence."[33] This statement sums up AoL philosophy, but is equally emblematic for the wider new age culture in Norway, which both AoL, TM and (to some extent) Acem are part of—and which is suffused with Indian ideas and practices. Although a part of new age culture, TM and Acem techniques (and other less "famous" yoga and meditation practices) have been present in Norway for about six decades—and are thus not so *new* anymore. Hindu-inspired Meditation Movements (the somewhat more organized part of the new religiosity field) have been instrumental in popularizing Indian practices in Norway, while simultaneously *localizing* them by various means. Norwegian-origin Acem with its rational and non-religious practice is in a process of growing and "re-globalizing," and Art of Living has made aspects of its organization more palatable to Norwegian clients by, for example, de-emphasizing guru devotion. AoLF Questionnaire respondents seem to interpret their practice primarily as therapeutic and health related, side by side with notions of self-spirituality, self-development and self-authority. AoL techniques are just few of many practices, activities and therapies the respondents are familiar with, which supports an analysis of HIMMs as an integral part of new age/ holistic health culture in Norway.

Norwegian consumption patterns of Indian techniques and practices, especially yoga, seem to be changing. A form of "dialogical" indigenization process or at least a degree of grounding or localization seems to have happened over the course of the last several decades, which at least partially explain the current mainstreaming of yoga and meditation practices—whereas other practices (like guru devotion) remain movement-specific and "esoteric." An interesting question may be whether these Indian-oriented new age practices are, as Campbell claims, aspects of a *spiritualization* of mainstream culture. Or, are they rather indicators of a (popular) culture increasingly focused on esthetics and personal development, instrumentally using Indian-derived practices understood to bring health and well-being (with the added benefit of a toned body), because they happened to be at hand and culturally available? Whatever the answers may be, these (and many other) questions open vast possibilities for further research on Hindu-inspired Meditation Movements, with a number of methods, and both in Norway and abroad.

---

33. http://www.artofliving.org/no-en (accessed 09.04.15).

References

Aadnanes, Per M. 1998. *Gud for kvarmann. Kyrkja og den nye religiøsiteten*. Oslo: University Publishing House.

Ališauskienė, Milda. 2009. "Spirituality and religiosity in the Art of Living Foundation in Lithuania and Denmark: Meanings, contexts and relationships." In *Subcultures and New Religious Movements in Russia and East-Central Europe*, edited by George McKay, Christopher Williams, Michael Goddard, Neil Foxlee and Egidija Ramanauskaite, 339–364. Oxford: Peter Lang.

Barker, Eileen. 1998. "New religions and new religiosity." In *New Religions and New Religiosity*, edited by E. Barker and M. Warburg. RENNER Studies on New Religions. Aarhus: Aarhus University Press.

Beckford, James A. 1994. "The mass media and new religious movements." In ISKCON Communications Journal (online) Vol 2(2), December 1994. Originally delivered at the International Conference on Religion and Conflict Armagh, 20–21 May 1994.

Campbell, Colin. 2007. *The Easternization of the West, a Thematic Account of Cultural Change in the Modern Era*. Boulder: Paradigm Publishers.

Diem, Andrea Grace and James R. Lewis. 1992. "Chapter 4: Imagining India: The Influence of Hinduism on the New Age Movement." In *Perspectives on the New Age*, edited by James R. Lewis and J. Gordon Melton, 48–58. Albany: State University of New York Press.

Frisk, Liselotte. 2002. "The Satsang Network, A growing post-Osho Phenomenon." *Nova Religio: The Journal of Alternative and Emergent Religions* 6(1): 64–85.

Gilhus, Ingvild and Lisbeth Mikaelsson, eds. 1998. *Skjult visdom—universelt brorskap: Teosofi i Norge*. Oslo: Emilia Forlag.

Hammer, Olav and Mikael Rothstein, eds. 2013. *Handbook of the Theosophical Current*. Leiden: Brill.

Hanegraaff, Wouter. 2013. "Enthenogenic esotericism." In *Contemporary Esotericism*, edited by Egil Asprem and Kenneth Granholm, 392–409. Sheffield: Equinox Publishing.

Hjelm, Titus. 2006. "Between Satan and Harry Potter: Legitimating Wicca in Finland." *Journal of Contemporary Religion* 21(1): 33–48.

Humes, Cynthia Ann. 2009. "Schisms within Hindu guru groups: The Transcendental Meditation Movement in North America." In *Sacred Schisms: How Religions Divide*, edited by James Lewis and Sarah M. Lewis, 372–396. Cambridge: Cambridge University Press.

———. 2012. "Hindutva, mythistory and pseudoarchaeology." *Numen* 59(2–3): 178–201.

Humes, Cynthia and Dana Sawyer. (unpublished) *Watering the Roots/ The Transcendental Meditation Movement and its History in the United States*. Albany: State University of New York Press.

Goodwin, Megan. 2014. "Gender." In *The Bloomsbury Companion to New Religious Movements*, edited by G. D. Chryssides and B. Zeller, 195–206. London: Bloomsbury Academic.

Kraft, Siv Ellen. 2011. *Hva er nyreligiøsitet.* Oslo: University Publishing House.

Kraft, Siv Ellen, Trude Fonneland and James R. Lewis, eds. 2015. *Nordic Neoshamanisms.* New York: Palgrave Macmillan.

Lewis, James R. 2014. "The youth crisis model of conversion: An idea whose time has passed?" *Numen* 61(5–6): 594–618.

Lewis, James R. and Jesper Aagard Petersen, eds. 2008. *The Encyclopedic Sourcebook of Satanism.* Amherst, NY: Prometheus Books.

Lewis, James R. and Inga B. Tøllefsen. 2013. "Gender and paganism in census and survey data." *The Pomegranate* 15(1–2): 61–78.

Løøv, Margrethe. 2010. "Fra Veda til vitenskap, en kulturanalytisk studie av meditasjonsorganisasjonen Acems utvikling." Unpublished MA thesis in the history of religion, Department of cultural studies and Oriental languages, The University of Oslo.

———. 2012. "Acems avfortrylling: Fra nyreligiøs motkultur til sekulær selvutviklingsteknikk." *Chaos. Dansk-norsk tidsskrift for religionhistoriske studier* 2: 9–34.

Lowe, Scott. 2011. "Transcendental Meditation, Vedic science and science." *Nova Religio: The Journal of Alternative and Emergent Religions* 14(4): 54–76.

Palmer, Susan J. 2008. "Women in new religious movements." In *The Oxford Handbook of New Religious Movements*, edited by James R. Lewis, 380–386. Oxford: Oxford University Press.

Rose, Stuart. 1998. "An examination of the New Age movement: Who is involved and what constitutes its spirituality." *Journal of Contemporary Religion* 13(1): 5–22.

Stenbjerre, M. and J. N. Laugesen. 2005. "Conducting representative online research." In Proceedings of ESOMAR Conference on Worldwide Panel Research; Development and Progress, 369–391. Budapest: ESOMAR Amsterdam.

Thurfjell, David. 2013. "Varför buddhismen är så omtyckt bland sekulära svenskar." In *Mystik och andlighet, kritiska perspektiv*, edited by Simon Sorgenfrei, 122–140. Stockholm: Dialogos Förlag.

Tøllefsen, Inga B. 2011. "Art of living: Religious entrepreneurship and legitimation strategies." *International Journal for the Study of New Religions* 2(2): 255–279.

———. 2012. "Notes on the demographic profiles of art of living practitioners in Norway and abroad." *Alternative Spirituality and Religion Review* 3(2): 95–110.

———. 2014. "Transcendental Meditation, the Art of Living Foundation, and public relations: From psychedelic romanticism to science and schism." In *Controversial New Religions*, Second Edition, edited by James R. Lewis and Jesper Aa. Petersen, 159–175. Oxford: Oxford University Press.

————. 2016. "Gender in New Religions." In *The Oxford Handbook of New Religious Movements, Volume II,* edited by James R. Lewis and Inga B. Tøllefsen. Oxforfd: Oxford University Press.

Trzebiatowska, Maria and Steve Bruce. 2012. *Why Are Women More Religious Than Men.* Oxford: Oxford University Press.

Wallis, Roy. 1984. *The Elementary Forms of the New Religious Life.* London: Routledge and Kegan Paul.

Walter, Tony and Grace Davie. 1998. "The religiosity of women in the modern west." *The British Journal of Sociology* 49(4): 640–660.

Williamson, Lola. 2010. *Transcendent in America, Hindu-inspired Meditation Movements as New Religion.* New York: New York University Press.

12

"Bumper Car Ride Through a Maze of Spiritual Trips":
Multiple Involvements, Changes across Time, and Deep Structure in the Alternative Spiritual Milieu

JAMES R. LEWIS AND OSCAR-TORJUS UTAAKER

Prior to the cult controversy of the seventies, sociologists of religion reserved the term "cult" for ephemeral spiritual groups that formed, attracted a following, and then declined and disappeared into what Colin Campbell termed the "cultic milieu" (the subculture that would later be referred to as the "New Age"). In his analysis of this milieu, Campbell carried out what was, in effect, a Copernican revolution by shifting the framework of analysis from individual new religious movements (NRMs) to the larger spiritual subculture out of which these groups emerged. The cult controversy, however, interrupted this revolution by prompting sociologists to refocus on the more solid, sect-like groups that were at the center of social conflict at the time. In the present chapter, we return to Campbell's paradigm shift, both by refocusing on the larger alternative spiritual milieu as our primary frame of analysis as well as by examining some of the dynamic patterns manifested by the memberships of select new religious movements.

Additionally, while participants in the New Age milieu are constantly shifting their involvements, there is a deep structure of values and self-understandings held by such seekers that remains stable, and that we will describe and analyze. This discussion will in turn provide a backdrop for an analysis of select questionnaire data gathered from members of three different NRMs (plus readers of the Norwegian New Age magazine *Visjon*) regarding their diverse, multiple spiritual interests, both previous and concurrent. Despite the apparent solidity of the three groups, memberships tend to ebb and flow, so that, for many participants, such NRMs are but one step in a much longer process of seeking. Additionally, participants are rarely focused exclusively on the practices of their respective spiritual group. Rather, most members also have a variety of other spiritual, divinatory, therapeutic, healing and alternative lifestyle interests that they simultaneously pursue—supplementary interests and practices that they nevertheless regard as being an integral part of their spiritual quest.

Beyond repeating and amplifying prior analyses of the alternative spiritual subculture, the thrust of our discussion will be to make an argument for understanding NRMs in terms of two contexts, one socio-cultural and the other temporal. On the one hand, members of new religions should be studied in the context of their varied alternative interests—many of which do not directly involve their specific NRM. Instead, though perhaps primarily focused in their religious group, their concerns and interests are likely more "spread out" within the larger alternative milieu. On the other hand, one needs to view NRMs as well as their participants processually—as organizations that are always changing in response to a variety of internal and external forces, and as participants whose interests, involvements and self-identities are in constant flux.

Dynamic milieus

In their "Seekers and Saucers: The Role of the Cultic Milieu in Joining a UFO Cult," Robert W. Balch and David Taylor quote an older member of what would later become Heaven's Gate who described his life-long religious quest as having been a "bumper car ride through a maze of spiritual trips." In the same paragraph, they also quote a younger member, who stated that, "Until I started talking to you, I never realized how much shit I'd been into" (1977, 848). These remarks highlight the dynamic, changing nature of the alternative spiritual subculture that has been labeled, variously, the cultic milieu, the New Age, occulture, *etc.*, in the sociological literature. Each of these different labels tends to highlight slightly different specific characteristics of this subculture. Though now over forty years old, "cultic milieu" has not lost its usefulness.

The expression "cultic milieu" is ultimately rooted in the discussion of modern religious classifications that began with Max Weber's distinction between church and sect (1949). Weber's student, Ernst Troeltsch, elaborated churches and sects into a set of analytic categories (1931). Churches in this schema were conceived of as national bodies that had reached an accommodation with the larger society, whereas sects were smaller groups that had broken away from churches in a quest for stricter and more intense forms of spirituality, somewhat withdrawn from participation in mainstream culture.

The American sociologist of religion H. Richard Niebuhr developed this distinction further by re-conceptualizing church and sect as opposite poles in a spectrum of dynamic possibilities (1929). He also inserted the category "denomination" to refer to the religious bodies that, similar to European national churches, had accommodated themselves to mainstream culture in the North American context. Another American sociologist, Howard Becker, introduced "cult" into this schema (1932). For Becker as for later sociologists of religion, cults were small, ephemeral, loosely-organized groups revolving around mystical doctrines taught by a charismatic leader. In contrast to sects, cults were generally not strict, and were not schisms from larger, pre-existing religious bodies. Though later theorists would articulate additional distinctions, the cult-sect-denomination (and/or church) schema became, in effect, the standard typology.

The groups that Becker and others referred to as cults emerged out of an alternative spiritual subculture that Colin Campbell influentially termed the "cultic milieu" in his "The Cult, Secularization and the Cultic Milieu" (1972). This essay quickly became a classic article, often cited in analyses of the alternative spiritual subculture. Part of the attractiveness of Campbell's notion was the emphasis he placed on the milieu as a kind of fertile socio-cultural "soup," out of which new organizations emerged, only to quickly lose their vitality and dissolve back into the milieu while simultaneously contributing elements to yet newer groups.

> Given that cultic groups have a tendency to be ephemeral and highly unstable, it is a fact that new ones are being born just as fast as the old ones die. There is a continual process of cult formation and collapse which parallels the high turnover of membership at the individual level. Clearly, therefore, cults must exist within a milieu which, if not conducive to the maintenance of individual cults, is clearly highly conducive to the spawning of cults in general. Such a generally supportive cultic milieu is continually giving birth to new cults, absorbing the debris of the dead ones and creating new generations of cult-prone individuals to maintain the high levels of membership turnover. Thus, whereas cults are by definition a largely transitory phenomenon, the cultic milieu is, by contrast, a constant feature of society. It could therefore prove more viable and illuminating to take the cultic milieu and not the individual cult as the focus of sociological concern. (Campbell 2002 [1972], 14)

Another analytic term that Campbell's article helped to popularize was the notion of seekership. Thus, in addition to the particular new religions which emerge out of the milieu, this subculture is constituted by a larger population of seekers who, in Lofland and Stark's words, are "searching for some satisfactory system of religious meaning to interpret and resolve their discontents" (1965, 868). By implication, these individuals have adopted lifestyles that prioritize seeking over finding, leading them to become temporarily affiliated with one group after another, in a pattern that has been referred to as a "conversion career" (Richardson 1978, 1980). This pattern of seeking simultaneously contributes, on the one hand, to the *fluidity* of the cultic milieu's contents and, on the other, to the *continuity* of the milieu's deep structure. We will elaborate on both the milieu's dynamism and its stability in the balance of the present paper.

Deep structures

The alternative spiritual subculture is notoriously difficult to delimit or to "characterize it in a decisive manner" (Lewis 1992, 6). One common approach has been to list core beliefs (e.g., Ellwood and Partin 1988, 14–15; Holloway 2000, 554–556), and to voice the caveat—along with an invocation of Wittgenstein's "family resemblance" metaphor—that most particular instantiations of the New Age will have some but not all of these core beliefs. This approach is useful for some purposes. For our analysis here, we are less interested in the metaphysical vision of the alternative spiritual subculture and more interested in the specific ideas and processes that give this milieu its stability—its deep structure, if we can borrow a useful, though sometimes contentious expression from linguistics.

To begin with, in several different places in his influential article, Campbell emphasizes that "the cultic milieu is united and identified by the existence of an ideology of seekership and by seekership institutions" (1972). In addition to Lofland and Stark, he refers to Dohrman (1958) and Buckner (1968) as his sources for the seekership notion. One of the more developed discussions of the seeker role can be found in Robert Balch and David Taylor's aforementioned discussion of Heaven's Gate (1977). After a brief overview and a discussion of the group's social organization, the authors provide an extended analysis of "The Social World of the Metaphysical Seeker." To begin with, they point out that, within the alternative spiritual subculture, the seeker role is not viewed as deviant. Rather, through a succession of different involvements—some of which might be shallow; others profound—spiritual seekers "organize their lives around the quest for truth" (1977, 848):

> This milieu consists of a loosely integrated network of seekers who drift from one philosophy to another in search of metaphysical truth. … Whether in a tipi in the Oregon woods or a mansion in Beverly Hills, their evenings are often spent with friends and acquaintances discussing metaphysical topics like psychic research, flying saucers, or Sufi mysticism. A significant part of their lives is devoted to the pursuit of intellectual growth, however undisciplined that may be in conventional academic terms. (Balch and Taylor 1977, 850)[1]

However, unlike our ordinary understanding of seeking, the goal of New Age seekership is continual growth rather than the attainment of a single, static end goal where one might finally stop seeking (Sutcliffe 2004, 477–478).

---

1. Compare this last statement with H. Taylor Buckner's remark about participants in "The Flying Saucerians," where he says that "Although they spend all their time learning, and they consider themselves "students," they do not learn things in an ordered and disciplined way" (1968, 228) and H. T. Dohrman's observation about participants in Mankind United: "through years of self-study they had drunk from mainsprings of knowledge that flowed only in cultic pastures outside the walls of schools and colleges" (1958,102).

In terms of the educational metaphors often used to describe this kind of spiritual growth, one might go from classroom to classroom and experience numerous graduations, but never a final graduation where perfection is reached—"because perfection means stagnation" (Balch and Taylor 1977, 853). It is the never-ending nature of the search that distinguishes seeking in the cultic milieu from what we ordinarily understand by seeking.

> One of Lofland and Stark's (1965) subjects aptly described the seeker's dilemma when she said: "The more I search, the more questions I have." The top of the spiritual mountain is an elusive goal, continually receding the higher the seeker climbs.... In short, the motivation to continue searching is built into the role. (1977, 854)

There are several closely related beliefs that support this notion of seekership. In the first place, though the New Age subculture appears, from one angle, to be dominated by static images of a single monistic truth, this static vision is offset by dynamic images that envision truth as the gradual unfolding of successive understandings. The most fundamental image is derived from the language of personal growth: "Life is seen as an infinite series of 'growth experiences'" (1977, 851). Another significant metaphor for the active spiritual life is education, and one often hears participants in the alternative spiritual milieu talk about their "learning experiences" (Lewis 2014). Other images include evolution (Kraft 2011), healing (Bowman 1999) and even an understanding of "progress" as "spiritual progress" (Partridge 1999, 80). And finally, one finds tropes of "journey," "search" and "adventure" (Sutcliffe 2013, 31).[2]

One religious notion that is especially compatible with this dynamic model of ongoing growth is reincarnation. Rather than developing within the framework of a process that comes to an abrupt end at death, most participants accept the idea that their quest continues after death in future lifetimes. Another important touchstone is what has been termed "epistemological individualism," the notion that "there are many paths up the mountain" and that each individual is, essentially, her or his own criterion of ultimate truth. Christopher Partridge has pointed out that, despite their assertions about the subjectivity of truth, many participants in the New Age implicitly hold absolutist views of truth. While this does indeed appear to be the case, the notion that something can be "true for me" (Partridge 1999, 88) while not true for others is nevertheless still held out as an ideal, allow-

---

2. It should be noted in passing that, despite the tendency among some commentators to drive a wedge of separation between alternative spirituality and Christian churches (e.g., Heelas and Woodhead 2005), many contemporary Christian bodies present themselves as "seeker churches," for whom faith is a "growth experience, a process of learning and exploring" (Roof 1999, 25). Expanding on these parallels is a topic for another paper, though Lewis has carried out some preliminary analysis of the Christian "sectarian milieu" in his discussion of movement milieus (2013).

ing one to become involved in a particular spiritual system without trying to convert others to the same system. It also means that, even when others within the larger spiritual subculture might disagree with someone's spiritual choice, they will typically not try to dissuade them from such choices (Balch and Taylor 1977, 851). Additionally, it implies that truth can be progressively unveiled in a stepwise fashion so that something that seems true and useful at one stage can later be dropped, rather like the Zen story about the seeker who leaves his raft behind after he reaches the farther shore.

Another part of the deep structure of alternative spirituality is what has been termed "self-religion." A notion originally put forward by Paul Heelas in his study of *The New Age Movement* (1996), self-religion refers to the idea that the ultimate goal of the seeker's quest is the divine source within, that we can contact through a deeper part of ourselves—our "real" self, which, because of the monism of most New Age thinking,[3] is already an integral part of the divine. Furthermore, what holds us back from realizing our true nature is a false sense of self that is the product of our socialization. Thus any methodology of spiritual "self-realization" necessarily involves peeling back the layers of our false self to realize our true self.

These understandings provide participants in the cultic milieu with a solid framework over which an ever-changing tapestry of different interests and a wide variety of spiritual fads can be spread. In an earlier study, Lewis described such overt, faddish changes as "indicative of the process of transformation" that the explicit contents of this subculture are constantly experiencing:

> This steadily changing nature is a trait in the movement's deep structure that researchers should carefully note. Without adopting such a perspective, the waning popularity of channeling and crystals—to take current examples—could be misinterpreted as indicative of a general decline in the New Age movement. Instead what is happening is that the New Age subculture is merely shifting its focus to such new topics as (at the time of this writing) "inner child" work, shamanism, and American Indian spirituality. (Lewis 1992, 10)

In other words, not only do the interests of individual participants shift from time to time, but also the collective focus of the larger subculture will periodically shift from one fad to another. Perhaps paradoxically, this constant dynamism is itself a stable process within the milieu. In Nigel Thrift's words, "the New Age circuit depends upon a constant throughflow of new ideas, even though these are often painted as rediscoveries of older knowledge" (1999, 48). One consequence of this pattern is that,

> Even star inspirational teachers, such as Louise Hay and Deepak Chopra, constantly reiterate their central messages of healing and awakening

---

3. See Rose (1998, 15) for a discussion of exceptions to monism.

with ever-new angles, prodigiously releasing clusters of books and tapes to tie in with their latest tours. (Redden 2005, 240)

In addition to sequential involvements, it should also be noted that the variety on offer within the alternative milieu allows many participants to hold a number of different serious interests simultaneously (Rose 1998, 15) —a pattern Steven Sutcliffe views as particularly characteristic of New Age seeking (2004, 477–478). Thus, for example, one and the same person might maintain an earnest daily Buddhist meditation practice, be studying Kabbalah and Sufi mysticism on free evenings, periodically drop in on a group of Qi Gong practitioners who meet every Saturday in the local park, and occasionally attend services at the Science of Mind church on Sunday mornings.[4] This hypothetical individual would likely consider herself or himself a serious spiritual seeker who sincerely feels that these diverse activities combine harmoniously to help her or him pursue the path to spiritual awakening.

From Counterculture to Consumption

Many contemporary observers—including academic observers (e.g., Heelas 2008)—have called attention to the close connection between this kind of seekership and consumer capitalism; e.g.,

> It could be argued that the term "New Age" refers principally to a set of dynamics in a socio-cultural field—*precisely those dynamics that ensure the continual instability of its constituent elements*. Marketization results not in the centralized control of ideology and practice, but their constant redefinition and re-direction. In other words, commerce actively shapes the diverse New Age milieu, allowing it to offer an ever-renewed array of alternatives to consumers in a range of fields.
>
> (Redden 2005, 241; italics in original).

The significance of consumerism and commodification for understanding many aspects of the contemporary alternative spiritual subculture has led some observers to dismiss the cultic milieu as trivial, viewing alternative seekers as shallow, acquisitive consumers and purveyors of New Age goods as greedy, amoral hucksters (e.g., Aldred 2000; Lau 2000). However, this kind of dismissive economic reductionism—a critical perspective that has its

---

4. For other examples of this pattern, refer to Sutcliffe (2000, 18) and McGuire (1988, 184–185). This sort of approach, of simultaneously holding "multiple associations with vastly different groups" (Roof 1993, 201), is not confined to the New Age subculture. For example, in his study of baby-boomer spirituality, Roof observes that "One man we interviewed thought it nothing out of the ordinary to describe himself as "primarily Catholic," and to tell us that while he attends mass weekly, he also belongs to an ecumenical prayer group in his neighborhood and frequently worships at a local evangelical church because of its "good preaching." (1993, 245). In this regard, also refer to Roof's example of an individual who combined Christian with alternative seeking (1993, 175).

place in moderate doses—ignores the fact "that much New Age commerce is value-driven. Most New Age commercial activity is small-scale (Hess 1993) and research suggests that many providers are highly committed teachers and entrepreneurs whose career choices signal their desires to realize their values in their life-styles and professions" (Redden 2005, 244).

As a comprehensive explanation for Western nations' alternative spiritual subculture, consumerist interpretations are also lacking in that they ignore the demographic roots of what later became the New Age in the counterculture of the sixties and seventies (Lewis and Melton 1992, xi). It is clear from glancing back at Balch and Taylor's 1977 article that their early piece is describing the same familiar spiritual subculture as the contemporary New Age milieu—minus the strong consumerist orientation. This is particularly evident in their description of the people who decided to follow "the Two," as the leaders of what would later become Heaven's Gate were called in the early days:

> A disproportionate number were remnants of the counterculture who preferred to avoid commitments that would unduly restrict their personal freedom. One man captured the protean flavor of this life when we asked him what he had given up to follow the Two: "I gave up a lot to come on this trip, man. I gave up my record collection, a set of tools, my old lady. But it's not the first record collection I've given up, and it's not the first set of tools. And I've had eight old ladies." Although a significant number of cult members had given up good jobs and comfortable homes to join the cult, most had not. For some of the younger members, the material aspects of life in the cult were not very different from what they had experienced before they joined. ... Many...had been traveling around the country with backpacks or in remodeled vans, rarely staying anywhere for more than a few weeks at a time.
>
> (Balch and Taylor 1977, 848–849).

Despite the obvious economic contrast between the counter-culturists of the early-to-mid seventies when Balch and Taylor conducted their interviews, the context for their research was still clearly an earlier manifestation of the same New Age subculture—one in which participants share "a metaphysical world-view in which reincarnation, disincarnate spirits, psychic powers, lost continents, flying saucers, and ascended masters are taken for granted" (1977, 850). Thus, however significant commercialism might be for understanding the contemporary alternative spiritual milieu, "a market model does not explain everything about the New Age" (Redden 2005, 243). And market forces cannot be the sole drivers of the constant changes found within this subculture.

New Religious Movements and conversion careers

Though some sociologists continue to use the term "cult," most specialists in the field utilize the expression New Religious Movements (NRMs) instead of cults, primarily because *cult* has become a negative term applied to stigmatized groups. The expression "new religion" is a direct translation of *shin shukyo*, which is the term Japanese sociologists applied to the many new religions that arose in Japan in the wake of the second world war. "Movements," on the other hand, appears to have been added by Western sociologists who wanted to study contemporaneous NRMs through the lens of categories developed within the study of social movements—hence the emergent expression new religious *movements*, as well as the expression New Age *movement*. And while the term "movements" implies dynamism, NRMs are often studied as if they were traditional sectarian churches.

As we noted at the beginning of this chapter, the emergence of the cult controversy in the seventies prompted sociologists to focus their attention on the least changeable of these NRMs, and they came to be studied as more or less static religious bodies. One of the few exceptions to this general pattern was Roy Wallis's early study, *The Road to Total Freedom* (1976), which traced the development of the early Dianetics movement (a "cult" in the older, sociological sense) into the Church of Scientology, in a process Wallis labeled "sectarianization" (1975). We might also mention that, using the influential audience cult-client cult-cult movement typology put forward by Stark and Bainbridge (1979), Paul Schnabel similarly analyzed the development of L. Ron Hubbard's movement from Dianetics to Scientology (1982). In the opposite direction, Anton LaVey's disbanding of the Church of Satan from a full-fledged religious organization into an audience cult in the mid-seventies has also been briefly discussed in terms of the Stark-Bainbridge typology (e.g., Lewis 2003, 111). And we might finally mention that ongoing organizational changes within the Family International have been discussed and analyzed (e.g., Shepherd and Shepherd 2010).

One of the reasons NRMs are infrequently mentioned in contemporary discussions of the cultic milieu is that they are not perceived as being a significant part of the alternative spiritual subculture. Thus, for example, Redden describes the nature of New Age involvement as being inimical to involvement in more structured religious organizations: "Group-doctrine-member models associated with more traditional religious collectivities do not adequately represent the ways in which participants tend to take on multiple affiliations, becoming involved in a number of groups, activities, and teachings as part of a personally determined trajectory" (2005, 240). This point can, however, be overemphasized.

On the one hand, not all of the people who offer content to the alternative spiritual subculture are primarily independent entrepreneurs. Rather, more than a little of what is on offer within the contemporary cultic milieu are lectures, classes and workshops held by organized religious groups. On the other hand, even the more structured New Age-style groups typically allow their members to get involved in other kinds of practices and teachings outside the boundaries of their specific organizations.

One of the few ways in which the dynamism of NRMs has been studied is with regards to what has been referred to as "conversion careers." This expression has come to mean a general approach to conversion research that takes a multi-factor approach to what is often pictured as a multi-step process of involvement, including disaffiliation (Gooren 2010; Gooren 2014). One of the earlier and, for present purposes, more important meanings of this expression refers to "sequential joiners who have "conversion careers" resulting from spiritual journeys that involve an experimental mode of seeking or searching" (Wright 2014, 707). In other words, "The notion of *conversion career* is tied to the idea of *serial alternatives*, by which is meant the sequential trying out of new beliefs and identities...." (Richardson 1980, 49; italics in original).

A number of different studies have presented data indicating that many people who disaffiliate from one new religion later join another intensive religious group (a pattern Sutcliffe refers to as "serial seeking" [2004, 476]). Thus, for example, Wright found that a full 78% of the disaffiliators he researched later joined another NRM or a conservative Christian church (1987), while Jacobs found the same pattern among half of the defectors she studied (1987). Other researchers have studied new organizations that formed in the wake of a group defection from a parent group (Rochford 1989; Lewis 2010). This pattern of successive involvements is described in H. Taylor Buckner's study of "The Flying Saucerians" as:

> A typical occult seeker will probably have been a Rosicrucian, a member of Mankind United, a Theosophist and also a member of four or five smaller specific cults. The pattern of membership is one of continuous movement from one idea to another. Seekers stay with a cult until they are satisfied that they can learn no more from it, or that it has nothing to offer, and then they move on. (1968, 227–228)

Picking up on Balch and Taylor's earlier work on disaffiliation from Heaven's Gate, Lewis has also utilized the seekership notion—plus the fact that most people who dropped out of "New Age"-oriented NRMs continued to participate in the larger New Age subculture—as a way of interpreting the largely positive post-involvement attitudes of ex-members of the Movement of Spiritual Inner Awareness (Lewis 1997, 199–203) and ex-members of the Order of Christ Sophia (Lewis and Levine 2010, 101–102). Thus, both for people who exchanged membership in one NRM for another as well as for people who dropped out of a New Age-oriented NRM to become an unaffiliated New Age seeker, their "primary religious framework remained in place, despite a shift in organizational affiliation" (Rochford 1989, 175).

While useful for overturning traditional ideas about conversion being an event that typically occurs only once in a lifetime, the weakness of the conversion career model is that it also seems to imply a religious parallel to "serial monogamy" (Richardson and Stewart 1978, 32) in which the seeker is sequentially loyal to a series of different religions. Because most members of New Age-style NRMs typically adhere to some version of the principle of epistemological individualism, we might anticipate that at least some members of such groups will be simultaneously involved in other strands of spirituality—which is perfectly possible within more decentralized movements. Thus, for example, in his early study of Mankind United, H. T. Dohrman notes that,

> In most cases the cult individual engages in the activities of several or more cult groups. ... In the over-all cult world a person might simultaneously belong to the Technocrats and the Rosicrucians; he might attend Flying Saucer Conventions in Hollywood hotels; in the meantime he might maintain his membership in the Mother Church of Christian Science while becoming familiar with stellar healing, induced emotion, and extrasensory perception at the Religion of the Stars services.
>
> (1958, 97–98)

Questionnaire research

Since 2009, Lewis has been gathering demographic and attitude data from members of a wide range of NRMs using online questionnaires on Survey Monkey (www.surveymonkey.com). Additionally, Inga Bårdsen Tøllefsen used the same basic approach in her study of the Art of Living Foundation (e.g., Tøllefsen 2011, 2012). Most of Lewis's questionnaires contained an open-ended item that requested respondents to identify "Other religions/ spiritual paths involved in, either now or in the past." The relevant item on the Art of Living (AoL) questionnaire was worded slightly differently, as: "If you have explored other practices or "spiritual paths," either now or in the past, what were these?" Additionally, there was a separate forced-choice item on all questionnaires that asked respondents to describe the religious tradition in which they were raised (if any). Though we knew we would not receive anything approaching crisp data from these kinds of open-ended questions, we nevertheless anticipated that we would obtain a suggestive impression of respondents' conversion careers.

From the available data sets, we chose to examine responses from 140 members of Andrew Cohen's Enlighten Next (which has gone under a number of different names over the years). Enlighten Next (EN), which publishes *EnlightenNext* Magazine (more familiar under its former title, *What is Enlightenment?*), participates in the alternative spiritual subculture, though it views itself as being in a more traditional spiritual lineage, associated with both Hinduism and Buddhism. We also decided to examine responses from 154 members of the Order of Christ Sophia (OCS), a group in the general lineage of the Holy Order of MANS (Lucas 1995) that sees itself in the mystical Christian tradition (Lewis and Levine 2010). Additionally, in line with the topic of the current volume, Tøllefsen allowed us to utilize data from 100 Norwegian residents who had responded to her survey of AoL members (2012).

Finally, we developed a questionnaire that collected responses from several dozen readers of the online magazine *Visjon* (*Vision*), an alternative magazine directed to Scandinavian—particularly Norwegian—readers.[5]

To briefly go over these groups' demographics, 78 (58%) of EN respondents were U.S. residents. Their average age at the time they took the questionnaire in 2011 was 50. Ninety-three respondents (or slightly less than two-thirds) were female. Seventy-seven, or somewhat more than half, were married or in some kind of committed relationship. Fifty-eight had children. And one hundred and eight (78%) were college graduates.

By comparison, 127 (83%) of OCS respondents were U.S. residents. Their average age at the time they took the questionnaire in 2011 was 44. One hundred and five respondents (68%) were female. Fifty-four, or somewhat more than a third, were married or in some kind of committed relationship. Fifty-three had children. And one hundred and twenty-one (79%) were college graduates.

We used the criterion of Norwegian residence to create our Art of Living subsample, so 100% of AoL respondents were Norwegian residents. Their average age at the time they took the questionnaire in 2011 was 44. Sixty-nine (or slightly less than 70%) were female. Fifty-nine, or 59% were married or in some kind of committed relationship. Sixty-one had children. And sixty-two (62%) were college graduates.

Finally, though the sample from *Visjon* magazine was quite small (twenty four), the characteristics of this sample were roughly comparable to the other samples, especially to the AoL sample. All were Norwegian residents. Average age when they took the questionnaire in 2013 was 48. Two-thirds (sixteen) were female. Fifteen (62%) were married or in a committed relationship. Eighteen had children. And fourteen (58%) were college graduates.

Findings and Discussion

Out of the Enlighten Next respondents, seventy three (52%) had been involved in groups other than EN. Thirty eight had been involved in one other group, eighteen in two other groups and seventeen in three or more other groups. Out of the Order of Christ Sophia responses, eighty four (54%) had been involved in other groups. Thirty had been involved in just one other group, twenty six in two other groups and twenty eight in three or more. Out of the Art of Living respondents, forty (40%) had been involved in other groups— twenty in just one, six in two and thirteen in three or more. And ten (40%) of the *Visjon* respondents indicated that they had been involved in specific traditions, three in one, one in two and six in three or more.

Buddhism or Buddhist meditation of some variety was the most popular alternative for all four samples: Thirty-four members of Enlighten Next,

---

5. For a discussion of *Visjon*, refer to Margrethe Løøv's chapter in the present collection.

thirty-five members of the Order of Christ Sophia, eighteen members of the Art of Living Foundation and five *Visjon* respondents. Hinduism or some form of Hindu-based meditation or involvement with a Hindu guru was next, with twenty-three members of EN, thirty members of OCS, sixteen members of AoL and three *Visjon* respondents. Some form of involvement with Christianity (not counting the tradition in which one was raised) ran a distant third place for Enlighten Next members (eight), and Christianity tied with New Age/New Thought/Esotericism for third for the Order of Christ Sophia (sixteen). Finally, other religious forms mentioned more than once included Paganism/Wicca, Shamanism, Sufism, Kabbalah and Scientology.

We were a little surprised to find that a number of respondents mentioned "Astrology" as being or as having been one of their spiritual paths. On similar questionnaires administered to members of other groups, respondents also mentioned Tarot and the *I-Ching*. Though some individuals might be involved in these divinatory systems in such depth that they effectively serve as spiritual paths in themselves, we assume that most respondents regarded such systems as providing insights that supplemented their work with other spiritual disciplines.

When Lewis worked with Helen Berger designing the questionnaire used for the 2009–2010 Pagan Census Revisited study (Berger 2010, 2011), she provided the phrasing for a general question about such divinatory systems, which was, "Which of the following have you found to really be of help to you?" This wording was useful for distinguishing between people who had casually dabbled in divination and those who felt they had received some sort of insight from at least one of these systems. Patterns of responses are recorded in Table 12.1, below.

The pattern indicates widespread interest in divination systems, with astrology coming out as the most popular for respondents in all categories. (It should be noted that one of the former leaders of the Order of Christ

Table 12.1 Percentage who found a given divination method "to really be of help."

	EN	OCS	AoL	*Visjon*
Tarot	18	21	16	32
Astrology	24	88	40	54
Runes	5	4	5	0
Palmistry	5	4	10	9
Numerology	4	10	9	18
I-Ching	16	5	7	4
Psychic Readings	16	9	20	46

Sophia wrote a book about astrology, which helps to account for the exceptionally high percentage of OCS respondents who found astrology to be helpful.) We should also note that while participants in the cultic milieu do use these systems for divinatory purposes, others utilize them almost exclusive for the purpose of what might be termed spiritual self-understanding. This is especially the case for astrology (Feher 1992).

If one focuses on holistic health rather than on phenomena that are overtly religious or divinatory, one can also make the case for a distinct "holistic milieu" (Heelas 2007) that is a subset of—or that, perhaps from other perspective, overlaps—the New Age milieu. As noted earlier, within the contemporary cultic milieu, "healing" has become more or less interchangeable with spiritual growth (Bowman 1999), meaning that involvement in different healing modalities and therapies that are part of the holistic milieu can also be an integral part of one's spiritual quest.

Over thirty-five years ago, James Richardson and Mary Stewart argued that various kinds of physiological activities should be considered as being a part of individuals' "conversion careers":

> For instance, the use of alcohol and such things as health food "trips,"
> dieting, vitamins, exercise, and other "body therapies" also should
> be included. The overriding ties among such activities is the doing
> of things that somehow include and affect the body in an attempt to
> achieve meaning, whether that meaning is derived from orgasms, jog-
> ging, natural foods, or some innovative combination of such activities.
> (Richardson and Stewart 1978, 29)

In the much-discussed Kendal Study, Paul Heelas and his co-researchers presented their subjects with a "holistic questionnaire" (Heelas *et al.* 2005). Part of that instrument consisted of a long list of alternative activities in which they might have been involved in the Kendal area (Kendal is a relatively small town in central England). Though we did not include all of the original items, a slightly edited version of the Kendal questionnaire was included in all of questionnaires discussed in this chapter. Expressed in terms of percentages to make comparisons more straightforward, findings from these are reported in Table 12.2, opposite. Note that the original questionnaire gave respondents a choice of "Rarely," "Sometimes," "Regularly" or "Frequently." For the purpose of juxtaposing and making comparisons between our different samples, we collapsed these responses into a single positive value, in contrast with "Never."

The pattern of responses to our truncated Kendal questionnaire was really quite striking, demonstrating more clearly than just about anything else how deeply situated these kinds of NRMs are in the surrounding alternative milieu. Though a few of the items are integral to a couple of these groups— e.g., yoga to the Art of Living—nothing else was a specifically AoL, OCS or EN practice.

Table 12.2 Which of the following groups, activities or therapies have you tried?

	EN	OCS	AoL	*Visjon*
Acupressure	63	59	44	65
Acupuncture	89	70	73	92
Aromatherapy	49	58	72	74
Astral travel	17	19	12	30
Chiropractic	78	81	55	75
Flower essences therapy	40	43	40	52
Healing/Spiritual healing	63	86	77	96
Herbalism	66	62	31	52
Homeopathy	84	87	73	82
Hypnotherapy	25	39	24	23
Massage	96	97	98	91
Naturopathy	47	58	24	23
Nutritional therapy	70	60	43	44
Polarity therapy	16	14	16	17
Psychotherapy	61	64	36	44
Qi Gong/Chi Kung	48	37	25	54
Rebirthing	23	16	20	30
Reflexology	47	42	25	26
Reiki	61	45	46	61
Shiatsu	46	21	11	26
Tai Chi	57	46	35	46
Sufi dancing	18	17	17	23
Yoga	90	89	100	83

All of the questionnaires also contained a set of five items from the General Social Survey (http://www3.norc.org/GSS+Website/) from the United States that measured parapsychological experiences, variables that the GSS labeled dejavu, esp, visions, spirits and grace, plus a sixth we have provisionally labeled prophecy.[6]

---

6. When Bainbridge administered a questionnaire composed of select GSS items to members of the Family International, he used these five paranormal items plus devised this sixth item in consultation with the Family (2002, 80–81).

Table 12.3   Have you had any of the following experiences?

	EN	OCS	AoL	*Visjon*
Thought you were somewhere you had been before, but knew that it was impossible.	78	84	62	83
Felt as though you were in touch with someone when they were far away from you.	90	92	73	88
Seen events that happened at a great distance as they were happening.	33	46	34	42
Felt as though you were really in touch with someone who had died.	72	67	64	79
Felt as though you were very close to a powerful, spiritual force that seemed to lift you out of yourself.	84	93	65	79
Received prophecy, visions, or messages from the spirit world.	46	78	49	50

Of these six experiences, the only one that might conceivably fit into the core teachings of AoL, OCS or EN is the fifth item, though even that one is not worded in a way one would find in the literature of any of the three NRMs (Table 12.3).

This does not mean that such experiences would not be acknowledged within these three organizations, but rather that their core teachings and practices would not discuss such experiences, or encourage, for example, trying to contact spirits of the dead. Once again, the fact that participants can acknowledge having had such experiences in a formal research questionnaire indicates their world views are rooted in the larger spiritual subculture, not just the teachings of the Art of Living, the Order of Christ Sophia or EnlightenNext.

Conclusion

There is a tendency for NRMs to be studied as if they were hermetically sealed off from the surrounding spiritual subculture. Researchers will, of course, typically examine the personal background of the founder and the various strands of spirituality from the larger milieu that were brought together to form her or his new synthesis in the early history of the movement. Additionally, observers will often briefly discuss the religious (or non-religious) backgrounds of the people who join. However, the time constraints of a typical fieldwork cycle normally prevent researchers from considering the activities and interests of members that lie outside the specific group being considered.

Thus if one is studying, for example, a neo-Hindu group, one is probably not even aware that a couple of members are receiving regular acupuncture or chiropractic treatments, or even that yet other members are participating in Sufi dancing or in a Qi Gong exercise group. Furthermore, one will likely remain unaware of such activities unless one explicitly asks. Similarly, a researcher might be aware that a couple of current members were once active in TM or some other spiritual group, but not consider that fact particularly relevant to her or his current research project. The fundamental problem is that we lack an orientation to larger frames of reference: Instead, as noted earlier, we study NRMs as if they were more or less static sect groups.

A common pattern within the field that creates a related set of problems along a temporal axis is that researchers will study one particular new religion, write a monograph on that specific group, and then begin the cycle all over again with another NRM (Lewis 2012, 159). Though this approach has certain advantages in terms of being able to contrast comparable patterns across different organizations, it also tends to cause one to remember such groups as being relatively stable organizations, fixed in memory at a specific stage of development rather than having experienced how they change across the course of longer temporal intervals. One also tends to miss the direct experience of watching people cycle into and out of NRMs—of seeing how a group that seems to be quite stable for an extended period of time actually undergoes an upheaval of personnel across the course of a decade or two. Thus while we have the notion of "conversion careers" in our conceptual toolbox, no one seems to have actually tried to establish ongoing contact with a sample of seekers and keep track of them across time[7] as they take their "bumper car ride through a maze of spiritual trips."

In a chapter on social theory and religious movements, James Beckford bemoans the lack of dialog between new religions specialists and those academicians who focus on broader theories of society, asserting that,

[D]evelopments in theories of social movements and of theoretical ideas about culture and identity tend to place religious movements near the

---

7. We have in mind is something along the lines of Saul Levine's approach as reported in his *Radical Departures* (1984), though Levine restricted himself to tracking NRM members from the period of their deepest involvement in a single group to their post-involvement re-adjustment period. Such "Panel studies are rare because they are costly and take so much time...." (Roof 1999, 11)

centre of some currently important problems for social scientists. It is no longer appropriate, then, to consign religious movements to categories of deviant or marginal phenomena. The movements' beliefs, values, forms of organization, kinds of activity, types of participation, societal reactions, and relations with agencies of social control all provide revealing insights into the dynamics of late modernity. (2003, 192)

In the case at hand, numerous theorists of late modernity—or, if one prefers, post-modernity or high modernity—have discussed contemporary society's current situation as characterized by a lack of certainty and stability, one in which people are always redefining themselves and whose sense of belonging is always changing (e.g., Bauman 2000; Giddens 1991). Assuming our analysis in this chapter is even partially correct, contemporary NRMs should be especially attractive to social theorists as they represent veritable hothouses of this kind of social dynamism—"quasi-laboratories in which profound cultural and social experiments can be relatively easily observed on a small scale" (Beckford 2003, 172).

References

Aldred, Lisa. 2000. "Plastic shamans and astroturf sun dances: New Age commercialization of Native American spirituality." *American Indian Quarterly* 24(3): 329–352.

Bainbridge, William Sims. 2002. *The Endtime Family: Children of God.* Albany: State University of New York Press.

Balch, Robert W. and David Taylor. 1977. Seekers and saucers The role of the cultic milieu in joining a UFO cult." *American Behavioral Scientist* 20(6): 839–860.

Bauman, Zygmunt. 2000. *Liquid Modernity.* Cambridge: Polity Press.

Becker, Howard. 1932. *Systematic Sociology.* New York: Wiley.

Beckford, James A. 2003. *Social Theory and Religion.* Cambridge: Cambridge University Press.

Berger, Helen A. 2010. "Preliminary finds from the pagan census revisited." Eastern Sociological Society meeting, March 18–21, Boston, MA.

———. 2011. "Goddess worship and political activity." Presented at the Eastern Sociological Society Meeting, February 24–27, Philadelphia, PA.

Bowman, Marion. 1999. "Healing in the spiritual marketplace: Consumers, courses and credentialism." *Social Compass* 46(2): 181–189.

Buckner, H. Taylor. 1968. "The flying saucerians: An open door cult." In *Sociology and Everyday Life,* edited by Marcello Truzzi, 223–230. Englewood Cliffs, NJ: Prentice-Hall.

Campbell, Colin. 2002. [1972.] "The cult, the cultic milieu, and secularization." In *The Cultic Milieu: Oppositional Subcultures in an Age of Globalization,* edited by Jeffrey Kapaln and Leléne Lööw, 12–25. Walnut Creek, CA: AltaMira Press.

Dohrman, H. T. 1958. *California Cult: The Story of "Mankind United."* Boston, MA: Beacon Press.

Ellwood, Robert S. and Harry B. Partin. 1988. *Religious and Spiritual Groups in Modern America*. 2nd edition. Englewood Cliffs, NJ: Prentice-Hall.

Feher, Shoshanah. 1992. "Who holds the cards? Women and New Age astrology." In *Perspectives on the New Age*, edited by James R. Lewis and J. Gordon Melton, 179–188. Albany: State University of New York Press.

Giddens, Anthony. 1991. *Modernity and Self-Identity: Self and Society in the Late Modern Age*. Stanford, CA: Stanford University Press.

Gooren, Henri. 2010. *Religious Conversion and Disaffiliation: Tracing Patterns of Change in Faith Practices*. New York: Palgrave MacMillan.

———. 2014. "Anthropology of religious conversion." In *Oxford Handbook of Religious Conversion*, edited by Lewis R. Rambo and Charles E. Farhadian, 84–116. Oxford: Oxford University Press.

Heelas, Paul. 1996. *The New Age Movement*. Oxford: Blackwell.

———. 2007. "The holistic milieu and spirituality: Reflections on Voas and Bruce." In *A Sociology of Spirituality*, edited by Kieran Flanagan and Peter C. Jupp, 63–80. Aldershot: Ashgate.

———. 2008. *Spiritualities of Life: New Age Romanticism and Consumptive Capitalism*. Oxford: Wiley-Blackwell.

Heelas, Paul, Linda Woodhead, Benjamin Seel, Bronislaw Szerszynski and Karin Tusting. 2005. *The Spiritual Revolution: Why Religion Is Giving Way to Spirituality*. Oxford: Wiley-Blackwell.

Hess, David J. 1993. *Science in the New Age: The Paranormal, Its Defenders and Debunkers, and American Culture*. Madison: University of Wisconsin Press.

Holloway, Julian. 2000. "Institutional geographies of the New Age movement." *Geoforum* 31: 553–565.

Jacobs, Janet. 1987. "Deconversion from religious movements: An analysis of charismatic bonding and spiritual commitment." *Journal for the Scientific Study of Religion* 26: 294–308.

Kraft, Siv-Ellen. 2011. *Hva er nyreligiøsitet*. Oslo: University Publishing House.

Lau, Kimberly J. 2000. *New Age Capitalism: Making Money East of Eden*. Philadelphia: University of Pennsylvania Press.

Levine, Saul V. 1984. *Radical Departures: Desperate Detours to Growing Up*. New York: Harcourt Brace Jovanovich.

Lewis, James R. 1992. "Approaches to the study of the New Age movement." In *Perspectives on the New Age*, edited by James R. Lewis and J. Gordon Melton, 1–14. Albany: State University of New York Press.

———. 1997. *Seeking the Light*. Los Angeles, CA: Mandeville Press.

———. 2003. *Legitimating New Religions*. Piscataway, NJ: Rutgers University Press.

———. 2010. "Autobiography of a schism." *Marburg Journal of Religious Studies* 15: 1–19.

———. 2012. "Cracks in the network conversion paradigm." *International Journal for the Study of New Religions* 3(2): 143–162.

————. 2013. "Free zone Scientology and movement milieus: A preliminary characterization." *Temenos: Nordic Journal of Comparative Religion* 49(2): 9–35.

————. 2014. "The Earth School: The movement of spiritual inner awareness." In *Controversial New Religions*, edited by James R. Lewis and Jesper Aagaard Petersen, 131–143. Oxford: Oxford University Press.

Lewis, James R., and J. Gordon Melton, eds. 1992. *Perspectives on the New Age.* Albany, New York: State University of New York Press.

Lewis, James R. and Nicholas M. Levine. 2010. *Children of Jesus and Mary: A Study of the Order of Christ Sophia.* Oxford: Oxford University Press.

Lofland, John, and Rodney Stark. 1965. "Becoming a world-saver." *American Sociological Review* 30: 862–875.

Lucas, Phillip. 1995. *The Odyssey of a New Religion.* Indianapolis: Indiana University Press.

McGuire, Meredith. 1988. *Ritual Healing in Suburban America.* Piscataway, NJ: Rutgers University Press.

Niebuhr, H. Richard. 1929. *The Social Sources of Denominationalism.* New York: Henry Holt.

Partridge, Christopher H. 1999. "Truth, authority and epistemological individualism in new age thought." *Journal of Contemporary Religion* 14(1): 77–95.

————. 2005. *The Re-Enchantment of the West.* London, T & T Clark International.

Redden, Guy. 2005. "The New Age: Towards a market model." *Journal of Contemporary Religion* 20(2): 231–246.

Richardson, James T. 1978. *Conversion Careers. In and Out of the New Religions.* Thousand Oaks: Sage Publications.

————. 1980. "Conversion careers." *Society* 17(3): 47–50.

Richardson, James T. and Mary Stewart. 1977. "Conversion process models and the Jesus movement." *American Behavioral Scientist* 20(6): 819–838

Rochford, E. Burke. 1989. "Factionalism, group defection, and schism in the Hare Krishna Movement." *Journal for the Scientific Study of Religion* 28(2): 162–179.

Roof, Wade Clark. 1993. *A Generation of Seekers: The Spiritual Journeys of the Baby Boom Generation.* New York: Harper San Francisco.

————. 1999. "Spiritual marketplace: Baby boomers and the remaking of American religion." Princeton, NJ: Princeton University Press.

Rose, Stuart. 1998. "An examination of the New Age movement: Who is involved and what constitutes its spirituality." *Journal of Contemporary Religion* 12(1): 5–22n

Schnabel, Paul. 1982. *Tussen stigma en charisma: nieuwe religieuze bewegingen en geestelijke volksgezondheid.* (Between stigma and charisma: New religious movements and mental health. Deventer: Van Loghum Slaterus.

Shepherd, Gordon and Gary Shepherd. 2010. *Talking with the Children of God: Prophecy and Transformation in a Radical Religious Group.* Champaign, IL: University of Illinois Press.

Stark, Rodney and William Sims Bainbridge. 1979. "Of Churches, sects and cults." *Journal for the Scientific Study of Religion* 18: 117–133.

Sutcliffe, Steven J. 2000. "'Wandering stars': Seekers and gurus in the modern world." In *Beyond New Age: Exploring Alternative Spirituality*, edited by Steven Sutcliffe and Marion Bowman, 17–36. Edinburgh: Edinburgh University Press.

———. 2004. "The dynamics of alternative spirituality: Seekers, networks and 'New Age'." In *The Oxford Handbook of New Religious Movements*, edited by James R. Lewis, 466–490. New York: Oxford University Press.

———. 2013. "New Age, world religions and elementary forms." In *New Age Spirituality: Rethinking Religion*, edited by Steven J. Sutcliffe and Ingvild Sælid Gilhus, 17–34. Durham, UK: Acumen.

Thrift, Nigel. 1999. "The place of complexity." *Theory, Culture and Society* 16(3): 31–69.

Tøllefsen, Inga B. 2011. "Art of Living: Religious entrepreneurship and legitimation strategies." *International Journal for the Study of New Religions* 2(2): 255–279.

———. 2012. "Notes on the demographic profiles of Art of Living practitioners in Norway and abroad." *Alternative Spirituality and Religion Review* 3(2): 225–252.

Troeltsch, Ernst. 1931 [1912]. *The Social Teaching of the Christian Churches.* 2 vols. Translated by Olive Wyon. Louisville, KY: Westminster/John Knox Press.

Wallis, Roy. 1975. "Scientology: Therapeutic cult to religious sect." *Sociology* 9(1): 89–100.

———. 1976. *The Road to Total Freedom: A Sociological Analysis of Scientology.* New York: Columbia University Press.

Weber, Max. 1949. *The Methodology of the Social Sciences.* New York: Free Press.

Wright, Stuart A. 1987. *Leaving Cults: The Dynamics of Defection.* Washington, DC: Society for the Scientific Study of Religion Monograph Series.

———. 2014. "Disengagement and apostasy in new religious movements." In *Oxford Handbook of Religious Conversion*, edited by Lewis R. Rambo and Charles E. Farhadian, 706–735. Oxford: Oxford University Press.

— Afterword —

New Age in Sweden:
A Comparison to Norway

LISELOTTE FRISK

Introduction

There are many cultural similarities between Sweden and Norway; they are neighboring countries and have a common history. In Sweden, the Swedish Church was the state church until the year 2000, when the church and state were separated from each other. Instead, *lagen om trossamfund*, ("the law of religious communities"), regulating registration of religious communities and state funding of these came into force. In 2013, 65.9% of the Swedish population were members of the Swedish Church, 48.5% of babies born were baptized, 30.1% of the youngsters went through confirmation, and the church performed 78% of burials (www.svenskakyrkan.se). Compared to Norway, the Norwegian church seems to have a slightly stronger position than its Swedish counterpart. Still, a majority of the Swedes are members of the Swedish Church.

As in Norway, New Age as a phenomenon has been a topic since the 1960s, with roughly similar waves of development, changes, and the influence of trends like globalization, individualism, and secularization. In 1972, the New Age book shop *Vattumannen* ("Aquarius") was opened by Per Frisk, who together with his wife Monica Katarina Frisk are significant persons associated with New Age in Sweden. Between 1984 and 2014, they were the owners of the publication *Energivågen* ("The Wave of Energy"), renamed *Free—din ledstjärna* ("Free—your guiding star") in 2010. This New Age magazine had originally been launched in 1982 by Tomas Frankell, another important person in the Swedish New Age milieu. Today *Free* is printed bimonthly in 25,000 copies, and is also available on-line. Per and Monica Katarina Frisk were the owners of the publishing house *Energica* between 1984 and 2008, which published several New Age-related titles, some of them bestsellers like *The Power of Now* by Eckhart Tolle, or *The Secret* by Rhonda Byrne.

A local mapping of New Age activities 2008–2011 (or, as referred to here, "popular religiosity") in the county of Dalarna in Sweden, an area of about 277,000 inhabitants situated about 300 km northwest of Stockholm, showed that 1.6% of the population engaged in New Age activities at least once a week (Frisk and Åkerbäck 2013). The New Age arenas in Sweden are very similar to those in Norway, with "alternative fairs" (in Sweden called "health fairs" or "harmony fairs"—"alternative" not being used as much as in Norway) being very significant, often taking place in minor villages as well. As in Norway, health centers or health institutes where several New Age activities—sometimes mixed with mainstream health activities—share space are common. For a couple of years in Sweden, there has been the possibility of obtaining state funding for private enterprises, which probably has been important for the increasing number of health enterprises, often conducted by women. Additionally, retreat centers with different orientations are common in Sweden, and are significant arenas for New Age activities.

In this short paper I will discuss some similarities and differences concerning New Age in Norway and Sweden, based primarily on the empirical study mentioned above.

Mediums and communication with the dead

The Swedish empirical material in the study conducted in Dalarna was compared to a similar study in Austria (Höllinger and Tripold 2012). One important difference that contrasted with the Austrian material was that the number of mediums and the extent of spirit communication was about three times higher in Sweden. Mediums and communication with the dead seem to be very popular in Sweden, probably as a result of the many popular TV serials, such as *The Unknown, Spirit Academy, Haunted Houses* and *Ghost Hunters* (Frisk, Höllinger and Åkerbäck forthcoming). This situation seems to be very similar in Norway.

Yoga and mindfulness

Neither yoga nor mindfulness has been addressed to any great extent in this book about New Age in Norway. Especially regarding yoga, Sweden scored significantly higher than Austria when the two empirical studies were compared (Frisk, Höllinger and Åkerbäck 2014). Sweden scores lower on most religious indicators than Austria (www.worldvaluessurvey.org). One explanation for the popularity of yoga may be its capacity to be interpreted both as a secular practice as well as a practice with non-secular or spiritual dimensions.

Another interesting matter in Sweden is that local Swedish yoga styles have developed. The abovementioned Tomas Frankell has, for example, developed his own style of yoga, influenced by the kundalini yoga of Yogi Bhajan. He calls this style *livsyoga,* meaning "yoga of life" (http://www. devanews.com/hem/startpage.php). We also came across other local yoga styles in Dalarna.

The practice of mindfulness may, similar to yoga, be utilized on both secular and spiritual arenas. In Sweden, mindfulness is practiced in various Buddhist contexts, as well as in the New Age milieu, but also within the conventional health-care sector (Frisk and Åkerbäck 2013, 151).

Human potential therapies

A vast range of holistic therapies are closely related to and included in the New Age concept, a phenomenon which is discussed in the Norwegian context earlier in this book. Not specifically discussed, however, are therapies with a clear connection to the human potentials movement that originated in the U.S. 1960s, closely connected with the Esalen Institute in California. The human potential movement has its roots in the humanistic psychology, but is more practice oriented. Examples of these methods are encounter groups and gestalt therapy. The most significant characteristics of the human potential movement are: an ideological framework focused on the human potential, or the importance of being "authentic" and free from restraints, such as defense mechanisms and social roles; the expression of emotions through catharsis; body therapies; focus on here and now; group therapy; and syncretism (Frisk 2014). In Sweden, Lena Kristina Tuulse has been the front person for this movement, between 1976 and 2007 running Wäxthuset ("The Growth House") outside Stockholm. One of her most important methods has been rebirthing, a therapeutic method using controlled breathing. Beginning around 1975, therapies from the human potential movement were integrated and used in the new religious movement led by the charismatic Indian leader Osho (1931–1990), at that time called Bhagwan Shree Rajneesh. Today, the Osho movement and especially its successors have become the main practitioners of human potential therapies in Sweden. The most well-known institute is Ängsbacka, which among other activities each year hosts a one-week festival which attracts about 1,000 people. The focus of the festival is on a variety of New Age/human potential activities, as well as cultural events (Frisk 2002, 2014). Another retreat center with this background is Baravara in Dalarna, engaging about 1,000 people each year (Frisk and Åkerbäck 2013, 113).

Neo-Shamanism

Sami religiosity seems to be both more significant and more integrated with New Age in Norway than in Sweden. There are, however, also currents of Neo-Shamanism in the Swedish New Age milieu, but these were especially prominent during the 1980s and 1990s. Characteristic of Neo-Shamanism in Sweden has been connections with the academic world, as some of the practitioners have been academics (Frisk, Höllinger and Åkerbäck 2014). Not much trace of Neo-Shamanism was, however, found in the Dalarna study.

Folk religiosity

Sweden has not had national folk healers like the Norwegian *Snåsamannen*. There are a few clairvoyants with no connections to the New Age who have attained a certain amount of fame. Some of these have their own question and answer columns in certain weekly magazines, mostly dealing with how to find lost items or animals. In Dalarna, we found only one such person, now in his 80s, specializing in finding lost animals. Not a single traditional healer was found.

Conclusion

Sweden is one of the most secularized countries in the world, independent of whichever parameters are used. New Age currents, however, seem to be as strong as in other countries. In comparison to other nations, some of these currents stand out as especially significant in Sweden. Practices in the cultural space between religious and secular arenas, like yoga, mindfulness, and human potential therapies seem to be especially prominent. Siv Ellen Kraft, at the University of Tromsø, describes how New Age arenas present many phenomena that are open to a number of interpretations. She calls these 'hybrid products', meaning that there are phenomena that can be understood as religious, but that each person can either choose, reject, or ignore these religious dimensions. Religious interpretations are thus but one potential choice for the individual among other choices (Kraft 2011, 78). Practices inviting this kind of choice seem to be successful in Sweden.

However, New Age currents are diversified in Sweden, and, as in Norway, come in different variations. Another strong current in Sweden deals with communication with spirits. This New Age current is closely connected to popular culture. As mentioned earlier, these phenomena seem to be as strong in Norway as in Sweden.

References

Published material

Frisk, Liselotte. 2002. "The Satsang network: A growing post-Osho Phenomenon." *Nova Religio* 6(1): 64–85.

———. 2014. "The Human Potential Movement in Scandinavia." In *Western Esoterism in Scandinavia*, edited by Olav Hammer and Henrik Bogdan, 195–202. Leiden: Brill.

Frisk, Liselotte and Peter Åkerbäck. 2013. *Den mediterande dalahästen: Religion på nya arenor i samtidens Sverige.* Stockholm: Dialogos.

Frisk, Liselotte, Franz Höllinger and Peter Åkerbäck. (2014). "Size and structure of the holistic milieu: A comparison of local mapping-studies in Austria and Sweden." *Journal of Contemporary Religion.*

Höllinger, Franz and Thomas Tripold. 2012. *Ganzheitliches Leben: Das holistische Milieu zwischen neuer Spiritualität unter postmoderner Wellness-Kultur.* Bielefeld: Transcript Verlag.

Kraft, Siv-Ellen. 2011. *Hva er nyreligiositet.* Oslo: University Publishing House.

Web sites

www.svenskakyrkan.se 141204
www.worldvaluessurvey.org 120128
http://www.devanews.com/hem/startpage.php 141212

— Afterword —

New Religions and "New Religiosity" in Denmark:
A Very Brief Subjective Note

Mikael Rothstein

In Norway, scholars of religion and folklorists have been fortunate enough to maintain a high-level research program on new and emerging religions, and what is sometimes termed "new religiosity." Dedicated senior researchers from the University of Bergen have, since the early 1990s, devoted considerable time and effort to the subject, and have over the years skilfully and admirably allowed young colleagues—who themselves gradually matured—to join their work. The result is a rare case of a long lasting, close-knit community of professionals dealing with contemporary, local religious innovations, and hence there is now a rather unique quantity of science on new religions and new religiosity in Norway.

We are unable to display anything of the kind in Denmark. The possibilities were there a long time ago, but scholarly and personal differences, and a disturbing lack of funding for the humanistic study of religion in Denmark, made the collective efforts to study new religions a road not taken. In effect, only a few scholars have continuously worked in this field of research in Denmark (as I have recently discussed, cf. Rothstein 2015). In terms of scientific results based on teamwork, I am sad to admit that no Danish initiative resembling what our Norwegian peers have built have come around, and that the Danish situation can therefore only indirectly serve as a comparative case. As for myself, I have moved my primary field of research to the religions of the rainforests of Borneo, and am no longer capable of keeping track of what is happening in the NRM-scene in general terms in Denmark (although I continue writing about specific NRM-related issues). In this brief presentation I shall, however, try to sum up what I would consider the most important features.

The Danish scene

We simply have no up-to date, comprehensive, overarching knowledge of new religions and "new religiosity" in Denmark. A considerable collection of materials has been established at the Centre for Present-day Religion (Centre for Samtidsreligion) at the University of Aarhus, where a sociological mapping of religious groups and movements in the city of Aarhus was published in 2013 (Ahlin *et al.* 2013).[1] This report, however, is precisely a *mapping* with sociological descriptions, and a rather acquiescent rendering of the various groups' belief systems, history etc. It never amounts to an actual analysis, and certainly not in terms of comparative religion or history of religions. Be that as it may, no overall picture of new religions and new religiosity in Denmark can be drawn. Since the death of the Christian apologist and foe of new religions, Johannes Aagaard, in 2007, and the subsequent demise of his organization, the notorious Dialogue Centre, not even counter- or anti-cult organizations are active in Denmark, and no systematic propaganda against new religions is being conveyed to the public.

How, then, to live up to the task put before me by the editors of the present volume? In the aftermath of an inspiring seminar at the Solstrand hotel close to Bergen, Norway, in November 2014, my hosts asked me to write a note regarding the differences between religious innovation in Norway and my own country, Denmark. During the seminar, the chapters featured on the previous pages of this book were discussed, and all agreed that a nation-focused comparative perspective from Sweden and Denmark would add to the value of the volume. The following reflections are my brief response to their invitation. Not based on a systematic survey, my few notes merely rest on a kind of informed hunch that builds after many years in the business of comparative religion. One thing, however, should be considered when dealing with this subject: Denmark is in many ways a thoroughly secularized country, and probably more so compared to Norway. This may have two implications: 1) There is, simply said, less Christianity to fight in Denmark when new religions wish to settle, but 2) it also means that the overall religious interest in Denmark is comparatively low in contrast to countries where religion has a stronger grip. As a consequence, the number of NRM-adherents is equally low in Denmark. Furthermore, it should be noted that the kind of religion entertained by most Danes, a rather easy-going version of Lutheran Protestantism, is closely linked with national, if not nationalistic, sentiments (Lüchau 2012). No new religion can offer this dimension as a part of its belief system.

---

1. An updated version (2015) is available at http://samtidsreligion.au.dk/fileadmin/ Samtidsreligion/Religion_i_Danmark/2015_e-aarbog/ReligioniDanmark2015.pdf

Mikael Rothstein

New religious groups in Denmark

Many new religions are present in Denmark, but only a few with considerable success. Most have remained small or quite insignificant. Among those thriving well in Denmark are Scientology. The organization has placed international centres and important administrative facilities in the country—most recently, in October 2014, when a "New Ideal Continental Headquarters" (a new "Ideal Org") opened in Glostrup close to Copenhagen—and made considerable investments in real estate. In effect, many Scientologists in Denmark (which in this case means Copenhagen) are foreigners who are in the country to join advanced courses not available elsewhere. The number of Danes who have been engaged in Scientology for an extended period of time (probably less than 1,000 individuals), therefore, is, with all likelihood, higher than it would have been if these kinds of resources were not available in the country. Scientology's presence in Denmark, consequently, is strong on the institutionalized level, but not equally impressive when it comes to Danish followers (references regarding Scientology in Denmark 1988–2009 are found in Rubin 2011). The fate of the Unification movement has been very different. Arriving in Denmark around 1970, this group never attracted a genuine following, probably never more than 50 dedicated people at one and the same time. Today, very few individuals represent this ever-changing organization in Denmark. Somewhere in between, the International Society for Krishna Consciousness (ISKCON) has managed to maintain a small temple at the rim of Copenhagen, where 5–10 monks live and where Sunday feasts are celebrated as everywhere where ISKCON has representatives. During the 1990s, when the organization had facilities in the centre of town, around 30 *brahmachary* monks and perhaps 10 nuns were living a communal life, and a smaller number of devotees lived in close proximity to, but not in, the temple. Sometimes up to 200 people would join their Sunday feasts, but this is hardly the case any longer. Also, Transcendental Meditation (TM), another old school NRM, has experienced a steady decrease in both numbers of people attending and a more general awareness. Remnants of the Osho-movements are still around, a few very small neo-Hindu communes still exist, as does a low-profile group of Sathya Sai Baba devotees. Natha offers yoga classes, while straightforward religious teachings (including those of a sexual nature) are downplayed in public. Ananda Marga runs a yoga and meditation centre in Copenhagen, and attracts ca. 200 people for their yearly "Prout Conventions." Sahaj Marg also has been present in Denmark for decades, since 1992 primarily working out of a rural meditation centre in Vrads Sande. Brahma Kumaris was established in the country in 1984 and presently has around 70 core members. Additionally, Siddha Yoga has a (rather modest) following in Denmark. On a minor scale, Amma satsang groups have formed in five Danish towns, but very few individual attend. Another guru-movement, the Narayanananda Universal Yoga

Trust, was founded in Denmark in the late 1950s by Swami Narayanananda (1902–1988) and still persists at Gylling Næs ca. 70 km. from Copenhagen. Various brands of the neo-Theosophical kind are around, but none on a large scale.[2] Among the older groups somehow (but increasingly irrelevant) termed "new" are the Jehovah's Witnesses (ca. 15,000), Unitarians, Mormons (ca. 4,500), Adventists and others, all living rather silent lives.

A few new religious groups are indigenous to Denmark. The oldest is probably the Theosophically-inclined *Vandrer mod Lyset* ("Walking Towards the Light"), which builds on channelled Jesus-messages received by Johanne Agerskov (1873–1946) in 1908–1914. The esoteric teacher, Jes Bertelsen (b. 1946), has been the head of a commune in the middle of the country since 1982 (Hinge 1995), but most impressively people promoting the spiritual work of neo-gnostic teacher and mystic, Martinus Thomsen (1890–1981) (knows simply as Martinus), have been running centres in Denmark since the 1950s, gradually developing from a modest start in 1932. Not posing as an actual organization, but rather as study groups, there is no organization to join. The Theosophical Fellowship, previously Shan the Rising Light, was founded by the rather controversial Theosophical leader, Danish born Ananda Tara Shan (nee Jeanne Morashti 1946–2002) but, following her death, the movement disintegrated (but presumably survives in Australia). New Age author and Theosophical teacher Asger Lorentzen (1949–2012), primarily known for his books, together with Yvonne Wassini, founded The Golden Circle in order to enhance the "Solar-Christ Impulse" believed to permeate the country at that time. Two significant Christian groups, apart from standard Evangelical movements, have emerged during the last decades: *Faderhuset* (House of the Father) headed by prophet Ruth Evensen (b. 1951), and "Evangelist" led by exorcist and "Conquerer of Death" Christian Hedegaard (b. 1966), both self-made religious leaders. *Faderhuset* rose to fame when the group confronted counterculture youth in Copenhagen (Rothstein 2009), while Evangelist attracted some attention due to its strong emphasis on exorcism and the fact that the group effectively bought most of a village in a remote part of the country. At this point in time *Faderhuset* is defunct (Evensen never managed to get another initiative, a hard-core Christian political party, working). As far as I know there are no new religions, hitherto unseen, appearing on the Danish scene at the time of this writing.

What *is* thriving in Denmark, not surprisingly, are the many non-institutionalized, popular kinds of religion usually labelled "New Age." The host of possibilities known throughout Europa, the US and many other parts of the world, are also available to Danish consumers in the same way as everywhere else. Also, although of another brand, neo-pagan movements and groups reinventing the old Norse religions are spawning to some degree,

---

2. My first book on new religions appeared in 1991. It is absolutely out of date now, but as a historical record is may still serve a purpose, cf. Rothstein 1991.

and perhaps more than other alternative religions right now. One prominent group is *Forn Sidr* ("The Old Ways"). I am, however, unable to identify phenomena that are particularly important to Denmark, and I have no way of determining the actual spread or popularity of these traditions as a whole. The aforementioned survey from the University of Aarhus is probably the best source available. What is certain, though, is that no prominent New Age personalities of any lasting importance, or anything of that kind, have emerged in Denmark.

Public personalities

One of the main differences, then, between popular religious beliefs in Norway and Denmark has to do with personalities—or the lack thereof. It appears that an array of significant persons have epitomized various aspects of popular religion, new religiosity or the "New Age" in Norway, thereby putting a face on otherwise unparented religious trends. From Joralf Gjerstad (b. 1926), better known as *Snåsamannen* (nicknamed after the place where he lives), a famous clairvoyant and healer, to the Princess Märtha Louise (b. 1971), who is (in)famous for claiming to be in contact with benevolent angels. With references to the solid roots of "Old Norway" to celebrated royalty, alternative spiritualities have been nourished in the public, making "warm healing hands" and the ability to communicate telepathically with animals household concepts. Comparable personalities have, as mentioned, never emerged in Denmark. Religious leaders of various brands have surfaced, and—as discussed above—on a few occasions new religious movements have actually emerged in this country, but it has happened outside the eyes of the public; i.e. as sectarian specialities in the religious underground, or on the religious fringe. The only common denominator, which, in terms of religion that has been able to reach society at large remains the National Protestant Church as an institution. This means that Denmark has no collective public awareness regarding so-called alternative religiosity, no common reference and therefore hardly any debate.

The media

The presence of significant Norwegian personalities has, in my opinion, allowed non-institutionalized religious currents to surface in the media in ways quite unseen in Denmark. Abstract, unintelligible religious notions are difficult to handle, but media celebrities representing such trends are easily approached by reporters, TV producers and the like. In effect, I believe that there is a far wider knowledge of "alternative religion" among average Norwegians compared to Danes. This does not imply that Norwegians are generally comfortable with this aspect of their culture, let alone obliging towards it. I am simply suggesting that the issue of new or emerging religions features more prominently in the minds of Norwegians compared to people in Denmark. On the other hand, another religious subject has been forcefully introduced in the Danish public during past decades: The negative debate on Islam and Muslims. Rather than continuing the debate on new religious movements, which was hot in the 1980s and 1990s, Islam has been positioned as the single most debated religion, and people tend to forget their fear and reluctance regarding the new religions. Islam soon became the new object of concern and fear. It appears to me that the Norwegian public has never quite abandoned old concerns regarding new religions, although Islam has been added to the bulk of presumed troubling religions in society. As always, whether in Denmark or Norway, Protestantism escapes any accusation and is understood to be the obvious, natural, pure and beneficial backbone of society. Any critical remark levelled against the Church is likely to be met with indifference, disbelief or confusion. There is simply nothing to complain about! Danish Nationalism is on the rise (a nationalistic party is the second largest in parliament), and Christianity is a strong component of the development.

The dominant religion

Religion however, no doubt, features more prominently in Norway compared to Denmark. Despite an undeniable Protestant groundswell during the past decades, Denmark remains quite easy-going in terms of religion. Of course there are devout Christians, but most people belong to the Church without believing. In fact, membership in the Danish *folkekirke* (a breed of National Church supported by the constitution; the word meaning "The People's Church") has more to do with "being Danish" than actual Christian devotion, hence the very high membership rate almost counting 80% of the potentially Christian population (Lüchau 2012).[3] Religious discourse in Norway appears to be stronger, more frequent and, not least, more generally acknowledged. Against this backdrop new religions in Denmark have very little to offer, while New Age-activities, which are easily combined with a laid-back kind of Protestantism, thrive. In this connection it should be mentioned that all religions are free to operate in Denmark, providing they do not violate the laws of the nation. It is possible, however, for a congregation to apply for formal recognition which, if given, will bestow upon the group the right to perform legally-binding weddings, and enjoy the benefit of certain tax deductions. A special committee (consisting of university scholars) was set up to evaluate applications ca. 20 years ago, and presently more than 160 different groups have been accepted (most Christian, Islamic and Buddhist, but also a few alternative and new religions—though strangely labelled as "Hindu" or "Buddhist").[4]

---

3. The number is steadily declining, partly because people abandon or disvow the Church, but from a statistical point of view more significantly due to non-Christian immigration: The population grows.

4. The application system, including detailed information regarding procedure, a full list of groups etc., can be accessed here: http://sm.dk/arbejdsomrader/trossamfund/godkendelse

Mikael Rothstein

The academics themselves

Finally we really cannot eliminate the possibility that Norwegian scholars of religion (be they historians of religion or folklorists) appearing in public have helped pave the way for a general understanding of new or esoteric religious notions. Norwegian scholars have been impressively good at presenting their findings to the public, and prolific as well. They have served as cultural translators in a situation where conflict always lurks around the corner. It is worthwhile considering to what extend this function (however unintended) has, in fact, helped non-orthodox religious trends gain a footing in Norway. My own experience in Denmark, after 25 years of media turmoil, is that the chances of conveying sound and scholarly-relevant information to the public are extremely difficult. The mass media are not designed to educate in this respect, but rather to uphold prejudice and ignorance. I have a feeling that scientific knowledge on religion somehow is taken more seriously in Norway.

References

Ahlin, Lars, *et al.* 2013. *Religion i Aarhus 2013. En kortlægning af religion og spiritualitet*, Aarhus: Center for samtidsreligion, Århus Universitet.

Hinge, Helle. 1995. *Jes Bertelsen-bevægelsen—New Age på dansk.* Copenhagen: Gyldendal.

Lüchau, Lüchau. 2012. "Seks teser om danskernes medlemskab af folkekirken." In *Fremtidens danske religionsmodel*, edited by Lisbeth Christoffersen, 311–327. Århus: Anis.

Rothstein, Mikael. 1991. *Gud er blå. De nye religiøse bevægelser.* Copenhagen: Gyldendal (and subsequent editions, including an extended Swedish translation).

———. 2009. "Kosmisk kamp på Nørrebro: De mytologiske forudsætninger bag kampen om Ungdomshuset." *Chaos—Skandinavisk tidsskrift for religionshistoriske studier* 51: 89–104.

———. 2015. "The Study of New Religions in Denmark: A brief and subjective research history 1985-2014." In *Nordic New Religions*, edited by James Lewis and Inga Tøllefsen, 13-35. Leiden: Brill.

Rubin, Elisabeth Tuxen. 2011. "Disaffiliation among Scientologists: A Sociological Study Of Post-Apostasy Behavior And Attitudes." *International Journal for the Study of New Religions* 2(2): 201–224.

Further Reading

Rothstein, Mikael. 2016a. "UFO Movements in Denmark." In *Anthology on Western Esotericism in Scandinavia*, edited by Olav Hammer and Henrik Bogdan, 630–639. Leiden: Brill.

———. 2016b. "The New Age in Denmark." In *Anthology on Western Esotericism in Scandinavia*, edited by Olav Hammer and Henrik Bogdan, 292-300. Leiden: Brill.

Index

Numbers in *italic* denote pages with figures, numbers in **bold** denote tables. Footnotes are shown in the form 4 n4. Footnote references are only used when the heading does not appear in the main body of the text.

Index

Index

Index

Index

Index

Index

Index

Index

Index

Lightning Source UK Ltd.
Milton Keynes UK
UKOW05f0152250417
299828UK00001B/33/P